Working with Words and Images

New Steps in an Old Dance

edited by
NANCY ALLEN

NEW DIRECTIONS IN COMPUTERS AND COMPOSITION STUDIES
Gail E. Hawisher and Cynthia L. Selfe, *Series Editors*

Ablex Publishing

Westport, Connecticut
London

Library of Congress Cataloging-in-Publication Data

Working with words and images : new steps in an old dance / edited by Nancy Allen.
    p. cm. — (New directions in computers and composition studies)
    Includes bibliographical references and index.
    ISBN 1–56750–608–9 (alk. paper) — ISBN 1–56750–609–7 (pbk. : alk. paper)
    1. English language—Rhetoric—Study and teaching—Data processing. 2. English
language—Rhetoric—Computer-assisted instruction. 3. English language—Rhetoric—
Computer network resources. 4. Report writing—Study and teaching—Data processing.
5. Report writing—Computer-assisted instruction. 6. Report writing—Computer network
resources. 7. Visual perception. I. Allen, Nancy (Nancy J.). II. Series.
PE1404 .W664 2002
808′.042′0285—dc21   2001053833

British Library Cataloguing in Publication Data is available.

Library of Congress Catalog Card Number: 2001053833
ISBN: 1–56750–608–9
ISBN: 1–56750–609–7 (pbk.)

First published in 2002

Ablex Publishing, 88 Post Road West, Westport, CT 06881
An imprint of Greenwood Publishing Group, Inc.
www.ablexbooks.com

Printed in the United States of America

The paper used in this book complies with the
Permanent Paper Standard issued by the National
Information Standards Organization (Z39.48–1984).

10 9 8 7 6 5 4 3 2 1

CONTENTS

COPYRIGHT
ACKNOWLEDGMENTS

—◆—

For material reproduced in this book, the following publishers are grate-
fully acknowledged:

Chapter 3

Figure 3.1, a constructed example of ransom note emphasis, from *Looking Good in Print* by Roger Parker, page 86. Copyright © 1988 by The
Coriolis Group. Reprinted with permission.

Chapter 4

Figure 4.1, Ojibwa love letter, from *Picture-Writing of the American Indians* by Garrick Mallery, page 363. Copyright © 1972 by Dover Publications. Reprinted with permission.

Figure 4.2, pictorial signs in the Sumerian, Egyptian, Hittite, and Chinese
languages, from *A Study of Writing*, 2d ed., by I. J. Gelb, page 98. Copyright © 1963 by The University of Chicago Press. Reprinted with permission.

Figure 4.3, examples of route directions, from "How Space Structures
Language" by B. Tversky and P. Lee, in *Spatial Cognition: An Interdisciplinary Approach to Representing and Processing Spatial Knowledge*, page 167. Copyright © 1998 by Springer-Verlag. Reprinted with
permission.

Figure 4.4, maps drawn by informants, from "How Space Structures Language" by B. Tversky and P. Lee, in *Spatial Cognition: An Interdisciplinary Approach to Representing and Processing Spatial Know-*

ledge, page 168. Copyright © 1998 by Springer-Verlag. Reprinted with permission.

Figure 4.5, bar and line graphs from "Bars and Lines: A Study of Graphic Communication" by J. Zacks and B. Tversky, page 1074, in *Memory and Cognition*. Copyright © 1999 by the Psychonomic Society, Inc. Reprinted with permission of the author.

Chapter 7

Quoted material from interviews with D. Foster, K. Scott, and E. Mitchell used with permission.

Figure 7.1, a page from the Introduction, page 31, from *Charlevoix* by D. Foster and K. Scott. Copyright © 1998 by Petunia Press. Reprinted with permission.

Figure 7.2, a page from the Section Two stories on Beaver Island, page 137, from *Charlevoix* by D. Foster and K. Scott. Copyright © 1998 by Petunia Press. Reprinted with permission.

Chapter 8

Figure 8.2, an actual photograph of the moon tipped as the frontispiece of an 1853 issue of the *Photographic Art Journal*. Smithsonian Institution Libraries. Copyright © 2001 Smithsonian Institution.

Figure 8.3, a 1854 daguerreotype of an annular eclipse reproduced as a salt print, then bound into book form in William Bartlett's photographs of the solar eclipse of May 26, 1854. Smithsonian Institution Libraries. Copyright © 2001 Smithsonian Institution.

Figure 8.4, a photograph of a relief map of the mountain of Teneriffe by C. P. Smyth, which was glued or "tipped in" to Smyth's *Report on the Teneriffe Astronomical Experiment of 1856*. Smithsonian Institution Libraries. Copyright © 2001 Smithsonian Institution.

Figure 8.5, photo-stereograph #4 from C. P. Smyth's 1858 *Teneriffe*. Smithsonian Institution Libraries. Copyright © 2001 Smithsonian Institution.

Figure 8.6, photo-stereograph #5, "The Sheepshanks Telescope," from C. P. Smyth's 1858 *Teneriffe*. Smithsonian Institution Libraries. Copyright © 2001 Smithsonian Institution.

Figure 8.8, image from De La Rue's 1862 "The Bakerian Lecture." Smithsonian Institution Libraries. Copyright © 2001 Smithsonian Institution.

Figure 8.9, image from De La Rue's 1862 "The Bakerian Lecture." Smithsonian Institution Libraries. Copyright © 2001 Smithsonian Institution.

Chapter 9

Figure 9.3, paragraphs as chapters, from Isidore of Seville, *Etymologiae* (1473). Courtesy of The Newberry Library, Chicago.

Figure 9.4, current chapter and paragraph format, from Wilbur S. Howell, *Logic and Rhetoric in England, 1500–1700*. Copyright © 1956, revised 1984, by Princeton University Press. Reprinted by permission of Princeton University Press.

Figure 9.5, ancillary illustration (early), from *De Magnete* (1600), page 139. By permission of the Folger Shakespeare Library.

Figure 9.7, correlative illustration using captions, from "The Origin of the Automobile Engine," page 114, in *Scientific Technology and Social Change* by Lynwood Bryant. Copyright © 1967 by the Estate of Mary E. and Dan Todd. All rights reserved. Reprinted with permission.

Figure 9.8, correlative illustration (early), from Oronce Finé, *Protomathesis* (1532). Courtesy of The Newberry Library, Chicago.

Figure 9.9, correlative illustration (modern), from *Laboratory Anatomy of the Alligator* by Robert B. Chiasson. Copyright © 1962. Reprinted with permission.

Figure 9.10, substantive illustration (early), from Isidore of Seville, *Etymologiae* (1473). Courtesy of The Newberry Library, Chicago.

Chapter 11

Figure 11.1, cover idea for the original proposal of *The Way of the Sorcerer*. Used with permission. Illustration © 2002 Mike Dringenberg.

Figure 11.2, thumbnails for the opening pages of *The Way of the Sorcerer*. Used with permission. Illustration © 2002 Mike Dringenberg.

Figure 11.3, finished artwork corresponding to the thumbnails for *The Way of the Sorcerer*. Used with permission. Illustration © 2002 Mike Dringenberg.

Figure 11.4, "Don Jose" from *The Way of the Sorcerer*. Used with permission. Illustration © 2002 Mike Dringenberg.

Figure 11.5, thumbnail sketch for "In the Circular Ruins," from *The Way of the Sorcerer*. Used with permission. Illustration © 2002 Mike Dringenberg.

Figure 11.6, "Teller," from *The Way of the Sorcerer*. Used with permission. Illustration © 2002 Mike Dringenberg.

Chapter 13

Figure 13.1, starting nodes for the Union Pacific Corporation, Union Pacific Railroad, and Union Pacific Technologies. Reprinted with permission of the Union Pacific Railroad Company.

Figure 13.2, Andrew Russell's photograph of the completion of the Transcontinental Railroad. Reprinted with permission of the Union Pacific Railroad Company.

Figure 13.3, Andrew Russell's photograph of the completion of the Transcontinental Railroad. Reprinted with permission of the Union Pacific Railroad Company.

Figure 13.4, "American Indians on horseback at Buffalo Run, Yellowstone, ca 1924." Reprinted with permission of the Union Pacific Railroad Company.

Figure 13.5, PQMPlus Highlights. Reprinted with permission of the Union Pacific Railroad Company.

Figure 13.6, Union Pacific Technologies. Reprinted with permission of the Union Pacific Railroad Company.

Chapter 15

The quoted material in the chapter prologue is used with the permission of Sean Cohen.

chapter one

RELATIONSHIPS BETWEEN WORDS AND IMAGES
an overview

◄━━━►

nancy allen

The dialectic of word and image seems to be a constant in the fabric of signs that a culture weaves around itself. What varies is the precise nature of the weave, the relation of warp and woof.

—W. J. T. Mitchell (1986, 43)

T HE LONG HISTORY OF INTERRELATIONSHIPS among words and images crosses disciplines, theoretical issues, practical considerations, and generations of researchers, practitioners, and thinkers. At times the definitions and uses of words and images have been so intertwined that the terms have become compounded. Chinese picture-writing, for example, was an early intermediary between pictographs and written language. Picture-writing so fascinated Ezra Pound that he saw it as a model for the poetic image (Mitchell 1986, 29). In the 1950s, painter Jasper Johns became known for turning numbers and letters into art. More recently, cultural analyst Tom Wolfe (1975) found words to be essential not just for interpreting but also for viewing late twentieth-century modern art: "In short, the new order of things in the art world was: first you get the Word, and then you can see" (p. 62). In a discussion of abstract expressionist painting in *The Painted Word*, Wolfe sees modern art becoming literature and words becoming art. Wolfe refers (1975, 111) to a piece by Lawrence Weiner that appeared in *Arts Magazine* in 1970. It consisted of a list of three steps and a sentence of explanation, but no other visual elements:

1. The artist may construct the piece.
2. The piece may be fabricated.
3. The piece need not be built.

Each being equal and consistent with the intent of the artist, the decision as to condition rests with the receiver upon the occasion of receivership.

According to Wolfe, these words were presented "as a work of art" (p. 111).

Today, writers and artists combine modes freely: a poet suspends a short piece of poetry in colored liquid inside a bottle; an artist constructs a wooden "bookworm" that bores its way through old books; a Czech photographer prepares handsome photographs from newspapers piled for recycling; and sculptor Tina Allen describes herself as writing Black American history in bronze (Allen 1999). Maya Lin's Vietnam War Memorial is a well-known combination of image and text: "The names are carved into black granite panels that form a large V at a 125-degree angle and suggest the pages of a book" (Hass 1998, 14). These exhibits attest to the importance the written word has for modern culture, while they simultaneously represent writing as part of their art—words as images.

Overlapping the functions of words and images is not confined to the creative arts. In advertising and flyers, for instance, we often find lettering used to inform us as it also catches our eye. Intertwining the uses of words and images occurs so frequently in our culture that it intrudes into our descriptions of events. According to Susan Sontag (1973), "It is common now for people to insist about their experience of a violent event in which they were caught up—a plane crash, a shoot-out, a terrorist bombing—that 'it seemed like a movie.' This is said, other descriptions seeming insufficient, in order to explain how real it was" (p. 16).

Few of us give serious thought to explaining the differences and relationships between words and images. Like the computers or telephones that we use daily, the actual inner workings of both words and images are complex, intricate, and, at times, fuzzy, but we don't really need to understand the intricacies in order to use words and images in our daily interchanges. However, if we want to use words and images effectively to achieve our purposes, and if we want to design intriguing uses of words and images together, we need to learn more about how they work and relate. They work in different ways, but they *do* work effectively together. Professionals and communicators who understand their workings can use the tensions created between them productively.

Among those who have attempted to explain word–image differences and relationships, W. J. T. Mitchell (1986) offers an analogy. He suggests we compare words and images to algebra and geometry: "Algebra works through arbitrary signs that have a grammar for how they should be read. Geometry works with its figures holistically. The relationships between words and images," Mitchell says, "are similarly complex ones that require translation and interpretation" (p. 44).

Other theorists have a far different view, seeing words and images as engaged in a mortal struggle for our attention and assigned value. Leonard Shlain claims that the superiority of words or of images within a society brings with it enormous accompanying effects:

> The introduction of the written word, and then the alphabet, into the social intercourse of humans initiated a fundamental change in the way newly literate cultures understood their reality. . . . Goddess worship, feminine values, and women's power depend on the ubiquity of the image. . . . Whenever a culture elevates the written word at the expense of the image, patriarchy dominates. When the importance of the image supersedes the written word, feminine values and egalitarianism flourish. (Shlain 1998, 7)

Mitchell Stephens (1998, 22), an advocate of moving images who is also a believer in the power of language, adds some support for part of Shlain's claim:

> When statements are written down, we gain the habit of pulling them out of the flow of experience and subjecting them to a narrow, rigorous analysis—noting their correspondences, connections or contradictions. Ong, Goody and others have come to believe that our system of logic— our ability to find abstract principles that apply independently of situa- tions—is to some extent a product of literacy, of the written word.

Daniel Boorstin (1987) does not connect interest in images and visual effects or the tedious analysis of language to gender, yet he also see words and images as though locked in a contest for our use and allegiance. In 1961 Boorstin first announced that our society was engaged in a "graphic revolution." Hank Corwin, a film editor, believes the revolution has already occurred. Talking about the preference for fast cuts and conden- sation found among today's film audiences, he said: "The war is over. The kids have won" (quoted in Stephens 1998, 149). He may be right. Matt Watroba, a schoolteacher and folk-music performer, recently told about a conversation he had with a ninth-grade student. Watroba had asked his students to choose a song with social significance for their assignment (Watroba 1999). The next day, when one student arrived at class, he handed Watroba a tape of a folk song that he believed had social signifi- cance. "Good," said Watroba. "What's the song about?" "I don't know," responded the student. "I haven't seen the video."

As appealing as these stories may be, viewing words and images as in perpetual debate serves us poorly in our attempts to use them in produc- tive collaboration, as today's media demand. Nor is the view of words and images as opposing forces historically accurate. Accounts of the develop- ment of written words and images show, in fact, that throughout their his- tories words and images have had much in common. As I introduce the issues concerning relationships between words and images that this book will address, I'll present a brief look at those histories to serve as background for the ensuing chapters. I'll also relate the issues raised to particular chapters in this volume in which readers can find a discussion of those issues focused in a particular field, theory, or research project; a presentation of the current status of particular relationships; or guidelines and pointers for practical application.

A Brief Historical Background

Use of language is considered to be a basic human ability. In fact, Noam Chomsky (1972, 70), arguably the most famous twentieth-century linguist, pointed to our use of language as the feature that most distinguishes humans from other members of the animal world:

> As far as we know, possession of human language is associated with a specific type of mental organization, not simply a higher degree of intelligence. There seems to be no substance to the view that human language is simply a more complex instance of something to be found elsewhere in the animal world.

Chomsky and Lev Vygotsky, a psycholinguist noted for his theories of human development, are among those who have related language to our ability to think and, in Chomsky's case, to human cognition: "It seems to me that today there is no better or more promising way to explore the essential and distinctive properties of human intelligence than through the detailed investigation of the structure of this unique human possession" (Chomsky 1972, 70).

To form a sentence is to think; one way to study thinking is to study language. But language may not be the only way in which human beings think. Language may simply be favored by those people who most often write and theorize about language and thinking—that is, by academic writers who have considerable ability with language and are aware of its importance in their own lives. As a result, they may be biased in language's favor. What's more, most of our educational system uses language as the primary tool to bring us through the various stages of academic learning. Drawing, used spontaneously by young children, in school becomes relegated to "art classes."

Language, however, has never been alone in its importance to thinking. To the classical Greek philosophers, images were also a central part of the thinking process, as Aristotle recognizes in this statement: "Images are to the thinking soul like sense impressions. . . . The soul never thinks without images" (Apostle 1981, 14). These connections persist in today's English language. According to the second unabridged edition of the *Random House Dictionary of the English Language* (1987), the word *idea* is related to the Greek word *idein*, meaning "to see." One definition of *idea* is "an impression," and another relates *idea* to Plato's use of Form, "an archetype or pattern of which the individual objects in any natural class are imperfect copies." One Middle English meaning of *idea* was "a mental image" (its spelling combined the *ide* stem of the Greek *idein* with the feminine noun-ending *a*). In everyday conversation we use "ideas" and "views" to refer to our thinking.

Artists and designers often say that they think in images; architects and design engineers, for example, sometimes hold brainstorming sessions by sketching out designs on one another's drawing pads. For his book *An Anthropologist on Mars*, Oliver Sacks (1995) interviewed Temple Grandin, who is autistic, about her experiences as a visual rather than a verbal thinker. Grandin teaches animal science at Colorado State University and believes her visual thinking not only gives her a special relationship with animals, but also makes her a clear thinker. Verbal thinkers, she believes, are often fuzzy thinkers (Sacks 1995, 244–94).

Technology has made the relationships between words and images even more intertwined. In a discussion of photography, Sontag (1973, 160) commented:

> Reality itself has started to be understood as a kind of writing, which has to be decoded—even as photographed images were themselves first compared to writing. (Niepce's name for the process whereby the image appears on the plate was heliography, sun-writing; Fox Talbot called the camera "the pencil of nature").

Moving pictures have added another layer of complexity:

> The first great box-office success . . . *Birth of a Nation* (1915) . . . attracted millions by its expansive battle scenes, its torrential action, and its close-ups of the faces of leering villains and of dead soldiers. This was the first movie ever shown in the White House. After seeing it, President Wilson is said to have remarked, "It is like writing history with lightning." . . . Scenes which before could be vividly depicted only in the pages of a book (but not on the stage) now for the first time could appear in another form: on the movie screen. (Boorstin 1987, 128)

Today we have such images in our living rooms and kitchens on television and computer screens. The combination of photography, film, and computers with all their imaging capability have brought us morphing and the 1999 film *The Matrix*, in which reality and images have become thoroughly mixed.

It is not surprising, then, that developing meaning from words and images is a challenge. Even without technology, interpretation is a challenge. Bill Nichols (1981, 26) echoes Sontag's concerns about interpretation and adds his own warning about the importance of learning to understand our systems of representation: "The environment becomes a text to be read like any other text. To not know the perceptual codes maintained by a given culture is tantamount to being an illiterate infant wandering through an unintelligible world." One place to begin increasing our facility with words and images is by trying to understand how they were related in their initial development.

DEVELOPING WRITTEN LANGUAGE

People have existed for at least a million years and perhaps longer. During much of that time, they have used spoken sounds to communicate, eventually developing these sounds into spoken languages. By comparison, writing is a relatively modern development. The earliest examples of what linguists consider to be written language date back only a little over six thousand years (Fromkin and Rodman 1998, 498). The leap from spoken to written language was a complex and significant one. Writing enables people to communicate over distance and time, to keep records, to support functions necessary to the culture and business of a modern civilization. The first person to use one tool, possibly a stick, to create another tool, a written sign that conveyed meaning, was our greatest inventor, but we don't know who it was. Members of early cultures believed language had divine origin, and every culture has its legend of how their language, especially their written language, was developed:

> Greek legend has it that Cadmus, Prince of Phoenicia and founder of the city of Thebes, invented the alphabet and brought it with him to Greece. (He later was banished to Illyria and changed into a snake.) In one Chinese fable, the four-eyed dragon-god Cang Jie invented writing, but in another, writing first appeared to humans in the form of markings on a turtle shell. In other myths, the Babylonian god Nebo and the Egyptian god Thoth gave humans writing as well as speech. The Talmudic scholar Rabbi Akiba believed that the alphabet existed before humans were created; and according to Islamic teaching, the alphabet was created by Allah himself, who presented it to humans but not to the angels. (Fromkin and Rodman 1998, 492)

These beliefs did not end with the development of literate civilization as we might think of it. Even as late as 1678, Cotton Mather's Harvard thesis claimed that language had divine origin (Sibley 1885), and some people may still hold to this belief.

Today, most language researchers believe that writing was more likely to have developed from early human drawings. Petroglyphs found in Chauvet Cave and LaFerrassie Cave in France date back 32,000 years, and those in Lascaux Cave in France and Altamira in Spain, 17,000 years. As Victoria Fromkin and Robert Rodman (1998) explain the process, the cave drawings appear to be illustrations of animals and events in the life of that time. Drawings from a somewhat later period that are believed to be direct images of objects are classified as pictographs, or "picture writing." Such images were literal representations of objects, but were not yet related to the words of a spoken language.

Pictographs have been found throughout the world, and, in fact, we still use them. For example, pictographs are used where international communication is required, such as on road signs to direct drivers and in transportation terminals to signal bathroom facilities (we all recognize the meaning of the person in a skirt or the one in pants regardless of what we may choose to wear). Once a pictograph becomes widely accepted within a culture, its meaning gradually expands to include concepts associated with the represented object. When pictographs become more abstract and are developed to represent ideas, they become what we refer to as ideographs. "Picture writing" becomes "idea writing" (Fromkin and Rodman 1998).

Earlier language researchers had reached similar conclusions. After extensive research concerning the relationships between pictographs and written language, Bishop William Warburton (1766) went so far as to state that all written languages were developed from picture writing (p. 71; also see discussion in Faigley 1999). To illustrate his point, Warburton described a process requiring hundreds of years to show how written communication moves from "picture writing" through hieroglyphics to institutionalized "arbitrary marks" and eventually to alphabetic writing. To illustrate picture writing, he used a large cloth painting showing a fleet of ships arriving on the shores of Mexico. In the early 1500s this painting had been sent to Montezuma by people stationed on the Mexican shore to notify him that the Spanish navy was arriving (Warburton 1766).

Although picture writing served the purpose of communicating important news, it was cumbersome and inconvenient, to say the least. To address such problems, cultures that were stable over time developed more efficient systems to make the information that was to be communicated more compact and easier to prepare. Warburton (1766) describes three primary methods, related to traditional rhetorical tropes, used in the process: 1) The principal circumstances or part could stand for the whole (synecdoche); for example, two hands holding a shield and bow could represent two armies at battle. 2) An instrument or symbol could stand for a thing (metonymy), as a scepter stands for a monarch or an eye for a god's omniscience. 3) One thing could represent another to which it bears some resemblance or analogy (metaphor). Thus a spotted serpent in a circle could represent the sky, the spots being stars, or a grasshopper could represent a mystery or an obligation to secrecy, since the grasshopper was thought to have no mouth (pp. 75–77). One of the best-known systems using these processes is Egypt's hieroglyphic system.

The obscurity of the characters used in these systems and the bulk of the communications produced led to further refinements. The Chinese threw out the full images and retained only tracings of the marks. Warburton (1766, 86) illustrated this development with an example showing

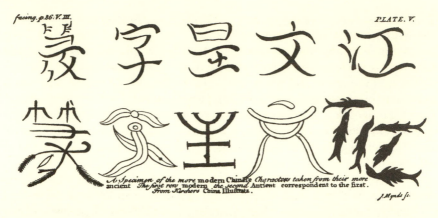

◆ **FIGURE 1.1** ◆

Chinese pictographic characters (bottom row) and their corresponding tracing marks (top row). FROM WILLIAM WARBURTON'S *THE DIVINE LEGATION OF MOSES DEMONSTRATED* (1766).

Chinese images of leaves and fishes moving from pictographic characters to tracing marks (see figure 1.1). Other developments, with the likely intention of making such a system even more efficient, led to "arbitrary marks" that stood for a meaning, and eventually to alphabetic writing. One result of these early developments is that a Chinese artisan, Pi Sheng, developed moveable type five centuries before Gutenberg (Stephens 1998, 28).

Though Warburton (1766) used examples from Mexico, Egypt, and China, he makes the point that "as all nations, in their ruder state, had hieroglyphic images or analogic or symbolic figures for marking things; so had they likewise simple characters or notes of arbitrary institutions, for mental conceptions" (p. 89). Today, the Sumerians, who left innumerable clay tablets of various document types, are generally considered the first to have developed written language (logographic writing)—that is, to have a system in which the marks, or signs, stand for words rather than objects. Linguists are now developing a dictionary of the Sumerian written language that is expected to extend to seventeen volumes (Fromkin and Rodman 1998, 495). This evaluation may change, however; new evidence from excavations in Egypt seem to indicate that Egyptians actually used written language earlier. Opinions as to which culture was first may depend to some extent on our definition of "written language." Warburton said, and most modern linguists would agree, that signs referring to "things" are hieroglyphic. It is when people develop signs that refer to "words" that we have true written language (Fromkin and Rodman 1998, 496–98; Warburton 1766, 94). This development, no matter which culture did it first, signals a significant step into abstraction, one that enables yet constrains, and sometimes completely derails, communication.

Modern linguists and psychologists have long worked to develop theories of how we relate meaning to words, one result of which has been development of the field of semantics. In chapter 2 of this volume, Arthur Glenberg brings our discussion of words up to the present with his newly developed theory of the Indexical Hypothesis. Glenberg first describes some current theories based on cognitive psychology concerning how we develop meaning from words; he then explains his own theory, which adds a new perspective to our understandings of language by relating the meanings we develop to the surrounding physical and cultural contexts within which words are used.

In chapter 3, James Kalmbach extends our understanding of how textual features influence our interpretive strategies by looking at the effects of letters themselves and their contribution to document design. Kalmbach discusses the stages students go through as they begin learning to use letters as design elements and offers insights that will help teachers work with students who are new to the capabilities computers offer us for working with text.

LEARNING TO SEE

> Like fish, we "swim" in a sea of images, and these images help shape our perceptions of the world and of ourselves. . . . We communicate through images. Visual communication is a central aspect of our lives.
>
> —Berger (1989, 1)

Images have been studied for several centuries. And just as the development of written language involved images, this history of images is entangled with words. One of the first books written about images as such, *Imagines*, is credited to Philostratus, of which there are actually two, grandfather and grandson, both of whom wrote about images between 200 and 300 AD. Philostratus son of Nervianus (the grandfather) has been credited with being the "father of criticism," though others of the time were also writing about painting and sculpture (Page, Capps, and Rouse 1931, xvi). Philostratus was a sophist who was as concerned with the form of his writing as with the images he viewed. Perhaps this is why in this early work of art criticism, Philostratus confounds the functions of words and images:

> Foreign as the procedure is to our point of view, it is the tendency of Philostratus to discuss paintings almost as if they were works of literary art. The scene or scenes are described for the story they tell, and for the sentiment they express in this story. The excellence of the picture for him lies in its effective delineation of character, in the pathos of the situation or in the play of emotion it represents. Its technical excellence is rarely mentioned, and then only as a means for successful representation.
> (Page, Capps, and Rouse 1931, xviii)

Philostratus's purpose in writing about art was twofold: to provide writing models for his students, and to train their aesthetic taste through the subject matter. However, he also saw much in common between words and images:

> Whosoever scorns painting is unjust to truth; and he is also unjust to all the wisdom that has been bestowed upon poets—for poets and painters make equal contribution to our knowledge of the deeds and the looks of heroes—and he withholds his praise from symmetry of proportion, whereby art partakes of reason. (Page, Capps, and Rouse 1931, 3)

In spite of Philostratus's testimony, images have been distrusted, in a tradition that has come down from Plato. The argument traditionally offered against images has been that they appeal to our emotions. Today, we have a new concern: Images mislead us into thinking they are reality. Many psychologists and philosophers fear we are replacing the reality in our lives with illusions. Yet Madison Avenue knows that we value the "real," the "homemade," and Hollywood counts on our willingness to perceive the world of images on a strip of celluloid as reality, at least for ninety minutes. Our suspension of disbelief is, or should be, a willed act, and, when we are caught unawares and swept into substituting illusion for reality, we should, if we wish, be able to will the illusion to stop. Despite psychologists' fears, surely we can distinguish images from reality when we actually focus our attention on it, can't we? Though Nichols (1981), too, worries about the potential for confusion, he believes we can exert control into this process: "We seldom mistake a menu for a meal or a map for a territory" (p. 21).

In chapter 4 of this volume, Barbara Tversky helps us unravel some of the complexities of our reactions to images. She describes how we develop meaning from graphics, their elements, graphic spaces, and depictions of abstraction, supporting her discussion with examples from her research. The guides she describes help us learn about how visual elements work. This knowledge becomes ever more important for both image producers and consumers as we enter a period in which images gain more power in our culture. From the perspective of those who see images and text as contesting forces, Stephens says: "Images are winning—materialistic, entertainment-besotting, civic-life-depleting images; vain, phony, surface-loving, fantasy-promoting, reality-murdering images" (Stephens 1998, 208).

If images exert such negative forces into our lives, perhaps Plato was wise in banning them. But if, instead, we look at words and images as collaborative means for understanding our world, we can believe that by increasing our knowledge of images and how they work, we can become alert to negative applications and be able to use images positively and productively.

In the remaining chapters of part one, Richard Johnson Sheehan and Ronald Fortune discuss various issues related to modern education and the ways we learn about images. In chapter 5, Johnson Sheehan describes a procedure he has developed from Arnheim's visual theories. He then explains how we can use this procedure to develop documents for media that are visually based, such as the World Wide Web. Finally, in chapter 6, Fortune assesses our lack of training for working with visual media and argues for visual thinking as a vital skill that is needed by any professionals who expect to work with the documents of the future.

Perception and Interpretation

Our attempts to understand the nature of imagery have been long and continuing. Linguists and psychologists, as we learn from Glenberg's chapter (chapter 2), have worked to develop theories for our interpretation of language. Our understanding of images, though also actively researched as Tversky shows us, is even less well understood by most of us. We know, for example, that we perceive images presented by the world and that we visualize images in our minds, but we should not assume that these perceptions and visualizations are innocent. That is, we do not simply perceive through a transparent window and visualize on a blank slate. Each of us brings our own perceptual and terminal screens developed through our particular biology and life experiences to this process, imposing a worldview over our sensory apparatus. We also attach meaning to each image through a very complicated process of translation. Nichols (1981, 12) offers this explanation:

> The world does not enter our mind nor does it deposit a picture of itself there spontaneously. . . . To be comprehended, the physical world must first be mediated and translated. Light waves, like sound waves, mediate between a distal object and a proximal stimulus. . . . The brain provides the translation service, organizing sensory impressions into patterns and then conferring meaning upon various kinds of patterns in order to construct a familiar, recognizable world.

The process of perceiving the world and imprinting what we see there as meaning in our minds is an active one in which we determine which pieces are chunked together, or as Nichols would say, it is a process for which we provide the punctuation. The relationship between a figure and its background is an example, one that Henry James used as the theme for a story, "The Figure in the Carpet." Nichols explains: "The boundary between figure and ground does not belong to either. . . . It is not *in* reality at all but *in* our perception, our punctuation of it" (p. 15). M. C. Escher attempted to show the changing relationship between figure and ground

as a continuum in his famous tessellation prints, such as one in which fish
turn into birds and fly away.

As complex and only partially understood as perception may be, a
central issue in our relationship to words and images is one of interpretation. Not only do our processes for interpreting words and images work
differently, there is also disagreement over which medium is more open
to interpretation:

> Few discussions of the relative merits of words and images get far with-
> out someone raising the question of imagination. Reading, they insist,
> requires it; watching doesn't. When we read, the assumption goes, scenes
> must be created in our heads. When we watch, that is not necessary; the
> scene is right there in front of us. I have problems with this argument. . . .
> In reading Dickens I'm mostly involved in trying to follow Dickens, not in
> painting mental pictures in my head. (Stephens 1998, 105)

Although written passages are open to interpretation and imagination,
some argue that images appear to be much more so. How to halt the end-
less possibilities of interpretation is an issue that has concerned many.
The solution is a function often given to the text that accompanies an
image. "Formerly, the image illustrated the text (made it clearer); today,
the text loads the image, burdening it with a culture, a moral, and imagination" (Barthes 1977, 26). I deal with this issue of relating images and
interpretive text in chapter 7, which describes the collaborative struggles
of three people to create and publish a photographic essay. Decisions
about how to caption its pictures were just some of the issues that faced
this group as it related a set of images and accompanying text to tell a
coherent story.

One source of our difficulty in interpreting images may be that they are
so much like the reality they *re*-present. Because images bear close resemblance to items in the real world, we sometimes have problems separating
them. "We think that it is the world itself we see in our 'mind's eye,' rather
than a coded picture of it, even more certainly than we believe that 'real'
people and objects populate the silver screen of a movie theater" (Nichols
1981, 12). Such a danger has also been noted by Boorstin (1987, 240), who
seems to echo Plato. In a discussion of images he wrote:

> In the height of our power in this age of the Graphic Revolution, we are
> threatened by a new and peculiarly American menace . . . the menace of
> unreality. The threat of nothingness is the danger of replacing American
> dreams by American illusions. Of replacing the ideals by the images, the
> aspiration by the mold.

Our distrust of images and confusion over how to relate to them are still
very real.

Conceptual Frames

As cognitive beings we impose structure on our perceptions in order to help us think about the world and function within it more effectively. We, in fact, use several variations of this tool in dealing with interpretation problems and the complex relationships between words and images. The following conceptual structures represent some of the ways in which we have represented contending views about our uses of words and images. In discussing each conceptual frame, I will refer to a chapter in this volume related to it.

MIMESIS VERSUS CONVENTION

A primary issue that has confronted the use of both words and images is the question of whether they are mimetic—that is, imitations of nature—or conventional—that is, arbitrarily established by agreed-upon usage. How words convey meaning has been a riddle attracting scholars from many schools. Giambattista Vico (1968) was one of the first theorists to champion "iconic" or "Adamic" language, in which words are believed to have direct ties to nature and to the early "naming" of objects in nature. Terry Eagleton (1983, 37) refers to a period in modern English history when there was a move "to safeguard the robust vitality of Shakespearian English. . . . This whole notion of language rested upon a naïve mimeticism: The theory was that words are somehow healthiest when they approach the condition of things, and thus cease to be words at all."

Such an organic view of language, which has waxed and waned throughout history, is related to the many rhetorical tropes and figures. By those who held to a natural view of language, these figures were thought to be essential forms of mythical expression that gave language its muscle and texture, rather than simply decoration. Skill at manipulating figures was considered an especially important part of one's writing ability during the sixteenth and seventeenth centuries. Sister Miriam Joseph (1947), for example, classified over two hundred figures used by Shakespeare. (For other books on rhetorical figures from the sixteenth to nineteenth centuries, see R. Sherry, 1550; T. Wilson, 1553; H. Peacham, 1593; J. Smith, 1657; S. M. Burnham, 1901; E. Holmes, 1966; and L. A. Sonnino, 1968. For modern examples of figures, see E. Corbett, 1965, and R. Lanham, 1991.)

Disagreements over the merits of various styles fostered arguments as to whether content could be separated from form or whether, as Comte de Buffon put it in the eighteenth century, "style is the man." By the 1960s, with advances in technology, we have Marshall McLuhan's related though differently focused declaration that "the medium is the message." With extensive linguistic and philosophic research on the development and use of languages and language theory, we have come to see words today as abstract signs, arbitrary markings that are defined by convention rather than by reference to nature.

Images went through a similar process. Early drawings were replications of natural objects, paintings depicted nature and people, and portraits of family members were the favored subjects for early photography. In chapter 8, Gregory Wickliff relates for us the process that photography went through in becoming accepted as a legitimate process for documenting events in nature, particularly astronomy, events which we could not view close at hand. As we learn about this process, we come to understand that the tension between mimesis and convention does not present a simple dichotomous choice. Understanding the conventions involved with the meaning of images does not mean that we eliminate their mimetic qualities. Along with abstractions and stylized drawings, we also see mimetic images every day—a common example, the icons on our computer screens.

PRIMARY VERSUS SUPPORT

Technical communicators have long held that graphics are included to support the surrounding textual arguments. Journalists would say that photographs are included to attract our attention to the important message in a story. The "net generation," as Don Tapscott (1998) calls today's young Internet users, might see the graphics as primary, as the best and fastest way to gain information. Newspaper editors now want to limit stories to less than 500 words, but they are interested in how the story will connect to the newspaper's web site (Ganter 1998). According to photographer Richard Avedon, "Images are fast replacing words as our primary language" (quoted in Stephens 1998, 11). It may be time for communicators to reinvestigate how these two modes relate in terms of primary and supporting roles for different audiences with an eye to reconsidering communication designs.

In 1990, Barry Pegg carried out just such a study to determine relationships between technical illustrations and the texts they were part of, developing a typology of the relationships he found. In chapter 9 of this volume he brings that study up-to-date by including electronic media in his analysis.

COMMUNICATION VERSUS DECORATION

Did people first draw pictures in order to provide information or decoration? Was the cave dweller who painted deer on the cave walls intending to educate the children about animals, create a record of a hunt, practice skills for paintings that would occur elsewhere, or decorate the living room? We don't know. Images serve all of these purposes and more. Just as we go through periods of preference for differing textual styles, we vary in our tastes for decoration on our tools and bodies and in our lives. During the recent modernist period, sleek, clean lines and minimalist approaches with little internal activity were very much in fashion. Since MTV, we have become accustomed to a different approach to editing images and in our uses of language; we want fast cuts and sound bites to avoid wasting time and to hold our attention. We have learned to process television news quickly; in 1996 the average sound bite was 8.2 seconds (Stephens 1998, 143). In a 1983 interview, television producer Quinn Martin stated:

> We used to play everything out; the exit walk, the long dissolve. I mean, people were very literal minded fifteen to eighteen years ago. . . . As commercials got people so used to absorbing information quickly, I had to change my style to give them more jump cuts or they'd be bored. (quoted in Stephens 1998, 149)

We demand more activity to keep us interested, and this is sometimes accomplished through what seems to be more decoration—the use of images and words in decorative ways. In magazines, especially but not exclusively the popular magazines, we find asymmetrical photos set on an angle and given blurred focus to add visual interest. It's okay now to let parts of the editing and creative process show around the edges of a production in a film or commercial; for example, in 1998 the Miller Brewing Company sponsored commercials signed by Dick, their supposed creator.

On stage, of course, the aside or turn to the audience has been with us for centuries. Nor is it new in theater to add decorations to hold the audience's interest. Some areas of theater that can be considered new are attitudes toward how particular elements contribute to a production, whether they are important in communicating ideas or as decoration. In chapter 10, Lisa Brock describes how the visual elements of a stage production act as the catalyst that turns text into theater. Though lighting, set design, and costumes may be seen by some as decoration, Brock explains their historical development into active elements of a play.

CONTEXT VERSUS INDEPENDENCE

During the first half of the twentieth century, New Criticism made popular the approach of treating words and images as if they stood alone, out of the stream of their surroundings. Poetry textbooks were published without authors' names attached to the poems. Photographs were consider to be unmediated, direct reproductions of what was shown. We still hear that "the data speak for themselves." Yet no scientist would actually think it appropriate to send a set of data to the National Science Foundation without first establishing the importance of the problem, the appropriateness of the research methods, and the importance of the results as they fit into or contradict other research in the field.

Today, we usually want to know the context and social conditions surrounding production of text, image, or even data in order to better interpret their meaning. Because there is no simple, direct reference between an image and the object it depicts, Mitchell (1986) says that we need to know much about an image in order to interpret it. To understand an image, for example, we need to know its language, its discourse community, its social context, and what can appropriately be said about it. The ways in which images and text are used within a culture influence what they say to us and what we can say about them. In chapter 11, Insu Fenkl and Mike Dringenberg describe how their interchanges of text and images operated in their development of a graphic novel. They used their interpretation of pictures to develop the story, and the story to develop the pictures. We have to have both the story and the pictures in order to fully understand either.

In our changing tastes, we are now demanding more visual interest from media in general. What's more, our aesthetic standards are changing. We're learning to read what some might call confusion and to find within it information that is meaningful to us. The simple, clean line isn't enough; today's audiences also want some pizzazz to keep them engaged. The implications for aesthetic standards in the twenty-first century are immense.

Where Are We Now?

According to Stephens (1998), we have had three communications revolutions: the introduction of writing, the introduction of printing, and now the moving image, an invention that Boorstin (1987) predicted would change our view of text. Stephens believes the moving image will eventually become twenty-first-century writing (1998, 201), although he admits we are still a long way from developing a lexicon and syntax for organizing moving images so that they may become a written language.

For years we have been hearing about the death of the novel. Television was supposed to kill it, and now moving images may replace words as a writing medium. Looking ahead toward possible effects of film on textual documents, Boorstin (1987, 129) said, "The novelist, then, has been encouraged to explore the boundless nonvisual world, as the movie maker has taken over much of his former jurisdiction over the fantasy world of sight, sound, and action." Yet the novel and writing remain healthy. A 1990 Gallup Poll found many more people who said they were reading a book or novel than they had found in 1957 (Stephens 1998, 9). Time-use studies conducted by John Robinson at the University of Maryland show that the amount of time per week people spend reading books and magazines increased by thirteen minutes between 1965 and 1985, even though magazine reading had suffered a dramatic dip when television first became popular. In spite of that increase, the decreases in time spent reading newspapers has brought the overall total reading time found by these studies down 30 percent, to a total of less than three hours per week (Stephens 1998, 10). Unfortunately, these reading statistics do not include newspapers online or informational web sites, to say nothing of chat rooms and UseNet groups, sources that many now read regularly.

Among those who see words and images as engaged in a contest, the choice of which position to defend is not trivial; according to researchers like Stephens (1998) and Shlain (1998), the implications for our future culture may be daunting. This present volume, *Working with Words and Images*, is not, however, intended to defend either position but rather to shift the focus of the argument. The important point is not which medium, words or images, is winning, but that each works in a different but often collaborative way to make a contribution to our overall making of meaning. It is these workings, these contributions and their interactions, that we need to understand. Writers who have created both novels and film scripts are very aware of the differences in what they can accomplish within each medium and the value of each. Boorstin's analysis of one film, *On the Waterfront*, and comments about it by Budd Schulberg, the scriptwriter, give us a good example of how these differences between a novel and a film are obvious to one who works with them.

After viewing the movie, Schulberg felt that he had more to say that could not be expressed in movie form, so he wrote a novel based on the same story:

> The film is an art of high points. I think of it as embracing five or six sequences, each one mounting to a climax that rushes the action onward. The novel is an art of high, middle, and low points. . . . The film does best when it concentrates on a single character. . . . It has no time for what I call the essential digression. The "digression" of complicated, contradictory character. The "digression" of social background. . . . [Film] cannot wander as life wanders, or pause as life always pauses, to contemplate the incidental or the unexpected. (quoted in Boorstin 1987, 147)

Summarizing the differences between novels and film, Boorstin concludes:

> The nuance, the perspective, the contradictions of historical development and social interaction were not made for the camera eye. . . . To be sure, the film can "speak-out," vividly and terrifyingly, as did *Waterfront*. But the novel is able, in Schulberg's phrase, "to speak-*in*," to search the interior drama in the heart and mind. (1987, 148)

When Stephens (1998) suggests that moving images may become the writing of the twenty-first century, he has much more than films in mind. Though still crude and not available to everyone, moving images are becoming common elements in electronic communications. Some have feared that computers are changing our patterns of entertainment and communication with dire results. Our tastes and interests may be changing, but writing, reading, and drawing are not disappearing because of computers. Thanks to web sites, email, discussion lists, chat rooms, and so on, as well as the ease with which we can use computers to compose, design, and revise, people are writing, creating their own art, and exchanging the results more than ever, a triumph of the GUI (graphic-user interface) over the command-line interface.

With electronic documents, particularly hypertexts, we are likely to approach our reading as we read newspapers or magazines, browsing through until something catches our attention—sometimes a heading or phrase, often an image. Hypertext fictions, which exemplify one application of electronic media to art, maintain many of the characteristics of paper fictions, yet they exist only as ghosts on a computer screen. Choosing a sequence of appealing links, each reader weaves an individualized story that may leap backward and forward through time and topics.

Hypertext fiction can solve some frustrations for writers: those intriguing side issues that can make a traditional story too long and tangled can be explored through links. With hypertext, a writer can come closer to telling the "whole" story. At the same time, however, hypertext fiction also presents new challenges for readers and, especially, for writers. How can a writer create a sense of place or time, which is often so important to fiction, when a reader's sequence-of-story passages can vary space-and-time patterns at a whim? How can an epiphany become a truly meaningful experience for a character when it might occur at any point in a story? How can there even be a coherent, progressive plot? Working within such an environment to create quality fiction requires a particular kind of genius, as it also raises a host of knotty questions about the nature of fiction. Is a plot or a sense of place necessary? Should images or sounds be included, as they are in the music videos that tell stories? What really constitutes a fiction?

Hypertext fiction is a genre that requires writers to develop an additional set of skills and a different sense of purpose, right alongside the talents and abilities more typically required of writers. It will also lead all of us to learn new reading conventions. Because hypertext has its being within the visual and highly linked medium of the computer screen, the best way to experience it is through an electronic context, such as a CD-ROM or on the World Wide Web (WWW). One imaginative discussion of creating hypertext fiction can be found at <paradoxa.com/excerpts/4-11joyce.hym>. At this site, Michael Joyce, one of the pioneers of literary hypertext, engages in playful speculation on the nature of hypertext fiction, where it has been and where it may be going.

These new areas and methods of communication present challenges for writers and designers, both culturally and technologically. Examples of one of these challenges will be found in this volume. Some of the illustrations in chapters 6, 12, and 13 are taken from the WWW. Consequently, they are copied at only 72 dpi and reproduce poorly in book print. Although this is regrettable, present technology offers no satisfactory solution.

Part three of this volume presents discussions of some of the other challenges and information on how we might deal more effectively with them. In chapter 12, Jonathan Allen and Greg Simmons discuss some of the technological challenges of designing documents for digital media, a mode of publication that they believe constitutes a revolution in document design. From their experience Allen and Simmons suggest problems to consider and offer some advice for meeting them. In chapter 13, Amy Kimme Hea deconstructs a web site to show the rhetorical implications for meaning found in its content and design. The insights she offers will help web-site designers see hidden implications in their own designs as well as those in sites they visit on the WWW. After these chapters of insights and skills focused on designing for digital media, we turn to two discussions of serious issues related to digital media presented in a more playful manner. In chapter 14, Rich Gold offers an oral presentation, albeit on paper, created with the common technologies of MicroSoft Office, Word, and PowerPoint. Gold raises issues related to reading, especially the unusual experience of group reading, and to the influence of one electronic medium on creative thought processes. He thinks, Gold says of himself, in PowerPoint. In chapter 15, Neil Kleinman brings together many of the strands that have traveled through this volume in his discussion of problems that arise when we combine text and graphics, a process he compares to trying to mix oil and water. Drawing on stories from his experiences, Kleinman tells us of problems professionals trained in new approaches now encounter in the work place and those that teachers face in developing programs to address today's communication challenges.

The computer's influence on writing, drawing, and reading cannot be overestimated, considering that "workplaces in which approximately 70 percent of jobs requiring a bachelor's degree or an advanced college degree now require the use of computers . . . [and] 87 percent of high school students are now writing on computers by Grade 11" (Selfe 1999, 415). Using computers may result in a different kind of reading, writing, and drawing than some traditionalists advocate, but these communication modes have always been on the move. We do not discard the old methods and styles, we enfold them, incorporate them into our new ways of doing things. As a counterpart to the minimalists' tenet, sometimes more is more.

We should keep in mind Boorstin's and Schulberg's comments about the different purposes that words and images can serve. Though they were talking about novels and film, two creative applications of these modes, their insights need not be limited to those endeavors. Their point is that we first evaluate our purposes and the audience we wish to address in any given situation; we then choose the mode of communication that works best within that context. Neither words nor images is blessed as "the way." As Fred Dretske put it, "In the beginning was information. The word came later" (quoted in Byrd 1994, 10). We could say the same of images: Drawing a line on a cave wall is information. Extending the line into a picture others will recognize as an antelope makes it an image.

This volume is not designed to define words or images nor to declare a victor in the perceived contest between them. Nor does our scope cover any of the many other influences on communication, such as those presented by our senses of touch, sound, and so on. What this volume *does* do is present examples, discussions, and research on intersections and relationships between words and images in several spheres of our professional and cultural experiences so that we might learn more about how these modes interact in the processes of communication. This volume addresses: current and historical theories of interpretation, visual thinking as a tool for writers, words and letters as visual images, and interactions of words and images in various professional arenas. It also explores ways in which electronic media are affecting the relationships between words and images and our uses of them. For those who are contemplating the issues raised here in terms of classroom procedures and professional preparation, Neil Kleinman has prepared a set of exercises focused on improving visual awareness and skills and a sample curriculum that integrates work with words and images. These appear in "Afterword: Experiments with Image and Word," the concluding section of this volume.

We do not have to view words and images as at war or attribute the cause of their variations in popularity to gender or time in order to agree that changes in our uses of words and images are occurring. If we want to become more effective at using words and images together as professional writers and web-site designers do, if we need to present complex ideas and make them clearer and more understandable as scientific researchers and architects do, we would do well to learn more about the workings of words and images and the interrelationships between them:

> The history of culture is in part the story of a protracted struggle for dominance between pictorial and linguistic signs, each claiming for itself certain proprietary rights on a "nature" to which only it has access. . . . Among the most interesting and complex versions of this struggle is what might be called the relationship of subversion, in which language or imagery looks into its own heart and finds lurking there its opposite number. (Mitchell 1986, 43)

References

Allen, Tina. (August 29, 1999). *CBS New: Sunday Morning*. CBS Television Network.

Apostle, Hippocrates G., trans., with commentaries and glossary. (1981). *Aristotle's On the Soul (De Anima)*. Grinnell, IA: Peripatetic Press.

Barthes, Roland. (1977). *Image. Music. Text.*, trans. Stephen Heath. New York: Hill & Wang.

Berger, Arthur Asa. (1989). *Seeing Is Believing: An Introduction to Visual Communication*. Mountain View, CA: Mayfield.

Boorstin, Daniel J. (1987). *The Image: A Guide to Pseudo-Events in America*, 25th anniversary ed. New York: Atheneum.

Burnham, Sarah Maria. (1901). *Figures of Speech*. Boston: A. I. Bradley.

Byrd, Don. (1994). *The Poetics of the Common Knowledge*. Albany: State University of New York Press.

Chomsky, Noam. (1972). *Language and Mind*, enlarged ed. New York: Harcourt Brace Jovanovich.

Corbett, Edward P. J. (1965). *Classical Rhetoric for the Modern Student*. New York: Oxford University Press.

Eagleton, Terry. (1983). *Literary Theory: An Introduction*. Minneapolis: University of Minnesota Press.

Faigley, Lester. (1999). Material Literacy and Visual Design. In Jack Selzer and Sharon Crowley, eds., *Rhetorical Bodies: Toward a Material Rhetoric*. Madison: University of Wisconsin Press, 171–201.

Fromkin, Victoria, and Robert Rodman. (1998). *An Introduction to Language*, 6th ed. New York: Harcourt Brace.

Ganter, J. Carl. (1998, August). Personal communication.

Hass, Kristin Ann. (1998). *Carried to the Wall: American Memory and the Vietnam Veterans Memorial*. Berkeley: University of California Press.

Holmes, Elizabeth. (1966). *Aspects of Elizabethan Imagery*. New York: Russell & Russell.

Joseph, Miriam, Sister. (1947). *Shakespeare's Use of the Arts of Language*. New York: Columbia University Press.

Lanham, Richard A. (1991). *A Handlist of Rhetorical Terms*. Berkeley: University of California Press.

Mitchell, W. J. T. (1986). *Iconology: Image, Text, Ideology*. Chicago: University of Chicago Press.

Nichols, Bill. (1981). *Ideology and the Image: Social Representation in the Cinema and Other Media*. Bloomington: Indiana University Press.

Page, T. E., E. Capps, and W. H. D. Rouse, eds. (1931). Introduction. In Philostratus, *Imagines*, trans. Arthur Fairbanks. London: William Heinemann.

Peacham, Henry. (1593). *The Garden of Eloquence*. London: H. Jackson. (Microfilm: Ann Arbor, MI: University Microfilms, 1947.)

Sacks, Oliver. (1995). *An Anthropologist on Mars: Seven Paradoxical Tales*. New York: Vintage Books/Random House.

Selfe, Cynthia L. (1999). Technology and Literacy: A Story about the Perils of Not Paying Attention. *College Composition and Communication* 50(3): 411–36.

Sherry, Richard. (1550). *A Treatise of Schemes and Tropes Very Profytable for the Better Understanding of Good Authors, Gathered Out of the Best Grammarians and Oratours*. London: John Day. Reprint, Delmar, NY: Scholars' Facsimiles & Reprints, 1977. (Microfilm: Ann Arbor, MI: University Microfilms, 1953.)

Shlain, Leonard. (1998). *The Alphabet versus the Goddess*. New York: Viking.

Sibley, John Langdon. (1885). *Biographical Sketches of Graduates of Harvard University in Cambridge, Massachusetts*, vol. 3: *1678–1689*. Cambridge: Charles William Sever.

Smith, John. (1657). *The Mysterie of Rhetorique Unvail'd*. London: George Eversden. Reprint, Menston (Yorks.) Scolar P., 1969. (Microfilm: Ann Arbor, MI: University Microfilms, 1953.)

Sonnino, Lee Ann. (1968). *A Handbook to Sixteenth-Century Rhetoric*. London: Routledge & Kegan Paul.

Sontag, Susan. (1973). *On Photography*. New York: Farrar, Straus & Giroux.

Stephens, Mitchell. (1998). *The Rise of the Image the Fall of the Word*. New York: Oxford University Press.

Tapscott, Don. (1998). *Growing Up Digital: The Rise of the Net Generation*. New York: McGraw-Hill.

Vico, Giambattista. (1968). *The New Science*, 3rd ed., trans. T. G. Bergin and M. H. Fisch. Ithaca, NY: Cornell University Press.

Warburton, William. (1766). *The Divine Legation of Moses Demonstrated*, 5th ed., vol. 3. London: A. Millar & J. & R. Tonson.

Watroba, Matt. (1999, April). Personal communication.

Wilson, Thomas. (1553). *The Arte of Rhetorique for the Use of All Suche As Are Studious of Eloquence, 1553*. London: Richardus Graftonus. Reprint, Gainesville, FL: Scholars' Facsimiles & Reprints, 1962. (Microfilm: Ann Arbor, MI: University Microfilms, 1953.)

Wolfe, Tom. (1975). *The Painted Word*. New York: Farrar, Straus & Giroux.

PART ONE

from media to meaning:
perception, interpretation,
and learning

Introduction: From Media to Meaning

"We allocate much of our energy to processing visual information," Arthur Berger (1989, 18) assures us and cites research by Jarice Hanson to support his claim:

> It is estimated that 75 percent of the information entering the brain is from the eyes, and that 38 percent of the fibers entering or leaving the central nervous system are in the optic nerve. Current research indicates that the eyes have 100 million sensors in the retina, but only five million channels to the brain from the retina. This means that more information processing is actually done in the eye than in the brain, and even the eye filters out information.

Berger extends his proposition beyond biological features to include social influences. He says, "We don't just 'see' but have to learn *how* to see and *what* to see. . . . And what we decide to see is determined by what we know and what we believe and what we want" (1989, 25). Visual processing, then, involves the physical perception and sorting performed by our biology as well as the adaptive skills and cultural values that we learn through education and social practices.

Our visual processing includes both words and images, since much of the language we process is read—from books, movie theater screens, computer displays, billboards, walls, newspapers, any of a host of sources. Words and images come at us constantly, and each presents its own special challenges to our brains (i.e., our personal CPUs) to process and develop meaning. A simplified view would say that we process words linearly, one word or phrase after another, and process images holistically, as a unit. But, actual processes are never that simple, including as they do the interaction of physical and social skills and influences.

Part one of this volume provides discussions of how we work with words and images to create both textual and visual meaning. The initial chapters present some of the issues raised by the processing we engage in daily and offer some new approaches to understanding these complexes of words and images and teaching others about them. These discussions bring up-to-date some of the issues presented in chapter 1 that arose during the historical development of words and images.

Arthur Glenberg, a psychologist at the University of Wisconsin, has studied human cognition and how we comprehend and develop meaning from language. In chapter 2, "The Indexical Hypothesis: Meaning from Language, World, and Image," Glenberg briefly describes cognitive psychology's standard approaches to language comprehension and then explains a very different approach he has developed. Glenberg's theory, which he calls the Indexical Hypothesis, explains how we develop meaning from language within contexts. According to Glenberg, understanding the meaning of a sentence involves combining (what he calls meshing) actions that underlie our understanding of words. When the resulting set of actions is coherent, that is, could actually be performed, then we believe we have understood the sentence. Glenberg describes three steps that produce meaning from language: indexing the words to appropriate objects in the world or analogical representations of those objects (e.g., images); deriving from the objects' possibilities for action within a given context (affordances); and meshing the possibilities as directed by the syntax of the sentence. Glenberg then applies his theory to documents that combine words and images, showing how the Indexical Hypothesis helps us to understand several cognitive phenomena and describing ways in which graphics facilitate text comprehension.

The letters that make up words also participate in how we react to a page of printing and to the meaning its words attempt to convey. According to Berger (1989, 151), "Design has, in a sense, the power to control people and to evoke certain desired responses. The size of print, the style of print, the heaviness or lightness of print, the size of margins, the arrangement of the block of type on the page—these and countless other seemingly minor matters have a profound impact on how we respond to printed matter." In chapter 3, "The Ransom Note Fallacy and the Acquisition of Typographic Emphasis," James Kalmbach, a professor of professional communication at Illinois State University, describes the process students go through when they begin learning to turn letters into design. As Kalmbach tells us, prior to schooling, children produce visually rich texts in which there is no easy way to tell where the story ends and the graphics begin. Once these children enter school, however, the urge to combine word and image is drilled out of them, and text is valorized almost exclusively. When such students enter professional and creative-writing classes, they are again asked to consider how the appearance of their text can help shape its impact. In his chapter, Kalmbach argues that writing novices and students go through an acquisition process very similar to the acquisition process children go through when first acquiring literacy. He documents four stages of achieving textual emphasis in the process of acquiring design literacy: scribal, additive, functional, and contrastive.

Developing meaning from documents, whether from paper or screen, also frequently involves interpreting images. Our interpretation of meaning from images can take on particular importance because of images' political and social potential. For example, our society argues about how the American flag can be used: As clothing? As a bedspread? Displayed over a school? Over a church? In a protest march? W. J. T. Mitchell (1986) stated the political implications of images in strong terms, concluding: "It is perhaps only a slight exaggeration to say that the English Civil War was fought over the issue of images" (p. 7). Susan Sontag (1973), with her own political agenda, declared the importance of images in our world: "A capitalist society requires a culture based on images. It needs to furnish vast amounts of entertainment in order to stimulate buying and anesthetize the injuries of class, race, and sex" (p. 178). How we respond to images may be complex, but it is not incidental.

In chapter 4, Barbara Tversky, a psychologist at Stanford University, attempts to untangle some of the complexities of our responses to images in various forms by describing her research into "Some Ways That Graphics Communicate." Tversky discusses what she has learned about how we understand images as both consumers and producers. In her research she analyzed how people responded to graphic representations and reconfirmed her findings by also asking them to produce graphics in response to verbal descriptions.

Richard Johnson Sheehan, technical communication professor at the University of New Mexico, draws on the field of visual presentation to develop a method that enables novices to expand their visual skills. Because Johnson Sheehan finds electronic texts to be essentially visual, he believes they require us to use a visual approach when we compose for them. In chapter 5, "Being Visual, Visual Beings," he shows us how, as teachers or practitioners, we can apply Arnheim's visual principles to the steps of developing documents. He begins by discussing the history and nature of electronic texts and concludes by showing how we can apply visual principles to designing our own documents.

Through visual images we are not only entertained, but we also learn and discover:

> The images we see, whether in our dreams or daydreams, in drawings and doodles, in our notebooks, or images we find in printed matter or films or the broadcast media—all are connected to our ability to focus our attention on something, to deal with it in other than abstract and intellectual ways, and ultimately to "break set" (escape from conventional ideas and beliefs) and come up with something new. (Berger 1989, 2)

In other words, visuals help us to think. Ron Fortune, a professor of writing at Illinois State University who has done considerable research on visual thinking, rounds out part 1 by bringing issues of visual and verbal skills together in chapter 6, "Image, Word, and Future Text: Visual and Verbal Thinking in Writing Instruction." Fortune discusses the kinds of training in visual thinking that students and practitioners will require if they are to produce the graphically rich documents envisioned for the future. As a guide, he sets up a detailed analysis of the processes through which instructors can pursue education in visual thinking to complement the development of students' learning through verbal representation.

References

Berger, Arthur A. (1989). *Seeing Is Believing: An Introduction to Visual Communication*. Mountain View, CA: Mayfield.

Mitchell, W. J. T. (1986). *Iconology: Image, Text, Ideology*. Chicago: University of Chicago Press.

Sontag, Susan. (1973). *On Photography*. New York: Farrar, Straus & Giroux.

chapter two

THE INDEXICAL
HYPOTHESIS
meaning from language,
world, and image

arthur m. glenberg

T HE RESEARCH IS AS CLEAR AS OUR INTUITIONS: Combining images and text can produce tremendous benefits for comprehension.[1] In fact, it is difficult to imagine programming a VCR, building a bookcase, or learning to use a compass without the help of both images and language. In contrast to the clarity of our intuitions, cognitive psychologists have had little success in producing clear explanations of the benefits. In this chapter, I will propose an explanation based on a recently developed account of meaning (Glenberg 1997) and language comprehension (Glenberg and Robertson 1999; Glenberg and Robertson 2000; Kaschak and Glenberg 2000). Explicating this account will take a bit of doing, because it differs dramatically from the standard approaches in cognitive psychology. In outline, I will sketch the standard approaches to meaning and language, as well as some reasons for discounting them. Then I will speculate on what sort of meaning can be relevant to the evolution of the cognitive system and how that sort of meaning leads to a new take on how language works, namely, the Indexical Hypothesis. This hypothesis will be applied to understanding how images and texts can combine to their mutual benefit, and I will offer some suggestions for how to maximize the effectiveness of images in texts.

Meaning I:
The Manipulation of Abstract Symbols

Cognitive psychology underwent a renaissance in the early 1960s in part because of the tremendous advances that were being made in computer science and artificial intelligence. Computers were, apparently, engaging in a type of thinking. Perhaps, it was thought, an understanding of computer thinking could be used to develop an understanding of human thinking. We know that computer programs are based on the manipulation of abstract symbols, such as binary digits. These symbols are abstract in several ways. First, a binary number (e.g., 1000001) may be used to represent a particular letter, such as "A." But this same number could be used to represent an "A" regardless of size, handwritten or typewritten, and so on. Second, the binary number is abstract in that it is an arbitrary representation of the letter "A"; that is, it doesn't look anything like the letter "A" or have any of the properties of an "A." These abstract symbols have wonderful properties in computers. First, because the perceptual details such as size and heft are stripped away, we do not have to worry about apparently irrelevant details interfering with computations using the symbols. Second, given that the symbols can be represented in an abstract format, we do not have to worry about the particulars of how a computer operates (e.g., does it use vacuum tubes, silicon, or neurons?) to guarantee the same result as long as the computer operates on the symbols the same way. Thus, computers "think" by manipulating abstract symbols using the rules of the software program, and using the same rules guarantees the same results no matter what computer is being used. Importantly, the meaning of an abstract symbol (e.g., 1000001) is given by its relations to other abstract symbols (e.g., 1000010) within the system, rather than by virtue of anything inherent in the symbol itself. In fact, given that the symbol is arbitrarily related to what it represents, it can have no inherent meaning.

If computers think by manipulating abstract symbols, perhaps humans do also. This analogy led to the development of Herbert Simon and Alan Newell's Physical Symbol System Hypothesis (e.g., Newell 1980) and a flowering of theories and experiments in cognitive psychology based on it and similar ideas. Even the briefest review of the most influential formal theories in cognitive psychology demonstrates that they are based on abstract symbols. This is true of production systems (e.g., Anderson 1993), neural networks and semantic networks (e.g., Masson 1995), memory theories (e.g., Hintzman 1986), high-dimensional space theories (e.g., Landauer and Dumais 1997), and theories based on propositions constructed from abstract symbols (e.g., Kintsch 1988). All of these theories base knowledge on abstract symbols; the symbols become meaningful through their relations to other abstract symbols; and thinking is the manipulation of the abstract symbols based on rules equivalent to computer software.

This framework seems to work well for language. Words *are* abstract symbols, and language manipulates them. Words are abstract because we use the same word, for example "chair," for a variety of different objects, stripping away their perceptual differences. Second, the word "chair" has an arbitrary relation to real chairs. That is, the word doesn't look like a real chair or have any of its defining properties such as backs and legs. Furthermore, we seem to generate meaning for language through the manipulation of the arbitrary symbols (words) by rules (grammar).

Thus, according to abstract symbol theories, language is understood by translating words into internal abstract symbols, and that these symbols are related to one another by a relatively small set of relations that reflect grammatical relations. For example, according to Walter Kintsch (1988), we understand a simple sentence such as "Erik dried his feet with a towel" by finding abstract symbols for Erik (e.g., 10001), feet (e.g., 10010), towel (e.g., 10011), and to dry (e.g., 00111), and then relating them using an internal proposition such as Rel 00111 (Agent 10001; Object 10010; Instrument 10011).

With this unanimity of opinion, what could be wrong? The answer is: Just about everything. First, the basis for the analogy between human and computer thinking is incorrect: Computers do not think. The only real thinking going on is that of the programmer and that of the user of the computer who interprets the abstract symbols. This is a contentious claim that I will not try to defend here, because it has been made eloquently by, among others, Hubert Dreyfus (1979), Gerald Edelman (1992), George Lakoff (1987), and Humberto Maturana and Francisco Varela (1987). Second, the thinking that people do, particularly when comprehending language, cannot be solely the manipulation of abstract symbols. This later claim is based on John Searle's (1980) Chinese Room Argument, and a variant of it discussed by Stevan Harnad (1990). Consider Harnad's thought experiment: You arrive at an airport in a country that speaks a language you do not know, say Chinese. At your disposal is a dictionary written in Chinese (not a Chinese/English dictionary). As you step into the airport terminal, you see a sign written in Chinese logograms (that is, abstract symbols), and you decide that you should figure out what the sign means. So, you pull out your dictionary and look up the first abstract symbol. Unfortunately, its definition is given in terms of other abstract symbols. So, you look up the first symbol in the definition, but its definition is also given in terms of other abstract symbols. Will you ever understand the meaning of the sign by tracing out relations among abstract symbols? Of course not. Similarly, it is hard to imagine how one could find the meaning of the proposition Rel 00111 (Actor 10001; Object 10010; Instrument 10011) from simply tracing relations to other propositions composed of abstract symbols.

As Harnad and Searle note, these abstract symbols must be grounded if they are to be meaningful. That is, somehow the symbols must be taken to refer to real things, such as letter "A"s or rabbits or feet or towels. But how does one go about grounding abstract symbols? Is there enough structure in the relations between the symbols to find the correct corresponding objects in the world? Hilary Putnam (1981; and see Lakoff 1987) has proven that there is not. That is, any set of abstract symbols and their relations can be mapped onto a variety of objects and their relations. In short, if we thought by manipulating abstract symbols, we could never be certain what we were thinking about, just as a computer engaged in manipulating abstract symbols may be playing chess or solving mathematical equations or simulating digestion. Thus to summarize: meaning cannot arise solely from the manipulation of abstract symbols (Searle 1980; Harnad 1990), they need to be grounded. But, if the mind consisted of nothing but abstract symbols and their relations, the symbols would be impossible to ground (Putnam 1981; Lakoff 1987). Given that almost all current models of meaning in cognitive psychology are based on manipulation of abstract symbols, there must be something seriously wrong with those theories.

But, as noted before, words *are* abstract symbols, and language manipulates them. So on the one hand, it appears that abstract symbols cannot underlie meaning, and on the other hand, the predominate human system for conveying meaning—language—seems to rely on just those abstract symbols. Is there a way out of this conundrum? The embodied approach to meaning and language is meant to do just that. The next section develops an "embodied" account of meaning. The section following that describes how language understanding results in embodied meaning.

Meaning II: Embodiment

Rather than starting from computer science (as do the abstract symbol theories), embodied accounts of meaning start with biology and evolution: Cognitive systems have almost certainly evolved, and attributes evolve because they contribute to survival and reproductive success. This is no doubt as true for cognition as it is for eyes and wings. Furthermore, survival and reproductive success require effective action in the environment. What does it mean for action to be effective? At the very least, it must take into account the constraints on action due to the actor's body. For example, when faced with a predatory snake, a bird can take the effective action of flying away. If a cat or a human were to try to fly away, that cat or human would be dead long before it had a chance to reproduce.

Given that cognition is designed to produce effective action, and given that meaning results from cognition, we can suppose that action and meaning are closely related. This supposition leads to an embodied approach to meaning as developed by Glenberg (1997) and Glenberg and Robertson (1999).[2] The meaning of a situation to a particular individual is the set of actions available to that individual in that situation. Furthermore, the set of actions is based on the mesh of affordances, experiences, and goals.

Affordances (Gibson 1979) are possibilities for action determined by the relation between the physical situation and the actor's body. For example, when faced with a snake, birds and cats need to act differently because of different actions the physical situation affords their different bodies. Similarly, the affordances of a chair are different for an adult and a toddler, because of their different bodily capabilities. For an adult, a chair affords sitting, but it also affords standing on (to change a light bulb), and hefting (to ward off a snake). The chair may afford sitting for the toddler, but if his or her balance is uncertain, it doesn't afford standing on, nor does it afford hefting.

Many affordances do not need to be learned. Instead, they are picked out by our perceptual systems that have co-evolved with our bodies to contribute to effective action. Nonetheless, some actions clearly benefit from learning based on our experiences and our cultures. Thus, you may choose not to sit in a particular folding chair because the last time you tried, it collapsed: you have learned new affordances of that chair. Or, you may choose not to sit in a chair because it is in a museum and our culture blocks that action.

Effective action also depends on goals. Thus, how one acts in regard to a chair depends on whether one needs to rest (so sit on it), change a light bulb (so stand on it), or scratch one's back (so sidle up to it).

Affordances, experiences, and goals can be combined, or *meshed,* because they are all realized in the same medium—the medium of bodily action. Combining these sources of action is not based on principles of association, statistics, or logic (as in abstract symbol theories). Instead, mesh satisfies intrinsic constraints on action—that is, constraints imposed by physics and biology. Thus, one can mesh the affordances of a chair with the goal of eating at a table; these actions fit together because of how our bodies work. But one cannot mesh the affordances of a chair with the goal of jumping rope. That is, the affordances of chairs do not mesh with the goal of jumping rope. Or, a mobile adult can mesh the affordances of a chair with the goal of scratching one's back, but one cannot (easily) mesh the affordances of a chair with the goal of drying one's back.

Thus the embodied claim is that the meaning of a situation is based on the mesh of affordances, experiences, and goals. Natika Newton (1996) discusses the philosophical underpinnings for basing meaning and understanding on action. Lawrence Barsalou (1999) demonstrates how a similar embodied account can be used to understand abstract concepts such as truth and exclusive-or.

The Indexical Hypothesis: Meaning from Words

The Indexical Hypothesis is a link between language and the action-based account of meaning. In making the link, the hypothesis provides a solution to the language comprehension conundrum that: a) meaning cannot be based solely on the manipulation of abstract symbols, but b) language, a prototypical abstract symbol system, conveys meaning.

By way of introducing the hypothesis, consider how we know whether a sentence makes sense. Sentence (1a) seems perfectly sensible, whereas sentence (1b) is nonsense, or at the very least bizarre:

(1a) After wading barefoot in the lake, Erik dried his feet using his shirt.

(1b) After wading barefoot in the lake, Erik dried his feet using his glasses.

Abstract symbol theories suggest several criteria for when a sentence is meaningful. First, of course, we need to know the meanings of the various words—that is, we need internal abstract symbols embedded in a web of other symbols—for each content word. For these example sentences, we certainly know what the words mean. Second, we must be familiar with the grammatical forms and relations; once again, no problem here. Third, the various components of the sentences must meet various "semantic selection" restrictions, so that agents (such as Erik) are animate, and so on. Fourth, the symbols must be in their proper relations, where "proper" means based on experience or grammatical class. All of the grammatical relations are acceptable, and for these examples most people have had no experience using shirts or glasses to dry feet.[3] Thus according to abstract symbol theories, the sentences are understood as two very similar propositions, differing only in the instrument component (I am using 10111 as the symbol for glasses):

(P1a) Rel 00111 [Agent 10001; Object 10010; Instrument 10011].

(P1b) Rel 00111 [Agent 10001; Object 10010; Instrument 10111].

Importantly, because the various criteria for meaning are met, abstract symbol theory asserts that the two sentences are equally understandable and equally sensible. But people, of course, see a striking difference. Sentence (1a) makes sense and sentence (1b) does not. The Indexical Hypothesis describes how the abstract symbols of language are turned into embodied meaning that discriminates between these sorts of sentences.

According to the Indexical Hypothesis, language comprehenders engage in three processes. First, noun phrases are indexed (or mapped) to actual objects or to analogical representations of those objects called "perceptual symbols" (Barsalou 1999). Thus, in a conversation with Erik, we might index "shirt" to the shirt he is wearing. Or, upon seeing in a museum a sign that says "Do not sit in the chair," we would index "the chair" to an object nearby. When actual objects are not available, we index the phrases to perceptual symbols, not abstract ones. These perceptual symbols do not have an arbitrary relation to their referents (in contrast to abstract symbols). Instead, they are based on perceptual details relevant to forming the symbol from experience. For our purposes, we can consider perceptual symbols to be mental images, although Barsalou is quite clear in pointing out how they differ from mental images.

In the second process, affordances are derived from the indexed objects or perceptual symbols. Thus we may note that a shirt can be used to keep someone warm, that it can make a tourniquet to stop bleeding, that it can be bunched up to prevent a draft from entering under a door, or it can be used to dry one's feet. The actual affordances derived depend on the third process, which is described next.

Finally, the affordances are meshed (combined) under direction of the syntax of the sentence. If the meshing process is successful—that is, if a doable set of actions is formed—then the sentence is understood.

So why is the sentence with "shirt" sensible, whereas the one with "glasses" nonsense? Because the affordances of a shirt can be meshed with feet to accomplish the goal of drying, whereas the affordances of glasses cannot be meshed with feet to accomplish the goal of drying. To put it differently, the Indexical Hypothesis asserts that understanding language requires using language to guide the construction of embodied conceptualizations, not the construction of abstract symbols.

Why is the difference in meaningfulness between sentences (1a) and (1b) beyond the ken of abstract symbol theories? There are several related reasons. First, because the symbols are arbitrarily related to what they represent, there is no way to examine the abstract symbols themselves (e.g., 10011 and 10111) and determine that one can be used for drying and one cannot. Second, the way abstract symbol theory would attempt to surmount this problem is by storing additional symbols and propositions meant to assert the equivalent of "a shirt can be used to dry things" and "glasses cannot be used to dry things." But given that the sentences used in Glenberg and Robertson (in press) were intended to describe novel situations, it is highly unlikely that the readers have actually had the opportunity to explicitly learn that "glasses cannot be used to dry things." Furthermore, given that the affordances of shirts and other objects are unlimited and generative (depending on changing goals and bodies), no list of explicit assertions could ever be sufficient to decide between sensible and nonsensical uses of objects. Instead, according to the Indexical Hypothesis, object knowledge consists of perceptual symbols from which we can derive affordances, and those affordances can change with the goal.

How Grammar Guides
the Mesh of Affordances

According to the Indexical Hypothesis, the third step in comprehension is to mesh affordances under the guidance of syntax. Kaschak and Glenberg (2000) propose that a particular type of grammatical information—grammatical constructions (e.g., Goldberg 1995)—provide the information that guides mesh. According to Adele Goldberg, constructions are form–meaning pairs. Thus, words are constructions that pair an abstract symbol (e.g., "chair") with a meaning (a thing you can sit on). Furthermore, Goldberg (1995) claims that basic sentence structures are also form-meaning pairings. Consider, for example, transitive sentences such as:

(2) Mike hit/threw/sent the feather.

Goldberg proposes that the transitive form (subject–verb–object) carries the meaning "act on," and that our understanding of (2) develops in part from meaning conveyed by the construction.

Another example of a construction is the double object construction, subject–verb–object1–object2. Goldberg suggests that the meaning of this construction is "transfer." For example, consider this sentence:

(3) Mike hit/threw/sent David the feather.

Thus, the subject (Mike) transfers the second object (the feather) to the first object (David). The double object construction seems to force verbs to take on a "transfer" meaning, even when the verbs normally do not have such a meaning. Consider, for example, "Mike blew David the feather," or even, "Mike sneezed David the feather." The fact that the last sentence is sensible is quite remarkable given that "to sneeze" is generally taken to be an intransitive verb that cannot take an object (let alone two).

Kaschak and Glenberg (2000) took Goldberg's ideas one step further. They proposed that the meaning conveyed by the construction provides the goal that guides the derivation and mesh of affordances. Consider again the sentence, "Mike sneezed David the feather." A limitless variety of affordances can be derived from the perceptual symbols for "Mike," "David," and "feather," and those affordances can be meshed in an equally limitless fashion. When put into a double object construction, however, the meshing process is constrained to produce a conceptualization in which transfer takes place: Mike has to start out with the feather and David has to end up with it.

We tested this idea using sentences like (4) that use innovative denominal verbs:

(4) Mike ballooned David the toy to help him out.

Denominal verbs are based on nouns (such as "bicycle") that are turned into verbs (such as "to bicycle"). Innovative denominal verbs can be made up and understood on the fly, such as "The newsboy porched the newspaper" or "My sister Houdini'ed her way out of the locked closet" (Clark and Clark 1979). We used innovative denominal verbs in the experiment, because these verbs have no conventional meaning: any meaning that is perceived must come from the interaction of the verb and syntax.

When the innovative denominal verbs were placed in the double object construction such as in sentence (4), the participants in our experiments overwhelmingly interpreted the innovative denominal verb as implying a type of transfer in which the noun (e.g., a balloon) is used to effect the transfer. We also placed innovative denominal verbs in transitive constructions such as in:

(5) Mike ballooned the toy to help David out.

In this case, people overwhelmingly interpreted the innovative denominal verb as implying "act upon" in which the noun (e.g., a balloon) is used to act on the toy. Thus, meaning of the innovative verb "to balloon" is determined by the construction in which it appears.

Importantly, we also demonstrated that syntax alone cannot generate meaning. Instead, the affordances of the noun underlying the denominal verb must be such that they can be used to accomplish the goals conveyed by the scene. Thus, if a previous context described the balloon referred to in sentence (4) as having been shredded, people don't know what to make of the sentence. Apparently, they do not understand the sentence as implying transfer, because they cannot mesh the affordances of a shredded balloon with the goal of transfer. Or as another example, most people cannot come up with a sensible reading of the double object sentence, "Mike sunned David the toy." Thus, it appears that grammatical constructions provide instructions for how to mesh affordances. But if the affordances do not mesh, a coherent meaning cannot be achieved. The experimental details supporting these claims are reported in Kaschak and Glenberg (2000).

How Image and Text Combine

The Indexical Hypothesis makes the relation between image and text almost transparent. According to the hypothesis, ordinary understanding of language always requires indexing to either objects or analogical representations of those objects (to derive affordances). When those analogical representations are mental constructs, we have been calling them "perceptual symbols." When those analogical representations are physical objects, they can be pictures, illustrations, graphs, and so on.

Indexing words to an image can benefit comprehension in both familiar and unfamiliar domains. Consider familiar domains first. Even when reading in familiar domains, language is inherently ambiguous; indexing to images can reduce that ambiguity and thereby enhance comprehension. Language is ambiguous because it uses abstract symbols (words) that intentionally ignore details. Thus the symbol "chair" can refer to an enormous variety of chairs, and if I say, "I threw the chair at the snake" and you index "chair" to your favorite stuffed chair, you may have a difficult time understanding how the throwing could be done. Much of the time we easily work out these problems, because the objects to be indexed are specified by the situation, are indexed by the speaker using gesture, or because you have enough experiences to work out an alternative indexing to another object or perceptual symbol (e.g., a plastic patio chair). A well-placed image can facilitate the process by providing the right affordances at the right time.

The benefits of a well-placed image multiply when reading in a technical domain (even a familiar one) in which excessively complex locutions would be required if language were to be completely explicit. For example, a molecular biologist needs to understand the detailed, complex foldings of a protein in order to understand how that protein interacts with other substances. The language needed to describe the details of even one fold and how that fold generates a functional shape might run for pages. Indexing the words "the fold" to the appropriate component of an image will give the biologist much of the information more quickly, more accurately, and with less ambiguity than the pages of text (cf. Larkin and Simon 1987).

The enormous benefits of indexing to an image are readily appreciated when reading or listening in unfamiliar domains. Imagine how difficult it would be to program a VCR in the absence of images and diagrams. Because the domain is unfamiliar, you may have no perceptual symbol from which appropriate affordances can be derived. Without an image to provide the affordances, understanding will be limited at best.

We studied an analogous situation using a compass (Glenberg and Robertson 1999) (see figure 2.1). The inspiration for the experiment came from my own preparation for a camping trip in the Rocky Mountains. I spent considerable time learning how to use a compass and topological map to identify landmarks (e.g., mountains). At first, the instructions that came with the compass seemed incomprehensible and bizarre. After I learned how to use the compass, however, the instructions seemed perfectly understandable. What produced this change? I think that I learned to index terms such as "direction-of-travel arrows" to the actual component part of the compass. Only after such indexing could I appropriately conceptualize instructions such as "Point the direction of travel arrows at the landmark."

Why should an instruction such as "Point the direction-of-travel arrows at the landmark" cause any difficulty? After all, we all know what an arrow is, what it means to point, and what a landmark is. As I noted before, how-

◆ **FIGURE 2.1** ◆

Suunto model M3 compass used in Glenberg and Robertson (1999). The direction of travel arrows are the two parallel arrows imprinted on the base of the compass and pointing to the right.

ever, the abstract symbols used by language are ambiguous. Consider the various ways that one can point depending on the affordances of "direction-of-travel arrows." It means one thing to point an index finger, another to point a rifle, another to point a car, and quite another to point the direction-of-travel arrows. If one indexes "direction-of-travel arrows" to a perceptual symbol of something like a rifle, then the type of pointing that is done with that sort of object will lead to confusion later when one is told to turn the 360-degree dial while pointing the direction-of-travel arrows; it would be very difficult to turn the dial if one were pointing as with a rifle. Once one has properly indexed "direction-of-travel arrows," however, how to point with them becomes less abstract and more explicit, because those types of arrows afford only certain actions.

In the Glenberg and Robertson (1999) experiment, two groups differed in their opportunity to index words to a video image of a compass. (In fact, there were four groups, but two of the four were relatively unimportant control conditions.) The Listen and Index group heard the audio track of a video tape describing the parts of a compass and map. The video image displayed the objects being described (see figure 2.1), thereby giving the participants the opportunity to index terms such as "direction-of-travel arrows." The Listen and Read group heard the same audio track and then read the script of the audio track, resulting in two exposures to the information. However, participants in this group did not see the video image, and so opportunities to index were reduced. After the two groups listened (and read) the information about the compass, we demonstrated that the groups were equivalent in their abstract knowledge about the compass. That is, the two groups performed equivalently on a verbal multiple-choice test covering parts of a compass described in the audio track (e.g., "When holding the compass in front of you, where do the direction-of-travel arrows point? a. magnetic north; b. true north; c. towards where you are facing; d. same direction as the orienting arrow"). Next, the participants in both groups read further instructions on how to use the compass to identify landmarks, and they were expected to follow the instructions—that is, to use the compass to actually identify landmarks. In contrast to equivalent performance on the verbal test of abstract knowledge, the Listen and Index group read these instructions more quickly and used the compass more accurately than did the Listen and Read group. Apparently, indexing the words to the image allowed the participants in the Listen and Index group to derive a type of meaning that is different from simply being able to recall the words and answer multiple-choice questions. We think that that meaning comes from the mesh of affordances that can be used to guide real action—in this case, the real action of using the compass to identify landmarks.

Barbara Tversky (2001; also see her chapter in this volume) notes that static images (such as those used in texts) easily and naturally convey static objects and some relational information, such as spatial proximity. Images do not naturally depict dynamic information, however. Thus, special training seems to be needed to extract information such as the rate of change from graphs (Gattis and Holyoak 1996). Also, people seem to have difficulty using a static depiction to imagine complex dynamical changes, such as how a series of pulleys act together (Hegarty 1992), or even what happens when a glass of water is tipped (Schwartz and Black 1999).

These observations, in conjunction with the Indexical Hypothesis, help us to understand why text and images make for an effective partnership: The image provides the opportunity to derive affordances, and the constructions provided by the text describe the dynamics—that is, how the affordances are meshed. The two mutually constrain one another to provide a more complete understanding than either could produce alone.

As an example, consider another instruction from the compass task used by Glenberg and Robertson (1999): "Turn the 360-degree dial until the red part of the magnetic needle and the orienting arrow are aligned." In the absence of an image (or the real compass), such an instruction is close to opaque for the naive reader: it is not clear what a 360-degree dial is, how it turns, or how the turning aligns anything. On the other hand, a static image, in the absence of the sentence, is equally useless. The image may give little indication of what turns and the consequences of turning. Even if some indications are given (e.g., with arrows that portray the direction of turning), as Hegarty (1992) has demonstrated, people cannot easily visualize the consequences of dynamic operations such as turning. Thus, it is difficult for the static image to convey a particular concept such as "until the red part of the magnetic needle and the orienting arrow are aligned" that requires the mesh of affordances in a particular sequence.

Putting the image and the text together permits each to play a constraining role in interpretation. The textural instruction, "Turn the 360-degree dial," situates the compass in the domain of human action and instructs the comprehender to consider interactions with the object that accomplish turning. The image of the compass and the 360-degree dial provide the affordances needed to know what sort of turning is required. Finally, the text describes the sequence of the meshing process and when it should end ("until . . .").

Suggestions for Design

The idea that images provide the affordances for meshing, and that texts provide instructions for meshing, leads to suggestions for design of texts with images. First, minimize the distance (in time and space) between text and image. Clearly, if the text is directing the mesh of affordances, and those affordances are being derived from the image, the image should be readily available while reading. Designers are at least partially sensitive to this advice, in that images often appear on the same page or an adjacent page as the relevant text. In some applications, it may be possible to integrate the two even further by embedding text within the image near the component relevant to the text (Mayer et al. 1995; Mayer et al. 1996). For example, consider how instructions for using a compass may be clarified. Most sets of instructions include images of the compass, but they are separated from the text. This separation requires the reader to somehow know that it is time to index the image and to stop reading. Also, the separation creates a problem in indexing: The reader must use the description of the to-be-indexed component to identify the component in the image. This process is potentially error prone, particularly when there are many components of the image that partially match the description. For example, a compass may have several types of arrows in addition to direction-of-travel arrows. Both of these problems can be eliminated by having small segments of text embedded in the image near the components that need to be indexed. Thus, an image of a compass may have printed near the 360-degree dial, "Turn the 360-degree dial until the red part of the magnetic needle and the orienting arrow are aligned," along with a line connecting the words "red part of the magnetic needle" to the image of the magnetic needle, a line connecting the words "the orienting arrow" and the image of that arrow, and so on. Thus, the spatial layout of the text (that it is close to the image) suggests when it is appropriate to index, and the connectors between phrases and the relevant component of the image facilitates the indexing.

The suggestion of minimizing temporal lag between reading the text and examining the image is difficult to implement in standard texts. Readers may not wish to switch attention from the text to the image, because it may lead to loss of one's location on the page, because the reader believes that further reading will disambiguate the text, or most likely because the reader does not realize that comprehension is suffering—that is, the reader may not appreciate that he or she is not constructing a meshed representation in sufficient detail to guide action (Glenberg et al. 1987). This problem can be solved in media other than print. For example, the auditory channel of film can provide the linguistic information needed to guide mesh, while the video channel focuses on the objects so that affordances can be derived. In instructional settings, sensitivity to the separate roles of image and words is part of what leads to a clear explanation: An instructor can be pointing to some object or its components (accomplishing the indexing for the student) while using language to describe how the affordances of the object should be meshed.

A second suggestion for design is to minimize the irrelevant in the image (Tufte 1983). From the point of view of the Indexical Hypothesis, there are at least two reasons for avoiding the irrelevant and the merely decorative. First, irrelevancies can produce unintended affordances or change the affordances of the depicted objects. For example, introducing solid, three-dimensional-looking bars on a graph can lead to confusion if, as is usually the case, it is only the height of the bar that is relevant. Second, irrelevancies can hide affordances, making it difficult to figure out how to mesh the objects as directed by the syntax (cf. Novick and Morse 1999). Nonetheless, some caution is in order. Stripping away what may appear to be irrelevancies may make it difficult for a novice to derive affordances. For example, if the image of a compass gives no indication of its size, then the reader may have a difficult time deriving affordances: Is it large enough to grasp? Is it too large to manipulate?

Summary and Conclusions

The Indexical Hypothesis describes how language—a system of abstract symbols and rules—is converted into embodied meaning: The set of actions available to the reader/listener. This translation occurs by indexing phrases to objects or images (or analogical representations in memory), deriving affordances from the objects or images, and then meshing those affordances under the guidance of grammatical constructions. Thus, the hypothesis helps us to understand how it is that words and images work together. The images provide a source of affordances that might otherwise be unavailable or difficult to retrieve from memory. The text provides the guidance for how to dynamically combine the affordances. Together, the text and image allow a level of understanding that could not be achieved from either alone.

Notes

1. Glenberg and Langston (1992) provide references to several hundred articles investigating the effects of images and texts.

2. This is an embodied account of meaning for two reasons: First, it supposes that meaning is based on biology, not computation; and second, meaning is based on how we use our bodies.

3. We know this for several reasons: First, these sentences were made up, along with many others reported in Glenberg and Robertson (2000), to reflect novel uses of items; second, if one were to ask a group of people to free-associate the phrase "dry one's feet," no one (before seeing these sentences) would ever say "glasses" or "shirt"; and third, a computer-based search of some 30,000 documents (see Glenberg and Robertson 2000) found that "dry," "glasses," and "shirt" are used in orthogonal contexts. Nonetheless, it certainly seems more sensible to use a shirt to dry one's feet. Must not that be based on experience? See the text for an alternative.

References

Anderson, John R. (1993). *Rules of Mind*. Hillsdale, NJ: Erlbaum.

Barsalou, Lawrence. (1999). Perceptual symbol systems. *Behavioral and Brain Sciences* 22: 577–660.

Clark, Eve, and Herbert H. Clark. (1979). When nouns surface as verbs. *Language* 55, 767–811.

Dreyfus, Hubert. (1979). *What Computers Can't Do*. New York: Harper & Row.

Edelman, Gerald M. (1992). *Bright Air, Brilliant Fire*. New York: Penguin.

Gattis, Meredith, and Keith J. Holyoak. (1996). Mapping conceptual to spatial relations in visual reasoning. *Journal of Experiment Psychology: Learning, Memory, and Cognition* 22: 1–9.

Gibson, James J. (1979). *The Ecological Approach to Visual Perception*. New York: Houghton Mifflin.

Glenberg, Arthur M. (1997). What memory is for. *Behavioral and Brain Sciences* 20: 1–19.

Glenberg, Arthur M., and William E. Langston. (1992). Comprehension of illustrated text: Pictures help to build mental models. *Journal of Memory and Language* 31: 129–31.

Glenberg, Arthur M., and David A. Robertson. (1999). Indexical understanding of instructions. *Discourse Processes* 28: 1–26.

———. (2000). Symbol grounding and meaning: A comparison of high-dimensional and embodied theories of meaning. *Journal of Memory and Language* 43: 379–401.

Glenberg, Arthur M., Thomas Sanocki, William Epstein, and Craig Morris. (1987). Enhancing calibration of comprehension. *Journal of Experimental Psychology: General* 116: 119–36.

Goldberg, Adele E. (1995). *Constructions: A Construction Grammar Approach to Argument Structure*. Chicago: University of Chicago Press.

Harnad, Stevan. (1990). The symbol grounding problem. *Physica D* 42: 335–46.

Hegarty, Mary. (1992). Mental animation: Inferring motion from static displays of mechanical systems. *Journal of Experiment Psychology: Learning, Memory, and Cognition* 18: 1084–1102.

Hintzman, Douglas L. (1986). "Schema abstraction" in a multiple-trace memory model. *Psychological Review* 93: 411–28.

Kaschak, Michael, and Arthur M. Glenberg. (2000). Constructing meaning: The role of affordances and grammatical constructions in sentence comprehension. *Journal of Memory and Language* 43: 508–29.

Kintsch, Walter. (1988). The role of knowledge in discourse comprehension: A construction-integration model. *Psychological Review* 95: 163–82.

Lakoff, George. (1987). *Women, Fire, and Dangerous Things: What Categories Reveal about the Mind.* Chicago: University of Chicago Press.

Landauer, T. K., and S. T. Dumais. (1997). A solution to Plato's problem: The latent semantic analysis theory of acquisition, induction, and representation of knowledge. *Psychological Review* 104: 211–40.

Larkin, Jill H., and Herbert A. Simon. (1987). Why a diagram is (sometimes) worth ten thousand words. *Cognitive Science* 11: 65–99.

Masson, Michael E. J. (1995). A distributed memory model of semantic priming. *Journal of Experimental Psychology: Learning, Memory, and Cognition* 21: 3–23.

Maturana, Humberto, and Francisco J. Varela. (1987). *The Tree of Knowledge: The Biological Roots of Human Understanding.* Boston: New Science Library.

Mayer, Richard E., William Bove, Alexandra Bryman, Rebecca Mars, and Lene Tapango. (1996). When less is more: Meaningful learning from visual and verbal summaries of science textbook lessons. *Journal of Educational Psychology* 88: 64–73.

Mayer, Richard E., Kathryn Steinhoff, Gregory Bower, and Rebecca Mars. (1995). A generative theory of textbook design: Using annotated illustrations to foster meaningful learning of science text. *Educational Technology Research and Development* 43: 31–43.

Newell, Alan. (1980). Physical symbol systems. *Cognitive Science* 4: 135–83.

Newton, Natika. (1996). *Foundations of Understanding.* Philadelphia: John Benjamins.

Novick, Laura R., and Deborah L. Morse. (1999). Building a bicycle, folding a fish: The role of diagrams in executing assembly procedures. Unpublished manuscript.

Putnam, Hilary. (1981). *Reason, Truth, and History.* Cambridge: Cambridge University Press.

Schwartz, Daniel, and Tamara Black. (1999). Inferences through imagined actions: Knowing by simulated doing. *Journal of Experimental Psychology: Learning, Memory, & Cognition* 25: 116–36.

Searle, John R. (1980) Minds, brains and programs. *Behavioral and Brain Sciences* 3: 417–24.

Tufte, Edward R. (1983). *The Visual Display of Quantitative Information.* Cheshire, CT: Graphics Press.

Tversky, Barbara. (2001). Spatial schemas in depiction. In *Spatial Schemas and Abstract Thought*, ed. M. Gattis (pp. 79–112). Cambridge: Massachusetts Institute of Technology Press.

chapter three

THE RANSOM NOTE
FALLACY AND
THE ACQUISITION OF
TYPOGRAPHIC EMPHASIS

james kalmbach

T HIS CHAPTER IS CONCERNED NEITHER WITH WORDS NOR IMAGES nor with the relationship of words to images; rather, it explores the ways in which words become images—that is, the ways in which the visual nature of text becomes part of that text's meaning and rhetorical purpose. Jay David Bolter and Richard Grusin (1999, 12) have described this process as "hypermediacy." It is a process during which a written text comes to be seen not as a transparent channel for communicating meaning, but as an opaque medium that can communicate meaning both through what is said and what is seen.

The argument that I will make is that because we have not studied the transition from transparent to opaque visual text, we do not know the process by which novice writers make this transition, and as a result, we have propagated a myth—the ransom note fallacy—that novice writers typically confound their texts with a wide variety of fonts, sizes, and styles when the truth is just the opposite: The visible texts of novice writers tend to be visually plain and become visually more complex in predictable ways as these writers develop fluency. Deconstructing the ransom note fallacy can help us to better understand this process and to better understand the social nature of visible text and typographic emphasis.

The Elements of Typographic Emphasis

Typographic emphasis means using visible text to call attention to some aspect of a document. Such emphasis is rhetorical in nature: visible text reinforces a particular meaning to a particular audience. Because emphasis is rhetorical and semiotic, it does not depend on any one of the technologies of writing. Handwritten documents, typewritten documents, as well as documents written on personal computers (and printed on inkjet or laser printers), all have their own grammar of visual emphasis. Handwritten texts, for example, communicate emphasis primarily through underlining, capitalizing all letters of words, and occasionally by making text larger. The devices available for visual emphasis using typewriters are similar. When typewriting, a writer can set headlines in capital letters, can underline for emphasis, and can add space between letters.

The introduction of personal computers that used typographically based operating systems in 1984 (the Macintosh and later Windows 95 and higher), as well as the widespread use of nonimpact printers (inkjet and laser), which incorporated the letter forms and emphasis devices of traditional typography into printing, have greatly increased the range of visual devices available for creating emphasis in everyday written communication, and has made these texts considerably more complicated and opaque.[1]

Today, whenever novice writers create texts on their personal computers, they have the option of using a variety of typefaces in virtually every major form: serif, sans serif, modern, traditional, transitional, decorative, handwritten, display, grunge, art deco, and so on. These novices, if they are using Microsoft Word, can choose from among nine different styles of underlining and eleven different typographic effects (from embossed to engraved to small caps to bold and italics). Finally, if these choices are not enough, they can set type in sizes ranging from 1 to 1,638 points.

In addition, modern word processors offer a variety of tools for manipulating space on the page, including tables, text blocks, finely grained controls to regulate the space between lines, and a variety of styles of text rules and borders. Moreover, because these typographic innovations are now part of every computer sold, typographic emphasis is available to most writers and novice writers, and typographic emphasis is part of the rhetoric of everyday written documents.[2]

The Ransom Note Fallacy[3]

Because devices for creating visual emphasis are now part of the most common and popular tools for writing, critiques of how novice writers use these devices have emerged. The most common of these critiques occurs under the banner of "ransom note typography." It is most often found in

◆ **FIGURE 3.1** ◆

A constructed example of ransom note emphasis. FROM *LOOKING GOOD IN PRINT* BY ROGER PARKER (1990). REPRINTED WITH PERMISSION.

books aimed at teaching would-be desktop publishers and novice writers how to format documents (see, for example, Litchy 1994; Parker 1990; 1995; and Williams 1992, 1994). Ransom note typography is said to occur when a variety of typefaces and typestyles have been used on the same page, creating a painful clashing that reminds readers of a ransom note (where every word has been cut from a different publication and pasted haphazardly on the page), and that leaves readers feeling that their aesthetic sense has been kidnapped.

Virtually all desktop design books include this critique in one form or another. Figure 3.1 is a constructed example of ransom note typography from Roger Parker's *Looking Good in Print*, which first appeared in 1990. Parker makes the following comment about ransom note emphasis: "The biggest single mistake most desktop publishers make is to include too many typefaces on a single page. This creates an amateurish, disorganized appearance" (p. 149). While Parker may not have been the first to use the term "ransom note" in relationship to the use of too many fonts and styles on a page,[4] his constructed example and the clear alternatives to ransom note emphasis that he presented in this and another book, *The Makeover Book* (Parker 1989), popularized this critique and his terminology. Most of the books on desktop design that have followed Parker make this point in one form or another. For example, Williams (1994, 69), in a self-quiz for readers, includes a constructed flyer that uses six different typefaces, and she offers a critique similar to Parker's of that document. Ransom note emphasis has even made its way into popular culture. In the comic strip *Foxtrot*, the oldest son is shown spending so much time picking fonts that he doesn't have time left to write a required paper. The *Chicago Tribune* recently ran this quote about ransom note emphasis in an article about fonts: "Many font-happy hackers . . . seek out wacky, virtually illegible type designs simply because they're eye-catching" (Keller 1999).

Ransom note emphasis has thus become symbolic of the damage that novice writers and desktop publishers can do to documents if they are given computers without instruction in visual design. What is remarkable about ransom note emphasis, however, is that it has become such a signifier while in real life, documents that actually make use of ransom note emphasis are rare, particularly in writing classes. I have been teaching writing, technical writing, and desktop publishing classes in computer-supported classrooms continuously since 1987, and I can count on one hand the number of real examples of ransom note emphasis turned in by real novice writers. What I see instead is page after page of Times New Roman type (the default typeface for Microsoft Office products), with headlines centered and set in capital letters. If something is particularly important, the writer may make the text a bit bigger and perhaps in bold-face or underlined, but still centered and all capped. Page after page after page. . . .

Why do trade books warn so vigorously against ransom note emphasis when real life examples are so difficult to find? One is tempted to attribute ransom note emphasis to urban legend much like the cookie recipes and virus scares that periodically sweep through the Internet. Perhaps the image of an out-of-control computer user adding font after font to his or her pages has become part of our mythology; or more cynically, perhaps the phenomena is the result of desktop-publishing authors trying to scare us into buying their books.

I would argue, however, that the fallacy of ransom note emphasis is the result of two things. First, the idea (if not the reality) of ransom note emphasis embodies a coming-of-age experience when the writer shifts from viewing the written text as a transparent medium that directly and unambiguously communicates meaning, to viewing the text as an opaque rhetorical form that communicates meaning not only through what it says but also through how it looks, where it is read, and who reads it. To use Bolter and Grusin's (1998) terminology again: it is the transition from "immediacy" to "hypermediacy"; it is the metamorphosis from modernity into postmodernity. Such a coming-of-age metaphor is so powerful and so useful in the abstract that it is easy to ignore the fact that ransom note emphasis rarely happens in real life.

Second, and more simply, ransom note emphasis may reoccur as a metaphor for what novice writers do with visible text because we have no other vocabulary. The vast majority of research on the role of typographic emphasis was done in the sixties, seventies, and eighties, prior to the personal computer revolution, when print documents where produced using offset lithography and photo-typesetting (and everyday documents were produced on IBM Selectrics and Smith-Coronas).[5]

Since then, as typography and typographic emphasis have become part of personal computing (and hence part of how most people write), there has been little research on how novice writers actually acquire these skills. Research on the effects of typography and typographic emphasis largely ended once typography become part of the writing process. As a result, there is no competing conceptual framework or terminology for talking about how novice writers learn to use visible text. Ransom note emphasis remains the only game in town.

In the spirit of offering an alternative vocabulary, I would like to use the remainder of this chapter to describe the three phases that I have observed novice writers progressing through as they learn to use typographic emphasis. While these stages lack the metaphoric power of typographic coming-of-age stories, they have the advantage of corresponding to what people actually do as they learn to compose visually.

Instead of filling their papers with many different typefaces and type styles, I have found that novice writers gradually learn to add emphasis devices to their texts following a consistent pattern that has three distinct stages:

- *Scribal Emphasis:* In the first stage, novice writers map strategies from handwriting to computer-mediated text, particularly in how they use capital letters.

- *Additive Emphasis:* In the second stage, novice writers create meaning by piling visual-emphasis devices upon one another.

- *Contrastive Emphasis:* In the third stage, novice writers begin to use contrast to systematically communicate meaning. This stage has two parts: simple and complex. Novices first develop simple contrastive emphasis strategies (also known as "less is more"), using fewer emphasis devices in a manner that systematically links visible text to meaning. Novices may then develop more complex contrastive strategies, extending the visual power of texts by combining visual emphasis along several different dimensions.

SCRIBAL EMPHASIS: ALL CAPS AND UNDERLINE

Although students and novice writers (at least at the college level) all write using computers with typographically based word-processing programs, in the initial phase of scribal emphasis they ignore the devices available in these programs and create emphasis by setting text in capital letters, often centered and occasionally underlined:

<u>MY SUMMER VACATION</u>

Years ago, it was possible to argue that this strategy reflected the influence of typewriting on computing, because typewriters only offered capitalization and underlining for visual emphasis. Today, however, most students make it through twelve years of public education without ever having once touched a mechanical typewriter, yet centered, capitalized headlines are as popular as ever. We can no longer blame this strategy on typewriters.

This strategy of starting with capitalized letters seems to reflect the historical manner in which new technologies for visually representing words have been introduced. As Paul Saenger (1982) points out, the original Greek alphabet and its Latin offspring used only capital letters. Upper- and lower-case letters did not evolve until the Middle Ages (Chappell 1980). Similarly, the first typewriters, introduced during the 1870s, used only capitals. Upper- and lower-case letters came several years later with the innovation of the shift key (Kleper 1976; Walker 1984). So too, the first computer monitors and mainframe printers also represented text using only all upper-case letters. Upper and lower case came later.

Harste, Woodward, and Burke (1984) have observed that as children learn to spell, they relive the evolution of writing systems. They start with a single symbol that represents a word. Often the first letter of their name is used to represent that name. They then progress to syllabic spelling, and then to alphabetic spelling. Perhaps novice writers, in learning to create visual emphasis, follow a similar strategy: They relive the history of how new technologies of the word have been introduced, starting with simple capital letters and then progressing to visually more complex forms.

As novice writers begin to push the limits of scribal emphasis, they start to add more emphasis devices to text that is already set in capitals and centered, but rarely do they add these devices in a manner that creates contrast. As a result, the page appears to be more visually complex but it still does not communicate rhetorical purpose.

The classic example of such transitional documents is a personal or organizational flyer announcing an event or an object for sale in which every line of type is set in 36-point boldface, centered, capital letters (see figure 3.2). The designer of this flyer has begun to move beyond simple scribal emphasis, but there is still no effort to use contrast to signal important information. Nothing on this page tells the reader/viewer where to look or what is important.

AMERICAN
          MARKETING
                    ASSOCIATION
MEMBERSHIP DRIVE

AUGUST 26-28
AUGUST 31 – SEPTEMBER 4

WILLIAMS HALL LOBBY
9:00-4:00

JOIN TODAY
ALL MAJORS WELCOME

◆ **FIGURE 3.2** ◆

An organizational flyer that uses transitional scribal emphasis.

ADDITIVE EMPHASIS

Figure 3.2, with its capital letters set in a typeface other than Times New Roman and in a type size larger than 12 point, is a transitional example of visual emphasis. The writer is moving beyond the simple capitalized forms of scribal emphasis into the second stage: additive emphasis. In this stage, the novice writer realizes that simply setting text to be emphasized in capitals does not give that text enough visual importance, so, casting around for a better strategy, he or she adds more and more emphasis devices onto the text to be emphasized. A simple capitalized header

SECTION 1: BACKGROUND

doesn't look strong enough so the writer adds an underline:

SECTION 1: BACKGROUND

But an underline still does not seem strong enough so the writer adds boldface:

SECTION 1: BACKGROUND

And then italic:

SECTION 1: BACKGROUND

Sometimes even that is not enough, so the writer tosses in outline and/or shadow:

SECTION 1: BACKGROUND

Finally, the writer makes the headline really big so that readers cannot possibly miss it:

SECTION 1: BACKGROUND

I have borrowed the term "additive" from a characteristic of oral cultures described by Walter Ong (1982). He argues that oral storytellers typically use "additive" styles, adding one clause after another in the textual flow of an oral narrative. Storytellers use additive conjunctions (she did this, and then she did that, and then she did some more, and so on) rather than using more complex subordinating conjunctions, relying on "pragmatics" to communicate meaning because listeners cannot effectively parse the sorts of complex syntactic structure that have evolved in a print culture (pp. 37–38). So also, novice writers, moving from scribal to additive emphasis, pile one visual device on top of another, rather than parsing the underlying grammar of emphasis, relying on the "pragmatics" of context to communicate intent.

CONTRASTIVE EMPHASIS

Scribal and additive emphasis can be found in many everyday documents. Visible text exists in discourse communities, and those communities map values onto the appearance of written documents. In small, closed, homogenous communities, writers may never receive the feedback they need to move beyond additive strategies for creating visual emphasis. When they do, however, the next stage is to use contrast to create visual emphasis. Initially, a novice writer will use fewer emphasis devices, but will use them in a more systematic manner so that the visual device corresponds to an intended meaning or purpose.

Contrastive emphasis is the first step in thinking about visible text as rhetoric. Both scribal emphasis and additive emphasis mask rather than highlight the relationship between meaning and the appearance of text. Using contrastive emphasis, however, means making the relationship explicit between visual device and intended meaning. Novice writers must conceptualize their audience and purpose and evaluate visible text against that audience and purpose to make this linkage.

Contrastive emphasis often develops in two stages. In the first stage, *simple contrastive emphasis,* novices realize that "less is more" and that their past practice of piling emphasis devices on top of emphasis devices, or using a single device over and over again, has not been effective, so they begin to use fewer emphasis devices in a more purposeful way. Instead of twenty lines of boldface text, they use boldface only once and discover that that one use jumps off the page.

This stage is marked by simpler, more visually plain pages. These pages often have emphasis hierarchies based on a single characteristic of type. For example, first-level heads may be boldface, second-level heads italic, and third-level, small caps; or the first level may be in 18 point, the second level in 14 point, and the third level in 12 point, and so on. It is as if the novice, just beginning to experiment with the connection between appearance and rhetoric, limits the different ways in which visible text varies in order to explore the nature of this relationship.

In the second stage, called *complex contrastive emphasis,* writers begin to vary the appearance of text simultaneously along several different dimensions. They may manipulate typeface, type size, and type style, as well as the space around headlines to create more visually complex hierarchies of emphasis. This sort of complex contrastive emphasis lies at the heart of the design strategies that are taught in desktop-design books. For example, Robin Williams bases her design advise in *The Non-Designer's Design Book* (1994, 14) on four principles:

- *Contrast.* The idea behind contrast is to avoid elements on the page that are merely *similar.* If the elements (type, color, size, line thickness, shape, space, and so on) are not the *same,* then make them *very different.* Contrast is often the most important visual attraction on a page.

- *Repetition.* Repeat visual elements of the design throughout the document. You can repeat color, shape, texture, spatial relationships, line thickness, sizes, and so on. This helps develop the organization and strengthens the unity.

- *Alignment.* Nothing should be arbitrarily placed on the page. Every element should have some visual connection with another element on the page. This creates a clean, sophisticated, fresh look.

- *Proximity.* Items relating to each other should be grouped close together. When several items are in close proximity to each other, they become one visual unit rather than several separate units. This helps organize information and reduces clutter.

Each of these principles extends the idea of contrastive emphasis into a different semiotic dimension. The goal of Williams's book is to teach the reader how to use combinations of these different dimensions in graceful ways to create complex, compelling, communicative pages.

Interestingly, the few real-life instances of ransom note emphasis that I have encountered have all been instances where novice writers have attempted to integrate complex contrastive emphasis strategies into documents without sufficient knowledge or training. Most often, these writers were designing an organizational publication such as a flyer, brochure, or newsletter (especially the latter). To create more contrast, they give each element of this document its own distinct typographic identity by setting each headline of each story in a different font.

Although complex contrastive emphasis offers many such opportunities to go awry, most writers can learn to complicate their visual patterns in interesting ways. A novice writer does not have to aspire to be a graphic designer to effectively use complex contrastive emphasis.

Emphasis Strategies and Unidirectional Development

Thus students and novice writers typically begin using scribal emphasis strategies, mapping the semiosis of handwriting onto a new writing space. They then progress to additive strategies in which they use new technologies to add one device on top of another to create emphasis and from there proceed to contrastive strategies of different degrees of complexity. These stages, however, are not the hard-wired stages of language acquisition (from single word to two-word utterance to telegraphic speech), nor are they like Piagetian developmental stages.

Instead, the process of growth seems to follow a pattern similar to what I. J. Gelb (1963) observed for the development of writing systems. He argued that a culture's writing system may be either logographic (using symbols to represent words), syllabic (using symbols to represent syllables), or alphabetic (using symbols to represent phonemes and morphophonemes), but as that writing system changes, it will always change in a single direction: from logographic to syllabic to alphabetic. Logographic systems do not evolve directly into alphabetic systems, and writing systems never move backwards. Alphabetic systems do not de-evolve into syllabic or logographic forms. He calls this the principle of "unidirectional development" (p. 201).

So also, novice writers may stop at scribal, additive, or contrastive emphasis, but when they change, they change in a single direction: from scribal to additive to contrastive emphasis. Writers who have learned to develop complex contrastive hierarchies to signal meaning do not go back to setting everything in centered capitalized letters.

The Ransom Note Fallacy in the Classroom

Because typographic choice is now a fundamental part of all personal computers, anyone teaching writing or working with novice writers comes in contact with the ransom note fallacy. Visual issues can be particularly frustrating for writing teachers, because as a group, we tend to have little training in visual communication. The many typographic choices available in Microsoft Word can be as paralyzing to writing teachers as they can be to writing students.

One obvious solution might be to ask students and novice writers to read a book on desktop design, perhaps Robin Williams's *The PC Is Not a Typewriter* (1992) or Roger Parker's *Looking Good in Print* (1990). Such an approach would seem to make sense. Williams and Parker know far more about typographic design than do most writing teachers. Why not let them do the heavy lifting? Unfortunately, I have tried this strategy on a number of occasions with, at best, limited success. I have assigned *The PC Is Not a Typewriter*, and students have raved about the book. They love Williams's clear prose and concise design principles; they admire her attractive pages and sensible design suggestions, but for the most part they go right on using scribal and additive emphasis strategies. A few students catch on and change their practice, but most do not. This is the dark side of the ransom note fallacy. Not only do students and novice writers fail to produce documents that exhibit the ransom note emphasis that desktop-design books warn against, but the books themselves have little appreciable impact on the visual practices of students and novice writers.

If Gelb is right about the nature of unidirectional development, then a book such as *The PC Is Not a Typewriter*, which focuses on the most complex forms of contrastive emphasis, is unlikely to be of much benefit to beginners. Students who come into a classroom using scribal emphasis strategies cannot jump directly from this to complex contrastive forms. They need to work through each of the stages (from scribal to additive to simple and then complex contrastive emphases) and need feedback geared to where they are. A book that concentrates on visual end-points does not help students work through this process.

Another reason for the failure of these desktop-design texts, however, is the social nature of typographic emphasis. It has to do with the nature of discourse communities, communities in the classroom, and the stance that many teachers and students alike take towards visual issues: To view visual issues as someone else's problem and as a result, keep these issues outside of the discourse community of the classroom.

This is a view that has historical roots. Writers traditionally wrote. They produced typewritten (or handwritten) text that publishers (with the help of copyeditors, typographers, graphic artists, and printers) turned into publications. It is also a view that is tied to issues of genre, status, and power (Berkenkotter and Huckin 1995). In our profession, the plain page is the high status page. One need only look at the journals *PMLA* (*Publications of the Modern Language Association*), *College English*, or *CCC* (*College Composition and Communication*) to see that this is so. Similarly, the highest-status publications in any business setting (the ones with the highest budget) will be produced by complex collaborative efforts in which writers have little if any involvement with visual issues.[6]

Assigning an attractive book written by a graphic-arts professional can have the effect of confirming this social reality. Because the visual advice is written by an expert in graphic arts who has far more knowledge about visual issues than anyone in the class would have, it confirms the feeling that visual issues belong outside of that classroom. Rather than encouraging students to attend more to the rhetorical strategies behind visual emphasis, books such as Parker's *Looking Good in Print* or Williams's *The PC Is Not a Typewriter* can send the message that these issues have nothing to do with the classroom. Rather than convincing students to take the leap from transparent to opaque, from immediacy to hypermediacy, these books can have just the opposite effect by convincing students that that leap is for others.

Indeed, the *real* fallacy of the ransom note fallacy is not ransom notes nor the cluttered aesthetic of ransom note pages; rather, it is the idea that learning about visual issues can take place outside of social contexts and discourse communities and the complex web of intention, actions, identities, and connections that such communities offer. If our understanding of typographic emphasis is to advance, we will need a much broader set of terms to described what writers do when they create visual emphasis (such as the ones suggested here), but we will also need a much greater sensitivity to the social context in which these visual transactions take place.

Notes

1. This technological transition is described in Kalmbach (1997).

2. Bernhardt 1986; Dragga and Gong 1989; Kostelnick 1989; Pegg 1990 and revised in this volume; and Sullivan 1988.

3. Arguing against various "fallacies" has a long tradition in English studies. We have railed against an "intentional fallacy" (Calhoun 1994), a "pathetic fallacy" (Hecht 1985), a "poetic fallacy" (Livingston 1995), and even a "technological fallacy" (Grusin 1996), among others.

4. See Poggenpohl et al. (1985) for one of the earliest and most insightful explorations by graphic-arts professionals of the impact of computers on the design of documents.

5. This research has its roots in structural linguistics (Hamp 1959; Waller 1982), in legibility research (Tinker 1963), in reading research (Haber and Haber 1981; Kolers, Wrolstad, and Bouma 1979), in instructional text design (Hartley 1980; Jonassen 1982), and in semiotics (Eiler 1987).

6. Although high-status documents may involve writers only in text creation, the reality for most professionals is that they also produce a significant number of reader-ready documents for which they are solely responsible for the appearance of the finished piece. These documents can range from internal memos, reports, internal procedure manuals, and style guides to end-user documentation in small companies. Even before computers, technical writers have been involved in such publishing. Murray made this point in an editorial about desktop publishing in the pages of *Technical Communication* (1988, 6): "[Technical Writers] have abused readers with typewritten documents for so long that desktop publishing systems and their output seem more revolutionary than they actually are."

References

Berkenkotter, Carol, and Thomas Huckin. (1995). *Genre Knowledge in Disciplinary Communication*. Hillsdale, NJ: Lawrence Erlbaum.

Bernhardt, Stephen A. (1986). Seeing the text. *College Composition and Communication* 37: 66–78.

Bolter, Jay David, and Richard Grusin. (1999). *Remediation*. Cambridge: Massachusetts Institute of Technology Press.

Calhoun, Laurie. (1994). The intentional fallacy. *Philosophy in Literature* 18: 337–38.

Chappell, Warren. (1980). *A Short History of the Printed Word*. Boston: Godine.

Dragga, Sam, and Gwendolyn Gong. (1989). *Editing: The Design of Rhetoric*. Amityville, NY: Baywood.

Eiler, Mary Ann. (1987). Semiotics of document design. In *Language Topics: Essays in Honour of Michael Halliday*, ed. Ross Stelle and Terry Threadgold (pp. 461–79). Amsterdam: Benjamins.

Gelb, I. J. (1963). *A Study of Writing*. Chicago: University of Chicago Press.

Grusin, Richard. (1996). What is an electronic author? Theory and the technological fallacy. In *Virtual Realities and Their Discontents*, ed. Robert Markley (pp. 39–53). Baltimore: Johns Hopkins University Press.

Haber, Ralph M., and Lynn Haber. (1981). Visual components of the reading process. *Visible Language* 15: 147–82.

Hamp, Eric. (1959). Graphemics and paragraphemes. *Studies in Linguistics* 14: 1–5.

Harste, Jerome C., Virginia Woodward, and Carolyn Burke. (1984). *Language Stories and Literacy Lessons*. Portsmouth, NH: Heinemann.

Hartley, James. (1980). Spatial cues in text. *Visible Language* 14: 62–79.

Hecht, Anthony. (1985). The pathetic fallacy. *Yale Review* 74: 481–99.

Jonassen, David H., ed. (1982). *The Technology of Text: Principles for Structuring, Designing and Displaying Text*. Englewood Cliffs, NJ: Educational Technology Publications.

Kalmbach, James. (1997). *The Computer and the Page: Publishing, Technology, and the Classroom*. Greenwich, CT: Ablex.

Keller, Julia. (1999). It takes all types. *Chicago Tribune* (September 8): B1, B7.

Kleper, Michael. (1976). *Understanding Photo Typesetting*. Philadelphia: North American Publishing.

Kolers, Paul, Merald E. Wrolstad, and Herman Bouma, eds. (1979). *Processing of Visible Language*. New York: Plenum.

Kostelnick, Charles. (1989). Visual rhetoric: A reader-oriented approach to graphics and designs. *Technical Writing Teacher* 16: 77–88.

Litchy, Thomas. (1994). *Design Principles for Desktop Publishers*. New York: Wadsworth.

Livingston, Paisley. (1995). The poetic fallacy. In *The Emperor Redressed: Critiquing Critical Theory*, ed. Dwight Eddins (pp. 150–65). Tuscaloosa: University of Alabama Press.

Murray, Phillip C. (1988). Desktop publishing: Another perspective. *Technical Communication* 35: 6–7.

Ong, Walter J. (1982). *Orality and Literacy*. New York: Methuen.

Parker, Roger. (1989). *The Makeover Book: 101 Design Solutions for Online and Desktop Publishers*. Chapel Hill, NC: Ventana Press.

———. (1990). *Looking Good in Print*, 2d ed. Chapel Hill, NC: Ventana Press.

———. (1995). *Desktop Design for Dummies*. Foster City, CA : IDG Books.

Pegg, Barry. (1990). Two-dimensional features in the history of text format: How print technology has preserved linearity. *Technical Communication Quarterly* 17: 223–42.

Poggenpohl, Sharon, Charles Owen, Roger Remington, and Michael Twyman. (1985). Graphic design/computer graphics: What do they mean? How do they fit? *Visible Language* 19: 180–219.

Saenger, Paul. (1982). Silent reading: Its impact on late medieval script and society. *Viator* 13: 367–414.

Sullivan, Patricia. (1988). Desktop publishing: A powerful tool for advanced composition. *College Composition and Communication* 39: 344–49.

Tinker, Miles. (1963). *The Legibility of Print*. Ames: Iowa State University Press.

Walker, Sue. (1984). How typewriters changed correspondence: An analysis of prescription and practice. *Visible Language* 18: 102–17.

Waller, Robert. (1982). Graphic aspects of complex texts: Typography as macro-punctuation. In *Processing of Visible Language*, ed. Paul Kolers, Merald E. Wrolstad, and Herman Bouma (pp. 241–53). New York: Plenum.

Williams, Robin. (1992). *The PC Is Not a Typewriter*. Berkeley, CA: PeachPit.

———. (1994). *The Non-Designer's Design Book*. Berkeley, CA: PeachPit.

chapter four

SOME WAYS THAT GRAPHICS COMMUNICATE

barbara tversky

A CENTURY AND A HALF AGO, a young Ojibwa woman sent the letter in figure 4.1 to someone she was interested in (Mallery 1972). The letter portrays a schematic map with a message superimposed. The map is to her home, marked by her totem, and is addressed to the man she wishes to visit her, marked by his totem. The message is her arm beckoning him to her home. Graphics such as these appear dispersed across space and time. They not only serve as messages, but also as geographic, historical, and economic records, as poetry, stories, and myths, and as proclamations, announcements, and orders. Everywhere, graphics preceded written language. Even today, graphics are in common use, as they are more readily understood by speakers of disparate languages than are written languages. This chapter presents an analysis of graphics produced by children and adults across time and across space. The primary interest is in the semantics of graphics—in particular, how they use space and the elements in it to communicate in cognitively natural ways. This is in contrast to words, which communicate primarily symbolically. The visuospatial nature of graphics, then, gives them both advantages and disadvantages relative to language. Graphics can use space and the elements in it to convey concrete concepts directly and abstract concepts metaphorically. However, many abstract concepts do not have natural analogs. Such

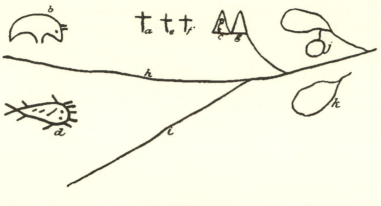

◆ **FIGURE 4.1** ◆

Letter from Ojibwa woman. FROM *PICTURE WRITING OF THE AMERICAN INDIANS* BY G. MALLERY ([1893] 1972). REPRINTED WITH PERMISSION.

concepts—for example, nonexistence or counterfactual—may be better expressed in language.

Kinds of Graphics

Consider the varieties of graphics humankind has produced. The prototypic graphic, of course, is a depiction of something in the world, or something imaginary that is similar to something in the world, a picture. Although such depictions bear enough resemblance to things in the world to be recognizable, they are not necessarily attempts to reflect the world as accurately as possible. On the contrary, many early depictions routinely violate spatial and temporal principles presumably in order to portray more than a particular view of a scene or object. Depictions, ancient and modern, from many cultures display inconsistent, often multiple, perspectives. Mixing or violating perspectives allows a communicator to convey more information than could be conveyed from a single consistent perspective. Thus multiple perspectives can relate more of the meaning or essence than a single consistent perspective, a device used to great effect by modern artists, notably Cézanne and Picasso. Similarly, many depictions mix time, portraying in the same painting or vase or relief scenes from different time periods, often ordered by importance rather than by time (Small 1999). In addition, depictions may exaggerate or distort certain features and omit others. The intent seems to be to convey conceptions of things rather than momentary perceptions of them.

Another common and ubiquitous graphic is a map. Like depictions of things that are real or resemble the real, maps also are not always designed to be spatially accurate. As for depictions, these violations of accuracy of appearance from a single viewpoint are presumably in the service of what their creators wished to convey. A device common in both ancient and modern maps is to present an overview of a street plan along with frontal views of important landmarks. This clever mixing of perspectives provides the traveler with routes to follow as well as allowing him or her to recognize the landmarks encountered en route. In addition to mixing perspectives, maps also often tell stories, especially the histories, real or mythic or both, of the cultures that created them. Migrations, genealogies, and battles are superimposed on an overview of the geography of the territory (see Harley and Woodward [1987] for examples from diverse cultures). Even contemporary maps created with the benefits of aerial photography and hi-tech GPS violate strict accuracy. If they did not violate size-scale constraints, for example, roads would not be visible on maps.

Diagrams, yet another common form of graphic, are not meant to reflect physical reality completely and veridically. Rather, they are meant to be schematized renditions of actual or abstract systems, from the structure of a chair or a house to the organization chart of a company or institution. As such, they are meant to reflect conceptual reality: They portray an analysis of the parts of a system and their interrelationships, structural, causal, or power.

Depictions, maps, and diagrams of actual systems are ancient and universal, or nearly universal, forms of graphics. Graphics of abstract systems and of data, in sharp contrast, are a modern (eighteenth century) Western invention (e.g., Beniger and Robyn 1978; Tufte 1983). Graphs appeared first and were first used to display a single variable against time—for example, balance of trade. In fact, despite the development of many creative visualizations, X–Y line graphs are perhaps still the most common form of data display (Cleveland and McGill 1985; Zacks et al. 2001).

No matter what their form or purpose, all graphics consist of elements arranged in space. Both the characteristics of the elements and their spatial arrangement are used to communicate. Cross-cultural studies as well as analyses of historical documents show communality in the way that elements and space are used in communication, suggesting that some graphic devices are cognitively natural. We will first examine elements, then spatial relations.

Graphic Elements

The oldest and easiest form of element is simply a depiction of the thing to be communicated. For example, the Ojibwa love letter depicted the tent of the young woman, the surrounding landscape, her totem, and that of her friend. But so many ideas we wish to express cannot be directly depicted. Then we resort to figures of depiction (e.g., Tversky 1995), such as synecdoche, where a part represents a whole, or metonymy, where a

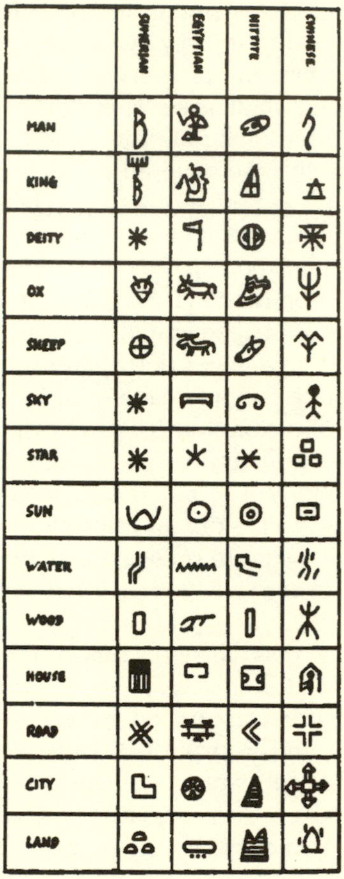

	SUMERIAN	EGYPTIAN	HITTITE	CHINESE
MAN	ß	🜨	⟐	⟩
KING	ß	🜨	⟐	⟐
DEITY	✳	⟨	⊕	✳
OX	☻	⟐	⟐	Ψ
SHEEP	⊕	⟐	⟐	⟩
SKY	✳	⊏	⟐	⟩
STAR	✳	✶	✳	品
SUN	⟂	⊙	⊚	⊡
WATER	⫽	∿∿∿	⟐	⟩
WOOD	▯	⟐	▯	⟩
HOUSE	▥	⟐	⊠	⟐
ROAD	✳	⟐	≪	⟐
CITY	⌐	⊛	◬	⟐
LAND	⟐	⟐	⟐	⟐

◆ **FIGURE 4.2** ◆

Pictorial signs in the Sumerian, Egyptian, Hittite, and Chinese languages.
FROM *A STUDY OF WRITING* BY I. J. GELB (1963, 2D ED.). REPRINTED WITH PERMISSION.

symbol represents the whole, such as the crosses indicated a graveyard in the love letter. These devices were common in early ideographic writing (see, for examples, figure 4.2). The head or horns of an animal represent the animal in several languages, and the symbol of office—a scepter—represents the ruler. Of course, these same sorts of figures of depiction are rampant in computer applications, where scissors are used to cut parts of documents and trash cans to eliminate unwanted files.

Importantly, graphics make use of elements other than depictions or icons that bear resemblances to or figuratively represent the things they signify. Some seemingly abstract graphic elements, such as lines, curves, crosses, blobs, boxes, and arrows, appear in many different kinds of graphics and seem to be readily and meaningfully interpreted within their contexts. Four case studies will illustrate the use of graphic elements to convey other ideas. The first is a study of children's inventions of arithmetic notation, which provides a suggestive comparison to the historical development of arithmetic notation. The next three projects come from our laboratory. They will elucidate the cognitively natural ways in which graphic elements are produced and interpreted. Each of our projects is based on a different kind of graphic: one on maps, one on diagrams, and one graphs.

CHILDREN INVENT ARITHMETIC

The notation system for arithmetic familiar to any grade schooler on the planet actually took hundreds of years to develop (e.g., Hughes 1986; Ifrah 1999). Curious about the difficulties of inventing such a system, Hughes investigated children's inventions. His informants were preschool and early school-age children. He gave them pencil and paper, then showed them various displays. The children's task was to "put something down on paper that represented" whatever was displayed. First, he displayed various quantities of bricks. The younger children, but even many of those already in school and learning the number system, put down forms of tallies; that is, they put one mark for each brick. The more rudimentary systems used by the younger children were iconic; that is, the marks represented objects—in many cases, bricks, but in other cases, other objects. The more refined systems used a simple line for each brick. The oldest children, with the benefit of schooling, put down a numeral corresponding to the actual number of bricks.

Inventing a way to represent the cardinal number of objects was not difficult for the children, and their solutions converged. A harder task, and one yielding more diversity of graphics, was to represent *no* bricks on the table. Some children left the page blank, some put a slash line, some made up a symbol, others—again the older, schooled children—put down a zero. Also difficult were representations of addition and subtraction. As for zero, there was little uniformity, though hands removing bricks were used by a number of children. At least one child used walking soldier-like icons to suggest that the bricks are walking away.

Intriguingly, what was easy and uniform for the children was early and uniform across cultures, and what was difficult and varied for the children was late to develop in cultures. Tallies appear widely across cultures, whereas numeral systems were developed later and more rarely; in fact, they were more often borrowed than invented. The zero appeared only in the seventh century, and symbols for addition and subtraction appeared even later, in the fifteenth century (Hughes 1986). These parallels between historical and individual inventions over time suggest that ontogeny recapitulates phylogeny (Hughes 1986).

```
DW 9

From Roble parking lot
R onto Santa Theresa
L  onto Lagunita (the first stop sign)
L  onto Mayfield
L  onto Campus drive East
R onto Bowdoin
L  onto Stanford Ave.
R onto El Camino
go down few miles.  it's on the right.


BD 10

Go down street toward main campus (where most of the buildings are as
opposed to where the fields are) make a right on the first real street
(not an entrance to a dorm or anything else).  Then make a left on the
2nd street you come to.  There should be some buildings on your right
(Flo Mo) and a parking lot on your left.  The street will make a sharp
right.  Stay on it.  that puts you on Mayfield road.  The first
intersection after the turn will be at Campus drive.  Turn left and stay
on campus drive until you come to Galvez Street.  Turn Right. go down
until you get to El Camino.  Turn right (south) and Taco Bell is a
few miles down on the right.


BD 3

Go out St. Theresa
turn Rt.
Follow Campus Dr. way around to Galvez
turn left on Galvez.
turn right on El camino.
Go till you see Taco Bell on your Right
```

◆ **FIGURE 4.3** ◆

Examples of route directions. FROM "HOW SPACE STRUCTURES LANGUAGE" BY B. TVERSKY AND P. U. LEE (1998) IN *SPATIAL COGNITION: AN INTERDISCIPLINARY APPROACH TO REPRESENTATION AND PROCESSING OF SPATIAL KNOWLEDGE*, EDITED BY C. FREKSA, C. HABEL, AND K. F. WENDER. REPRINTED WITH PERMISSION.

LINE, CURVES, CROSSES, AND BLOBS: CONVEYING ROUTES

Lines appearing in one-to-one correspondence to the number of things, then, have been invented by children and by many cultures to represent numbers of things. Lines have been used to represent other concepts as well—for example, segments of roads. A number of years ago, we stopped passers-by near a student dormitory and asked them if they knew how to get to a popular fast-food place off campus (Tversky and Lee 1998, 1999). If they said they did, we asked them either to sketch a map or to write down directions to the restaurant. Figure 4.3 contains two of the route directions, and figure 4.4 contains two of the maps given by informants. Note that route maps differ from regional maps in that they only include the information needed to get from the start to the destination, meaning that much detail, even of the roads followed and structures encountered, is omitted.

Following an analysis developed by Michel Denis (1997), we coded both depictions and descriptions into their elements. Significantly, al-

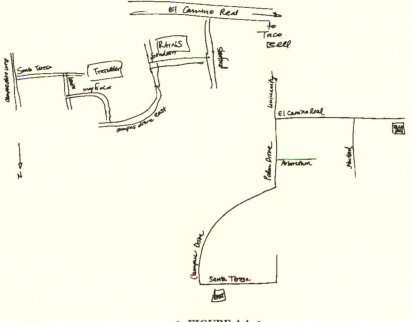

◆ **FIGURE 4.4** ◆

Maps drawn by informants. From "How Space Structures Language" by B. Tversky and P. U. Lee
(1998) in Spatial Cognition: An Interdisciplinary Approach to Representation and Processing of Spatial
Knowledge, edited by C. Freksa, C. Habel, and K. F. Wender. Reprinted with permission.

though depictions are concrete and potentially analog, whereas descriptions are symbolic and discrete, there were a number of striking parallels between depictions and descriptions that served as route directions. Lines, curves, crosses, and blobs, for example, were all used to designate portions of paths or routes from start to end points. Corresponding to each in the descriptions was a small set of verbal instructions. The lines in the maps corresponded to the expressions "go down" or "go straight" in the descriptions. The curves in the maps corresponded to the expression "follow around" in the descriptions. The crosses signifying intersections corresponded to "make a" or "take a" or "turn." Lines, curves, and crosses are simple diagrammatic components of routes that have apt correspondences between forms of lines and forms of motion along paths. Blobs were schematized bounded regions and for the most part served to represent buildings or other environmental structures that, in overviews, appear as regions of varying shapes.

Each of these graphic devices schematizes the visual information much as subway maps do, rather than presenting it more accurately metrically. Roads and paths, for example, take many more forms than just straight or curved line segments. Yet this is all the information the depictions encoded—thus apparently all the information that is needed to adequately communicate the route. Likewise, for directions, "go down" or "follow around" are sufficient for most cases. The same sort of schematization occurred for depictions and descriptions of turns. Although the actual intersections varied considerably, most were schematized in the drawings to approximately 90 degrees. Those cases where the depicted intersections differed from 90 degrees did not necessarily correspond to the deviations from 90 degrees found on the ground. Similarly, the language of the descriptions did not distinguish the degree of turn. Finally, blobs, usually circles or ellipses, were used to represent landmarks, typically buildings, irrespective of the shapes or appearances of the actual landmarks. Depicting a solid figure was apparently sufficient, just as the names for landmarks in the descriptions denoted solid figures, usually without specifying appearance in greater detail.

The pragmatics of communication, linguistic or pictorial, demand that where more information is needed to distinguish one path or landmark from another, both descriptions and depictions would be expected to provide it. The parallels between descriptions and depictions of routes, both for the segmentation into elements and for the semantics of the elements, give encouragement to the possibility of automatic translation between sketch maps and route directions. Indeed, participants given parallel tool kits, either descriptive or depictive, were able to use the tool kits to construct comprehensible directions (Tversky and Lee 1999). Of course, the routes participants selected to describe or depict were known to them; otherwise, they could not have produced coherent maps or directions. Schematic maps like these, using straight and curved lines, crosses, and blobs, are found in cultures all over the world (e.g., Harley and Woodward 1987). Those maps, like these, portray actual space more or less schematically.

BARS AND LINES: CONVEYING DATA

An example of natural uses of graphic elements in an abstract domain comes from studies of productions and interpretations of bars and lines for portraying data (Zacks and Tversky 1999). As noted earlier, lines are one-dimensional features that can form paths, thereby serving to connect one place to another. Lines can also serve to signify paths between abstract rather than concrete entities, such as different values on the same dimension. Bars, on the other hand, are two-dimensional containers. They naturally serve to include some things within, separating those things from things in other containers. Lines connecting A and B seem to say that A and B are similar in sharing a dimension in common, but differ in having different values on that dimension. Bars, by contrast, seem to say that things that are contained in one bar share a feature or set of features that differ from the feature or features shared by things contained in another bar.

Does the underlying notion of connectors and separators affect how lines and bars are interpreted or used? In one study, students were pre-

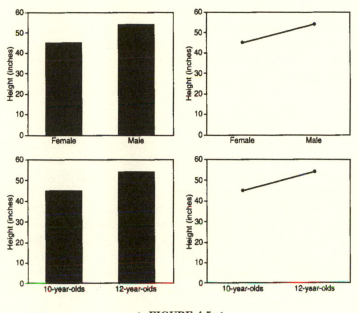

◆ **FIGURE 4.5** ◆

Bar and line graphs used by Zacks and Tversky in "Bars and Lines: A Study of Graphic Communication" (1999). From *MEMORY AND COGNITION*, COPYRIGHT © 1999 BY THE PSYCHONOMIC SOCIETY. REPRINTED WITH PERMISSION OF THE AUTHOR.

sented with one of the graphs shown in figure 4.5. Both bars and lines display imaginary data for height over a discrete variable—sex—or a continuous variable—age. The students were asked to write a brief description of the information portrayed in the graph. The interpretations were scored as trends or discrete comparisons by judges blind to condition. Trend descriptions included: "height increases from women to men," "height goes up with age," and even, "as people get more male, they get taller." Discrete comparison descriptions included: "men are taller than women" and "older kids are taller than younger." Because lines connect and bars separate, we expected more trend descriptions for lines and more discrete comparisons for bars. This is exactly what happened. In fact, the effect of graphic display was stronger (accounting for more variance) than the effect of the underlying variable, discrete for men versus women or continuous for age.

Mirror-image results were obtained when we asked participants to construct data depictions from descriptions. We gave participants descriptions of discrete comparisons: "height for males (12 year olds) is greater than height for females (10 year olds)"; or descriptions of trends: "height increases from females (10 year olds) to males (12 year olds)." Participants tended to produce bar graphs for discrete descriptions and line graphs for continuous ones, again overriding the underlying nature of the dependent variable.

The ways in which lines and containers are interpreted and used to communicate abstract information, then, is cognitively compelling. Lines connect and bars separate. These perceptual units carry conceptual meaning, affecting how depictions are interpreted and how descriptions are visualized.

ARROWS: CONVEYING ORDER

Arrows are another perceptual unit that appears in depictions, both concrete and abstract. In route maps, they are used to indicate direction of movement. In fact, about half the participants in the study of Tversky and Lee (1998) used them for that purpose. In diagrams of systems, arrows appear to indicate direction of power or control or causality. As for maps of environments, diagrams of systems by themselves are structural and neutral with respect to direction. Are arrows a cognitively natural perceptual unit comparable to lines, curves, and bars? A case can be made that they are. One place that arrow-like figures appear in nature is in river junctions or, on a smaller scale, in water runoff. In both cases, the arrow-like form created from the juncture indicates the direction of flow of the water. Another place arrows commonly occur is as tools created by humans. Here, too, the arrowhead point indicates the direction of movement—in this case, of the projectile. The transition from movement in space to movement in time to movement in causality seems to be a natural one, certainly one reflected widely in the ways people talk.

To ascertain whether arrows serve to indicate causal direction in diagrams, in ongoing research Julie Heiser and Barbara Tversky (Tversky et al. 2000) presented students with one of three diagrams: of a bicycle pump, a car brake, or a pulley system. Arrows were added to half the diagrams. Students were simply asked to interpret the diagrams. When there was no arrow, students' descriptions were more structural. For example, for the pulley system without arrows, one student wrote: "A three-pulley system with a load/weight." In contrast, when arrows were present, the descriptions were more causal or functional. For example, for the bicycle pump with arrows, one student wrote: "Pushing down on the handle pushes the piston down on the inlet valve which compresses the air in the pump causing it to rush through the hose." Interestingly, most of the time, the structure was implicit in the functional descriptions. This suggests that it may be easier to infer structure from function than function from structure, a possibility we are now testing. We are also investigating the mirror-image situation, asking students to produce diagrams from either structural or functional descriptions. The expectation is that arrows are more likely to be included in the diagrams produced from functional rather than from structural descriptions.

UNDERLYING CONCEPTUAL STRUCTURE: DEPICTIVE AND DESCRIPTIVE UNITS

These three studies point to powerful correspondences between depictions and descriptions of the same conceptual material. The correspondences in turn suggest that depictions and descriptions are similarly schematized, because both are driven by the same conceptual analysis of the domain. For example, in order to construct an external representation of instructions to get from A to B, the route is first schematized to an ordered list of actions around landmarks and route segments. Either a depiction or a description can then be constructed from the schematization. For route directions, then, the correspondence between depictions and descriptions is at the level of words or phrases and the structured linking of them.

For graphs, the correspondence between depictions and descriptions is at a level more general than the level of words. For interpreting or producing bars and lines, the common underlying conception is of the relationship between the variables, as a trend or discrete comparison. For diagrams, the correspondence between depictions and descriptions is yet more general, at the level of conceiving of the entire system as a structural one or a causal one.

Despite these variations in the generality of the correspondences between depictions and descriptions, in all cases, perceptual units—lines, curves, containers, arrows—map onto conceptual structures. The underlying meaning suggests a natural way of interpreting graphics as well as a natural way of constructing graphics from an interpretation.

Graphic Space

Like the graphic elements themselves, the space between graphic elements has also been used to convey meaning in cognitively compelling ways. An example so obvious that it typically goes unnoticed is the space between words. There was a time when language was written as strings of letters without breaks between words. Grouping the letters that belong to one word separately from those that belong to another by a spatial device, an empty space between the letters, makes it easier to distinguish the words. Written language has other examples of spatial devices that convey meaning naturally. For example, ideas are separated by paragraphs, which are signaled by indentation and/or skipping a line, and outlines make successive use of indentation to signal subordination.

Space can be used meaningfully at several levels, depending on the degree of spatial information that is intended to be conveyed. The weakest level is the nominal, or categorical, level, where things are merely separated into groups by a common feature or features, like the letters that belong to different words (see Stevens [1946] for a discussion of scale types). Stronger constraints come when order is indicated spatially, as in indentation for paragraphing or successive indentation in outlines. Order can be indicated in other ways. A straightforward way is to order things in a list in the way they are ordered on some other variable: children by age, scientific discoveries by dates, countries by GNP, groceries by route through the store. Partial orders are commonly represented by hierarchical trees, where one direction, usually horizontal, is meaningful, and the other is not. Still more information is represented when space is used intervally. In many X–Y graphs, not only is the order of elements in space meaningful, but also the distances between the elements. Interval representations allow inferences such as that the lag time between scientific discoveries and commercial applications is getting shorter and shorter. Finally, when a zero point located in space is meaningful, then ratios of spatial distances between elements are also meaningful. Ratio representations allow inferences such as that the distance between Chicago and San Francisco is more than twice the distance between Chicago and New York. With the notable exception of pie charts, which are appropriate for ratio relations but not for interval ones, uses of space to represent interval and ratio relations are often the same, differing in the interpretation.

Let us now turn to some examples of graphic inventions that use space in these ways. The examples come primarily from cross-cultural studies on children of varying ages. The historical inventions that will be discussed echo those of the children.

CHILDREN INVENT WRITING

In a series of studies, Lilianna Tolchinsky Landsmann and Iris Levin asked preliterate children from several different cultures, all with alphabetic scripts, to take dictation (Tolchinsky Landsmann and Levin 1985, 1987). Of course, there was no expectation that they would write real words. Rather, the goal was to characterize the graphic symbol systems the children would invent. Naturally, their inventions were not pure, as the children had been exposed to writing even if they did not know how to decipher the code, or even what the code was. Early on, children wrote down one mark for each word, much like the ideographic scripts that preceded the alphabet in which each character corresponded to a word. Older children often used several characters for each word, much like the scripts they would eventually learn. The words children invented often resembled the concepts they were representing. For example, larger concepts got larger words, and when a choice of colors was given, the choice corresponded to the color of the thing represented. In some cases, written words were longer for concepts that took longer to say, again indicating that the children were absorbing something of the nature of the alphabetic scripts they would acquire. In all cases, spaces separated words. Children began writing from the top of the page and always placed words on a line.

These features characterize all written languages as well, although sometimes the lines are horizontal, sometimes vertical, sometimes beginning at the left, sometimes at the right, but always from the top.

The devices that children inventing writing produce, then, strongly resemble the devices invented across cultures for the same purposes. Of course, children's exposure to the writing systems of the surrounding culture may have biased at least some of their inventions, but nevertheless, the ubiquity of the inventions suggests that they are cognitively compelling.

CHILDREN INVENT GRAPHS

How do children use space to convey abstract concepts? We investigated this by providing children with square pieces of paper and stickers, and asking them to arrange the stickers in space to represent a number of relative concepts: time, quantity, and preference (Tversky, Kugelmass, and Winter 1991). Children were first acquainted with the task by representing spatial relations—specifically, the arrangement of small dolls on a line. Then, to elicit representations of time, the experimenter sat next to the child and asked the child to think about the times of day when the child ate breakfast, lunch, and dinner. The experimenter then put a sticker down in the middle of a blank, square piece of paper to represent the time for eating breakfast, and asked the child to put down a sticker showing the time for eating lunch and another sticker for the time for eating dinner. Other time questions followed. One question about quantity asked the child to think about the amount of candy in a handful, the amount of candy in a bagful, and the amount of candy collected at Halloween. A preference question asked the child to think about a food the child loved, a food the child didn't like, and a food somewhere in between. The participants included Hebrew-speaking Israelis, Arabic-speaking Israelis, and Americans. These cultures are of interest partly because of the directions of their writing systems. English is written from left to right, whereas Hebrew and Arabic are written right to left. The right to left tendencies are much stronger in Arabic than in Hebrew for several reasons: Arabic script is connected and each character is formed from right to left, whereas Hebrew has no script and most letters are formed from left to right. In Hebrew, the arithmetic system follows the Western left-to-right order, but in Arabic, arithmetic is taught from right to left until the middle-school years when the Western conventions are adopted. Participants ranged in age from preschool to college.

One question of interest was how much information from the conceptual relations the children preserved in the spatial mappings? Would this vary with age or culture? In fact, the amount of information preserved in the mappings increased with age, but did not vary across culture. Some of the youngest children only preserved nominal or categorical relations in their mappings; that is, they regarded time for breakfast, lunch, or dinner or preference for television shows as different, but not as on an ordered continuum. These children placed their stickers haphazardly on the page. Such children were unusual. Most of even the youngest children ordered the stickers on a line, mappings that preserved ordinal information. Some of the relations children were asked to map had clearly unequal distances between the items; for example, time to wake up, time to go to school, and time to go to bed. Despite the clear differences, only the older children's mappings preserved interval information. To test the limits of this, a new group of children were given special procedures designed to call attention to the different intervals and to elicit interval mappings. For the most part, these failed. By twelve years, however, children began to map intervals spontaneously.

Another question asked of the data concerned the directionality of the increases. Would they vary with language or with concept? In fact, directionality varied both with language and with concept. For preference and quantity, increases were mapped approximately equally across cultures from right to left, from left to right, and from bottom to top. The only direction to indicate increases that was avoided was top to bottom. These practices reflect what seem to be biases about horizontal and vertical space. Horizontal space is neutral—the right and left halves of the body are relatively symmetric, especially in comparison to the top and bottom or front and back halves, which are clearly different. What is on the right and what is on the left in the space around the body are for the most part arbitrary, an accident of one's current point of view. What is up and what is down in the world, by contrast, are no accident. What is up defies gravity, exhibits strength. People grow stronger as they grow taller. Larger piles, of goods or money, are higher. So "up" is associated with more, better, stronger. This apparently natural association between space and meaning is reflected in language and gesture as well. We say that someone is at the top of the world or the top of the heap and we give a thumbs up or a high five.

Spatial displays of temporal relations, however, were different. All groups mapped temporal order from down to up. They also used the horizontal axis, but the specific direction depended on the direction of writing in the language. Many English speakers plotted increases in time from left to right, whereas Arabic speakers tended to plot temporal increases from right to left. As noted, in Hebrew, writing is less lateralized than in Arabic; similarly, the graphic mappings of Hebrew speakers were also more evenly distributed from right to left and from left to right. Some of the Arabic speakers, and only the Arabic speakers, mapped later times to lower. This, of course, corresponds to the way calendars and date books are organized: the beginning, the earliest time at the top.

Spatial relations, then, can be used spontaneously to convey abstract, nonspatial relations by children and adults in different cultures. Space is readily used to convey categorical and ordinal relations; it may also be used to convey interval relations. There is some consistency in the spatial direction used to convey increases. First, increases are nearly always conveyed vertically or horizontally, not diagonally or circularly. The particular horizontal direction is neutral except for the case of temporal increases, wherein horizontal direction tends to follow writing order. As for the vertical axis, increases in quantity and preference (but notably not in time) overwhelmingly correspond to upwards direction, in correspondence with language and gesture, where up indicates more, better, and stronger. Moreover, these correspondences seem grounded in the world, where, in general, more things make higher piles and stronger things are taller.

Depicting Abstractions

Graphics have been produced by different cultures throughout history for different ends. They portray reality and myth; they record history and present proclamations; they convey models of things and systems. To convey these various meanings, they use characteristics of elements as well as the spatial relations among elements. Many of these depictive devices have been invented and reinvented across cultures and ages for similar meanings. As such, they are readily interpreted, even if novel; thus they appear to have a degree of cognitive naturalness. Elements may resemble the elements to be mapped, or they may represent them figuratively. As the preceding studies have shown, a small group of geometric forms may be used to convey abstract meanings directly. For example, in sketch maps, straight-line segments indicate straight roads, curved-line segments indicate curved roads, crosses indicate intersections, and blobs suggest environmental structures. Note that these depictive units, like language, are schematic or categorical; none normally captures exact metric relations. In graphs, lines link and bars separate, so that line graphs are interpreted and produced for trends, whereas bar graphs are interpreted and produced for discrete relations. In diagrams, arrows indicate temporal sequence from which causal sequence is readily inferred. The presence of arrows in diagrams encourages causal—over and above structural—interpretation.

Spatial relations among elements are also readily produced and interpreted using the basic underlying metaphor that proximity in space reflects proximity in an abstract dimension. Graphic space may preserve abstract spaces at several levels of information.

At the nominal or categorical level, items are separated into groups that share a common feature or features, but there is no relationship implied between groups. At the ordinal level, items have differing values on the same underlying feature, yet the distance between them is not intended to be meaningful. Distance between items is meaningful at the interval level (and ratios of distances at the ratio level, where zero is meaningful).

General abstract meanings may also be expressed in depictions. Equivalence, for example, can be expressed by grouping items that are equivalent and spatially separating them from items that are not. Equivalence can also be indicated pictorially, by various frames such as boxes, bars, and parentheses and by similar appearance, as in fonts, sizes, colors. Connections between items can be depicted by lines of various sorts. Order among items may be indicated both spatially and pictorially as in indentation of paragraphs or in outlines as well as the order in which a set of items is listed—for example, children in order of age, groceries in order of a path through the supermarket. Pictorially, orders, especially partial orders, can be represented as trees. Similarly, degrees of relationship such as similarity, salience, or strength can be suggested, for example, spatially by degree of proximity, or pictorially by degree of appearance, color, or size. Proportion can be indicated by spatial proportion. Direction is conveniently conveyed by arrows, whether the direction is spatial, temporal, causal, or other.

Change can be easily expressed by actual change, as in animation, though animations can present both perceptual and cognitive difficulties (see Tversky, Morrison, and Betrancourt [forthcoming]). Other effective ways to indicate change are by artfully selected successive stills, as in comics (McCloud 1994), instructional materials (Zacks and Tversky [forthcoming]), or flowcharts with arrows.

Conclusion

Words are certainly the prototypic medium of communication. They can be concrete or abstract, succinct or expansive. They can be audible or viewable and are portable. But words bear only symbolic relations to the concepts they represent—therein lies their limits and their power, the power of abstraction. By contrast, depictions use elements and the spatial relations among them to convey concrete and abstract meanings quite directly. Using space and the elements in it to convey meaning also capitalizes on the impressive capacity people have to process and store spatial and visual information—therein lies the powers of depictions. They can grab and keep attention by being attractive or humorous or frightening. They can demonstrate knowledge directly rather than indirectly, as in maps and models. They can promote inferences based on spatial and visual reasoning. They can serve as external representations of thought, alleviating the mental-processing load. As external representations, they are open to a community of users who can inspect, reinspect, and revise them. There is more to depictions than meets the eye.

References

Beniger, J. R., and D. L. Robyn. (1978). Quantitative graphics in statistics. *American Statistician* 32: 1–11.

Cleveland, W. S., and R. McGill. (1985). Graphical perception and graphical methods for analyzing scientific data. *Science* 229: 828–33.

Denis, M. (1997). The description of routes: A cognitive approach to the production of spatial discourse. *Cahiers de Psychologie Cognitive* 16: 409–58.

Gelb, I. J. (1963). *A Study of Writing*, 2d ed. Chicago: University of Chicago Press.

Harley, J. B., and D. Woodward (Eds.). (1987). *History of Cartography*, vol. 1: *Cartography in Prehistoric, Ancient and Medieval Europe and the Mediterranean*. Chicago: University of Chicago Press.

Hughes, M. (1986). *Children and Number: Difficulties in Learning Mathematics*. Oxford: Blackwell.

Ifrah, G. (1999). *The Universal History of Numbers: From Prehistory to the Invention of the Computer*. New York: Wiley.

Mallery, G. (1972). *Picture Writing of the American Indians* (1893). Reprint, New York: Dover.

McCloud, S. (1994). *Understanding Comics*. New York: HarperCollins.

Small, J. P. (1999). Time in space: Narrative in classical art. *Art Bulletin* 81: 562–75.

Stevens, S. S. (1946). On the theory of scales of measurement. *Science* 103: 677–80.

Tolchinsky Landsmann, L., and I. Levin. (1985). Writing in preschoolers: An age-related analysis. *Applied Psycholinguistics* 6: 319–39.

———. (1987). Writing in four- to six-year-olds: Representation of semantic and phonetic similarities and differences. *Journal of Child Language* 14: 127–44.

Tufte, E. R. (1983). *The Visual Display of Quantitative Information*. Cheshire, CT: Graphics Press.

Tversky, B. (1995). Cognitive origins of graphic conventions. In *Understanding Images*, ed. F. T. Marchese (pp. 29–53). New York: Springer-Verlag.

Tversky, B., S. Kugelmass, and A. Winter. (1991). Cross-cultural and developmental trends in graphic productions. *Cognitive Psychology* 23: 515–57.

Tversky, B., and P. U. Lee. (1998). How space structures language. In *Spatial Cognition: An Interdisciplinary Approach to Representation and Processing of Spatial Knowledge*, ed. C. Freksa, C. Habel, and K. F. Wender (pp. 157–75). Berlin: Springer-Verlag.

———. (1999). Pictorial and verbal tools for conveying routes. In *Spatial Information Theory: Cognitive and Computational Foundations of Geographic Information Science*, ed. C. Freksa and D. M. Mark (pp. 51–64). Berlin: Springer-Verlag.

Tversky, B., J. B. Morrison, and M. Betrancourt. (Forthcoming). Animation: Can it facilitate? *International Journal of Human Computer Studies*.

Tversky, B., J. Zacks, P. U. Lee, and J. Heiser. (2000). Lines, blobs, crosses, and arrows: Diagrammatic communication with schematic figures. In *Theory and Application of Diagrams*, ed. M. Anderson, P. Cheng, and V. Haarsley (pp. 221–30). Berlin: Springer-Verlag.

Zacks, J., and B. Tversky. (1999). Bars and lines: A study of graphic communication. *Memory and Cognition* 27: 1073–79.

———. (Forthcoming). Event segmentation in instruction.

Zacks, J., E. Levy, B. Tversky, and D. Schiano. (2001). Graphs in use. In *Diagrammatic Reasoning and Representation*, ed. M. Anderson, B. Meyer, and P. Olivier (pp. 187–206). Berlin: Springer-Verlag.

chapter five

BEING VISUAL, VISUAL BEINGS

—◆—

richard johnson sheehan

I N *The Electronic Word* (1993), Richard Lanham argues that "[d]igitized communication is forcing a radical realignment of the alphabetic and graphic components of ordinary textual communication" (p. 3). Indeed, as Lanham suggests, what it means to be "literate" in our society is changing dramatically as we shift from a print-based culture to an electronic culture. More and more, the long-guarded divisions between "content" and "design" are dissolving as image and word become interchangeable. An important consequence of this image–word coalescence is that *how* we say something is increasingly *what* we say. Or, to restate Marshall McLuhan's mantra yet again, the medium *is* the message. If so, our definitions of "text" need to be emended to suit the visual nature of electronic texts, and we need to rethink what it means to be literate in a postprint culture. Moreover, when we teach people to write or compose, we need to address the increasing importance of design and visual thinking to the invention, organization, style, and delivery of text.

   In this chapter, my premise is that electronic texts are essentially "visual" texts—much as printed texts are "literal" and speeches are "oral." Of course, elements of the visual, literal, and oral play a role in all texts. My argument, however, is that the controlling rhetorical element (i.e., visual, literal, oral) shifts to suit the medium. Therefore, I argue, if the medium is electronic, the controlling rhetorical element is visuality. If this is true, I believe we should begin developing pedagogical strategies that help people compose visually as well as literally. Visual composition, however, involves more than paying attention to the surface layout of texts. Instead, it would involve teaching people how to approach writing as a form of "visual thinking," in which they invent texts spatially rather than linearly. I will begin by discussing the history and nature of the electronic-visual texts. Then I will define visual thinking in relation to visual communication. Finally, I will conclude with some remarks about using gestalt principles of design to invent and organize three-dimensional visual text.

What does it mean to be a visual being? What does it mean to compose visual texts? To answer these questions, this chapter will argue that we need to use our understanding of visual thinking and design to help us learn how to better express ourselves through electronic media.

The Electronic Word

There has been a great amount of debate regarding the changes to our culture since John Vincent Atanasoff's invention of the digital computer at Iowa State University in 1942. Most commentators see the invention of the computer as a starting point for the "electronic revolution" or "the information age." In reality, though, the invention of the computer was only an important event in an "electronic" revolution that was already well underway. The revolution of the "electronic word," as Lanham dubs it, took its prerevolutionary steps with the nineteenth-century inventions of the telegraph and telephone. In the twentieth century, the inventions of mass-market wireless radio (1916) and television (1929) brought the electronic word into its own. Often, the electronic word is mistakenly used as a synonym for computer-based text, but this association of electronic media with computers is overly simplified. Electronic media, after all, are defined by their *broadcasting* capabilities, through which information can be sent and received almost instantaneously by a great number of people (McLuhan 1964, 248). The inventions of computer-based media like the hypertext, Internet, and multimedia texts are only the most recent advents of broadcast media.

My intention, however, is not to downplay the importance of the invention of the computer and computer-based texts. Rather, it is to point out that many of the predictions about how computers will change our society have already come true—and have been true for some time. With a sense of alarm, media pundits often predict that people will no longer turn to books or newspapers for knowledge, preferring electronic sources of information like the Internet or CD-ROMs. A look around at our culture, however, shows that these kinds of predictions are hardly risky. After all, long before personal computers burst onto the scene in the 1980s and

1990s, people were already turning to electronic media like radio and television for a significant amount of their knowledge and learning. Those of us who are professors are quite aware that very little of our students' knowledge and understanding has been gathered from print sources, such as books and even newspapers. We acknowledge that our students gather most of their knowledge and values from television and computers. Moreover, once alerted, even die-hard defenders of the codex book come to recognize that few of their everyday thoughts and conversations are based in print sources; rather, much of our thought and discourse are dominated by the electronic word. Indeed, the electronic word has *already* forged intellectual and behavioral changes that are deeply ingrained in our culture. Whether we like it or not, print media has already been replaced by electronic media as the primary learning source for most people.

The electronic word has restructured our society over the past hundred years. One example is the fading of geographical distinctions among people. Despite the claims that the Internet will allow people to reach out "across physical boundaries" and form nongeographical communities, in reality, radio and television have already more-or-less dissolved these boundaries. My neighbor who listens to conservative talk radio probably has more beliefs in common with someone thousands of miles away in Vermont than he has with me, an addict of National Public Radio. Indeed, my neighbor and I view the world differently and talk differently, even though we live in the same geographical community. Television, of course, has greatly streamlined the communal differences among social groups in the United States (and the world for that matter). Though academics may resist the centrality of television in our culture, we must concede that television shapes what most people wear, how they talk, what they talk about, and even how they think. Of course, there are opportunities for the expression of individual tastes; but whereas people in pre-electronic cultures typically dressed, talked, and thought much like their geographical neighbors, today people dress, talk, and think like the electronic communities with whom they identify. The broadcasting capabilities of the computer will probably further these trends, but we need to acknowledge that these trends started long before the invention of the computer, hypertext, or the Internet. Indeed, the electronic word has already been changing our culture for almost a century.

So, what is the impact of the invention of computer-based media on the electronic revolution or information age? Put simply, the computer is to the electronic culture what the printing press was to the literal culture. The computer democratizes the electronic word by making electronic literacy more available, much as the printing press democratized the written word. Moreover, just as the printing press freed literal text from exclusionary parochial and royal hands, the computer is freeing broadcasting from the elite hands of wealthy media conglomerates based in New York, Chicago, and Los Angeles. For the most part, the invention of the computer has kicked the electronic revolution into a higher gear, much as the invention of the printing press greatly accelerated the final evolution of Western culture from an orality-based society to a literacy-based one. And, just as the printing press allowed most people to learn how to read and write and thus become active members of the literate society, the computer is allowing more people to become participants in the electronic revolution by offering them the opportunity to broadcast their thoughts and ideas. If you have access to the Internet, you don't need an expensive studio and megawatt antenna to broadcast to millions of people. All you need is a personal computer and Internet access. All these years, the majority have been spectators in the electronic revolution, passively listening to their radio and staring at their televisions. Now, the once-silent can produce their own visual texts, offering them the ability to reach millions of people.

The most significant change brought about by the invention of the computer is the final psychological shift of Western culture into a visual age. That is, we are finally completing the change, begun in the early twentieth century, from a literal culture into a visual one. The history of Western culture has experienced these kinds of shifts before, as new communication technologies came into use. Eric Havelock argues that the Greek alphabet was "a piece of explosive technology, revolutionary in its effects on human culture" (1982, 6). The invention of the alphabet shifted an oral culture to a literal one by recasting text into an enduring artifact to be studied, reflected on, and preserved. The written word opened the path for studies of literature, mathematics, logic, and law. Moreover, as Havelock points out, the written word restructured Greek culture, opening the door for a Platonic notion of absolute truth and morality (pp. 4–15). Elizabeth Eisenstein (1979) and Walter Ong (1982) point out that the invention of the moveable-type printing press launched the European Renaissance, completing the transition of Western culture from its oral/mythic basis to a literal mindset. Until the invention of the printing press, written texts were primarily created to recycle written text back into the oral culture. "It was print," Ong argues, "not writing, that effectively reified the word, and, with it, noetic activity" (p. 119). In other words, Western culture did not fully make the transition from an oral to a literal culture until the invention of the printing press promoted the widespread proliferation of written texts. In *Understanding Media* (1964) and *The Medium Is the Message* (1967), Marshall McLuhan showed how broadcast media, from the telegraph to the television, were profoundly changing our culture by creating nongeographic communities, or even a "global community." Havelock, Eisenstein, Ong, and McLuhan convincingly demonstrate in three different eras how new inventions in communication technology do not merely change the way we relate to words or texts—they change the way we conceptualize and discourse about reality.

Until recently, however, electronic media have been viewed as the dimmer shadow of print media. Commercial radio started as a means for newspapers to broadcast bits of their articles to tease listeners into buying the paper form (e.g., WGN in Chicago stands for "World's Greatest Newspaper"). Radio and television have always deferred to books and articles as the privileged source on the subject being covered. And, even today, television news anchors still glance down strategically at the papers on their desk to remind readers that they are relying on the written word, even though everyone knows they are reading from a teleprompter. But after the invention of the computer, especially the Internet, we see less deference to the written word and more reliance on the image as a way to present thought. Indeed, newspapers like *USA Today* are designed to look like television broadcasts. Internet versions of newspapers and magazines are becoming increasingly popular, as people move from paper to electronic sources for news. Meanwhile, books are quickly being transformed into screen-based or CD-ROM multimedia packages with graphics, video, and sound.

The invention of the personal computer seems to be the catalyst for finally shifting the literal culture into a visual one, much as the printing press was the catalyst for shifting the oral culture to a literal one. Indeed, the electronic word and the moorings for a visual culture have been around for some time, but it is the computer that is finally moving us beyond print literacy as the primary source of belief and knowledge. In essence, we are taking the important final steps of our transformation into visual beings, as the electronic word replaces the literal word as a privileged means of interpretation and expression.

But if the computer is indeed only a recent medium for the electronic word, what sets it apart from other media like radio and television? Why is the computer such an important development when the electronic word has been around for so many years? Indeed, many of the claims of a "New Orality" or "New Visuality" that are now being made for computer-based texts echo the same claims that were made for radio and television decades ago. And, similar to the early days of radio and television, we are also hearing the same eulogies for the book and anxieties over the corruption of our values and children. What sets computer-based electronic text apart from radio and television, however, is the ability of almost anyone to *compose* a visual text, not just view it. It is the act of composing hypertexts that finally restructures consciousness, much as Ong (1982) claims that print, not merely writing, restructured Western consciousness. In other words, as people continue to introduce and manipulate more visual texts, they will become active members of a burgeoning visual culture, not just passive observers. It is the act of composing texts visually that completes the restructuring of consciousness, remaking us into visual rather than literal thinkers.

Visual Thinking

The visual nature of electronic texts, including radio, is not hard to demonstrate. That television is a highly visual medium need not be proven here, but the visual nature of radio is not as apparent. Nevertheless, writers for radio have long known that the secret to effective scriptwriting, news reporting, and sports announcing is the ability to help the listeners visualize what is being described. In one major radio-production textbook, for example, the author begins by describing radio in the following way: "Radio makes pictures. It is a blind medium but one which can stimulate the imagination so that as soon as a voice comes out of the loudspeaker, the listener attempts to visualize what he hears and to create in the mind's eye the owner of the voice" (McLeish 1988, 1).

Other radio-writing textbooks offer repeated advice to "write visually" with descriptive, colorful words. Indeed, writers for classic radio programs like *Vic and Sade* or *Fibber McGee and Molly* understood that listeners must be able to "see" the action being described. These programs were salted with lines like "Well look at that over there" or "Here comes Molly with her blue hat." News radio similarly exploits visual cues like "I'm standing in the middle of Times Square, confetti and reveling people all around me." In the case of sports: "The Cyclones are dressed in their road red uniforms, and the Jayhawks in their home white uniforms." Are the colors of the uniforms important to understanding the game? They are, if the listeners want to visualize the game rather than just know the literal details.

From radio and television, we have learned that effective composing for electronic media requires the writer to think visually in order to help the readers see the text. But what is visual thinking? Rudolph Arnheim's influential writings on this subject, especially his landmark books *Art and Visual Perception* (1964) and *Visual Thinking* (1969), make a most convincing argument that visuality itself is a form of thinking. At first glance, Arnheim's premise that people "think visually" might seem like a rather self-evident assertion. After all, our sense of sight dominates our everyday existence. But, as Arnheim points out, when the histories of Western philosophy, science, and education are considered, one soon realizes that visuality has traditionally been defined as the antithesis of thought (1969, 1–12). The origin of this distrust goes as far back as Plato, who in the *Republic* argued that the senses, especially sight, only offer illusory and distorted shadows of truths. Plato praised nonsensory disciplines such as mathematics, geometry, and logic, because he believed they allowed humans to reach beyond the senses to an objective universe. Meanwhile, Plato mistrusted and counseled against the visual arts, because he believed artists were imitators and deceivers of the truth (1961, 597). Indeed, in Plato's work we see the origins of a shift toward literalist ways of thinking based on the written text, and we see the shift away from mythic ways of thinking that were based in the oral text (Havelock 1963, 10).

Much of Western philosophy has maintained this tacit separation between "seeing" and "reasoning," leading to a devaluation of visuality as a form of thought. Seeing is assumed to be the inert window through which humans observe reality—a fogged-up window that tends to blur or distort that reality (Kinross 1985, 18–20). Reasoning, on the other hand, is often defined as the ability to reach beyond the human senses to discover an objective reality that is structured by truth, logic, and mathematics. Indeed, Western philosophy has long assumed that proper reasoning overcomes the distortion of the senses, allowing humans to refine what they perceive into knowledge. Even in empirical science, where the experiment is paramount, scientists' careful observations are intended to lessen the obscurity and uncertainty of the senses in order to develop data that can be analyzed through logic and statistics. In the sciences, visuality is a means for collecting information; but the assumption persists that knowledge will take its final form in numbers, logical arguments, and formulas. Truth is never *seen* in philosophy and science, it is only derived.

The bias against visual thinking is also ingrained in the way we educate our children. Arnheim points out that our educational system actively works toward eliminating visual means of interpreting the world (1969, 294). For example, in early grades, children typically start out by learning about language and the world through images and drawing, but it is not long before the visual is replaced by literal words and numbers. "Some teachers," Arnheim writes, "have collected together numbers, dates, lists of famous people, lists of events. . . . But to children, the world does not look like that. When their eyes see the world, they see happenings, people, and things acting upon each other" (1993, 94). Indeed, it seems as though our educational system is designed specifically to wean children off their inclination for images, pictures, drawings, and color, only to replace these visual fancies with increasingly nonvisual texts and methodologies. Consequently, whereas thinking for young children is defined by what they can see or perceive, the educational system rapidly redefines thinking in terms of what can be compiled into a list, computed with a formula, or argued out with words.

The end result of this shift toward literal thought, as Arnheim points out, is the assumption that seeing and reasoning are two entirely different activities (1993, 95). Essentially, perception is assumed to be a lesser form of thought in which the senses passively supply the mind with interesting images and experiences; meanwhile, literal reasoning is the privileged form of thought, forging those raw sensory images into theories, formulas, statistics, and logical proofs. As a child moves further into the educational system, he or she finds that the visual arts, such as painting, film, dance, design, and even architecture, are viewed with increased skepticism, typically consigned to the realm of fancy or entertainment—and budget cuts. Then, in advanced grades, the literal realm almost wholly replaces the visual as the primary mode of reasoning and expression. Indeed, when you consider the makeup of the modern university, you will notice that few departments actually stress visuality or visual thinking. Even fine-art departments emphasize the "appreciation" of art, often requiring their students to write essays, minus design and images, about their experiences with paintings, sculpture, theater, and dance. All but a few departments stress literal reasoning as the basis for truth and knowledge.

The persistent detachment of perception from thought, especially in a culture that increasingly relies on visual texts for knowledge, seems to be a prescription for intellectual bankruptcy. In an increasingly visual world, few people have been actually taught how to reason and express themselves visually. Even worse, people have been taught to shun the visual as a resort to stupidity or deception. As a result of this bias against visuality, the ability to think visually and communicate with images has atrophied, as reasoning and rationality are equated with the literal mindset. In a literal culture, to be "rational" is to use images as little as possible, relying heavily on the written word as the arbiter of truth and reason. In the coming visual culture, however, rationality will probably be realigned around images as well as words. As long as our educational system persists in requiring strictly literal modes of thought and communication, we will increasingly be teaching students to think and write for a nonvisual world that no longer exists.

The issue, however, is not visual thinking versus literal thinking, which preserves the false premise that there are two separate modes of thought and that one must dominate the other. Rather, the issue is how we can re-integrate visuality into our understanding of thought and reasoning. In other words, we need to find out how we can break down the barriers that separate the senses from thought, and perception from reasoning. One way to break down these barriers is to start acknowledging that to *see* is to *think*. In *Visual Thinking*, Arnheim offers three principles that can help guide us toward understanding the visual nature of thought and composition (1969, 19–27):

- Vision is selective
- Fixation solves problems
- Shapes are concepts.

These three principles offer a basis from which we can start teaching people how to interpret and express themselves visually. Moreover, as I will show in the next section, they form a platform for using gestalt theories of design to teach students to "compose visually" in both paper-based and on-line texts. Let us consider each of Arnheim's principles individually.

VISION IS SELECTIVE

By selective, Arnheim suggests that the act of viewing requires the active interpretation of what one is seeing. He writes:

In looking at an object, we reach out for it. With an invisible finger we move through the space around us, go out to the distant places where things are found, touch them, catch them, scan their surfaces, trace their borders, explore their texture. It is an eminently active occupation. (1964, 28)

As proof of this visual selectivity, Arnheim points out that animals and humans are conditioned to pay attention to changes in their environment. If something starts moving, changes color, assumes a familiar shape, or transforms into something unfamiliar, animals and humans will tend to fixate on that changing element. Meanwhile, the unchanging parts of the creature's surroundings typically become part of the background, which is more or less unnoticed. Arnheim's point is that seeing is not merely a passive recording of what the eyes are experiencing; rather, seeing is a selective process in which some things are noticed and the limitless other visual stimuli recede into the background and are not noticed. This inborn visual selectivity is not something learned, suggests Arnheim; instead, it is a central mainstay of the thinking process.

The act of driving a car offers a good example of selective perception and visual thinking. As you drive, you tend to notice the changing elements around you. You look at that blue truck approaching from the left. Then you shift your attention to the station wagon in front of you because it is growing larger (i.e., it is braking or driving slower). Then the green light ahead changes to yellow, signaling for you to stop. As you wait for the green, you pay attention to some children skating on the sidewalk next to the road. As you drive, your eyes focus selectively on moving or changing objects, allowing you to react almost instantaneously to changes in the environment. Since driving is not a natural activity, learning to drive often requires us to train ourselves on how to govern our selective visuality. The admonition "keep your eyes on the road" is a warning to avoid being distracted by the moving or changing things outside the driving path. Our instinctive visual selectivity often works against our efforts to concentrate on the road, so we need to train our selectivity to concentrate on only the changes that are important.

In texts, especially hypertexts, this type of visual selectivity greatly influences how the content of the text will be interpreted by the readers. Much like the driver of a car, a reader of a hypertext pays most attention to the things that change or are changing as he or she is working through the text. For example, after a page or two in a site, the button bar at the top of the page will no longer be noticed. Rather, the changing information in the center of the screen is what the reader will pay attention to. In other words, the reader will selectively concentrate on the new, changing parts of the text while the consistent features of the hypertext will shift into the background, rarely noticed.

Essentially, reading a hypertext on screen requires users to think visually more than they would with print-based texts. When reading a hypertext, readers will start by look for focal points on the screen or page. In a typical book, the focal points tend to show up in rather predictable places, such as at the top left of the page or perhaps in a subhead or picture, if available. But hypertext pages, being far more fluid in structure, often present a variety of possible focal points in the form of graphics, tool bars, links, various colors, and even moving images or movies. And yet, as people become more familiar with reading hypertexts, they learn to scan strategically for those focal points. Soon, only the changing parts of the web site are noticed by the readers. To stretch the driving analogy a bit further, reading a hypertext is like moving down a road in the car. As the readers choose links, they move further and further into the text. Eventually, the peripheral items (typically at the edges of the screen) are noticed less, because they are familiar and unchanging. At the same time, the changing items (typically in the middle of the screen) come to the foreground, because the readers selectively fixate on the new information on each screen.

FIXATION SOLVES PROBLEMS

Of course, seeing is not a simple stimulus-response process; so let us consider Arnheim's second principle of visual thinking, "fixation solves problems." Arnheim points out that higher life forms—of which humans are debatably one—gain an increasing ability to willfully control their visual selectivity. In other words, humans are not merely slaves to something flashing or moving in their field of vision, even though it may be distracting. Rather, how a person sees something is driven by their reasons for looking at it. Indeed, Arnheim demonstrates that one attribute of "intelligence" is the ability to shift the "center of vision" to the "center of interest" (1969, 25). That is, your interests in keeping the car on the road will tend to keep you from looking at the many changing objects around you. Arnheim points out that humans are always framing what and how they see the world according to their goals and interests. And, because visual thinking is ultimately driven by the problem to be solved, humans prioritize the changing elements in their field of vision to help them meet their goals (Bernhardt 1986, 70–72).

This second principle also comes into play as a person reads a hypertext. For example, when surfing the Internet to find some information, a reader's selective interests can overcome the annoying moving icon in the banner above the text. The advertiser knows that the reader's eye will be attracted to something moving, but the reader's selective interest will typically urge him or her to look for the information that will address the problem he or she is seeking to solve. Moreover, if desired, the reader can willfully choose to look at the oft-repeated button bar at the top of the screen if it will allow him or her to move to a place that will address required needs. Scanning selectively according to their interests, readers will immediately focus on the items that will suit their needs.

SHAPES ARE CONCEPTS

Arnheim's third principle suggests that prior experiences with common shapes govern the way humans view new experiences. Few objects, Arnheim points out, will take on an exact shape that is familiar. Rather, from prior experiences with similar objects, perception will "impose" a familiar shape on that object. Arnheim writes:

> Only rarely does this material conform exactly to the shapes it acquires in perception. The full moon is indeed round, to the best of our viewing powers. But most things we see as round do not embody roundness literally; they are mere approximations. Nevertheless, the perceiver does not only compare them with roundness but does indeed see the roundness in them. Perception consists in fitting the stimulus material with templates of relatively simple shape. (1969, 27)

Arnheim's point is that perception uses prior experiences with particular objects to help us recognize what they are. For example, the shape of a book would be familiar to most people, so a new book would not require a completely new visual interpretation. By imposing a familiar shape onto the book, perception allows the reader to ignore the idiosyncratic qualities that might distinguish each book from the others. This reliance on prior visual experiences allows humans to fit objects into visual categories with minimal hesitancy. Each object is not experienced wholly new. Rather, perception streamlines what we see into familiar shapes, governing how and what we see.

Arnheim's "shapes are concepts" principle also highlights the human ability to visually "complete" objects. If a book is partially hidden beneath a desk, for example, most people will easily fill out the unseen shape of the book. Relying on prior experiences with books, perception allows people to impose the remainder of the shape on the object. Indeed, few people would assume that the book's shape is determined by the part that can actually be seen sticking out from beneath the desk. Humans will invariably conceptualize the shape as a whole. Or, as Arnheim's principle suggests, the shapes themselves are concepts, and we tend to conceptualize reality through these types of shape-concepts.

Composing Visually

My argument to this point has been that the emergence of the electronic word in the twentieth century has already shifted our culture into a visual age. In many ways, we are already visual beings. Until recently, however, the shift toward visual thinking has been limited, because radio and television have restricted most people to a passive consumer position. But computers have allowed us to become *composers* of visual texts, accelerating our evolution into visual beings. The challenge we face is to use what we know about visual thinking and design to guide us toward an understanding of visual composition.

Arnheim's principles, based on gestalt design theories, give us a good start. Using Arnheim's three principles of visual thinking, an initial premise of visual composition is that writers need to learn how to conceptualize texts "spatially" rather than linearly. In most literal texts, the goal is to linearly convey a reader from one point to another. Novels, for example, lead readers from an initial scene, through a complication, to a resolution. An argumentative essay, meanwhile, is intended to persuade an audience to move linearly from an initial point of view, through reasoning, to another point of view. Visual texts, on the other hand, need to be created spatially, inviting the writer to conceive a three-dimensional "writing space" much as architects, landscape designers, or city planners conceive three-dimensional physical spaces (Bolter 1991). An architect, for example, designs a building spatially by conceptualizing various rooms, their different functions, and the way they relate to one another. Similarly, a landscape designer first imagines how the available space for a garden will be carved into areas and then fills them with appropriate plants, trees, fountains, furniture, and so on. Likewise, city planners envision a variety of physical spaces with different functions, such as residential areas, parks, school zones, and shopping districts. The issue in visual composition is not how to move the readers from point A to point B; rather, the issue is how the designer can devise areas of information that are functionally interconnected. In this type of three-dimensional writing space, linearity would be a design choice of the composer, similar to hallways in a building, paths in a garden, or streets in a city. But, linearity would not be a given, as it is in literal texts.

Arnheim's three principles of visual thinking allow us to reconceive composition as a visual gestalt, conceptualizing writing in terms of whole spaces rather than lines. Gestalt theory emerged from the field of psychology in the 1910s and 1920s with the writings of three influential psychologists, Max Wertheimer, Kurt Koffka, and Wolfgang Kohler. Out of their initial studies of perception, gestalt psychologists soon came to realize that humans perceive reality in whole shapes rather than isolated parts (*gestalt* means "shape" in German). Wertheimer (1938) defines Gestalt theory in the following way: "There are wholes, the behavior of which is not determined by that of their individual elements, but where the part-processes are themselves determined by the intrinsic nature of the whole. It is the hope of Gestalt theory to determine the nature of such wholes" (p. 2). To illustrate the concept of gestalt, notice how figure 5.1 is perceived to be a square, even though it is actually made up of a collection of individual circles. As Arnheim's principle "shapes are concepts" suggests, viewers of this figure will naturally "close" these various individual parts (circles) into a shape (square), or a gestalt. It is quite difficult to look at individual cir-

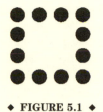

◆ **FIGURE 5.1** ◆

The mind will "close" items into a familiar shape. When interpreting a hypertext, the reader will seek to create order in hyperspace by closing the shape of the whole text.

cles without also noticing that they are part of a larger whole. Meanwhile, the "nonshape" in figure 5.2 is chaotic, resisting the readers' attempt to close the circles into a shape. The same gestalt applies to reading and writing. Most readers would grow increasingly frustrated if, while reading, they were handed individual pages, one at a time. Instead, readers prefer to have a sense of the whole text, knowing how the page they are reading fits into the larger whole. The genre of a text can provide this sense of wholeness, but in most cases the simple fact that pages are bound together assigns a place for each page within the whole text. The overall text forms a conceptual and physical context for each page, much as the square in figure 5.1 offers a larger sense of wholeness to the individual circles.

In on-screen documents, awareness of a text's gestalt becomes even more acute. Often, it has been suggested that reading a poorly designed hypertext feels like reading a newspaper through a paper-towel roll. Usually this "paper-towel-roll effect" comes about because each page in a poorly designed hypertext only allows the readers to experience an isolated part of the text without a sense of the whole. Without contextual cues built into each page, readers soon lose a sense of the shape, or gestalt, of the text. Unless the designer of the hypertext takes the human need for gestalt into account, the readers soon lose a sense of the text's wholeness. For this reason, it is common for readers to feel that they are lost in poorly designed hypertexts, because they lose track of how the page on their screen relates to the remainder of the text. If these isolated

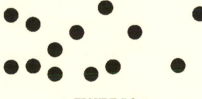

◆ **FIGURE 5.2** ◆

This shape is chaotic. A shape of a chaotic hypertext is harder to conceptualize because space is harder to close.

pages were our circles in figure 5.2, we might say that the readers are having trouble "closing" them into the whole shape.

Numerous articles and books have discussed using gestalt principles to help people become more critically aware of the design of texts (see especially Barton and Barton 1985, 1993; Bernhardt 1986). Meanwhile, other articles and books have suggested using gestalt principles to help people design paper-based texts (see especially Bernhardt 1986; Kostelnick and Roberts 1998; Moore and Fitz 1993). But gestalt principles can also be used to guide the composition (i.e., invent, organize, design, and deliver) of texts in a variety of visual media. How do we teach people how to compose appropriately for visual texts? When visually composing a text, whether paper- or screen-based, writers need to learn how to satisfy the readers' need for the text's gestalt. Toward this end, gestalt theory offers us some key principles that we can follow toward a theory of visual composition. Let us consider them separately.

GOOD SHAPE (FAMILIARITY)

Arnheim's principle "shapes are concepts" is based on the Law of Good Shape in gestalt theories. This law suggests that humans tend to make sense of complex images by perceiving them as collections of simple shapes (Koffka 1935, 141–43). In figure 5.1, gestalt theory suggests that humans will perceive the square, because it is a familiar shape into which the collection of circles can be closed. Figure 5.2, on the other hand, is chaotic or noisy, because it is hard to discern familiar shapes, except the circles. Nevertheless, if one stares long enough at this scattering of circles, the outlines of familiar shapes such as squares, triangles, and circles start to appear. At the very minimum, one begins to perceive invisible lines that connect different circles together. As the mind attempts to make sense of the scattering, another of Arnheim's principles, "fixation solves a problem," comes into play as the mind attempts to create order out of chaos.

In a visual text like hypertext, the Law of Good Shape suggests that three-dimensional documents should be designed using familiar shapes. Many poorly designed hypertexts leave the readers uncomfortable, because their haphazard structures force the readers to attempt to reconceptualize disparate parts of the document into more familiar shapes. The immediate problem faced by the readers is the chaotic nature of the text itself, compelling them to expend more energy trying to sort out the irregularities of the text's structure into simpler forms. In a well-designed hypertext, simple three-dimensional shapes (e.g., cubes, pyramids, spheres, quadrilaterals) can be used to structure the text, allowing the readers to more easily "close" the shape of the text. When the reader successfully closes the text, the structure of the document seems intuitive, offering a sense of wholeness to the contents and organization of the document. Soon, the readers can navigate the text easily, because they can conceptualize its basic structure and shape.

The Law of Good Shape, however, does not merely involve the use of simple shapes. Designers of hypertexts are increasingly using "design metaphors" to impose a familiar shape on the contents of a hypertext. For example, the desktop metaphor on any Windows-based screen interface allows readers to conceptualize the shape, structure, and boundaries of a seemingly infinite gathering of data. By sorting files (documents, spreadsheets, presentations) into folders or trash cans, the viewers can organize the space conceptually, because most people are familiar with this kind of office environment. Metaphors like tabbed notebooks, buildings, a wizard's workshop, elevators, and bookshelves are being used to organize multimedia texts, interfaces, and web sites. For instance, the design metaphor for Timothy Leary's web site, before he died, was organized around his house, allowing people to find different information or conversations by going to different rooms in the house (<http://www.leary.com/home>). These kinds of design metaphors effectively impose a familiar shape on the potentially infinite amount of space and data in hyperspace. Such familiarity allows readers to move through the text smoothly, anticipating where information can be found by making intuitive guesses about the types of information that might be found in a familiar place. For example, as one might guess, the "living room" in Leary's house is the place to find the "chat room." The "library," as one might also expect, makes available on-line versions of Leary's books, articles, and works about him. Metaphors create "good shape" by structuring documents around familiar places and shapes.

When composing a visual text, simple shapes and familiar metaphors aid the invention process as well as providing an intuitive organization for a text. If an artist, for example, wants to create a forum for his or her artwork, he or she might consider using a gallery metaphor. Basic features of the text, like various exhibit rooms, immediately come to mind; however, the artist would soon find that the metaphor urges the creating of an information desk, a gift shop, a critics chat room, an office, and even an artist's studio to show off some works in progress. The metaphor becomes a locus for inventing more content to flesh out the hypertext. Even thinking about a text as a simple shape, like a pyramid, might allow the composer to identify horizontal or vertical gaps in the content of a document. Ultimately, the shape of the document helps the writer compose a balanced text, and it helps the readers to intuitively close the document and anticipate the scope, shape, and structure of the entire document.

FIGURE–GROUND (CONTRAST)

In design, it is important that the viewer be able to discern the figure (the object being looked at) from its ground (the object's context). Gestalt theorist Koffka refers to this phenomenon as the Law of Contrast, although most designers speak of "Figure–Ground Separation" (1935, 605). Similarly, Arnheim's principle "vision is selective" also relates to the abil-

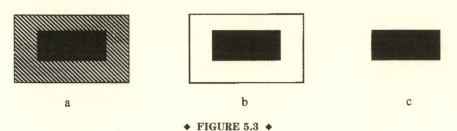

a   b   c

◆ **FIGURE 5.3** ◆

A busy hypertext does not allow the readers to easily distinguish a specific page from the other pages in the site. An orderly web site, on the other hand, allows the reader to concentrate on the page being viewed.

ity of humans to fixate on objects (figures), isolating them from their contexts (grounds). For example, if we are looking out on a busy street, we might fixate on a moving bus, mentally pulling it off the background of the remainder of the scene around it. The more the ground behind the object is visually complex, however, the more difficult it will be to "pull the figure off the ground." In these cases, designers will talk about the "visual noise" in the ground that makes the figure less distinguishable. For example, figure 5.3a shows how a noisy ground can make the figure harder to see. The issue is one of contrast. If the figure does not contrast sufficiently with the ground, it becomes far more difficult for the readers to determine how the figure is supposed to be interpreted. Conversely, the ground is also important for understanding the figure. Without a ground, the figure hangs in empty space, lacking reference to a whole (see figure 5.3c); or, as Koffka writes, "[t]he figure depends for its characteristics upon the ground on which it appears. The ground serves as a framework in which the figure is suspended and thereby determines the figure" (1935, 184).

In visual composition, the challenge is to distinguish an individual page from the rest of the text without losing the sense of the ground. To avoid these figure–ground problems, authors of hypertexts need to recognize a few things:

- Each page should contain a specific whole topic that can stand on its own. In other words, in order for the figure (page) to come off the ground (rest of the hypertext), each page needs to be able to exist as a separable entity from the rest of the text. Otherwise, the readers cannot "close" the topic into its own conceptual shape.

- Each page should also contain some visual elements of the ground so the readers understand how the individual page relates to the other parts of the hypertext. This can be accomplished by maintaining a predictable template for the entire hypertext; or a consistent set of buttons or a standardized color scheme will reassure the readers that they are staying in a congruous text. By stressing consistent design features in every page, the writer avoids confusing the readers with "visual noise" or "chaos."

- As mentioned in the above discussion of Good Shape, the hypertext should be organized in a predictable structure, preferably a familiar shape. Too many hypertexts are built like urban sprawls, with subdivisions slapped up and connected with erratic links. Just as it is difficult to find your way around in a shapeless urban sprawl, so too is it difficult to navigate hypertexts that have unpredictable structures. The ground becomes too noisy, so it is difficult to conceptualize how an individual page is framed within the overall text.

Overall, thinking spatially about a text helps a designer avoid figure–ground problems. Rather than thinking of text as a means to take the readers linearly from A to B, writers should carve up the text into topics and topic areas that are placed in a predictable shape.

EQUILIBRIUM (BALANCE)

Composing a balanced text is again a matter of conceptualizing writing spatially rather than linearly. In gestalt design, an unbalanced text layout gives the reader a sense of uncertainty or incongruity. Gestalt theorists recognized that an unbalanced visual field led to a sense of imbalance by the perceiver (see Koffka 1935, 311–17). Because readers expect a sense of balance in any text, a lack of equilibrium adds tension to the reading process. For example, if a large color photograph dominates the upper-right corner of a page with nothing on the other side of the page to counterbalance it, the reader will feel that the text is unstable and chaotic (see figure 5.4a). On the other hand, even a nonsymmetrical text such as figure 5.4c has a sense of equilibrium, because it is balanced. Both figures 5.4b and 5.4c are balanced, because the items with "weight" are spread evenly on the page.

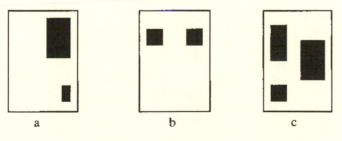

a   b   c

◆ FIGURE 5.4 ◆

Web sites can feel unbalanced in structure, much like page "a" on the left. Equilibrium can be reached with a symmetrical or balanced hypertext.

In visual texts, especially hypertexts, the problem of unbalanced writing might seem subtle until one is made aware of it. In an unbalanced hypertext, one link on a nodal page might lead the readers to a few hundred pages of information. A second link on the same page, however, leads to only a couple of pages of information. For most readers, this lack of equilibrium in the text creates the sense that the site is unfinished, unstable, or unpredictable. Imbalance in a visual text creates an unsettling feeling for readers, even if they are unaware of the reason why they feel uncomfortable.

To avoid these balance problems when composing a text, a writer should think of a text as a design space, like a building or garden, in which the design components need to be spread out evenly. In a building, an architect will typically spread rooms of similar functions evenly throughout the building, often using symmetry and balance to create an even framework. In a landscape, if the designer wants to put a large pond on one side of the garden, it is usually counterbalanced with some larger bushes or trees on the other side. In a hypertext, the text should be balanced topically, avoiding sprawl in one area and cramped space in another. Meanwhile, topics of equal importance should be allocated relatively equal amounts of space in the overall text. If one topic requires more space than others in the text, it should receive more links on a nodal page to signify the amount of content in that area. Moreover, where possible, larger topics should be cut into smaller topics to give the text an overall sense of equilibrium.

To compose a visual text with a sense of equilibrium, the writer needs to balance the coverage of the topics as much as possible. One way of checking balance is to draw a map of the site to check for sprawl or cramped space. Attention to equilibrium will also help the author decide which topics lack coverage or provide too much.

GROUPING (SIMILARITY AND PROXIMITY)

Gestalt theorists have discussed grouping at great length. When looking at a page or a landscape, people will tend to group items by similarity or proximity. Koffka referred to these principles as the Laws of Equality and Proximity. Put simply, these principles of grouping suggest that people will perceive items of similar shape, color, function, or place as a set. For example, in a garden, yellow flowers of different types will be grouped together because they are similar in color. Trees will be grouped together because they are similar in shape. Meanwhile, items that are placed in close proximity will also be viewed as a group. For instance, a bed of different colored flowers and bushes will be grouped together visually, because they are in close proximity to each other.

Consider the working of *similarity* and *proximity* in figure 5.5. In this figure we see two types of grouping at work. A viewer can selectively group the items that are similar (e.g., the circles with circles) or the items

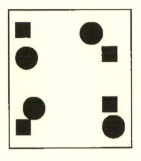

◆ **FIGURE 5.5** ◆

Grouping by *similarity* and *proximity*. In a hypertext, pages that look similar or appear in the same part of hyperspace will be grouped together psychologically by the reader.

that are close together (i.e., a circle with a nearby square). How the viewers choose to look at the page depends on whether they will group the different figures by *proximity* or *similarity*.

In the design of documents, including hypertexts, grouping plays an important role in creating a feeling of coherence within a text. For example, effective page layouts often include repeating elements, like a red circle or a blue square, that are placed strategically on a particular page or throughout the document. Repeated icons or standardized subheads serve to draw a page or document together into a whole. Meanwhile, if a designer places a subhead close to a paragraph, the gestalt principle of proximity ensures that the subhead will be grouped with the paragraph below it. In a hypertext, grouping works in some additional ways. It can be used to employ basic shapes to organize the larger parts of the text. If, for example, one part of the hypertext is structured around a cube matrix, by similarity other parts of the text of equal value should be structured into a cube also. Meanwhile, the organization of the hypertext should position related topics in close proximity on nodal pages, so that readers see them as belonging to a set. Perhaps a design metaphor could be used to place areas of related function together in a site, so the readers can conceptually group them together. By grouping the contents of the hypertext through attention to similarity and proximity, the writer will make the entire text for the readers easier to conceptualize. Readers will experience much less chaos, because the document is visually coherent.

GOOD CONTINUATION (ALIGNMENT)

The gestalt principle of *continuation* suggests that humans will tend to complete shapes, even if they are interrupted by other lines or shapes. So, when a shape is broken, as in figure 5.6 (left), a viewer will complete the shape; or in some cases, as in figure 5.6 (right), the viewer will actually perceive ghost shapes by continuing shapes and lines that appear to be

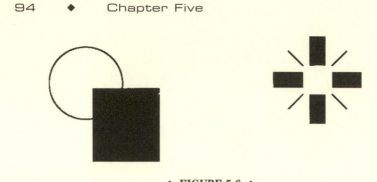

◆ **FIGURE 5.6** ◆

Continuation. When parts of a hypertext overlap (in three dimensions), the readers will extrapolate wholes among partial items in hyperspace.

broken. As Arnheim's principle, "shapes are concepts," suggests, humans will often seek out familiar shapes to overcome potential chaos. Continuation is important, because it often determines how the readers will interpret the relationships among pages in a hypertext. In figure 5.7 we see good and bad examples of continuation. In figure 5.7a viewers will typically use good continuation in two ways: First, they will join all the black squares together to create the standard shape of the larger square; they will also align the smaller squares, visualizing lines that connect the sides of the smaller squares. In figure 5.7b, on the other hand, continuation is difficult because there is minimal alignment. The eye seeks to group the squares into some kind of shape (a circle, a face?), but ultimately fails because the standard shape is broken in too many places. Also, the haphazard layout of the squares means that there are only a few places where continuous lines can be drawn. In essence, this second figure creates a sense of disorder and chaos.

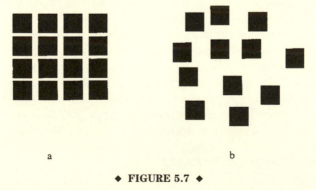

a   b

◆ **FIGURE 5.7** ◆

Good continuation (a) helps the reader conceptualize a predictable structure in hyperspace. A lack of good continuation (b) will urge the reader to fabricate their own structure out of the chaos, sometimes in ways that the hypertext writer did not anticipate.

In a hypertext, a lack of alignment also creates this sense of chaos as the reader attempts to visualize the gestalt of the text. If a hypertext suffers from sprawl in all different directions, the reader has difficulty figuring out how different parts of the site align and relate to one another. Again, there is a lack of continuity to the text, because pages are linked erratically. Writers of hypertexts essentially need to learn how to impose alignment on spaces. Pages of equal or similar importance should be aligned into a familiar shape so that the reader can "close" them into a framework. Otherwise, the site is far more difficult to conceptualize for the readers. Moreover, when a writer detects chaos in a text, he or she should seek out ways to make pages parallel in content, so that the alignment of the work is easier to comprehend. Ultimately, the goal is to create an orderly, familiar layout in which the contents and the pathways through that content are intuitive to the readers.

Conclusion

The gestalt principles discussed in this chapter are only a first attempt to create a path for thinking about texts visually. Certainly, they only offer a few steps in a potentially helpful direction. We are in a time much like that of the ancient Greeks, I believe. We live in a period of transition in which visual texts are not new, but they are working their way into our culture. Composing these kinds of text seems to urge us to rethink how we conceptualize the invention, organization, and style of them. Thinking spatially helps writers conceptualize the content and shape of visual texts. Meanwhile, as in radio, writing visually shifts us away from an emphasis on literal facts toward image-based descriptions. In all, thinking in shapes and metaphors invites writers to approach composition spatially rather than linearly. In their book *Rhetoric and the Arts of Design*, David Kaufer and Brian Butler recast rhetoric as a "design art." They write:

> The activity of design involves formulating future states of affairs in one's
> head and then designing products that are externalized representations
> of these futures. In the case of an architect, there is the future state of a
> building under design and its gradual realization in material form. In the
> case of rhetoric . . . the speaker must plan ahead to control the events in
> the here and now of an audience. (1996, 37)

Or to put it another way, a writer of visual texts needs to spatially envision the future state of a hypertext document. Then the writer needs to bring the document into its material form. Kaufer and Butler seem to be describing how we will think about composition in the near future.

Admittedly, many of the concepts and suggestions in this chapter are abstract. However, my essential point has been that the composition of visual texts is transforming us into visual beings. Much of this transformation has already taken place with the saturation of radio and television in our culture. Nevertheless, in so many ways we are still linear composers of text, even though we live in a visual age. Our writing is still structured on linear understandings of logic, rationality, and reason, often causing visual texts to appear illogical, irrational, and unreasoned. But as we continue to evolve into visual beings, we will begin seeing texts as design spaces. Perhaps a new logic, rationality, and reason will be created with that shift into a visual age.

References

Arnheim, Rudolph. (1964). *Art and Visual Perception*. Berkeley: University of California Press.

————. (1969). *Visual Thinking*. Berkeley: University of California Press.

————. (1993). Learning by looking and thinking. *Educational Horizons* 15: 94–98.

Barton, Ben, and Marthalee Barton. (1985). Toward a rhetoric of visuals for the computer era. *Technical Writing Teacher* 12: 126–45.

————. (1993). Modes of power in technical and professional visuals. *Journal of Business and Technical Communication* 7: 138–62.

Bernhardt, Stephan. (1986). Seeing the text. *College Composition and Communication* 30: 66–78.

Bolter, Jay David. (1991). *Writing Space*. Hillsdale, NJ: Erlbaum.

Eisenstein, Elizabeth. (1979). *The Printing Press as an Agent of Change*. New York: Cambridge University Press.

Havelock, Eric. (1963). *Preface to Plato*. Cambridge, MA: Harvard University Press.

————. (1982). *The Literate Revolution in Greece and its Cultural Consequences*. Princeton, NJ: Princeton University Press.

Kaufer, David, and Brian Butler. (1996). *Rhetoric and the Arts of Design*. Hillsdale, NJ: Erlbaum.

Kinross, Robin. (1985). The rhetoric of neutrality. *Design Issues* 2: 18–30.

Koffka, K. (1935). *Principles of Gestalt Psychology*. New York: Harcourt.

Kostelnick, Charles, and David Roberts. (1998). *Designing Visual Language*. Boston: Allyn & Bacon.

Lanham, Richard. (1993). *The Electronic Word*. Chicago: University of Chicago Press.

McLeish, Robert. (1988). *The Technique of Radio Production*, 2nd ed. Boston: Focal Press.

McLuhan, Marshall. (1964). *Understanding Media*. New York: McGraw-Hill.

McLuhan, Marshall, and Quentin Fiore. (1967). *The Medium Is the Message*. New York: Bantam.

Moore, Patrick, and Chad Fitz. (1993). Using gestalt theory to teach document design and graphics. *Technical Communication Quarterly* 2: 389–410.

Ong, Walter. (1982). *Orality and Literacy*. New York: Routledge.

Plato. (1961). *Republic*. In *Collected Dialogues*, ed. E. Hamilton and H. Cairns. Princeton, NJ: Princeton University Press.

Wertheimer, Max. (1938). Gestalt theory. In *A Source Book of Gestalt Psychology*, ed. W. Ellis (pp. 1–11). New York: Harcourt.

chapter six

IMAGE, WORD, AND FUTURE TEXT
visual and verbal thinking in writing instruction

ronald fortune

T HE INTRODUCTION OF COMPUTERS into composition instruction fifteen or more years ago opened up for teachers and students alike a range of new possibilities for presenting ideas and information and, in the process, redefined for many what a writing course should entail. Central to this redefinition was an interest in the impact of computer technology on what we consider to be a text and on perceptions of how we read and write. The earliest discussions pursuing these issues anticipated a rhetorical revolution that in many ways hinged on the relationship between the image and the word.[1] In fact, from one angle, the history of the uses of computers in writing instruction can be viewed in terms of an effort to articulate how reading and writing instruction would have to change, because of the ways in which computer technology was opening the door to more visually rich documents. Tracking the development of computer-based composition instruction from the early days of word processing to the more recent work with hypermedia reveals that, each time a new kind of application that bears on text production has been introduced, there has been a corresponding acceleration in efforts to extend our views of rhetoric and writing instruction by articulating a new understanding of the relationship between word and image. Any effort to discuss where we are today with efforts to describe the relationship between computers and writing and, more particularly, the interplay between image and word in electronic texts should begin with this history, since, in various ways, the discussions that constitute this history isolate the terms of the problem in an especially useful way.

Historical Overview

In "Redefining Literacy: The Multilayered Grammars of Computers," Cynthia Selfe (1987) describes how students learning to write using word processing at her institution "invented and exploited a new set of literacy skills that their teachers never imagined" (p. 13). These skills included using "different fonts, font sizes, symbols, highlighting, and graphic elements" (p. 13). She follows her observations on the new directions she saw her students taking with a challenge to the entire profession: "Our profession will have to work diligently in the next few years to identify and explore the changing nature of literacy within a computer-supported writing environment, and to consider the implications of these changes for our teaching" (pp. 13–14). What is significant about Selfe's discussion is, first, her recognition that students who were writing on the computer had already begun to manifest a sensitivity to the visual dimension of electronic documents, and second, that writing instructors were lagging not only in their ability to recognize this but also in their ability to adjust their teaching to provide appropriate instruction.

Selfe's discussion is also noteworthy because, even though her students were working with what now seem to be the relatively limited features of a word-processing program, she still sees strong evidence of a verbal–visual interaction in their efforts. She sees students using color "as a visual cue to underlying logical content and structure" (p. 13). She is careful to point out that, in student documents, color became much more than a way to decorate the text; rather, it functioned visually to signal how the verbal text was working:

> Students, for example, used three different colors to signify primary, secondary, and tertiary headings; used two different colors to "paint" contrasting arguments contained within a single paragraph; and used color-coding to identify thesis or topic statements and the evidence that supported these central ideas. These painting strategies are important because they go beyond mere decoration of text to represent a visual revelation of logical structures. (1987, 13)

Color thus allowed a word to operate in two ways at the same time—the *verbal* (as a word in the lexicon) and the *visual* (as a color in the spectrum)—with each operation working differently to point to the same thing.[2] The issue here is not so much an interplay between word and image, since coloration modifies the appearance of words minimally and the colored words still function predominantly as words. Rather, word processing at the time that Selfe was writing accommodated the treatment of word as image in fairly basic ways, which meant that, for the most part, this manipulation of the word only began to suggest the potential for word–image interaction. Subsequent developments have complicated the issue by investigating how word and image work independently, and then have used what was learned about each independently to explore how the two could interact more complexly in a computer-generated document. At the same time, however, as technology made it easier to incorporate distinct words and images into a single document and to manipulate both in ways previously unimagined by most writers, the question of their interaction became foregrounded, and the treatment of word as image evident in Selfe's research has served as a foundation for subsequent efforts.

Following closely on the heels of the introduction of word processing into writing instruction was the advent of desktop publishing and a renewed effort to explore how this technology altered our understanding of writing and rhetoric. Patricia Sullivan's (1991) "Taking Control of the Page: Electronic Writing and Word Publishing" traces the shift from word processing to what she called "word-publishing," which requires the writer to "internalize the role of the designer" (p. 55). The need to internalize the role of the designer raises the visual stakes, so to speak, and significantly enlarges the range of visual elements that the writer would have to know and employ for the greatest rhetorical effect. Recognizing that writers traditionally have been taught to focus on making verbal meaning, Sullivan argues that they would increasingly need to view their work in terms of constructing a page, rather than writing words on a page. As they do so, she argues further, they would have to recognize how word and image as distinct signs on the page together participate in the making of meaning. Sullivan describes a model for representing the integration of word and image on the page that views their relationship as running along a continuum, "with the point of visual–verbal integration as a fulcrum that moves along the continuum depending on the type of document being produced" (1991, 57). Figure 6.1 represents the point of visual–verbal integration in a document. Sullivan views the problem of integrating word and image as a matter of balance relative to the text's rhetorical purpose. Hers is a more generic analysis because, rather than looking to how specific words and images interact, she establishes a general principle for explaining how they coexist and influence one another on the same page. Nevertheless, her analysis alerts us to the need to investigate exactly how the word and the image interact by observing and then problematizing their coexistence. Significantly, she locates the source of any potential interaction between word and image in the larger rhetorical purpose of the document, so any subsequent effort to articulate a word–image dialectic would have to begin here.

The emergence of hypertext and the growing popularity of the World

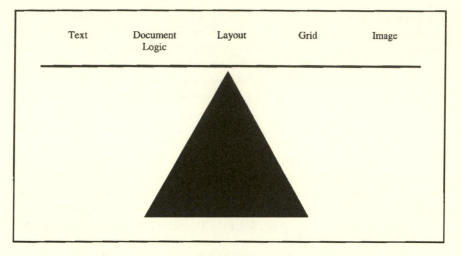

| Text | Document Logic | Layout | Grid | Image |

◆ **FIGURE 6.1** ◆

Sullivan's representation of the point of visual–verbal integration in a document.

Wide Web offered new opportunities to explore the relationship between word and image. Since these technologies moved us beyond the page-bound document and into the territory of screen-based electronic documents, they complicated exponentially the issue of the interplay between word and image in writing instruction. Yankelovich, Meyrowitz, and van Dam (1991), in an early discussion of the role of hypertext in literary studies comparing the advantages and disadvantages of the print medium relative to the electronic medium, single out the prominence of graphic elements in the latter as a distinct advantage of this medium:

> Perhaps the greatest advantage of electronic documents over paper ones is their ability to handle many more graphic elements. By combining a variety of media, electronic books can provide not only static images, but also dynamics (e.g., computer animations and computer-controlled video sequences), interactivity (e.g., ability to move objects, change and edit objects, and change states), and sound (e.g., computer-generated or audio disk recordings). These features all help in creating better audiovisualization. (1991, 56)

This analysis attends less to the dynamics of the interaction between image and word and instead concentrates on how doing various things with images in an electronic document—things that are not available in a paper document—affects our understanding of what texts are and how they work.

At the same time that scholars were identifying the features that would define hypermedia as a new kind of writing, others were discussing how the graphic options that electronic documents make possible should influence rhetorical theory and theories of the writing process. George Landow (1991) was one of the first to articulate a rhetoric for hypertext in an essay titled "The Rhetoric of Hypermedia: Some Rules for Authors." He begins by picking up the same argument heard in the studies reviewed above and applies it to hypermedia: "Hypermedia, which changes the way texts exist and the way we read them, requires a new rhetoric and a new stylistics" (p. 81). Although he stills sees hypermedia as a text-dominated form of communication, he includes in his rhetoric several rules for authors that focus on the relationship between word and image. So, while asserting that the "defining characteristics of this new information medium derive from its use of blocks of text joined by electronic links" (p. 81), a segment of his rhetoric (rules fourteen through seventeen) is dedicated to explaining the function of graphic images within a hypertext. These graphic rules implicitly concede the primacy of text. The relationship between word and image in this analysis generally involves having the word explain the image; text orients the reader to the graphic. Landow appropriately attends to the relationship between image and word, but because his orientation is predominantly textual, the relationship he allows for in his rhetoric limits how images can be expected to work.

Subsequent discussions of the relationship between word and image in hypertext have attempted to elaborate and complicate not only how graphic images work within an electronic document but also, within the framework of this elaboration and complication, how words and images interact. It is noteworthy that, as these subsequent elaborations and complications have evolved, they have not dismissed the conclusions of earlier work. Rather, they have extended the earlier work so that the relationship between the verbal and the visual found in the Selfe, Sullivan, Yankelovich et al., and Landow studies are included implicitly and explicitly in more recent studies, even as the latter attempt to go beyond what the former have done. The "word-as-image" representation found in Selfe's study, then, must be accommodated in more recent studies, because the verbal medium can still be handled visually as well as verbally, just as Selfe describes. Or, the verbal explanation of a graphic that Landow discusses still obtains, because this is one way in which word and image can interact in a hypertext document.

In a discussion that more or less represents where we are now, Gunther Kress (1998) offers an especially interesting elaboration and complication of earlier discussions concerned with the relationship between word and image that illustrates this cumulative process, even as it moves the issue to the next level of analysis. His essay frames the problem in many of the same terms found in the essays discussed above, but it also elaborates these terms into a new set of problems, a set that focuses on exactly how distinct words and images intersect in a hypertext:

We should begin by asking: Are language and image doing the same? Can
they ever do the same?

A second set of questions concerns the interaction/interrelation of the
two languages or semiotic modes between which translation takes place.
Do they merely coexist? Or do they interact? To what degree do they
interact? If language and image do not merely coexist, but interact, what
are the consequences? If they have different potentials, will they serve
different functions, and then inevitably become specialized, both repre-
sentationally and communicationally? (1998, 67)

His response to these questions, in brief, calls for "changes in the semiotic
landscape." Specifically, he sees a need for a new theory of semiosis capable of explaining how different semiotic modes function dialectically,
which requires an understanding both of how the different modes function
individually and of how their differences can be productive interactively.
The key to this challenge for Kress lies in the concept of "synaesthesia."
He asserts that "[a] new theory of semiosis will have to acknowledge and
account for the processes of synaesthesia, the transduction of meaning
from one semiotic mode in meaning to another semiotic mode, an activity
constantly performed by the brain" (1998, 76). That is, in an electronic
document, if the word narrates information and the image displays information, as Kress argues, they necessarily communicate differently so that,
as we engage their operations separately and synaesthetically, we develop
a larger and more complex comprehension of the communication than
would be the case if we understood that communication solely or predominantly in terms of either the word or the image.

At this point in the evolution of computer-generated writing and the
relationship between the verbal and visual in writing instruction, two
problems require our attention. The first involves exploring how the word
and image work differently and similarly and how, as a result, they can
interact synaesthetically. The second requires deciding how the capacity
to work with words and images interactively develops over time; that is,
just as student writing and graphic abilities must follow a developmental
curve, their abilities to work with the two together must be allowed to
mature gradually. Answers to these questions should help to determine
how to build an attention to the interaction between word and image into
a writing course. This agenda appropriately assumes an understanding of
a point suggested to varying degrees in the studies examined above: that
writing instructors do not already possess and therefore must develop the
knowledge about visual communication and its relationship to verbal
communication that teaching writing in the terms described here will
require.

Differentiation, Density, and Synaesthesia

Understanding how words and images interact in an electronic document requires first that we recognize how they differ fundamentally, and
then, within the framework of their differences, how they are sufficiently
alike for each to provide a lens through which the other might be appre-
hended. One fairly established analysis that helps to address the first problem is to see the difference between the written word and the visual image
in terms of what Nelson Goodman (1968, 226) has called "differentiation"
and "density": "Nonlinguistic systems differ from languages, depiction
from description, the representational from the verbal, paintings from
poems, primarily through the lack of differentiation—indeed through density (and consequent total absence of articulation)—in the symbol
scheme." Goodman explains that both the word and image are a part of
systems and have meaning only within the systems in which they participate. W. J. T. Mitchell (1987, 67) elaborates on Goodman's explanation of
how the word and the image and the systems to which they belong differ:

> [In a picture] every mark, every modification, every curve or swelling of
> a line, every modification of texture or color is loaded with semantic
> potential. . . . The image is syntactically and semantically dense in that
> no mark may be isolated as a unique, distinctive character (like a letter
> of an alphabet), nor can it be assigned a unique reference or "compliant."
> Its meaning depends rather on its relations with all the other marks in a
> dense continuous field. A particular spot of paint might be read as the
> highlight on Mona Lisa's nose, but that spot achieves its significance in
> the specific system of pictorial relations to which it belongs, not as a
> uniquely differentiated character that might be transferred to another
> canvas.

Visual images such as graphs and charts operate somewhere between
the relatively dense and undifferentiated nature of the picture and the relatively differentiated word. Some features of graphs and charts (e.g., the
notation for segmenting a pie chart) are differentiated in that they entail a
syntax that carries over from one occasion to another. Other features (e.g.,
the use of color in a pie chart to express something about its constitutive
segments) lean more toward functioning as the undifferentiated feature
that relies on the system inherent in the total image for its communicative
power. Of course, the graphs and charts that use pictures to signify different points and thereby become more pictorial increase the undifferentiated dimension of the overall image.

Claude Gandelman (1991), in *Reading Pictures, Viewing Texts*, offers
a basis for connecting the visual processing of words and images by representing all visual processing as involving two fundamental operations—the
optical and the haptical. Drawing on the work of Alois Riegl, Gandelman
explains that one way of seeing—the optical—scans objects "according to

their outlines," while the other—the haptical—"focuses on surfaces and emphasizes the value of the superficies of objects" (p. 5). Gandelman adds that "the optical eye merely brushes the surface of things. The haptic, or tactile, eye penetrates in depth, finding its pleasure in texture and grain" (p. 5). Gandelman cites the work of the eighteenth-century British philosopher George Berkeley to explain how the interplay between the two ways of seeing make perception an essentially synaesthetic operation:

> There is no vision in the performative meaning of the term—that is, in the sense of seeing as a potentiality of acting over the objects that surround us—without a transfer of the sense of touch to the operations of vision. . . . It is only through a transference of the sense of touch to the eye that one is able to locate and identify things and evaluate one's position in relation to them. Purely optical vision by an eye devoid of the synaesthetic sense of touch would be a vision without pattern recognition in which only points, or at best two-dimensional extension, would be perceived. (1991, 6)

Gandelman's analysis balances the analyses of Goodman and Mitchell in that, while the latter examines how letters and drawings as marks on a page work differently systemically, the former stresses the synaesthetic nature of all-seeing. So, while the optical may be more prominent in seeing the written word on the page because the word is linear and angular, and the haptical more prominent in seeing an image because an image is textured, in both instances seeing combines the optical and haptical. In this there may be the basis for understanding how the written word and the image interact in an electronic document.

Viewing the work of the word and image synaesthetically in an electronic document would have us process a letter as if it were an image, and process an image as if it were a word. This does not mean that we don't process words as words and images as images, but rather that we enhance the processing of words by seeing them as images, and images by seeing them as words. Combining the above analyses, this means that we would see words as being dense as well as differential and would view them haptically as well as optically. Conversely, we would examine the features of an image for their differential aspects and would view them optically as well as haptically. The proliferation of font types and the libraries of clip art available for use in electronic documents certainly invite such an approach, especially since many of the font families are textured and much of the clip art works differentially. In the following font type, for example, we are as aware of the textured density of the characters as we are of their alphabetic function:

a b c d e f g h i j k l m n o p q r s t u v w x y z

◆ **FIGURE 6.2** ◆
Quasi-alphabetical images.

At the same time, the lines and curves in much clip art are standardized to the point that they seem more alphabetic than pictorial, as the examples in figure 6.2 suggest. While these signs may seem to be extreme examples because they are obviously designed to transfer from one situation to the next as letters in an alphabet do, they share with clip art in general a kind of predictability characteristic of the differentiation that Goodman and Mitchell talk about and the optical processing that Gandelman discusses.

Analyzing the relationship between word and image in these and other terms provides a useful foundation from which students can learn to make critical decisions, as writers and as readers, about how these features of a multimodal text work interactively. In delineating a theory of the relationship between words and images, this analysis allows students to see the whole text in terms of the equal and related though differing contributions of its components, which can keep them from formulating a reductive or distorted view of the respective roles of word and image that often results when they consider the two in isolation. Certainly, problems arise when writers do not understand how words and images work separately and interactively. In the early days of desktop publishing this was a theme repeated again and again in discussions about the relative quality of the documents novices were producing. When Henrietta Shirk (1991) considered the need to establish standards for hypertext design, she was largely reflecting a general concern over the "proliferation of poor design techniques as novices began to apply the many publication design tools that technology made available to them" without "a firm grounding in the basics of document design." This state of affairs, she argued, led to texts "typically lacking in professional quality" and therefore communicatively ineffective (p. 197). Our efforts to address this concern have mostly focused on educating students in the dynamics of visual representation to supplement their learning in verbal communication. However, we need to go beyond this and make sure that, in addition to teaching them about the ways in which words and images function independently as discrete systems, we also bring these together and study how they function interdependently.

A Developmental Perspective

A necessary part of following through on the above agenda includes attending to how an understanding of the interplay between word and image must develop over time. Studies of the writing process and its teaching have for a long time accepted that half of the work of learning to write is developmental. That is, study after study has not only reminded us that language abilities develop over time, but has also attempted to chart the lines along which this development can best occur through a succession of writing experiences. Although we might expect a parallel situation in the literature on the development of visual abilities, Howard Gardner (1980) argues that there is surprisingly little on the subject. Nevertheless, he asserts that drawing, and by extension visual thinking generally, "cannot—and should not—be considered apart from the rest of the child's evolving capacities," and he broadly describes the contours that this progression would follow from the infant to the adolescent (p. 14). A part of the difficulty in tracing the development of children's visual-rendering abilities derives from a tradition that at best separates verbal and visual expression at an early age, and at worst represents the two in actual opposition to one another. Gardner (1980, 155) roughly describes the way in which verbal expression gradually diminishes and finally dissolves any commitment to developing visual expression:

> And so until the task of writing has been mastered, the system of drawing is the only one sufficiently developed to permit expression of inner life. Once writing mechanics and literary accomplishment have advanced sufficiently (as they ought to have by the age of nine or ten), the possibility of achieving in words what was once attempted in drawings comes alive: the stage is set for the decline—or demise—of graphic expression.

In other words, development itself is perceived to be predicated on the substitution of one kind of expression for another rather than on the elaboration and complication of their interaction over a period of years. In the early grades, the ability to move "beyond" drawing to verbal expression is construed as a sign of progress and therefore dooms efforts to develop students' abilities in verbal expression and, by extension, in managing creatively and constructively the interaction between word and image.

Articulating a developmental strategy for cultivating an interaction between word and image in computer-based writing instruction might benefit from understanding the historical progression evident in discussions of the effects of computer technology on our notions of text, reading, and writing. That is, recalling how the introduction of each new kind of software application triggered new analyses of how writing and writing instruction would have to change offers a frame for approaching the integration of word and image developmentally. Such a progression would begin with the treatment of word-as-image exemplified by Selfe's students and would move through the synaesthetic rendering of the word–image relationship that Kress suggests.

Applications

The remainder of this discussion will examine several specific examples of efforts to apply the principles outlined above. Of course, these limited examples come nowhere near containing all of the possibilities that the principles discussed above would allow for; however, even though they are limited themselves, the examples may suggest a range of other possibilities. The more we understand the nature of the task, the more readily we will be able to develop instructional approaches that will address the need that Selfe and others alerted us to more than ten years ago.

One way of helping students in a writing course understand how word and image interact is to use images to represent the lessons they are learning visually as well as verbally, and then to encourage them to see how the verbal and the visual expressions can interact to render a more complete comprehension than would be possible through either by itself. The analyses of how word and image interact such as those found in Goodman, Mitchell, and Gandelman provide a means for framing the discussion.

The role of revision in writing has received extensive attention in composition studies over the last twenty-five years. As drafting, peer response, and portfolios have reshaped the pedagogical landscape of the composition classroom, they have served to remind us how difficult this aspect of writing can be for students and, indeed, for all writers. This difficulty marks revision as one aspect of writing instruction that especially invites a verbal–visual approach, since a multimodal approach multiplies the ways in which an individual accesses an issue and therefore facilitates understanding. This argument is implicit in Mina Shaughnessy's (1977) discussion of how to present drafting to basic writers. She suggests the value of showing students facsimile copies of Keats's drafts for "The Eve of St. Agnes," because these manuscript facsimiles reproduce for students "a map of the writer's debates, which, in turn, encourages the student to hesitate over his own words" (p. 222). The visual nature of the map, combined with the verbal instruction students receive and their actual practice in drafting, combine to help them see what the task requires. Shaughnessy does not single out the Keats manuscript because it offers more or better lessons on drafting and revision than other manuscripts; rather, the drafts of "The Eve of St. Agnes" or the draft of any other work simply allows students to visualize the dynamic of the process and thereby helps them to understand what they should see on the pages on which their own efforts are recorded.

Using manuscript materials from published writers in a writing course can fulfill two functions at the same time: While it allows students to visu-

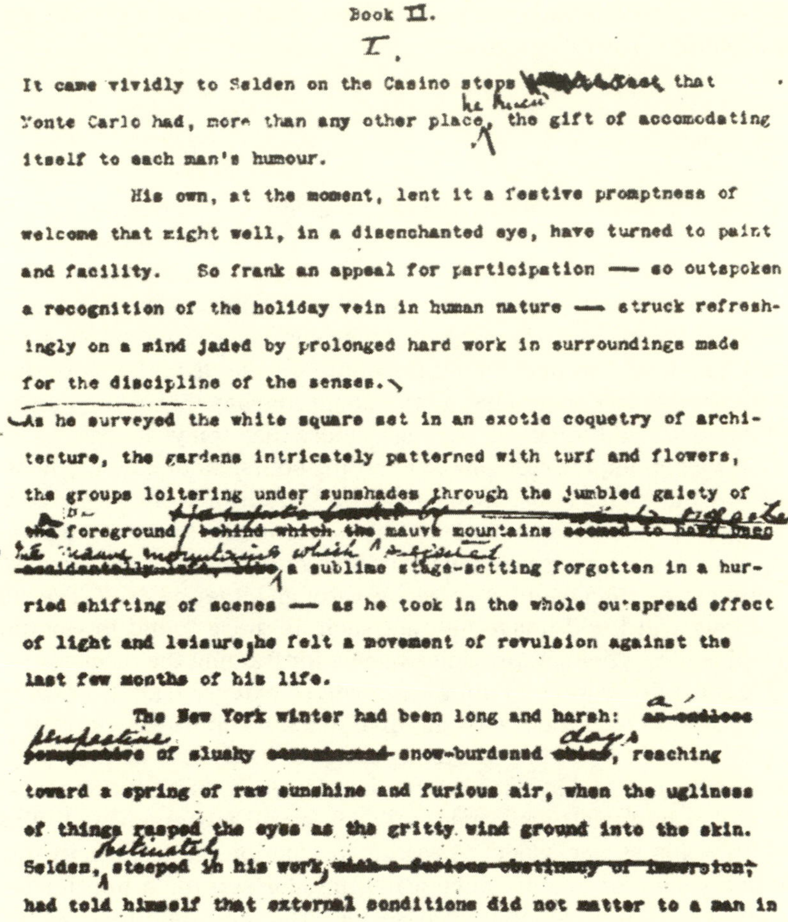

Book II.

I.

It came vividly to Selden on the Casino steps ~~that the~~ that
          he knew
Monte Carlo had, more than any other place, the gift of accomodating
itself to each man's humour.

His own, at the moment, lent it a festive promptness of
welcome that might well, in a disenchanted eye, have turned to paint
and facility. So frank an appeal for participation —— so outspoken
a recognition of the holiday vein in human nature —— struck refresh-
ingly on a mind jaded by prolonged hard work in surroundings made
for the discipline of the senses.

As he surveyed the white square set in an exotic coquetry of architecture, the gardens intricately patterned with turf and flowers,
the groups loitering under sunshades through the jumbled gaiety of
the foreground ~~behind which the mauve mountains seemed to have been~~
~~accidentally~~ ~~like~~, a sublime stage-setting forgotten in a hur-
ried shifting of scenes —— as he took in the whole outspread effect
of light and leisure, he felt a movement of revulsion against the
last few months of his life.

The New York winter had been long and harsh: ~~an endless~~
~~perspective~~ ~~of~~ slushy ~~surroundings~~ snow-burdened ~~skies~~ days, reaching
toward a spring of raw sunshine and furious air, when the ugliness
of things rasped the eyes as the gritty wind ground into the skin.
Selden, steeped in his work, ~~with a furious obstinacy of immersion~~
had told himself that external conditions did not matter to a man in

◆ FIGURE 6.3 ◆

Typescript page from Edith Wharton's *The House of Mirth*.

alize what writing looks like, it also provides an opportunity to illustrate
how word and image interact and how students can conceptualize the
integration of the two in their own writing. The reproduction of the typescript facsimile for the first page of the first chapter in part II of Edith
Wharton's *The House of Mirth* (figure 6.3) provides a basis for demon-
strating the point. This image communicates the experience of revision
with a depth and texture to the experience of revising not evident in the
abstract language we use to discuss the subject. In presenting revision verbally, we might draw on, for example, the analysis of the process found in
Faigley and Witte's study of the revision processes of experienced and in-
experienced writers to introduce students to such concepts as microstruc-

tural and macrostructural revisions. These concepts are highly useful in helping students to organize their understanding of the different kinds of tasks that revision entails. Here the language abstractly narrates the experience of revision, an experience consisting of a succession of choices broadly classified as having microstructural and macrostructural consequences for a text. Our ability to read the narration depends on our familiarity with the linguistic symbols used to communicate it. This ability in turn is a function of our having experienced the symbols in a wide range of other contexts. The image, however, exhibits the density and texture that Goodman, Mitchell, and Gandelman discuss. Certainly, the words on the typescript page are a part of the image, but the image's ability to communicate the experience of revision does not depend primarily on our processing this language. Instead, we respond to the texture of the image, looking at the evenness of the typed line operated on by uneven scribbles that run across the typed text and the interlinear insertions that disrupt the feel of order suggested by the typed lines. In short, the image captures the erratic and irregular character of revision in a way that narrating the experience verbally does not.

The advantage of using a draft of a published text that students might already know is that it makes the visual more striking, since the students' prior experience with the text has been so dominated by the unbroken and unblemished linear line of verbal text. At the same time, working with some other kind of text, including sample pages from the instructor's own drafts, would also be effective as long as the pages used are approached as visual images of the drafting process. As soon as the discussion moves toward the relative advisability of a particular word change between early and late drafts, the discussion ceases to treat the facsimile as an image and becomes a linguistic analysis.

Although it is beyond the scope of this chapter to develop a semiotics of synaesthesia of the kind that Kress calls for, the need for such a semiotics is apparent. Certainly, the analyses of Goodman, Mitchell, and Gandelman suggest issues that such a semiotics would need to explore; a more fully theorized analysis would go much farther in helping to address questions regarding the impact that seeing the crossed-out text and the interlinear insertions at uneven angles to the typed line would have on a student's ability to understand the vocabulary of revision and the processes this vocabulary represents. In effect, it would explain how the visual image of the page informs and shapes the processing of the language about revision, and how the language of revision conditions what a student sees of significance in the facsimile of the typescript. The arrow moving the unindented third paragraph to the end of the second paragraph in *The House of Mirth* typescript does not simply illustrate what Faigley and Witte would call a "mean-preserving" change. Rather, as a visual lens through which the phrase "meaning-preserving" is viewed, it helps to determine how and what the phrase signifies. In addition, because the arrow as visual can function more fluidly than language, it can condition how other language—the term "paragraph" for example—is understood. Similarly, a semiotics of synaesthesia would reveal how the language of revision operates on what a student sees in the arrow. Unlike language, arrows are not highly differentiated signs and thus are highly dependent on the system of signifiers in which they appear on a given occasion. Language that accompanies and interacts with the visual in which an arrow appears, therefore, can substantially influence how a reader allows the arrow to function within the visual system. The phrase "meaning-preserving change" used in connection with the facsimile page, in turn, can frame how the arrow between the two paragraphs is allowed to mean.

Caution must accompany any effort towards approaching the problem of the developmental path students follow in mastering the interaction between word and image through the succession of word–image relationships highlighted in the different kinds of software programs that have become available over the years. There is no inherent connection between how individuals develop and the technological options available to programmers at successive points in the evolution of software. A potential parallel between the two, examined in the discussion below, is based on the coincidental observation of a correlation in the work of students enrolled in two courses at significantly different grade levels. One course was a general education one examining the relationship between technological changes and the evolution of narrative technique in literary works dating from the invention of the printing press. All of the students enrolled in the course were college freshmen and had no knowledge of or experience with hypertext as authors before enrolling in the class, though most had used the Internet and were familiar with its characteristic methods of operation. The other course was a graduate course dedicated to investigating the evolution of English studies in a digital age. The students enrolled in the class generally had considerable experience with theories of text, including theories that analyze such issues as the nature of the printed page, problems of visual and verbal design in a text, and the ways in which different critical theories define text. However, only one had previous experience creating a hypertext, and most had no experience at all of this kind. An assignment shared by both groups required the students to build hypertexts. In the general-education course, students were asked to write a story conventionally and then to create a hypertext version of that story, changing it as they saw fit. Students in the graduate course, which included assignments covering the short fiction of William Faulkner and F. Scott Fitzgerald, were asked to draw on the theories of language, rhetoric, and literature covered earlier in the course. Neither assignment constrained the students in the manipulation of word and image allowed in hypertext.

Observations of the students while in the process of creating their hypertexts and analyses of the final products suggest three preliminary conclusions regarding the developmental paths the two groups followed. First, as they accumulated more experience in viewing the hypertexts of others and in constructing their own, their development generally followed the same trajectory: text-as-image, the coexistence of text and image on the same page, the interaction between text and image in a text-dominated hypertext in which the image illustrates the word, and finally the synaesthetic interaction between word and image in which each acts on how the other is processed and understood. Second, complete progress along this trajectory was a clear exception in the freshman course, but was more common in the graduate course. Third, while the developmental paths that some students in the two groups followed approximated one another, the graduate students traveled this path at a much more accelerated pace than did the students in the general-education course. Throughout their developmental work, however, both groups exhibited a propensity to do certain things with words and images less because they saw a need for these in the hypertexts they were creating, but because they were intrigued by the fact that the program being used allowed them to do these things. In other words, the developmental path for both groups involved considerable experimentation that was driven less by rhetorical need and more by a sense of curiosity about the power of the application being used.

The two most prominent features of the hypertexts among students in the undergraduate course were colored fonts and the juxtaposition of stock or personal photographs with text, often depending on the story they were telling. Fonts were colored both to mark out, as Selfe notes, the different ways in which the designated text participated in the underlying logic of the text and to signal a link to another portion of the hypertext. One of the most interesting aspects of the word–image relationship in these hypertexts was the selection of the photographs included, especially when the student was drawing on a stock photograph. Often, the relationship between a photograph and text was relatively arbitrary, but at other times students worked hard to find photographs that communicated something about the stories they were telling, even though these photographs were not taken with their stories in mind. In these instances, the students came the closest to achieving a synaesthetic relationship between word and image. This was most apparent in the drafting, as a dialogue between word and image was reflected in the changes that occurred in the text because of some feature in the selected photograph, which was later replaced because the writer had chosen a new direction for the story as a result of the change originally precipitated by the introduction of the now-replaced photograph. In situating words and images on the page, most writers in the general-education course simply placed text and photograph next to one another, inviting the reader to infer the connection (see figure 6.4). In this case, the story encapsulates modern isolation and boredom within the experience of people riding a bus. As this screen illustrates, there isn't a very specific relationship between this text and this

The time tick tocks pasts endlessly, and unerringly. The people are worn as well. Pay your money old man, poor woman, all you who would. Pay and sit. Wait and leave.

Back   Next

1 3 4 5 6 7 8 9 10 11 12

◆ **FIGURE 6.4** ◆

Web page from an undergraduate general-education course.

photograph; rather, the relationship is between the whole story and all of the photographs. In effect, the writer could have included all of the text in one part of the text and all of the photographs in another, which suggests a more general synaesthesia. Nevertheless, the links between the story and photographs are not arbitrary or simply illustrative. The photographs collectively frame how we read the text and vice-versa, again at least in a general sense.

The hypertexts generated by students in the graduate course exhibit both more visual material (e.g., backgrounds and icons) and a much more specific synaesthetic relationship between word and image on each page. This latter especially signals their greater progress on the developmental trajectory described above. One of the hypertexts developed in this course focused on Faulkner's story, "A Rose for Emily," and aimed to show how theories of the composing process were evident in the work Faulkner engaged in on his way to completing the story (see figure 6.5). This particular page in the hypertext focuses on the character of Tobe, Miss Emily's black servant. The page not only provides a photograph specifically selected to communicate this character visually, but to work with three different texts: 1) the much more elaborated description of the character as rendered in the typescript of the story, 2) the heavily edited version of the character as presented in the published version of the story,

Clues to the Writing Process

Faulkner reinforces that Emily is an isolated figure by creating a situation in which Emily has no one to rely on and no one to turn to. Faulkner creates a black servant--Tobe-- equally isolated by race, class, and economic situation. He has served Emily faithfully for more than twenty years. The parallels between these two characters underscore the marginalization of both Blacks and women in the South.

Read both the typescript and the published version of "A Rose for Miss Emily" to better understand the relationship Faulkner considered between Emily and Tobe.

HOME

UP

◆ FIGURE 6.5 ◆

Web page from a graduate course on the study of English in a digital age.

and 3) the text offering the writer's interpretation of this character within the frame of this particular story, but also within the contexts of Faulkner's work generally and of the general cultural milieu in the South at the time when the story is set. Simultaneously, the picture joins the three texts by providing a common lens through which to read them, even as the three texts invite us to view different features of the picture to the point that each text renders a different picture by interacting with different aspects of the image. The graduate students' accelerated progress along the developmental path and the increased complexity and sophistication with which they rendered word–image relationships within their hypertexts reinforce Gardner's observation that development in visual abilities cannot be considered apart from the evolution of an individual's evolving capacities, though one wonders how much farther along they would be if their visual abilities had been actively fostered after the shift to an emphasis on verbal performance in the early grades.

Conclusion

As the above discussion demonstrates, the call for writing teachers to build a greater attention to the relationship between the verbal and the visual into their instruction has a relatively long history, at least to the extent that computers in composition instruction have a history. That we are not farther along than we might wish to be may result from the fact that we are dealing with something of a moving target. First, the target moves as we increasingly recognize the need to articulate better than we have the relationship between image and word in a way that gives each its due, while at the same time representing how the two function coextensively. Second, once we understand that the ability to integrate the verbal and visual follows a developmental path consisting of several complex operations, we realize that progress will require the best continuing efforts of both instructor and student. Yet, as study after study has insisted, this is not a path that we can choose to follow or not. With the growing influence of technology on all forms of human communication, we recognize the fundamental necessity of preparing students to take full advantage of this technology in their efforts to learn to communicate most effectively, even as the software and hardware constantly change, always extending and complicating the task before us.

As the above discussion has noted, the major challenge at this point is to articulate a semiotics of synaesthesia that can serve as a foundation for explaining how word and image interact. Studies such as Kim Sydow Campbell's (1995) *Coherence, Continuity, and Cohesion: Theoretical Foundations for Document Design* offer detailed analyses of document design that contribute to our understanding of the dynamics of the page, which includes an attention to the relationship between the visual and verbal. However, these analyses focus less on the processes involved in viewing the word through the image and the image through the word than on the rhetorical effect of their combination on a page. In Kress's terms, they do not account for the "transduction from one semiotic mode in meaning to another semiotic mode, an activity constantly performed by the brain" (1998, 76). Ultimately, we need both kinds of analysis. However, since much has been done on one kind, the greatest urgency at this point is to invest in the other as well and then to use what we learn to improve our students' abilities to compose electronic documents, which will be increasingly the kinds of documents that they will be called on to create most effectively in the future.

Notes

1. Throughout the ensuing discussion, the term, "word," should be taken to refer to the written word. Although computer technology invites opportunities to integrate the spoken as well as the written word with the visual image, the context for this discussion is writing instruction, and therefore slanting the discussion toward the interplay between the written word and the visual image is appropriate. At the same time, the interplay between the spoken word and visual images in a hypertext document, for example, raises a number of interesting issues that are related to but differ from the issues addressed here, and this interplay would be worth exploring in another study.

2. Of course, the written word itself is an image in the sense that it consists of marks on the page with shape and texture. However, while one could explore how the written word gets treated as an image in calligraphy or in painting (expressions that most obviously foreground the visual nature of the written word), within the context of a writing course it is generally not treated as an image. As Selfe points out, it is with the graphic possibilities introduced by word processing that students begin consciously to manipulate the written word as an image. For a historical review of the treatment of the written word as a visual element in a painting, for example, see Meyer Schapiro, *Words, Script, and Pictures: Semiotics of Visual Language* (1996).

References

Campbell, Kim Sydow. (1995). *Coherence, Continuity, and Cohesion: Theoretical Foundations for Document Design*. Hillsdale, NJ: Erlbaum.

Faigley, Lester, and Stephen Witte. (1981). Analyzing revision. *College Composition and Communication* 31: 400–414.

Gandelman, Claude. (1991). *Reading Pictures, Viewing Texts*. Bloomington: Indiana University Press.

Gardner, Howard. (1980). *Artful Scribbles: The Significance of Children's Drawings*. New York: Basic Books.

Goodman, Nelson. (1968). *Languages of Art: An Approach to a Theory of Symbols*. Indianapolis: Bobbs-Merrill.

Kress, Gunther. (1998). Visual and verbal modes of representation in electronically mediated communication: The potentials of new forms of text. In *Page to Screen: Taking Literacy into the Electronic Era*, ed. Ilana Snyder (pp. 53–79). London: Routledge.

Landow, George P. (1991). The rhetoric of hypermedia: Some rules for authors. In *Hypermedia and Literary Studies*, ed. Paul Delaney and George P. Landow (pp. 81–103). Cambridge: Massachusetts Institute of Technology Press.

Mitchell, W. J. Thomas. (1987). *Iconology: Image, Text, Ideology*. Chicago: University of Chicago Press.

Schapiro, Meyer. (1996). *Words, Script, and Pictures: Semiotics of Visual Language*. New York: George Braziller.

Selfe, Cynthia. (1987). Redefining literacy: The multilayered grammars of computers. In *Critical Perspectives on Computers and Composition Instruction*, ed. Gail Hawisher and Cynthia Selfe (pp. 1–15). New York: Teachers College Press.

Shaughnessy, Mina. (1977). *Errors and Expectations*. New York: Oxford University Press.

Shirk, Henrietta Nickels. (1991). Hypertext and composition studies. In *Evolving Perspectives on Computers and Composition Studies: Questions for the 1990s*, ed. Gail Hawisher and Cynthia Selfe (pp. 177–202). Urbana: National Council of Teachers of English.

Sullivan, Patricia. (1991). Taking control of the page: Electronic writing and word publishing. In *Evolving Perspectives on Computers and Composition Studies: Questions for the 1990s*, ed. Gail Hawisher and Cynthia Selfe (pp. 43–64). Urbana: National Council of Teachers of English.

Yankelovich, Nicole, Norman Meyrowitz, and Andries van Dam. (1991). Reading and writing the electronic book. In *Hypermedia and Literary Studies*, ed. Paul Delaney and George P. Landow (pp. 53–79). Cambridge: Massachusetts Institute of Technology Press.

PART TWO

mixing media in the arts
and professions:
design and performance

When words and images are combined, each influences how we perceive the other, making the process of developing meaning even more complex, but also opening the door to a potentially rich outcome. Modern technology has allowed writers and designers to become multimedia artists who relate image and language practices. Part two presents discussions of particular issues raised by our difficulties with interpreting words and images and the contextual frames we have developed as aids to the interpretation process. In these chapters we find these issues presented as they have occurred in particular areas of the arts and professions.

Photography was one of the earliest visual art technologies to be explored for its storytelling capabilities. The continuous-frame camera of the 1940s could combine a series of pictures into a kind of pictorial documentary that encouraged viewers to create a narrative interpretation. A series of enlarged pictures taken at different moments of a process could be joined together to present a life-sized version of an event, something as simple, for example, as the American-icon activity of preparing and eating a peanut-butter sandwich. Books of photography that we sometimes refer to as "coffee-table books" have called themselves "photo essays," implying that they have something to say and that it is being said through photographs. Questions then arise as to what kind and how much text is needed, how the text should be related to the pictures, and how text and image each influence our interpretation of the situation presented. In chapter 7, "Telling Our Stories in Pictures: Case History of a Photo Essay," Nancy Allen, professor of written communication at Eastern Michigan University and editor of this volume, explores the experiences of one group that prepared a volume they labeled as a "photo essay." The chapter describes their struggles as a group to develop their project and their discussions of the issues that influenced their decisions concerning text, photographs, design, and the relationships among them.

Chapter 8 further explores the influences of photography, this time the special part photography played in setting the context for a new professional field. Photography was originally developed as a tool for mirroring nature. When Louis Jacques Mandé Daguerre used silver iodide to fix an image on a coated metal plate, he was looking for a method to produce realistic images of nature that more accurately represented details of natural items than those created through other means. Photography brought us "far seeing"; that is, the ability to see things that were too far away to be seen directly—and "close-up views" through which we could see details more closely and clearly than we could otherwise. As Émile Zola put it, "You cannot claim to have really seen something until you have photographed it" (Stephens 1998, 75). Gregory Wickliff, professor of professional communication at the University of North Carolina–Charlotte, has researched photography's rhetorical and epistemic roles in creating "new" knowledge, through which photography participates in conceptual structures of both mimesis and convention. In his chapter on nineteenth-century photography, "Astronomical Rhetoric: Nineteenth-Century Photographs as Models of Meaning," Wickliff examines arguments made for photography as a knowledge-making tool in developing both contexts and conventions of interpretation. In presenting the range of claims made for early astronomical photography, Wickliff explores historical trends in Western culture linked to the credibility, logic, and emotional power of photographic rhetoric in technology and science.

In 1391, Chaucer penned what is considered the earliest recorded technical document in English, his *Treatise on the Astrolabe*. The visual elements of this text include not only illuminated letters but also graphics, which aided the reader's understanding of this technology, which was complex for its time. At about the same point in history, the publication of Gutenberg's printed Bible helped to standardize several visual features of a printed text that we now take for granted, such as punctuation and initial capital letters on sentences. Such features of the relationships between text and graphics have developed in all periods. In 1990 Barry Pegg, a writing professor at Michigan Technological University, wrote a history of text format and print technology in which he described a three-part typology of text–image relationships, exploring the primary and supportive roles of words in relation to images. In chapter 9 of this volume, "Two-Dimensional Features in the History of Text Format: How Print Technology Has Preserved Linearity," Pegg extends his typology to include today's movement of texts and images into electronic media.

Theater, another area of intersection between verbal and visual representation, has historically been a showcase for the playwright, an artist at creating conversation. But the theater is a visual venue as well. In developing their arts, actors and public speakers have long studied gesture as an important part of their delivery. As early as 1727, John Henley published a book on pronunciation and gesture for use in the legislature, theater, court, and pulpit, and more recently, in 1994, Desmond Morris produced *Bodytalk: A World Guide to Gestures*. We speak through bodily images as well as with words, in person and on stage. The theater also speaks visually through other modes. For example, the first impression an audience receives as the curtain opens is a created setting—built and painted to evoke place, time, and an emotional as well as physical setting. Lighting, from the lanterns of Shakespeare's time and the gaslights that followed to today's electronics, adds another major component of the visual imagery on stage. Electrical lighting can be varied in intensity, focus, color, and illumination and can move about on stage, almost becoming an actor in the cast. *A Chorus Line*, which opened in 1975, was the first Broadway show to have its lighting controlled by computer, using a system designed by Gordon Pearlman (1999), and such technology has now grown into an important theater industry. The visual effects can hardly be dismissed as mere decoration for the script.

According to Lisa Brock, a playwright and theater critic in Minneapolis, theater exists in the interrelationships between language and image. The text, or script, is not theater, but a blueprint for theater, which only becomes realized when it exists in the present tense, within a context of images. In chapter 10, "The Concrete Word: Text and Image in the Theater," Brock discusses the balance of power within the interrelationships of text and images, a balance that has been debated since the late nineteenth century; it has shifted as technological advances have created new possibilities for presenting images onstage. Her discussion assesses the ways in which these practical advances have impacted and been shaped by parallel philosophical debates on the nature of interrelationships among words and images in the theater.

As the provinces of words and images become more intertwined, the nature of what we think of as a book changes and expands. What is called "book art" now includes three categories: *fine-press books*, which are done in traditional book form with artistic levels of workmanship; *artists' books*, which incorporate innovative design that may, for example, display pictures on satin or metal pages; and *book-objects*, which combine media in sculptural structures that extend beyond book form. With the advances in technology now available to writers and designers, images have gained greater importance for telling stories in several media. These new forms create new conventions for writers and new contexts for interpretation that prompt us to think about books and art in new and more visual ways. Graphic novels, a variation on comic books, are a special medium for which the process of production generally involves a series of interlinked (and often unconscious) collaborations. In most cases, an editor "orchestrates" the relationships among a penciller, inker, colorist, letterer, scripter, and plotter and in the process tacitly controls the rhetorical and aesthetic resonances of the final product. In chapter 11, "'The Way of the Sorcerer': An Etiology of Two Images from a Lost Graphic Novel," creative-writer Insu Fenkl and graphic artist Mike Dringenberg present a behind-the-scenes reflection on their process of collaboration in producing the graphic novel *The Way of the Sorcerer*. In a back-and-forth interchange, the writer scripted and "thumbnailed" the book, the artist prepared sketches of the action he envisioned from the thumbnails, and then the writer rewrote the text based on the artist's visualizations in rough sketches, which were later realized as full-scale paintings. Fenkl and Dringenberg examine their process of mutual reading and how it affected their underlying consciousness in the writing of their mixed-media text. Neither text nor graphics operated independently, but instead required the context of the other in the development of this book and for our interpretation of it.

References

Henley, John. (1727). *The Art of Speaking in Public*. London: N. Cox.
Morris, Desmond. (1994). *Bodytalk: A World Guide to Gestures*. London: J. Cape.
Pearlman, Gordon. (1999, August 3). Personal communication.
Stephens, Mitchell. (1998). *The Rise of the Image, the Fall of the Word*. New York: Oxford University Press.

chapter seven

TELLING OUR STORIES IN PICTURES
case history of a photo essay

———◆———

nancy allen

W HEN WE THINK ABOUT PREPARING a document that seriously explores a topic, an essay perhaps or some other declaration of viewpoint, we focus on words. Handbooks, rhetorics, guidelines, and writing curricula since Aristotle's peripatetic instruction have shown speakers and writers how to consider their topics, develop their points, and present their arguments with words. It wasn't that images weren't considered by classic writers and speakers; they were condemned. Plato had refused images admission into his republic because they were false representations, thrice removed from reality and capable of impairing reason. Many traditional scholars followed suit, discrediting images as tools of emotion. In following tradition, formal essays have focused on rational appeals presented through words as the most valid method for presenting issues. Because images create emotional appeal, they have typically been discredited as poor, if not invalid, elements for meaningful presentation of serious issues.

The negative stance toward images has never been unanimously held, however. Thomas Aquinas, though he agreed that images excite emotions, nevertheless credited them as having some communicative advantages over words. Images were easily accessible to "unlettered" members of an audience, and they could be powerful as elements of a discussion

(Stephens 1998, 61, 180). Communicators who needed to present technical information have for centuries found drawings and other images useful for clarifying details that were difficult to describe in words. Think, for instance, of the sketches of war machines da Vinci prepared for potential benefactors. Images in technical communication have focused not on the emotional but on the factual: they have presented concrete examples of machinery, tools, or statistics and follow a practice that can date its English roots back to 1391 with Chaucer's illustrations of the astrolabe. For today's audiences, photographs and other images help to clarify details and demonstrate points as well as attract attention and create a focus for discussion.

In this chapter I will present a case for which images are the major elements in an essay, in this case a photo essay, that combines photographs and text, and I will describe the techniques that this project group used to bring their use of images and text together effectively. Though accompanied by words, the photographs carry the weight of their discussion, establishing the context and telling the story of the subject for these communicators. In presenting this case, I will first discuss issues that researchers and theorists have raised concerning the use of images and words in discourse. I will then show how these issues played out for one group—a writer, a photographer, and a design firm, who collaborated to create a photographic essay about a small city.

Photographic Books and Essays

Photographs and photojournalism seem to have long been with us, but the invention of photography and its use in public communication are relatively recent. "The first reproduction of a photograph in a newspaper appeared as recently as March 4, 1880, when a picture entitled 'Shanty-Town' was printed in the New York *Daily Graphic*" (Boorstin 1987, 125). Since this appearance, photographs have become a standard part of newspaper journalism, and their domain has broadened to include several types of publications. We are, for example, now familiar with book-length collections of photographs commonly referred to as "coffee-table books." Though photographs had been used as illustrations in books, it wasn't until twentieth-century technology made viable photographic collections in book form that they became widely published.

Some of the most famous photographic books are those published by the Sierra Club in the 1960s. We enjoy leafing through these books, which usually contain text passages as well as photographs, because they are beautiful to look at. Yet as we look, these books also make strong statements in support of conservation. Earlier, in the 1930s, the Farm Security Administration (FSA) had sponsored a series of photographic books prepared by some of the best photographers of the day along with accompanying text that varied from captions to poetry. While this series was ostensibly created to present a record of 1930s life in the countryside, the books also had the serious social purpose of presenting important issues concerned with the living and working conditions of people in small towns and rural areas. The books are credited with having affected legislation associated with farm life and workers during that period (Hunter 1987, 88).

One example of a more recent photographic collection is *A Pictorial Celebration of the American Woman*, published in 1989. This book, a collection of a hundred winning photographs from a Parade-Kodak National Photo Contest, includes both color and black-and-white photographs with very short captions identifying the person pictured, the photographer, and the situation shown. One page of the book's 138 pages contains five quotations about women, printed in large white letters on a black background. With or without these quotations, the other 137 pages stand as testimony to the strength, versatility, and contributions of women to American culture. A 1999 photographic collection similarly draws attention to men in American culture. This book, *Fathers and Sons: Stories of How Sport Builds Lifelong Bonds*, allows James Beckett to make a positive statement about the influence of sports on relationships at a time in our society when sports are the subject of contesting opinions.

Some books of photographs are called photo essays, a label that Plato would probably have considered an oxymoron, since essays deal with ideas and, to Plato, photos deal with emotions. An essay, however, is not conventionally expected to offer conclusive truth. The term "essay" comes from *assay*, meaning "to weigh," a term we apply to ideas as much as to ore samples. In their theoretical analysis of writing, Wayne Booth and Marshall Gregory (1987) say of essays: "In an essay, writers appraise ideas or problems, trying out solutions but seldom, if ever, resolving them once and for all" (p. 52). James Kinneavy (1971), another textual theorist, reaches a similar conclusion: "Undoubtedly the very best term which history offers for the text of a discourse that was merely exploratory, not conclusive, in aim is the term 'essay'" (p. 97). Frederick Crews, author of the widely used *Random House Handbook*, defined the essay even more loosely as "a fairly brief piece of nonfiction that tries to make a point in an interesting way" (Winterowd and Blum 1994, 34).

One feature all of these definitions of essays have in common is that they refer to words. Words are what we commonly use to express our positions on a topic. Of course, we are familiar with the common expression that "a picture is worth a thousand words," but the traditional attitude concerning persuasive discussion is more likely to agree with William Saroyan's remark: "One picture is worth a thousand words. Yes, but only if you look at the picture and say or think the thousand words" (Hunter 1987, 6). To explore a topic or prepare persuasive arguments about it, communicators have traditionally used words.

In contrast with tradition, an essay, to ascribe to its definition as "an exploration of a topic" or "an attempt to make a point about something in an interesting way," need not be constructed of words. In some cases, in fact, an essay may use words in only a minimal way or perhaps not at all. In 1972 the British Broadcasting Corporation published *Ways of Seeing*, a book that John Berger developed in conjunction with a television series. This book consists of seven parts labeled as essays: four combine words and images, but three are made up almost entirely of images. Two of the three image essays have single-line identifying captions for the pictures, and the third has no added captions nor any words other than those contained within a few of the pictures. Berger refers to these three as "pictorial essays." They tell us about ways of viewing women and about contradictory aspects of the oil-painting tradition. They are, Berger says, "intended to raise as many questions as the verbal essays. Sometimes . . . no information at all is given about the images reproduced because it seemed to us that such information might distract from the points being made" (1972, 5).

Walter Benjamin's (1969, 237) comment on moving images makes clear the sort of contribution images can make to exploring a topic or making a point:

> Even if one has a general knowledge of the way people walk, one knows nothing of a person's posture during the fractional second of a stride. The act of reaching for a lighter or a spoon is familiar routine, yet we hardly know what really goes on between hand and metal, not to mention how this fluctuates with our moods. Here the camera intervenes with the resources of its lowerings and liftings, its interruptions and isolations, its extensions and accelerations, its enlargements and reductions. The camera introduces us to unconscious optics as does psychoanalysis to unconscious impulses.

Rudolph Arnheim made a similar comment about still photographs: "The enlargement of a snapshot does not simply render more precise what in any case was visible, though unclear: it reveals entirely new structural formations of the subject" (Benjamin 1969, 236). Clearly these theorists believe that photographs have an important contribution to make toward exploring a subject or making persuasive statements about important topics.

Creating a Photo Essay

To investigate how these theoretical insights worked in an actual publishing situation, I conducted individual interviews with members of a group that produced a photographic book they refer to as a "photo essay." The book, titled *Charlevoix*, explores the area and ambiance around Charlevoix, Michigan, using interplay between words and pictures to make a statement about a geographical area in what the creators hoped would be an interesting way.

The project was initiated by book-store owner Dianne Foster, who had frequently been asked by her customers for a book that did more than simply give historical facts about the Charlevoix area. After an initial two-and-a-half-hour meeting over coffee with Ken Scott, a photographer, Foster enlisted him to join her in producing a photo essay. In his work Scott typically used one camera and two lenses, avoiding gimmicks to produce photography with a purity Foster admired. Since he was from the northern region but not from Charlevoix, Scott also brought a fresh eye to the subject.

To design the book, they worked with Tim Nielsen, Emily Mitchell, and Darren Shroeger of the Nielsen Design Group, whose business it is to create publications involving both words and images. The Nielsen Design Group has produced several projects for a museum and thus frequently "get into real nitty-gritty issues of what's the message in the relationship of text to images" (Mitchell 1998).

Foster decided to self-publish in order to maintain control of the project and to apply her management skills in a new area. Consequently, her next step was to establish Petunia Press. She had worked in critical care nursing and hospital administration before establishing the book store and so had had extensive experience with business and project planning. She developed what she called "probably the most comprehensive business plan ever done for a book" (Foster 1998) and secured a loan from a local bank that was familiar with her successful track record at the book store.

Foster, Scott, and the Nielsen designers constituted a group with a variety of skills and approaches to a project. As Foster (1998) explained it:

> My underlying philosophy when putting a team together in health care was to seek out diversity. I looked at resumes for strengths and accomplishments, but my decisions were based on interviews. I was more interested in *how* the person accomplished, in their thinking and their behaviors, than in *what* they accomplished. If we were all in a room together and were all thinking alike, we would never achieve the benefits of the group process, where our ideas are challenged and our thinking is stretched. When I first met Ken, my initial reaction was, "oh, we're too different. He's real laid back and I'm real driven." But then this became the strength of the whole project. Ken balanced my intensity, and I kept our project on task.

THE DESIGN PROCESS

The process for developing the project involved individual as well as group work and was fed by both words and images. Working from customers' requests, Foster and Scott first developed a table of contents, choosing subjects that were visually interesting in themselves or that represented characteristic features of the area. Examples of special features would be "a picture that says petunias," to represent the petunias that

Charlevoix citizens plant along the town's main street each year, and one that included the screen door on the Horton Bay General Store, whose familiar slam announced customers. After working individually on text and photos, Foster and Scott met again to revise their lists for logistical and time constraints, and they continued to revise, compare, and add as the project progressed.

On one subject, photographs of people, Foster and Scott had different perspectives. Foster felt strongly that people are life, and she didn't want Charlevoix to look like no one lived there. Scott, on the other hand, didn't like to photograph people because of their tendency to pose. In addition, pictures of vehicles and people other than children tend to date a publication because their styles change more quickly than do landscapes and buildings. Then, too, there was always the possibility of "immortalizing" on film a couple who thought they were on a "lost weekend." Foster concluded, "Ken's sensitivity to 'people issues' made me much more aware of the potential for problems" (Foster 1998). In the end, Scott worked out a way to include children and well-known town characters in natural ways and in settings that would not negatively affect their book's shelf life. The result satisfied both of their interests.

They worked on text and images for thirteen months so that they could capture all four seasons. In that time Scott took 3,500 shots, though they expected to have only 145 pictures in the finished book. According to Scott, "I try to do things, I don't even know how it will turn out" (Scott 1998).

Emily Mitchell (1998) explained that there are two primary ways in which projects like this are handled by designers. Most often, the author/photographer brings in copy and photographs, talks with the designers about the purposes for the project, and then the designers try to put something together from the words and images. In the second process, which Mitchell prefers, the author/photographer meets with the designers before the text and images are prepared, and they talk about ideas for the project, together forming some preliminary concepts that become a platform for the whole. Mitchell's position is that "the earlier the designers are brought into the conceptual work, the better. It's their job to give a forming hand" (Mitchell 1998). Either process involves some risks. If the designers are brought in late, the project may not be as strong as it could have been with their creative input. On the other hand, if the designers are brought in early, their preliminary concept, if too heavy-handed, could curtail some of the freedom and creative insight the author/photographer brings to the project.

Foster had expected to go into the project with a blank book designed by the Nielsen Design Group, with slots for words and photos that she and Scott could simply plug their work into. In actuality, the Charlevoix project more closely followed the first process, in that Scott and Foster had most of the photos and text prepared before meeting with the designers.

On the other hand, the Nielsen Design Group allowed Foster and Scott more participation in the actual design portion of the project than is typical. Foster (1998) recalls:

> We put in a lot of eight- and ten-hour days in that office. And it worked for us. There were tough days, there were great days. It basically was a new experience for all of us. As difficult as it was, us sitting together and trying to come up with the design, that whole process could be so exhilarating and exasperating all in the same day. I still think it was the best process. Never would I approach a project now where we would just take photo shots and plug them in.

Leadership on the project fell mainly to Foster, who had initiated the book and obtained the backing. But she continuously emphasized the partnership between herself and Scott, and as the project progressed, leadership shifted among Foster, Scott, and Mitchell as different needs called for particular expertise. Foster said that at times she wanted to step in on a decision but held back, forcing it to be a group operation. According to Mitchell (1998), "each piece of expertise was respected as such, and when that was needed, it came forward, and others deferred." The times when Foster did force a decision were ones in which she felt the project could become bogged down indefinitely.

This project had dual stated purposes: to provide documentary scenes and information on the Charlevoix area, and to present artistic photography. These correspond to functions that art historian Alan Gowans ascribes to pictorial art or graphic images. Art and images, Gowans said, can serve us as 1) *substitute imagery* to preserve the appearance of some item of interest; 2) *illustration*, when the art is intended to record events or tell stories; 3) *persuasion/conviction*, when shapes can be associated with ideas, concepts, or convictions; and 4) *beautification*, when the art is intended to provide us with visual pleasure (Berger 1989). The documentary purpose for this book meant preserving familiar scenes for reader-viewers, but in a way that would make them interesting. Scott explained: "I was taking pictures of things people see everyday, so I wanted to get different angles, different times, so they would see them in a different way" (Scott 1998). His comment is reminiscent of Arnheim's claim, reported earlier, that photography can show us reality in a new way. An unstated purpose of the project, which the bank administrators were undoubtedly aware of, was one of persuasion, the promotion of the Charlevoix area for vacation, business, and residence.

Foster and Scott whittled Scott's collection of shots down to two hundred, and then asked the designers to eliminate the rest to reach the goal of 145. Instead, Mitchell (1998) took a different tack:

> They brought in the pictures, I did the statistics [picture-to-text proportions], we allocated and kind-of formed some concepts from that, a two-

section book. Then once we put that structure together and knowing they had plenty of documentary shots, we said, "Now, we need *more* pictures. We want more magic. It's a book of Ken Scott's artwork, in addition to being about Charlevoix, and we'd like to see more shots that represent his unique vision of things. Let's get more shots like that one," and we identified one that was pure abstraction and had nothing to do with documentation. Those are some of the shots that we ended up using to present the project and to divide the book up into sections.

These pictures added visual interest and fulfilled the artistic purpose that Gowan lists as the "beautification function." It was an intended purpose for the project that Foster and Scott had temporarily lost track of. With this redirection from the Nielsen Design Group, the book finally contained 241 photographs.

RELATING WORDS AND IMAGES

The Nielsen Design Group was also primarily responsible for orchestrating the relationships between words and images. Scott, who says that he speaks primarily through his images, expressed his motivation for participating in a book that joined his images with words. "People have wanted words. If they could have words or pictures, they'd rather have pictures. They want to have the 'now' of what they enjoy. But they like to have words with it" (Scott 1998).

The conjunction of words and images brought up the problem of how to present both in a single volume. The Nielsen designers came up with a creative layout that divided the book into a primarily visual introduction and a more-documentary second part that included fifteen sections of text with pictures, sections they referred to as "stories." Mitchell explained that when Foster and Scott brought in the pictures and designated which ones went with the introduction and which with the remaining stories, she first did an analysis to find the ratio of words-to-pictures. She discovered that the ratio of words-to-pictures in the introduction was very off-balance:

> There were fifty or sixty photographs allocated to the introduction, but only three hundred words, which would ordinarily need only a few pages. The other pictures were balanced with their stories—for instance, lots of pictures of stone houses, but also lots of words. If we wanted the pictures in the introduction to be of a certain size, that section needed to be fifty pages long. So I knew from the analysis that the book had a very strong visual introduction, that there was a lot to say visually. The front section should really become a photo essay, and the words should be distributed sparingly, sprinkled in among the photographs. If it's fifty or sixty pages long with only a small number of words, so be it. (Mitchell 1998)

To create an appropriate mix, she made the text more dominant by making it bigger than the text in the stories and more concentric on the page. She then broke the introduction text into a series of thoughts and

In the wake of explorers came fur traders, fishermen, settlers, farmers,

lumber barons, and manufacturers. Tourism and summer resorts followed in the late

nineteenth century and brought an economic balance to the region.

◆ **FIGURE 7.1** ◆

A page from the introduction emphasizing the photograph, which is accompanied by two sentences. NOTE: FROM *CHARLEVOIX* (PAGE 31), BY D. FOSTER AND K. SCOTT. CHARLEVOIX, MI: PETUNIA PRESS, 1998, REPRINTED WITH PERMISSION.

distributed them near related photographs. Figure 7.1 shows one page from the introduction and figure 7.2 one from the story section, illustrating the differences in appearance and density of text. Both sections also include several full-page photographs with no text. Mitchell said her layout represented the modernist tenet, "form follows function," which she believes in (Mitchell 1998). The atypical form of the first section was determined by the function it fulfilled in the book as a whole, a visual orientation to the book and to the city of Charlevoix.

The issues concerning placement of photographs and text were not over. The layout in the second section needed to accommodate larger blocks of text with directly related pictures. These pictures Mitchell classified as illustrations and considered their relationship to text as much more straightforward. In the visual introduction, readers could browse; in the second section's stories, they could settle down and read. So the next step Mitchell took was to sketch a grid for the section's page layout. She explained:

time, money, advanced planning, and cooperative weather. The island has two airports with several twenty-minute flights departing and arriving throughout the day. For convenience, many islanders keep a vehicle on the island as well on the mainland.

Always a thrill for islanders, the arrival of the first spring ferry generates a bustle in the harbor as long-awaited freight is unloaded from the boat. The Beaver Island Boat Company operates two passenger, vehicle, and freight ferries out of Charlevoix from April until the end of December. The 95-foot *Beaver Islander*, built in 1962, carries 200 passengers and ten vehicles. The old, tuckered *South Shore* ferry was retired in late 1997 with the arrival of the new *Emerald Isle*. The 130-foot stern-loading Emerald Isle is named for a ferry from years ago. However, the new boat is the grandest ferry Beaver Island has known. She has a capacity for 300 passengers, twenty vehicles and one heavy truck, and is equipped with the latest comforts and conveniences. The Ferry service transports many tourists to

Beaver Island is a simpler, less material world. Yet, it is a progressive place.

and from Beaver Island. The nearly three-hour cruise across Lake Michigan is a wonderful way to make the transition to the slower motion of the island.

Beaver Island is a simpler, less material world. Yet, it is a progressive place. It merely progresses at its own pace, by its own standards, and without sacrificing traditional values along the way. Part of the island's charm is that its residents are more inclined to act on what feels right rather than what might be considered "politically correct" by the rest of the world. Interestingly, much of the rest of the world is racing about, at breakneck speed, desperately seeking some semblance of balance, harmony, and simplicity which are the same qualities that islanders found generations ago. It's an unruffled repose that still exists today on Beaver Island.

Yes, island life has a special quality. It is tranquil, nostalgic, and healing. As day fades into night, there's an ease to the island's silence and a gentleness in its darkness. The moon-washed trees seem to whisper messages from far away. You feel the need to answer, and you cannot, except in spirit. So you drift off to sleep with only the soothing rhythm of the island flowing through you.

◆ FIGURE 7.2 ◆

A page from the section-II story on Beaver Island. Words received more emphasis in these stories and occupied a larger percentage of page space.

NOTE: FROM *CHARLEVOIX* (PAGE 131), BY D. FOSTER AND K. SCOTT. CHARLEVOIX, MI: PETUNIA PRESS, 1998, REPRINTED WITH PERMISSION.

With the statistics, you kind-of figure out how space is filled, you get a feeling for it, make a first round of assumptions. Then you can design a grid to accommodate what you're observing. In this section of the book [the second section], I needed a way to have running text, thousands of words, with pictures right along side it. (Mitchell 1998)

Mitchell's grid established boundaries and a horizon line for each page. In general, text was to go below the horizon and photographs above. Some pages, however, had text that was higher on the page and a small photograph. Mitchell explained the variation in layout as, once you establish the grid, then you can break the rules. One page with much more text than picture was one for which Foster didn't want to cut text, so they added a little variety to the layout. The height of the picture was then determined by the height of the text. Mitchell (1998) added: "The margin was established, and there are certain rules we don't break, like the space between a picture and the rule or between the rule and a section title. These give a book consistency." The grid provided a baseline, but the layout then required aesthetic judgment. According to Mitchell (1998), "You set up the grid, you've got the structure, and then the rest of it you feel."

Interestingly, Mitchell believes that her approach to layout would apply to a technical document as well as to an artistic one. When asked about the Jet Propulsion Laboratory page design that was established to help soldiers find information easily, Mitchell (1998) responded:

> That kind of institutional book-design process frequently does not con-
> sider the end-user well enough. The process is so often operations-ori-
> ented and isn't driven by objective thinking about the content. Like
> myopia. It's thoughtless to put something in a structure like that and to
> never change it and to never let the content dictate how it's presented.
> An organization approaches it with expediency *of preparation* as a goal,
> not expediency *of understanding*. They do it to save time and money. If
> the issue is how fast someone can understand something, I would wager
> that a thoughtfully designed jet propulsion book would be more quickly
> understood than one that isn't thoughtfully designed.

The issue for her was one of engagement. Readers become more engaged with thoughtfully designed documents and consequently learn from them more quickly and effectively:

> They may need something that doesn't have any words in it at all. Maybe
> it's all pictures with diagrams that show what buttons to push. Maybe it's
> not a book; maybe it's a movie. The issue is more like planning—solving
> the problem and planning it well, understanding what needs to be done,
> and then doing that. Cookie-cutter solutions just aren't thoughtful.
> (Mitchell 1998)

Even with variation in their page layout, sometimes text needed to be cut to fit into the space available. Foster recalled one instance when Tim Nielsen asked her to cut thirty-four words from the train depot section:

> I just about cried. You have no idea how many times I've edited this. You
> can't just cut thirty-four words; you have to rework the whole thing, tran-
> sitioning and rearranging sentences. But everybody has their area of ex-
> pertise, and you have to respect that. If Tim said we needed to cut thirty-
> four words, then we needed to cut thirty-four words. There's only so
> much space. So I just hung up the phone and did it. (Foster 1998)

Another difficult decision was whether to include captions for the pho-
tographs, and if so, how to handle them. One issue was placement. Captions presented with the photographs might compete with the words in the text sections. Another issue was the function of captions. Foster and Scott were reluctant to add specific identification to the pictures. Scott felt that "In an image driven book, the story is written by the people

who buy it. Of course, some people feel put on the spot about what that story is, so they want words" (Scott 1998). Foster approached captions similarly: "I had the feeling that we didn't want to caption the photographs because then we were telling people what they were seeing, and I didn't want to do that. I wanted it to be whatever it was for that person" (Foster 1998). One example of a labeling issue concerned Charlevoix's stone houses, a group of structures with unusual architecture. When Foster wrote that story, she consulted an architect on how to write about them. His suggestion was, "Tell people about the picture, but don't tell them what they're seeing. Don't describe them as gnome houses, don't give them that character. Let readers come to that conclusion if that's what they want. Just stick to describing the architecture" (Foster 1998). This advice supported Scott's and Foster's reluctance to label items too completely in their text.

A third issue related to captioning was one of page design. "Captioning photographs is awkward," said Foster (1998). "It's clumsy, it makes so many words, it impedes the flow. As you turned the page, you'd find words here and then words there, and the eyes don't know where to go."

In the end they did not include captions with the photographs. Photos in the second section appear on the same pages with text, but there is no exact correspondence or identifying caption. Instead, the photos and text relate in terms of mood and general subject. For example, pictures of the shore are placed near discussions of sailors and fishermen; shots of a quarry and a farm appear near a statement about what came in the wake of the explorers. With these general topical relationships, readers can draw their own associations between photographs and text as they go through the book.

For those readers who really wanted the pictures identified, Foster and Scott added an index at the back of the book, but even then, they were very careful about the wording, trying not to be specific when it wasn't warranted. As Foster (1998) said, "If someone wants to believe that it's their field or a place they've been, then let them have that. Don't tell them it's on this road and destroy that for them." She likes the same nonspecific approach for museum displays as well: "It bothers me when I walk through an art museum and I look at a painting and right next to it is the interpretation from the artist of what it is. I don't want to know that. Maybe later, but I don't want to know that right then because then I stand there trying to see what they see" (Foster 1998). Mitchell believed their nonspecific style of identification in the index also avoided some privacy issues they might otherwise have faced. Foster and Scott had, however, been careful to obtain permission whenever any person or place was recognizable in the pictures or included in the text.

Another design feature that involved the relationship between words and images was their decision to include "pull quotes," small segments of highlighted text, in the second section stories. Pull quotes can fulfill several functions: attract a reader-viewer's attention, feature a key piece of information, and add visual interest to a page. Mitchell proposed that they include them and asked Foster to select which quotes she'd like to have, but Foster found herself struggling. As she tells it: "I just dumped that one back on her. I said 'I wrote it. They're all important words to me. You're a person reading it for the first time, and you're a person not familiar with Charlevoix.' So she did all of that for me. I thought they should all be pull quotes" (Foster 1998).

All of these decisions affected much more than simply the attractiveness of a page. The design also influenced the content and usability of the book as a whole. The book's overall design with an introduction that consisted primarily of photographs brought readers into Charlevoix visually before getting them involved with learning the facts and history found in the second section's stories. The group believed this design might cause some readers, used to heavily structured texts, to wonder where they were going, but ultimately they felt the design fit their combination of artistic and documentary goals. "It does something to the mood. That was Nielsen Design that did that. They really pushed on it, and I really appreciated that" (Foster 1998).

ESTABLISHING A FIRST IMPRESSION

Although overall design is very important to a book's success, any book, essay, or report needs an opening impression that will bring readers into the subject and interest them enough to pursue it. For a book, the cover jacket's design is a large part of that first impression, and this group was divided over what would be most effective on the jacket. Foster was anticipating a photograph that was beautiful but traditional; for example, the raised bascule bridge in the center of town with a sailboat passing through it. Mitchell felt that the book contained a lot of artistic photography, so the jacket should reflect the artistic approach. She wanted a picture that would compel people to open the book. Scott was frustrated because he had expected that, as they went through the selection and design processes, a picture would stand out as the obvious best choice for the cover, and that had not happened. They only knew that, because Charlevoix is a lakeside city, they had to have a boat on the cover, and they needed to include a lot of blue.

In actuality, they needed not just one photograph, but two, because the front and back of the cover jacket needed to work together. To select them, Foster, Scott, and the Nielsen designers sat together and put up a number of pairs of pictures, then switched them, creating various scenarios. After spending some time at this, Foster began to think that they could probably spend the next three months going back and forth. The cover selection became an occasion when she felt she needed to assert leadership in order to avoid an impasse. In the end, they picked two shots of boats; Foster asked each participant whether he or she was comfortable with these, and when they all agreed, the decision was made. They would use this pair and move on, though they did continue to worry at times whether they had made the right choices.

The photographs they selected represented both Scott's photographic ability and scenes specific to Charlevoix. Both were somewhat abstract night scenes, one in a marina and the other during a Venetian boat parade, and thus showed attractive and unusual lighting effects. In the parade shot, for example, the dark form of a boat has its decks lined with luminaria that reflect orange ripples in the water. As time exposures taken at night, both shots include some fuzzy lines of light. From Mitchell's perspective, these were good examples of Scott's photography:

> Ken's documentary stuff is first rate—very professional, well-focused, interesting perspective. But the pictures of Ken's that I like best are the abstractions that present something universal—that's what abstraction does—and pick up on the light. His work is definitely taking pictures of light. (Mitchell 1998)

Scott was surprised by the final decision: "I see images differently than other people do. They pick out images I never would have thought they would. Like the mood piece on the cover. I expected they'd choose a crisp piece, bright blue sky, white clouds. But they picked a blurry piece. I don't know why" (Scott 1998).

Choosing pictures was not the only problem concerning the cover jacket. The major issue was the color, and that entailed an extended consensus process. In addition to the dark blue within the picture and as a block behind the title, the jacket draft used an intense yellow as the primary color on the spine, the jacket flaps, and some portions of the marina picture. Foster didn't like it:

> I don't like that color. I've never liked that color. . . . I kept trying to get them to go soft. And Emily said, "Big snooze," and Ken wanted bold, the primary-color look. So for about four months both of them had to listen to me whine about the yellow. One night Ken and I went to dinner after we had met with the Nielsen Group, and he had this little mini-book jacket on a thumb-board book. He set it right on the table and said, "By the time we are through dinner, you will like yellow." But I didn't like it. I showed my neighbor some jackets, and he said, "Wow, colorful." And I said, "The designers are really pushing it, and I'm uncomfortable with it. What would you do?" And he said, "Well, if I go to a designer for something about art, I'd probably go with them because there's a reason why they're saying that." . . . That yellow against the dark blue was a shock for me, but Emily's feeling was that it makes people want to go further. That was one where I said, "OK, you guys do what you want." Now I do like it, but I think because it was bold and daring to some degree to use that combination. (Foster 1998)

Scott's conclusion about this decision reflects his visual perspective: "Color is so subjective. We all see colors differently, so there's going to be give-and-take about color. You can't have it perfect, so pick your battles" (Scott 1998).

THE EFFECTIVE AND THE PLEASING

As might be expected, each of the collaborators had different ideas as to what they thought were the most effective and most aesthetically pleasing pages. The pages they selected reflect their individual approaches and responsibilities on the project as well as their personal tastes. Foster, who had asked for pictures with people in them, particularly liked a full-page photograph showing the inside of a fishmarket and Kellie, the worker there. "Kellie is third generation at this family fishery. She runs around all over town with her rubber boots on, and everybody knows her. There's a lot of action that happens around this" (Foster 1998). A small picture on the opposite page shows some of the action as workers clean and prepare the fish. The group included this shot because it portrays the reality of what people do in a fishery, but they kept the picture small because they considered the content to be somewhat gruesome.

Scott also selected the picture of the fishmarket as a favorite, but for different reasons. Scott was drawn to the contrasting lighting effects. The florescent lights in the rear gave a green background, and the incandescent lights in the foreground accentuated the golds and browns of the smoked fish. Scott was happy to have gotten the green and golds together. He also found the pictures on a pair of adjoining pages, a Dairy Queen drive-in and an old car, to be effective because the two photographs worked well together in what he called a "marriage of images." Both photographs recall a bygone time as well as the present. Like the fishery, the photograph of the car is bathed in green light, though Scott had not used any filters or washes. He explained that what looked like a green wash occurred because of the mercury street lights, which sometimes give off a green color.

Mitchell found the functional spreads—the title pages and section dividers, the directory, table of contents, and index—to be powerful, because they are so full of "juicy details." These pages establish the book's design and content, and tasteful handling of such material can be a challenge to a designer. She pointed out a spread on one divider page that she believed was an unusual image. "The light. It's absolutely blue, and then the light from the boat brings purple and green shadows that have an otherworldly feeling" (Mitchell 1998). Mitchell also chose two two-page spreads in which she felt the colors resonated together beautifully. One pair shows two fall scenes of yellow and gold leaves with white and dark tree trunks, the other shows two scenes of ice and clouds. Looking at them, she said: "These have to be two of my favorite parts just because of the beauty of the photographs. They just make me go 'ahhhh'" (Mitchell 1998).

Defining a Photo Essay

The jacket flap identifies *Charlevoix* as a photo essay. Though the book is not making an overt argument for a position on an issue, the producers all view it as an essay presented in photographs and text. When I asked Foster about this label, she said:

> We had a lot of discussion about that. When I hear the words "photo essay," I just think that's images and words. People can paint a portrait with words beautifully, and that's not a photo album, that's an essay. Here it was words enhanced by photography and photography enhanced by words. (Foster 1998)

Mitchell thinks of a photo essay as

> a story told—it's a visual story. In the end I think it's fair to say that it's a photo essay and it's a visual story supported by a text. That's the way I think human beings are; I think visual things, pictures, are always more attractive than the text. They get the attention before the text does, so visuals always dominate. (Mitchell 1998)

In visual books done without any text, Mitchell believed the "story" would be in the pictures. They would provide the structuring that we expect from a text. According to Mitchell, "To a visual person, you're guided in the same way, really. Just as directly." She suggested it might be interesting to research the brain-wave activity of people who are looking at images, in comparison with those of people who are reading text. Scott brought the viewer into his understanding of the term "photo essay." In a photo essay, he believes, you tell a story with pictures, but it's really the people looking at the pictures who write the story.

Though Foster and Mitchell thought that neither photographs nor text dominated the book, Scott did feel that the photos were dominant. But since he thinks of himself as speaking through images, the separation between photographs and text may not be a major one for him. An example of a statement Scott made in images is in the book's dedication. It includes a line of small figures in silhouette. One of the figures is a person that Scott wanted to remember in the dedication; he feels that this statement does so in images.

Learning from Experience

The group got together when the book was finished to evaluate the project and their process for completing it. This experience had been a new one for all of them—new for Foster because she had never worked on a book before, new for the Nielsen Design Group because they had never involved clients in the design process to such a degree, and espe-cially new for Scott, who had not previously worked in collaboration with others. Foster reported:

> They learned, and we learned. I learned not to be so procedure-driven when sometimes I wanted to be. You want to set deadlines, and you want to have an outline, and you want to just go in. I had to let go a little bit because others may not think that way, and you can't make them think that way. I needed to accept their style, and they needed to accept mine. I was very open with Ken and Tim and Emily, and I think that's one of the objectives. When Ken said he didn't need to know about the budget we were working with, I'd say, "You do need to know all this because it will help you to understand when I have to make decisions." (Foster 1998)

Mitchell believed that one reason Foster's and Scott's different styles worked together was because "[t]hey're both very gracious and generous and appreciative of each other, so they each gave where the other felt strongly" (Mitchell 1998).

Foster said that the only change she would make in the business plan would be to allow more time for the design process. On this project, the estimated six weeks for design became twelve or fourteen weeks. She said: "I think if you develop a good process, a creative process, it takes more time, and I underestimated the time on that." She would also try to set the budget for the graphic designers on a "for-project" basis, as she had for other parts of the project, rather than as an hourly rate. She reported: "I'm distracted by the clock running, that makes me a little bit nervous. It interrupts creativity. And yet I didn't let that stop us. I just figured this was important. We'd go back later and do less of something else, but this was critical" (Foster 1998). In the end they exceeded the design portion of the budget by about 30 percent, due in part to the increase from 145 to 241 images. Now, nearly a year after publication, Foster reported that the book's sales have been even more brisk than she had projected in her plan, and they passed their break-even point early.

This group worked both from experience and by "learning as you go"; in doing so, they reached conclusions about project work that coincide with those found in textbooks and advocated by trainers. For example, collaborative projects produce rich results but consume extra time and energy. For another, groups made up of members with a variety of skills increase the chances for quality in the project results. And third, to reach quality decisions and establish a comfortable working process, opinions and ideas need to be openly expressed but also graciously treated. There were times when each of this group's members pushed for a strongly held position, and other times when, after discussion, each yielded to another's expertise.

Members of this project also repeatedly spoke of the value of up-front planning. The planning may take various forms, from a formal business proposal and conceptual structure to lists of subtasks and page grids, but the people working on this project found all of it valuable. They agree that input from designers at the beginning would have been helpful as well, but as Mitchell and Foster both noted, the designer's guiding hand also needs to allow freedom for the project to evolve with creativity.

As is often the case with research, some of the most interesting points to come from this case study are the ideas for future research. In this case, Mitchell suggested two research areas: the effectiveness of thoughtful design versus standardized design for instructive documents; a comparison of brain activity when reading versus viewing images. Both of these would involve complex, multifaceted research but could produce provocative results.

The research reported here looked at the effectiveness of telling a story through photographs and how that effort might be supported by text. In *The Rise of the Image, the Fall of the Word*, Mitchell Stephens (1998) makes strong arguments for what he sees as a developing language of images, yet he sets a combined goal: "The power of the image, not in lieu of words but in partnership with words" (p. 129). The photo essay that tells the story of Charlevoix uses both photographs and text, each working with and supporting the other, yet maintaining independent functions. The group members were very conscious of how the relationships between images and words influenced the attractiveness of the pages, the presentation of material to their reader-viewers, and the possible reactions these reader-viewers might have to connections created between words and a particular photograph. We communicate through images, through words, and through how we relate them to each other.

Of course, we also communicate through various media. Stephens (1998) argues that as we advance into a more visual culture, "We can finally imagine a form of communication that is, to use Rabelais's words, better than print" (p. 183). For Stephens, that form of communication is video. Today's film directors feel that they "write" in film, and sculptor Tina Allen (1999) says that she "writes" in bronze. Maya Lin is an artist-architect who often combines images and words in her work, such as the much-visited Vietnam War Memorial in Washington, D.C. Columnist James Kilpatrick's comment about this memorial echoes Scott's comments on readers of photo essays. Kilpatrick wrote: "This will be the most moving memorial ever erected . . . each of us may remember what he wishes to remember—the cause, the heroism, the blunders, or the waste" (Hass 1998, 16–17). Kristin Hass (1998) commented: "Visitors to this memorial would take on the responsibility for the memory of the war. . . . People come to this memorial and they make their own memorials" (p. 20). The visual images created by the sculpture provide the guidance, and the viewers write their own stories. This relationship between images and their viewers is what Scott imagines for his photographs.

As we prepare our essays or statements of our views, we need to consider the possibilities offered by the many media available to us. We speak through the images we present as well as through the words. Perhaps the part of this process most often forgotten is that we also speak through the ways we relate images and words to each other. John Berger (1972, 33) expressed the power of images well: "If the new language of images were used differently, it would, through its use, confer a new kind of power. Within it we could begin to define our experiences more precisely in areas where words are inadequate. (Seeing comes before words.)"

References

Allen, Tina. (August 29, 1999). *CBS News: Sunday Morning*. CBS Television Network.

Beckett, James. (1999). *Fathers and Sons: Stories of How Sport Builds Lifelong Bonds*. Dallas: Beckett Publishing.

Benjamin, Walter. (1969). *Illuminations*, ed. and introduction by Hannah Arendt; trans. Harry Zohn. New York: Schocken Books.

Berger, Arthur A. (1989). *Seeing Is Believing: An Introduction to Visual Communication*. Mountain View, CA: Mayfield.

Berger, John. (1972). *Ways of Seeing*. London: Penguin Books.

Boorstin, Daniel J. (1987). *The Image: A Guide to Pseudo-Events in America*, 25th ann. ed. New York: Atheneum.

Booth, Wayne C., and Marshall W. Gregory. (1987). *The Harper & Row Rhetoric: Writing as Thinking, Thinking as Writing*. New York: Harper & Row.

Foster, Dianne. (August 1998). Personal interview. Traverse City, MI.

Foster, Dianne, and Ken Scott. (1998). *Charlevoix*. Charlevoix, MI: Petunia Press.

Hass, Kristin Ann. (1998). *Carried to the Wall: American Memory and the Vietnam Veterans Memorial*. Berkeley: University of California Press.

Hunter, Jefferson. (1987). *Image and Word: The Interaction of Twentieth-Century Photographs and Texts*. Cambridge, MA: Harvard University Press.

Kinneavy, James L. (1971). *A Theory of Discourse: The Aims of Discourse*. New York: Norton.

Mitchell, Emily. (August 1998). Personal interview. Traverse City, MI.

Parade Publications, Inc. (1989). *Pictorial Celebration: The American Woman*. New York: Continuum.

Scott, Ken. (July 1998). Personal interview. Traverse City, MI.

Stephens, Mitchell. (1998). *The Rise of the Image, the Fall of the Word*. New York: Oxford University Press.

Winterowd, W. Ross, and Jack Blum. (1994). *A Teacher's Introduction to Composition in the Rhetorical Tradition*. Urbana, IL: National Council of Teachers of English.

chapter eight

ASTRONOMICAL RHETORIC
nineteenth-century photographs as models of meaning

gregory a. wickliff

I N THIS AGE OF DIGITAL IMAGING, the definition of what constitutes an acceptable photograph is being pushed and pulled by electronic technologies. The digital image is now assumed to have been manipulated before publication. The contrast has been adjusted, the image has been cropped and sized electronically, the file has been compressed for electronic transfer, often through "lousy" processes. The sheer ease of electronic manipulation of photographs makes contemporary arguments for the verity of photographs seem naive. But this was not always the case. In the nineteenth-century context of emerging sciences, proponents of early photographic processes had first to establish that the photo-chemical image was an accurate one, a representation of an observation that was susceptible to measurement and verification. Because of the success of early rhetors, entire scientific disciplines have been defined and legitimized by the ethos of photography as a technology for recording what is "really there" in nature, even when the reality being depicted exists beyond the realm of direct human perception (e.g., the infrared or the ultraviolet).

For no discipline of inquiry is this more the case than for astronomy in general, and astrophysics in particular. While we now accept digitally manipulated composite images transmitted from the surface of Mars as superior to the earth-bound representations, early rhetors had to demonstrate that any astronomical photograph was as acceptable as mathematically recorded, direct human observation.

Histories of nineteenth-century astronomical photography emphasize both the experimental and systematic nature of scientific inquiry. They may center around the development of photographic processes (the daguerreotype, the wet collodion process, the dry collodion process), around the development of ever larger telescopes (refractors and reflectors), the development of improved clock drives, around the chronology of important short-term astronomical events and their photographic images, around the initiation and completion of systematic celestial mapping projects, around the lives of astronomers, and around the conventions and proceedings of international astronomical congresses. But irrespective of the criteria for analysis, one rhetorical trend is clear among nineteenth-century astronomical texts and their histories: that of a movement toward increasing acceptance of and reliance upon photography as a satisfactory means of representing astronomical observations.

In 1938, Daniel Norman, a historian of astronomy, was able to claim for the first century of photography: "There is no exaggeration whatsoever in the statement that our present picture of the Universe is due wholly to the power of the photographic plate" (1938, 591). His claim is in large measure confirmed by the measurements taken from photographs of the 1919 eclipse that were used to confirm Albert Einstein's relativity hypothesis. From measuring the distance to the sun, to mapping the entire visible night-sky and the invisible motions of distant stars, photography in the nineteenth century came to represent another way of modeling the cosmos, a representational method that eventually became amenable to mathematics, measurement, and the rigors of intellectual scrutiny and validation through duplication, repetition, and prediction. It created models of relations in the distant universe that centered the observer behind the eyepiece of an earth-bound telescope, but that projected a dispassionate and objective celestial scientist who could reduce "self-registering" images on photographic plates to pure mathematical relations with great precision. Through photography and spectroscopy (the study of the spectra of light), nineteenth-century astronomers posited the chemical nature of the sun and other stars, the presence of increasing numbers of asteroids, the shape and contents of nebulae and comets, and so eventually earned disciplinary status for a new branch of scientific inquiry, astrophysics. Photographic images of the sun, moon, and, eventually, planets and stars, led to protracted debates about what constituted a satisfactory representation of a thing or a process: the solar spectrum, a star field, the transit of a planet across the face of the sun.

This historical review of the photographically illustrated literature of nineteenth-century British and American astronomy reveals through close readings how early astronomical rhetors were active agents in challenging assumptions behind nineteenth-century photographic practices, even while they simultaneously built a new and highly situated discipline upon those practices. Early astronomers who experimented with photography attended to the devices and the processes in their writing in ways that period scientists in other disciplines, except perhaps microscopy, most often did not. Astronomers wove more precision into their language describing photographic processes and made somewhat fewer assumptions than scientists in many disciplines about appropriate photographic technique and device designs. Almost without exception and from the first, they resisted the romantic rhetoric of "naturalism" in photography that so dominated the popular reception of the daguerreotype, perhaps because the objects of nature for their observations were so remote and distanced, both literally and intellectually. As individuals and collectively, they reflected in writing on the weaknesses of photographs—their lack of color, the blurring of motion due to long exposure times, the chromatic aberrations of lens and emulsions, and the difficulty of securing satisfactory lithographic prints from photographic images. The early identification of these weaknesses helped to set rhetorically a technological agenda for photographic inventors and astronomers, an agenda that would not be realized until the century's end with color photography, increasingly shorter exposures, better clock drives for telescopes to track the apparent movement of celestial objects, and improved photomechanical printing processes.

In the Beginning . . .
A Short History of Photography

In January 1839, Louis Jacques Mandé Daguerre announced to the French government his development of a successful photographic process. Dominique François Arago, French minister of science and director of the Paris Observatory, made an elaborate argument before the French Chamber of Deputies in July of that year for a life pension for Daguerre and the son of Nicéphore Niépce, his deceased collaborator, in return for any patent claims. Arago's rhetoric of 1839 reveals his belief in the essential value of systematics and scientific inquiry. He goes on to suggest that some forms of intellectual property like the photographic process have a value that transcends the profit motive, and claims, as Mary Warner Marien (1997) has noted, a certain nationalistic pride in Daguerre's claims for priority over the competitive photographic process developed by William Henry Fox Talbot in England. His comprehensive arguments, successful with the French government, included large claims for the scientific value of photographic images and proved especially prophetic for astronomy. The daguerreotype, claimed Arago, would record observations from nature in detailed and archival forms that could be distributed easily, and would open up new areas of scientific inquiry, including spectroscopy and photometry, precursors to astrophysics. In

SWEEP, *Oct.* 17, 1825.

No.	Monkey Clock	F	Index Arc	Pos	Diagram, Name, &c.	Description, Remarks, &c.	Reductions.	Æ 1825·0	N. P. D. 1825·0	No.
	h m s		° ′ ″			Monkey set with transit. Began sweep.	In Æ.	° ′ ″	° ′ ″	1
1	21 48 38,6	2	+0° 4′ 16″	8		An indifferent observation.	By m s			2
2	22 13 42,0	1	+0 59 40	8	d Pegasi		2 −0 51,4	22 16 45,4	80 12 53	3
3	16 1,5	2	2 33 0	D		35° n f 30″ 9 and 11 or 8 and 10 m.	6 −0 52,5	22 25 3,2	78 24 13	4
4	25 16,0	1	0 43 20	D		87° s p 30″ 10 and 10½ m.	37 −0 57,8	22 28 47,1	80 21 53	5
5	29 39,0	M	2 41 0	N	Not in M.S. Cat.	Extremely faint. Elongated perpend. to merid.	41 −0 57,4			6
6	33 24,6	2	2 23 40	8	ζ Pegasi					7
7	37 40,0	1	1 25 10	D		50 s p 20″, 11 and 12 m.	The rate of the clock is evident-	22 36 5,4	79 17 3	8
8	40 9,0	1	1 37 40	N	III. 216	R. F. g b M, a star precedes.	ly accelerating,	22 41 9,7	79 18 33	9
9	45 34,5	2	1 33 40	D		60° s p, 9 and 12 m., 4 or 5″.	and the gain is	22 44 35,7	80 4 33	10
10	50 39,0	2	0 8 0	N	III. 465	Extr. F. R. b M.	1″ in 36″, so that	22 49 13,0	77 48 53	11
11	21 4 13,0	2	0 20 0	N	Not in M.S. Cat.	Extr. F. R. Seems to have a star in centre.	we have Mean Reduction in Æ for 1st wire	23 2 57,7	78 0 53	
						Windy.	= −0ᵐ 51ˢ,5			12*
12	7 54,0	2	0 5 0	N	III. 222	R. sm b M. p B. Small, has a B. st. near.	clock−Æ+15ᵐ 1ˢ	23 6 38,8	77 45 53	13†
13	———	...	−0 2 0	N	III. 221	A neb. in field with the last, and pre-ceding it about 5′ of time. R. F. p M. half a minute in diam.	30ᵐ	23 6 33::	77 38 23	
14	19 18,0	1	+0 49 20	N	III. 226	R. p B. was b M. almost to a star.		23 18 24,7	78 30 13	14
15	22 48,0	2	0 38 20	D		0° s f, 10″, 10 and 11 m.	Reduction from	23 23 30,0	78:29 13	15
16	27 40,0	2	0 8 0n	D			2d to 1st wire	23 26 30,0	77 48 53::	16
17	30 14,0	1	2 30 50	N		R. B. n B star foll.	= −0ᵐ 24ˢ,5	23 35 20,2	80 11 43	17
18	34 9,±	1	0 18 ±	N	II. 255	Looked for the "Suspected Nebula" of M.S. Catal. It is verified. It is however, so nearly a star in appear-ance, as to be easily mistaken for the 3d star of a trapezium (tri-angle ?) The place is here put down as in the working list, but it was found in the middle of the field by it.		23 53 15±	77 59 ±	18
19	9 1,45	2	0 45 10	D		65° s f, 15″, 9 and 10 m.	Reduction in N. P. D.	0 7 55,6	78 26 3	19
20	14 40,0	2	2 48 30	N	II. 257	s F. p L. R. g b M.	By ° ′ ″	0 13 20,7::	80 29 23	20
21	17 43,0	2	0 4 30	8		7 m.	2 +77 41 0			21
22	22 38,0	1	2 32 40	D		20° s p 25″ 10 and 11 m.	6 +77 40 59	0 33 28,2	80 13 33	22
23	27 19	1	0 45 40	D		45° s f 10″, 9 and 10 m.	37 +77 41 10	0 36 23,5	78 26 33	23
24	31 59	2	0 34 40	D		40 s f, 5 or 6″, 12 and 13 m. a 3d s p.	41 +77 40 43	0 39 29,8	78 15 33	24
25	37 34	2	1 17 45	D		10 s f 12 or 15″ 9 and 9½ m. nearly equal		0 44 13,8	78 58 38	25
26	40 5	1	1 11 20	Cl		A small cluster of pretty close stars.	Mean +77 40 53	0 47 9,7	78 52 13	26
						Calm and Clear.				
27	57 16	2	0 25 20	Tr		A very elegant triple star, 1 and 2 40° n p, 3″ ; 1 and. 3 40° s f 7 or 8″. 1−8 m, 2−10 m, 3−9 m.		0 55 55,5	78 6 43	27
28	1 14,0	2	0 24 20	D		3° n p, 5″, 11 and 12 m.		1 1 58,3	78 5 23	28
29	3 40,0	2	0 19 30	D		45° s p 10″, 10 and 11 m.		1 5 2,7	78 0 23	29
30	14 5,0	2	0 40 0	N	II. 252	Irr. R. v L. eg a little b M. has a neat D st. foll.		1 14 42,0	78 0 53	30
31	16 45	2	0 40 0	D		40° n p, 10 or 12″, 8 and 13 m. immedi-ately following the nebula II. 252.		1 14 54,0	78 0 53	31
32	22 40,0	2	0 35 20	D		5° n p 8 or 9″, 9 and 10 m, very neat.		1 20 56,3	78 16 13	32
33	25 16,0	1	0 11 40	D		30° n f, 12″, 10 and 13 m.		1 23 57,7	78 52 13	33
34	29 11	2	1 24	D		60° s f or n p, 20−25″, equal, 10 and 10 m.		1 27 37,1	79 4 53	34
35	31 40	2	1 1 50	D		5° n p, 5−7″, 9 and 10 m. neat.		1 29 49,5	78 41 53	35
36	36 0	2	0 50 50	D		50° n p, 20−25″, 9 and 10 m.		1 34 27,8	78 46 43	36
37						7 m or 5?.(marked 8 m in Bode).				37
38	40 54,1	2	1 36 0	N	Not in M.S. Catal.	Extremely F. taken at 41ᵐ 45ˢ about 1ᵐ after the transit, which was missed.		1 40 ±	79 10 45	38‡
39	44 3	1	0 54	4		6 or 7 m.				39
40	50 5	2	1 14	D		85° s p 20″ 12 and 18 m. Index taken at 49°.		1 46 31,6	79 4 44	40
41	52 2	1	0 53 0	8	Arietis 26 Bode.	v B. 5 m. (N.B. marked 8 m. in Boos).				41
42				D		75° n f, 25″, 10 and 11 m.		1 53 16,4	78 17 43	42
43				D		45° n p, 30″, 8 and 15 m.		1 57 22,3	80 21 43	43
44				D		40° n f, 7 or 8″, 10 and 11 m.		2 5 57,0	78 44 53	44
						Quadrant read off 40° 8′ 40″. Transit clock s 11ʰ 0ˢ. Monkey fast on transit +7ˢ.				

◆ **FIGURE 8.1** ◆

A table of astronomical measurements representing direct observations from John F. W. Herschel's *Account of Observations Made with a Twenty-Feet Reflecting Telescope.* LONDON: RICHARD TAYLOR, 1826.

more general terms, Arago argued that encouraging technological and sci-entific innovation was good for France—that such technical achievements would surely increase national prosperity.

Prior to 1839, astronomers had relied upon detailed observations recorded as scaled drawings and measured positions recorded in large tables with high numerical precision to represent their key findings, such as J. F. W. Herschel's (1826) *Account of Observations Made with a Twen-ty-Feet Reflecting Telescope* (see figure 8.1). What photography offered was potentially a way to both arrest the best moment of observation, archive it for repeated later study (during daylight hours), and to verify observations by comparing multiple photographs taken of the same event and series over time. For scientists like Arago, daguerreotypes were more than the equal of the direct observation of nature, because as he foresaw, they also provided a way to record spectra beyond human perception— prismatic bands representing colors that the daguerreotype plate could record, but that the unaided human eye could not perceive.

Arago convincingly cataloged the potential uses of the new medium in 1839. For archeology, he spoke of the time required to record the hiero-glyphics on the great monuments of Thebes, Memphis, and Karnak, con-cluding that "by daguerreotype, one person would suffice to accomplish this immense work successfully" (Arago 1839, 17). For cartography and architecture, he explained how the camera lens, designed around geomet-ric principles of Renaissance perspective, would allow one to determine "the exact size of the highest points of the most inaccessible structures" (Arago 1839, 17).

For astronomical photography in particular, Arago made important claims. He suggested the possibility of mapping the moon with daguerreo-types, "one of the most protracted, difficult, and delicate tasks in astron-omy" (Arago 1839, 21). He spoke of photographically comparing the absolute intensities of the light of stars (photometry), and of recording the sights of the spectroscope. And he pointedly argued for the value of unan-ticipated applications, saying that with an invention such as the daguerre-otype, "it is surely the unexpected upon which one especially must count" (Arago 1839, 22). His arguments prevailed with the French Chamber of Deputies, and in August 1839 a more-than-comfortable life pension of 6,000 francs annually was granted to Daguerre, and 4,000 francs annually to Niépce's son.

An Ever More Satisfactory Representation

Even the most critical of nineteenth-century authors approached "viewing" or "reading" a photograph with a great number of assumptions. The most common of these continue to revolve around a "naturalistic" set of assumptions: that the photograph represents quite well a direct obser-vation from nature, or perhaps even, through the magic of modernist tech-nology, creates another instance of the thing itself. On one hand, to recog-nize the force of this claim, one need only look at a well-focused photograph of the face of a loved one to feel the pathos a photographic image can invoke. But on the other hand, if the image is one made through wavy glass and angled up and focused narrowly upon the boot soles of the beloved sitter, then it begins to become clear how large and important are the number of technological and conventional assumptions made about any one "satisfactory" image.

Professional photographers understand that the two-dimensional image that a photograph presents invariably embeds assumptions. In the context of nineteenth-century books, the glued or "tipped-in" photographs in general embed the notions that have largely survived to the present day. To demonstrate the range of conventional assumptions made when viewing a "naturalistic" photograph, I've compiled the following list, paying special attention to what we expect and do not expect to be made explicit in textual explanations of bound photographs.

- Monocular vision is satisfactory.

- Two-dimensional representations of three-dimensional objects are satisfactory.

- Limited depth of field and acceptable focus are satisfactory.

- The range of tones and colors represented in daylight is satisfactory (not infrared or ultraviolet, for example), and monochrome (black and white) representations are generally considered satisfactory in the nineteenth century. Even in black-and-white emulsions, the range of available tones and color sensitivity is a product of both lens and film properties and varies in response to the duration of the exposure in a phenomenon called "reciprocity failure." The daguerreotype lens and photographic plate were most sensitive to the blue, or "actinic," wavelengths of white light. Nonetheless, it is conventionally not expected that the film type, lens type, and exposure duration be noted for every satisfactory image.

- Short exposures are generally desirable over the apparent blur of motion seen in longer exposures—a special problem for astronomers.

- Camera stability in a single point of view is generally desirable, or if in motion, the camera should pan at a rate parallel to that of the subject relative to the viewer. In astronomy, this is the motive behind the development of ever-more-accurate clock drives for photographing long exposures of the planets, moon, and stars.

- The normal viewing distance for the resulting photographic print is assumed to be about 18 inches, a reflection of arm length and conventional reading distances.

- An image that persists longer than one average human lifetime can be considered "permanent."

- A lens should be designed to represent normal Renaissance perspective on a flat surface and not, for instance, on a concave, convex, or irregularly textured surface, and the image on that surface should not expand, contract, or change shape (stability of the base).

- The film plane normally describes a rectangular image, while the lens throws a circular image large enough to cover that rectangle.

- No need generally exists for an absolute image scale so long as the subject exists in a three-dimensional field with normal perspective, but a scale often distinguishes scientific images from others by its assumption of the role of measurement for image analysis.

- It is not necessary to see or completely understand the operation of the photographic instrument or processes in order to evaluate and understand the result—that is, a detailed process may not be required before determining if the image is satisfactory. Astronomers, on the other hand, paid much textual attention to photographic processes.

- The focus distance need not be explained.

- The camera pitch need not be noted, and is generally assumed to be level and perpendicular with the horizon at head- or waist-level.

- The kind, color, and placement of light sources need not be noted (including the sun's position described as the calendar date, the time of day, or the latitude and longitude for outdoor work), nor need the use of reflectors be explained.

- The time interval between related images need not be carefully noted.

- The collaboration of lens designers, camera-makers, film- and paper-makers, and print-makers need not be acknowledged explicitly—the image framer/camera operator (photographer) can claim a sole by-line for an image.

- Captions may or may not be present, and may exist only by reference to figure numbers in the text, in a textual paragraph.

- No need exists to acknowledge the number of and process of creating photographic duplicates of an image—an assumption that works against the art tradition and toward that of commercial printing and publishing.

- Although a direct process may yield a negative or negative/positive view (as do the daguerreotype and ambrotype), the published version is almost invariably the positive, in imitation of tonal shades as we see them.

- A laterally inverted image may be an acceptable image, so long as typographic characters are not reversed.

A more contemporary list of assumptions might include those about the enlarging process from gelatin negatives, the use of filters and toners, the naturalistic registration of colors, and the effects of digital rendering. Put bluntly, and from the viewpoint of the late twentieth century, interpreting a photographic print is no more natural than other cultural constructs such as exercising table manners, making a violin, setting up a carnival, or visiting a landfill. A still photograph is a product of human craft and the division of labor, a talisman that must be interpreted through learned conventions, and is a rather fragile artifact of an individual's momentary sensibility.

The astronomer's photographic task is often especially difficult, as the subjects are celestial objects that are optically small, dim, and that may exist both in huge numbers and in optical arrangements that may only rarely occur such as a total solar eclipse, or the twice-in-a-century transit of Venus across the face of the sun. Nineteenth-century astronomers could pose their photographic subjects, adjust the lighting, or easily shift the camera position to make their images. What they could do was to experiment with cameras, lens, shutters, and telescopic designs. They explored types of emulsions and developed new and experimented with printing processes. They expanded the range of colors recorded photographically and divided and analyzed spectra for the chemical and physical information they contained. They invented new ways to measure the fine details of images, and better clock-drives to guide the telescope and camera in panning through long exposures. The unusually demanding constraints under which astronomers work led immediately in the mid-nineteenth century to critiques of photographic technology and its products. If astronomical photography were to succeed, a host of improvements would be needed in the original daguerreotype photographic process.

Daguerre himself had experimented with an image of the moon even before Arago's 1839 public announcement of the photographic process (Vaucouleurs 1961, 14). Although he did not consider the resulting image to be satisfactory, the mere ability to record moonlight on the daguerreotype plate encouraged Arago to claim that photography might soon be used to map the moon in detail. But because of insensitive emulsions, the exposure times were too long, and the manual panning process required by the moon's apparent movement was too difficult. With images of the sun, opposite problems arose because of the intensity of light and the need for extremely short exposure times. Without rapid shutters, the excess light caused a "solarization" effect that blurred the image and shifted colors and tones. But the potential of photography was too tempting to be ignored by those astronomers most familiar with experiments in optics and chemistry. One by one, the problems posed by nineteenth-century lunar, solar, and even planetary and stellar photography were solved, at least to the satisfaction of younger leading astronomers who made up an epistemic jury that worked to overcome a bias toward direct observation among its elders.

The Moon, Sun, Planets, and Stars Rendered

From the first, astronomers perceived in photography the ability to: 1) accurately and systematically record the appearance of celestial bodies, 2) measure the relative brightness of objects (photometry), and

3) record and analyze spectra to determine discrete qualities in celestial light sources (spectroscopy).

Prior to the late nineteenth century, astronomy had been defined narrowly as the study of the motions and magnitudes of celestial objects. After 1839, photography made new kinds of information available about celestial objects. Used in conjunction with other astronomical and optical devices, the camera and its photographic plate created the means to study the spectroscopic and photometric information contained in light itself, to separate out and measure its components, even for extremely dim light sources like distant stars. A review of the claims made for images in photographically illustrated texts shows the movement toward an increasing ethos for photography in astronomy.

THE MOON

It was not long after Daguerre's unsuccessful attempts to capture an image of the moon that a satisfactory photograph was made. On March 23, 1840, John William Draper exposed his daguerreotype plate for twenty minutes to capture an image of the moon. Yet it would be another ten years before acceptably sharp images of the moon could be routinely made. The first published photograph of the moon was a result of the collaboration between William Cranch Bond, director of the Harvard Observatory, and John Adams Whipple, a well-known daguerreotypist in Boston. Together, they made a set of daguerreotypes of the moon that set a new standard for astronomical photography in 1850. Reproduced as a saltedprint positive by Whipple's wet-collodion "Crystallotype" process, an actual photograph

◆ FIGURE 8.2 ◆

Reproduced as a salted print positive by Whipple's wet collodion "Crystallotype" process, an actual photograph of the moon with an exposure time of thirteen seconds tipped as the frontispiece of an 1853 issue of the *Photographic Art Journal* by John Adams Whipple.

with an exposure time of thirteen seconds was tipped as the frontispiece of an 1853 issue of the *Photographic Art Journal* (see figure 8.2). In the accompanying article, Whipple reflected openly about the challenges of early lunar photography, especially the clock-drive:

> The governor that regulates the motion of the telescope although suffi-ciently accurate for observing purposes was entirely unsuitable for daguerreotyping; as when the plate is exposed to the moon's image, if the instrument does not follow exactly, to counteract the earth's motion; even to the nicety of a hair's breadth, the beauty of the impression is much injured or entirely spoiled. . . . I might obtain one or two perfect proofs in the trial of a dozen plates, other things being right, but a more serious obstacle to my success was the usual state of the atmosphere in the locality. . . . When the moon was viewed through the telescope it had the same appearance as objects when seen through the heated air from a chimney, in a constant tremor, precluding the possibility of successful daguerreotyping; this state of the atmosphere often continued week after week in a greater or less degree, so that an evening of perfect quiet was hailed with the greatest delight. (Whipple 1853, 66)

Whipple looked to the technology of the clock-drive to solve in large meas-ure the imaging problem, writing: "I have not the least doubt, that when Prof. Bond applies his Spring Governor, (a remarkable invention of his own, for regulating motion) . . . we shall be able to present as perfect daguerreotypes of the moon ten or fifteen inches in diameter as we have in our possession of three inches" (Whipple 1853, 66).

THE SUN AND PLANETS

Astronomers soon found that the sun could be captured on the daguerreotype plate during times of reduced light such as during total or annular eclipses. Daguerreotype images had been successfully made by August Ludwig Busch of the 1851 eclipse, and William Holmes Chambers Bartlett of the 1854 event, but daguerreotypes could not be easily copied or distributed with texts. To overcome this, Bartlett (1854) has his daguerreo-type images rendered as salt prints by Victor Prevost, a photographer trained in the waxed-paper negative process of Gustave Le Gray, and bound into book form (see figure 8.3). Unlike William and Frederick Langenheim's daguerreotypes of the same event (Thomas 1997, 189), Bartlett's 1854 images were carefully timed and so subject to measurements.

Because of its brightness, the sun was the first suitable astronomical subject for study by means of the daguerreotype process. The earliest pho-tographically illustrated work in this line was C. Piazzi Smyth's *Report on the Teneriffe Astronomical Experiment of 1856, Addressed to the Lords Commissioners of the Admiralty* (1858a). This report and its longer and more populist version, *Teneriffe, An Astronomer's Experiment: or, Speci-alities of a Residence Above the Clouds Illustrated with Stereographs*

◆ **FIGURE 8.3** ◆

1854 daguerreotype by William Bartlett of an annular eclipse reproduced as a salt
print by Victor Prevost, a photographer trained in the waxed-paper negative
process of Gustave Le Gray, then bound into book form in Bartlett's photographs
of the solar eclipse of May 26, 1854. Washington, DC: Smithsonian Institution.

(1858b), both contain tipped-in photographs made from glass plates
through the "wet-plate" collodion process. Smyth's was a British astronomical expedition to determine the effects of altitude (reduced atmos-
pheric effects like Whipple's chimney tremors) on observation. Significantly, Smyth's attempts to make solar and lunar photographs largely
failed, and no astronomical images are included in either text. Yet the
author and publisher chose nonetheless to include tipped-in stereo views
of the telescope, the encampment, the topography, and members of the
expedition party. In this way these early publications participate in the
travelogue tradition of illustrating topographic and ethnographic texts for
distant audiences. But the author also reflects directly on the qualities of
astronomical representations. Whereas a single drawing might obviously
be a poor record of an observation, Smyth argues that multiple drawings
provide a means of astronomical verification. For support, he refers to the
tipped-in stereo photographs, arguing that a blemish on one half of the
plate will be confirmed or disproved by comparison with the other half. In
support of his hypothesis that the higher altitude would afford better viewing, Smyth pointed to his recognition for the first time that the colored
bands of Jupiter were in fact products of its atmosphere, cloud-like
masses of what he termed "cumuli, cumuloni, and cumulostrati—the drift

doubtless of the Jovian trade-wind" (Smyth 1858a, 484). He at once made multiple drawings:

> Three drawings of these appearances—they might almost be called reve-lations—in Jupiter are inserted in Plates XXXIII and XXXIV. The originals were begun and finished at the end of the telescope, and each was made on a different evening, and without any reference to the previous views; so that the one may be used against the other, in determining the proba-ble error in the representation of any particular feature of interest. (Smyth 1858a, 484)

Smyth explicitly cautions astronomers against the weakness of making a single drawing, writing that "a single drawing should not be looked on, by itself, as of importance in the present state of astronomy; for how can others than the artist prove the reality in nature of anything they may find in that one document, when this alone is before them? A bad designer will often unconsciously give an erroneous figure" (Smyth 1858a, 484).

Interestingly, Smyth assigns little if any more credibility to a single photograph than to a single drawing:

> If astronomical drawing is to take a similar trustworthy and trusted place to numerical observation, in its own branch of subjects, we must in the first place with every man's work, eliminate errors in drawing and imper-fections of the means and medium employed. How easily much if this may often be accomplished by two drawings, may be well seen in some of the photographs in the book of illustrations; for having been taken with stereoscopic intentions, they are all double. Hence, is there some doubtful mark in one? We have only to look to the other; and if the mark was in the scene itself in nature, it will likewise appear in the second view as well; but not so if it were merely a fault or imperfection in the surface of the plate. (Smyth 1858a, 485)

According to the Brucks (1988), the 1856 Teneriffe expedition cost £500. The 144-page *Report* opens with a tipped-in stereo view of a relief map of the mountain of Teneriffe (see figure 8.4). The three-dimensional model was created by James Nasymth, a retired engineer and inventor with a reputa-tion for his modeling skills and an amateur British astronomer. Nasymth's relief model of the peak and crater was then photographed by C. P. Smyth and printed in an edition of 350 by his wife Jessica and glued or "tipped-in" by the printer of the *Report*. Significance of the model or its photograph is not insisted upon by the text, but it suggests an "aerial balloon view," the first of which was realized in Boston in 1860 by James Wallace Black. The images' captions in both volumes acknowledge the collaboration between camera operator, photographic printer, textual printer, and publisher. This *Report*, arguing for the success of the Teneriffe expedition by demonstrat-ing the superiority of high-altitude observatories, earned for Smyth a fel-lowship to the Royal Society, being elected in June 1857 (Bruck and Bruck

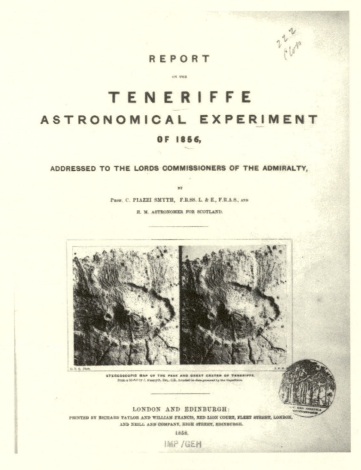

REPORT

ON THE

TENERIFFE
ASTRONOMICAL EXPERIMENT
OF 1856,

ADDRESSED TO THE LORDS COMMISSIONERS OF THE ADMIRALTY,

BY

PROF. C. PIAZZI SMYTH, F.R.SS. L. & E., F.R.A.S., AND

H. M. ASTRONOMER FOR SCOTLAND.

STEREOSCOPIC MAP OF THE PEAK AND GREAT CRATER OF TENERIFFE.

LONDON AND EDINBURGH:

PRINTED BY RICHARD TAYLOR AND WILLIAM FRANCIS, RED LION COURT, FLEET STREET, LONDON, AND NEILL AND COMPANY, HIGH STREET, EDINBURGH.

1858.

◆ **FIGURE 8.4** ◆

A photograph of a relief map of the mountain of Teneriffe. The three-dimensional model was created by James Nasymth, and then photographed and printed by C. P. Smyth in an edition of 350. LONDON: RICHARD TAYLOR AND WILLIAM FRANCIS.

1988, 67).

In "Photo-Stereograph #4," Smyth's wife and colleague Jessica is seated in the foreground of their tent, enclosed by makeshift rock walls, with a small telescope behind her (see figure 8.5). Her presence personalizes the image, making it a hybrid portrait: landscape, domestic architectural, and technological image.

A similar image, "Photo-Stereograph #5," shows the large "Sheepshanks" (named for its owner) refracting telescope carried to an altitude of 10,000 feet (see figure 8.6). The parallax shift is demonstrated by the stereoscopic effect of the two-lens camera, with the rope cutting across the face of the sailor in the right-hand image but not in the left. Of course,

◆ **FIGURE 8.5** ◆

Photo-Stereograph #4 from C. P. Smyth's *Teneriffe*, an astronomer's experiment, or, specialites of a residence above the clouds illustrated with stereographs, showing the hybrid portrait/documentary image that substituted for unsatisfactory astronomical photographs. LONDON: LOVELL REEVE, 1858.

◆ **FIGURE 8.6** ◆

Photo-Stereograph #5, "The Sheepshanks Telescope" from C. P. Smyth's *Teneriffe*, an astronomer's experiment, or, specialites of a residence above the clouds illustrated with stereographs, showing the effects of parallax shift in the two images. LONDON: LOVELL REEVE, 1858.

the two images are designed to optically converge, as the appended advertisement explains, "with the use of an ordinary stereoscope, open below, and well adapted for a new form of the instrument, *The Book Stereoscope*, constructed to fold up in a case like a map, without detriment to its stereoscopic action" (Smyth 1858b, 24).

Notice that the print on the shipping box is not laterally reversed, but rather "CPS," Smyth's initials, are clearly legible. Also, in the caption is a small reference in italics to the corresponding page number, made by printing the caption and border in relief as part of the gathers, then later pasting in the appropriate images. This sophisticated book design provides in this way a cross-reference to the fuller context provided in the body of the book, a textual feature that was not taken up by most subsequent texts with photographic illustrations, whose designers rely instead upon captions and simple proximity to textual information for reference purposes, or, who assert textual primacy over the image by incorporating references by figure number alone into the text, but do not include cross-page references from the photograph to the accompanying text.

The textual description of "Photo-Stereograph #6" narrates the colors, absent of course from the monochrome photograph, of rock outcrops on the plain below the telescope: "In the middle of the day they gleamed again with bright greens, reds, blues, purples, and whites, as well as with yellows and browns. The greens, and likewise all those other colors being due to the nature of the rock" (Smyth 1858b, 144).

Smyth's astronomical texts about the Teneriffe expedition, in which the ethos of photography was oddly both central and ancillary, was followed by the impressive photographic results of Warren De La Rue inspired by the vision of George Biddell Airy, astronomer royal at Greenwich.

In 1860, De La Rue succeeded in photographing a total solar eclipse in ways that yielded measurable results. De La Rue was a printer, an astronomical photographer, a microscopist, and like Smyth, a friend of James Nasymth. But it was Airy, who, with Sir John Herschel, encouraged De La Rue and helped define an early agenda for photography in astronomy. The first steps were De La Rue's monocular, then stereoscopic views of the moon, sun, and planets. His success was tied to the greater sensitivity of the wet collodion glass process over the daguerreotype process, and a preference for the reflecting telescope, which brings the light of all colors to a common focus point, unlike refractors. He selected the best glass available as a base for the collodion. Writing in 1859, De La Rue explained that:

> At the latter end of 1852, I made some successful positive lunar photographs in from ten to thirty seconds on a collodion film, by means of an equatorially mounted reflecting telescope of 13 inches aperture, and 10 feet focal length, made in my own workshop, the optical portion with my own hands; and I believe I was the first to use the then recently discovered collodion in celestial photography. . . . Although these photographs

were taken under the disadvantage referred to, namely, the want of an automatic driving motion, excellent results were nevertheless obtained, which proved how perfectly the hand may be made to obey the eye. (De La Rue 1860, 131)

For De La Rue, the mind acted as an image stabilizer, compensating for optical defects in direct observation, but not in photography:

When the telescope is employed optically, the mind can make out the proper figure of the object, although its image dances before the eye several times in a second, and is able to select for remembrance only the states of most perfect definition; on the other hand, a photographic plate registers all the disturbances. The photographic picture will consequently never be so perfect as the optical image with the same telescope, until we can produce photographs of celestial objects instantaneously; we are still a long way from this desirable end. (De La Rue 1859, 133)

Yet even a simple lunar portrait possessed photographic qualities that, for De La Rue, exceeded what was otherwise possible by direct observation:

Portions of the moon, equally bright optically, are by no means equally bright chemically; hence the light and shade in the photograph do not correspond in all cases with the light and shade in the optical picture. Photography thus frequently renders details visible which escape observation optically, and it therefore holds out a promise of a fertile future in selenogical researches; for instance, strata of different composition evidently reflect the chemical rays to a greater or less extent according to their nature, and may be thus distinguished. (De La Rue 1860, 145)

De La Rue's early success with lunar photography, and the larger cultural fascination with stereophotographs, encouraged him to experiment with making stereo images of the moon. His method of producing lunar stereo images was explained in detail in a long 1859 article written for the British Association for the Advancement of Science titled *Report of Celestial Photography in England*. This report demonstrates De La Rue's command of the history of astronomical photography, explains the photographic theory behind his lunar stereo pairs, and looks ahead to his plans to photograph a total solar eclipse in the year ahead. But as with the 1856 and 1858 Smyth work, the report itself contains no astronomical photographs but only woodcuts based on line drawings of geometrical relations (see figure 8.7). The difficulty and expense of duplication seem not yet to have warranted the distribution of astronomical images that were important photographically, but did not yield measurable images. In justifying his stereo views, De La Rue's argument is for both the novelty and the "gigantic," albeit metaphoric, implications for science photography in general. De

would no longer be semi-circles, but semi-ellipses, whose conjugate diameter is equal to 0·2263, and whose transverse diameter is inclined 90° to the pole.

Stereoscopic Pictures of the Moon.—Taking advantage of the libration, we may, by combining two views taken at sufficiently distant periods, produce stereoscopic pictures which present to the eyes the moon as a sphere. It has been remarked by the Astronomer Royal, that such a result is an experimental proof of the rotundity of our satellite. A dispute has been going on between photographers as to the proper angle for taking terrestrial stereoscopic pictures, and I infer that one side of the disputants would consider my arrangement of moon-pictures to produce stereographs unnatural, because under no circumstances could the moon itself be so seen by human eyes; but, to use Sir John Herschel's words, the view is such as would be seen by a giant with eyes thousands of miles apart: after all, the stereoscope affords such a view as we should get if we possessed a perfect model of the moon and placed it at a suitable distance from the eyes, and we may be well satisfied to possess such means of extending our knowledge respecting the moon, by thus availing ourselves of the giant eyes of science.

It does not follow as a matter of course that any two pictures of the moon taken under different conditions of libration will make a true stereoscopic picture; so far from this being the case, a most distorted image would result, unless attention be paid first to the selection of the lunar pictures, and then to their position on the stereoscopic slide. It is possible to determine beforehand, by calculation, the epochs at which the two photographs must be taken in order to produce a stereoscopic picture; but so many circumstances stand in the way of celestial photography, that the better course is to take the lunar photographs on every favourable occasion, and afterwards to group such pictures as are known to be suitable.

A little consideration of what has been before stated will show that two lunar pictures, differing only by libration, either in longitude or in latitude, will give a true stereoscopic effect, provided the angular shifting is sufficiently great.

On the other hand, if the two pictures differ both by libration in latitude and in longitude, they will give a true stereoscopic picture provided they satisfy the following condition. Suppose a point in the centre of the equator, when the moon is in a mean state of libration, has become shifted at the epoch of picture A in any given direction, and let an imaginary line pass through that point and the centre of the lunar disc, if at the epoch of picture B the point lies anywhere in the direction of that line, then a true stereograph will be obtained, provided the two pictures be suitably placed in the stereoscope.

◆ FIGURE 8.7 ◆

A woodcut based upon line drawings of geometrical relations showing De La Rue's photographic theory behind his lunar stereo pairs, from his 1860 "Report of Celestial Photography in England."

La Rue anticipates that some viewer will consider his stereographs

> unnatural, because under no circumstances could the moon itself be so seen by human eyes; but, to use Sir John Herschel's words, the view is such as would by seen by a giant with eyes thousands of miles apart: after all, the stereoscope affords such as view as we should get if we possessed a perfect model of the noon and placed it a suitable distance from the eyes, and we may be well satisfied to possess such means of extending our knowledge respecting the moon, by thus availing ourselves of the giant eyes of science. (De La Rue 1860, 143)

De La Rue's stereophotographs of the moon were not true simultaneous stereo pairs, but rather were crafted from two images taken at distant periods apart. To explain the theory behind the images, one must understand that the moon, like the earth, wobbles on its axis. This means that if two images of the full moon are timed so as to allow the greatest amount of wobble between the images, the effect when pasted beside each other and viewed with a stereoscope is an effective illusion of the space between our eyes and three-dimensionality. In explaining the design of his stereo pairs, De La Rue says that: "Assuming the space between the eyes to be two and three-quarter inches, and the nearest distance for distinct vision to be about ten inches, we find 15° 48′ as the maximum stereoscopic angle" (De La Rue 1860, 144).

But simply to render the moon in three dimensions was not to advance fundamental astronomy, based as it was on close and repeated observations and modeled with great mathematical precision. What Airy hoped for from photography as early as the 1840s was for photographic observation to reduce or remove errors introduced by human observers from the astronomical record. Airy convinced the Admiralty to offer a prize of £500 for the development of photographically based self-recording astronomical machines (Rothermel 1993, 144). In an 1857 article for the *Monthly Notices of the Royal Astronomical Society*, Airy argued that when astronomical photographers could "obtain collodion finer in grain and still more sensitive, it will supersede hand-drawing altogether, and even now the results obtained are much more accurate than anything hitherto done by mapping or hand-drawing" (quoted in Rothermel 1993, 145).

Airy and De La Rue both saw an opportunity to establish a strong foundation for photography with the eclipse of 1860. But by 1860, De La Rue and Airy had hopes for taking "instantaneous" collodion wet-plate negatives in the direct focus of the telescope, with enough apparatus to yield measurable results of several solar phenomenon, including the size and nature of the solar prominences, their positions on the sun, and the path of the moon. Rothermel points out that successfully photographing the eclipse was of the utmost importance for Airy, so much so that he forced all the other members of the expedition to Spain to "embark earlier in order that De La Rue might have sufficient time to set up and take sample photographs" (Rothermel 1993, 155). The use of photography to record the eclipse was a gamble, and De La Rue and Airy were forced to make many informed guesses about the intensity of light during the eclipse. De La Rue chose to take his photographs with the Kew photo-heliograph, a telescope designed to yield images of the sun as large as four inches in diameter. But in doing so, the light was reduced in intensity 64 times. As De La Rue (1862, 334) phrased the question in his long narrative article for *Philosophical Transactions*:

> Would it be possible with such an enfeebled image to get even a single impression during the whole duration of the totality? This was an extremely doubtful matter. By employing the Kew heliograph one would evidently run the risk of returning without any pictures of the *totality*, however many might be procured of the other phases of the eclipse.

De La Rue had a portable observatory constructed, and, as the collodion wet-plate glass negatives had to be developed immediately upon exposure, it contained a wooden darkroom, covered by a tent of canvas that "was kept wetted with water, in order that the evaporation might lower the temperature of the stratum of air between it and observatory" (De La Rue 1862, 336).

Because of the large degree of uncertainty involved, De La Rue writes (1862, 338) that he was convinced by Airy

> to make preparations for eye-observations (which I did not originally contemplate), partly in order that I might be in a position to interpret from my own sketches and recollections the results of the photographs, and partly because in case I should fail in making photographs, I might still be able to contribute something to the series of observations.

He also hoped to record extra-photographic information like the color of the prominences, and to that end had a prepared color scale to use for comparison. When the totality began, De La Rue was engaged in making measurements through the optical telescope, but when he learned that the first image of the totality was successful, he "made no further measurements, knowing full well that I should get them far better in the photographs." And the photography did succeed; De La Rue was able to claim that "upwards of forty photographs were taken during the eclipse, and little before and after it—two being taken during the totality, on which are depicted the luminous prominences, with a precision as to contour and position impossible of attainment by eye-observations" (De La Rue 1862, 339).

In analyzing the photographs, De La Rue writes at length about the issues of enlarging and duplicating the glass-plate negatives. Far from being dim, the solar image, even with the instantaneous shutter, was extremely dense and so difficult to print from. Both contact prints and enlargements were made from the original negatives, then duplicate negatives from those positives. Because the ethos of photography was central to De La Rue's article, the illustrations in the article take this as their thesis. Yet, in the general issue of the journal, again no direct positive photographs were included. Instead, messotint facsimiles and carefully measured "electro-duplicates" were published along side De La Rue's hand-colored sketches. A small set of special editions were printed with positive copies of the original totality images, these being distributed only to observatories and selected societies (Rothermel 1993, 158) (see figure 8.8). As Rothermel has noted, Airy, more so than De La Rue, was aware that the authority of the photographs was central to the scientific claim of the article. Airy thought that any intervention beyond printing positive images would reduce the credibility of the photographic process. He wrote to De La Rue:

> I insist on having as infinitely more important exact facsimiles of the two Totality Photographs. It is the amount of measurable change on those which possesses such a peculiar value. . . . [The originals] and not

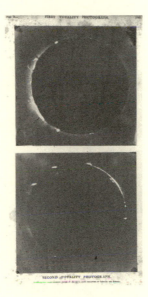

◆ **FIGURE 8.8** ◆

De La Rue's "The Bakerian Lecture" (1862) was illustrated primarily with engravings based upon photographs, but this image of one from a small set of special editions printed with positive copies of the original totality images distributed only to observatories and selected societies. The authority of the photographs was central to the scientific claim of the article.

> the touched-up photographs, contain the evidence on the case. The interpretation . . . may be fallible (I do not believe that it is), but the whole question about the prominences is strongly debated, and you must proceed with exactly the same caution as in a disputed case in a court of law. (quoted in Rothermel 1993, 158)

In response to Airy's concerns, De La Rue's report is very explicit about the photographic history of each image published in the article. For example, he notes the difficulties occasioned by working from copies and from emulsions that don't have the exposure latitude to record both the brightest and darkest areas: "The corona, for example, which is depicted on the original negatives, is to a great extent lost in the copies, because in bringing clearly out the details of the prominences, the corona in most cases becomes over-printed" (De La Rue 1862, 399). In his explanation of the illustrations, De La Rue shows his awareness of levels of representational ethos defined as layers of removal from direct experience. Verity, he argues, persists despite the possibility of technical faults in the emulsions or processes, but he also notes its economic costs, weighed against a value for the permanence of the reproduced image, silver salts versus inks:

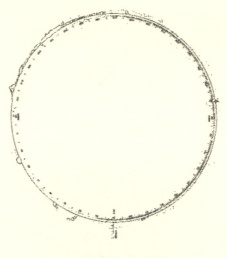

◆ **FIGURE 8.9** ◆

De La Rue's "The Bakerian Lecture" (1862) also employed the technique of electro-duplication of photographs on glass to reproduce measurable astronomical images.

> In Plate IX are given mezzotint facsimiles of the two totality-pictures the size of the originals; although they will serve to give a general idea of the photographs, and to illustrate what has been said respecting them, they are, after all, but imperfect substitutes for the photographs themselves. Copies of the photographs would have been inserted in this memoir, had past experience of the permanence of such pictures warranted the Council in doing so*. *In the Author's copies, Plate IXa, photographic copies from the originals are given. They are two removes from the originals. (De La Rue 1862, 399)

De La Rue also reflects his momentary dismay at comparing his eclipse photographs to those of Secchi. In the positive prints of Secchi's images, a major prominence appeared to be missing. But by traveling to Italy to view the original negatives, De La Rue determined that the apparent discrepancy was not in the negatives, but only in the reproductions (Rothermel 1993, 156).

De La Rue also used a new method for illustrating his article that was a middle ground between the unretouched photograph and the messotint lithographs called the "electroduplicate" (see figure 8.9). In this zinc-based process, the printing plate is chemically etched directly from the emulsion onto the glass negative. It was this method that De La Rue selected for presenting the outline of the solar prominences on a ruled circle.

Because the measurements taken from the photographs needed to be precise ones, another issue was whether the wet collodion emulsion shrank when drying. De La Rue conducted repeated experiments and argued that "there was no appreciable contraction, except in thickness, and that the collodion film did not become distorted" (De La Rue 1862, 368). In short, he established the ethos of his photographs successfully, and by extension, convinced a British epistemic jury of his claim for the solar origin of the prominences that had been observed during eclipses for centuries.

In a final gesture that harks back to Smyth's Teneriffe work and De La Rue's crafted images of the moon, he again suggests that binocular vision possess more verisimilitude than a monocular image can:

> In conclusion, the two totality-pictures No. 25 and No. 26, when reduced to a suitable size and placed in the stereoscope, No. 25 on the left, and No. 26 on the right, afford a very beautiful view of the phenomenon of totality, and one which could not be enjoyed by mortal eyes in looking at the real eclipse. (De La Rue 1862, 415)

Notice that the claim here is one that cannot be tested by readers who do not possess copies of the special author's edition that included actual photographs. Even for those who do, it suggests that further photo-manipulation is needed: the reduction to an appropriate size, pasting the images side by side with the correct orientation, and engaging the use of the stereoscope.

THE TRANSIT OF VENUS

Twice in a century, at eight-year intervals, Venus passes directly between the earth and the sun. This event, called the transit of Venus (across the sun's face), creates an opportunity to carefully time the passage of the event, and by extrapolation, to calculate the distance to the sun. But while a transit and an eclipse are similar, the astronomical goal for the 1874 transit of Venus was not to observe general phenomena, but rather to reduce the chance of error in these calculations to less than 1 percent. Precision in both observation and measurement was paramount. As George Forbes (1874) explained in a volume written to prepare for the upcoming transit:

> This method is looked forward to with much interest, because it is the first time that photography has been extensively employed in delicate astronomical measurements. The method has been employed in America to measure the distances between double stars. The double star is photographed and the distance is afterwards measured as accurately as possible. Prof. Bond finds that the probable error of similar measure is $0'072''$ or one-third of the probable error of a similar measure made with a filer micrometer as estimated by Struve. (Forbes 1874, 31–32)

Forbes argued that the value of the photographs would also reside in the ability to make repeated and careful measurements, "when the observer cannot be carried away by the excitement of the moment" (1874, 56). But he also foresaw the dangers of overexposure—the solarization effect that would enlarge the apparent area of the sun and make precise measurements impossible.

This is, in effect, what happened, and the enlarged images of the transit failed to yield consistently measurable results that would reduce the margin of error from that of direct observations. In the short term, this was a blow for astronomical photography, and photography was not systematically used for the next transit of Venus, eight years later in 1882.

Conclusion

Despite the failure of photography in the transit of Venus in 1874, the concept of using photography to carefully document astronomical events had been established, and by the century's end, an ambitious international project to map the entire visible sky was begun. The "Carte du Ciel," or map of the sky, would not be completed until 1964, long after much of the visual data had been determined with more precision through other methods. But by 1900, photographic technology was a primary rather than a secondary method in astronomy. As photographic spectroscopy and photometry became more widespread, new concepts of the nature, size, and motions in the universe were propounded. Measurable images became the basic tools of astrophysics, a new discipline that was fundamentally underpinned with data derived through photography. By the end of the nineteenth century, astronomical photography had established its credibility as a method of inquiry, and established the foundations that Albert Einstein would look to for his hypotheses about the relativity of matter and energy—a hypothesis that would be confirmed in 1919 by photographs of a solar eclipse that demonstrated the bending of light by the gravity of the sun. After an uncertain start, photography by the turn of the century was looked to to confirm the observations most fundamental to a new theory of the universe itself.

References

Arago, D. F. (1839/1980). Report. In *Classic Essays on Photography*, ed. A. Tractenberg. New Haven, CT: Leete's Island Books.

Bartlett, W. H. C. (1854). *Bartlett's Photographs of the Solar Eclipse of May 26, 1854*. Washington, DC: Smithsonian Institution.

Bruck, H. A., and M. T. Bruck. (1988). *The Peripatetic Astronomer: The Life of Charles Piazzi Smyth*. Philadelphia: Adam Hilger.

De La Rue, W. (1860). Report of celestial photography in England. *Reports of the British Association for the Advancement of Science for 1859*, 131–53.

————. (1862). The Bakerian lecture—on the total solar eclipse of July 18th, 1860, observed at Rivabellosa, near Miranda de Ebro, in Spain. *Philosophical Transactions*, 333–416.

Forbes, G. (1874). *The Transit of Venus*. London: Macmillan.

Herschel, J. F. W. (1826). *Account of Observations Made with a Twenty-Feet Reflecting Telescope*. London: Richard Taylor.

Marien, M. W. (1997). *Photography and its Critics*. Cambridge: Cambridge University Press.

Norman, D. (1938). The development of astronomical photography. *Osiris* 5: 560–94.

Rothermel, H. (1993). Images of the sun: Warren De La Rue, George Biddell Airy and celestial photography. *British Journal of the History of Science* 26: 137–69.

Smyth, C. P. (1858a). *Report on the Teneriffe Astronomical Experiment of 1856, Addressed to the Lords Commissioners of the Admiralty*. London: Richard Taylor & William Francis.

————. (1858b). *Teneriffe, An Astronomer's Experiment, or, Specialites of a Residence Above the Clouds Illustrated with Stereographs*. London: Lovell Reeve.

Thomas, A. (1997). *Beauty of Another Order: Photography in Science*. New Haven, CT: Yale University Press.

Vaucouleurs, G. (1961). *Astronomical Photography: From the Daguerreotype to the Electron Camera*, trans. R. Wright. London: Faber & Faber.

Whipple, J. A. (1853). Untitled article. *Photographic Art Journal* 6: 66.

chapter nine

TWO-DIMENSIONAL FEATURES IN THE HISTORY OF TEXT FORMAT
how print technology has preserved linearity

———◆———

barry pegg

U NILLUSTRATED TEXT HAS, throughout the part of history known to us, progressively developed in form to show its cognitive structure on the two-dimensional medium of the page. In illustrated text, however, images have maintained the same relationships with their text. (I have simplified these into three types: *ancillary*, *correlative*, and *substantive*.) If we can assume that human systems that change spontaneously over time evolve in the direction of efficiency, and if we can further assume that systems that spontaneously stay the same do so in obedience to the rule, "If it ain't broke, don't fix it," then we might think that there is something inherently more effective in print communication in which relationships among ideas are presented spatially (in the case of print, two-dimensionally).

The records of written texts considered apart from illustration reveal, though not of course in tidy historical succession, a progression in roles for texts: from cues for oral performance, through the silent reading invented, according to Paul Saenger (1982, 301), some time in the fourteenth century, to the multiple uses text is put to today, whether for instructions (routine or emergency), information, persuasion, or entertainment.

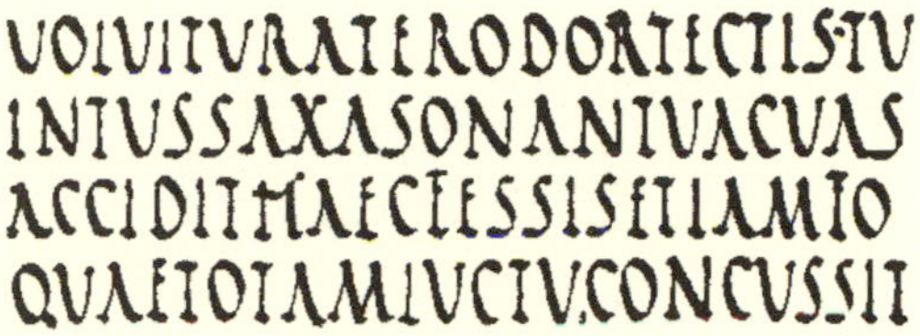

VOLVITVRATEROĐOŘTECTISTV
INTVSSAXASONANIVACVAS
ACCIDITTIAECTESSISETIAMTO
QVALTOTAMIVCTVCONCVSSIT

◆ **FIGURE 9.1** ◆

Continuous text: Virgil, *Aeneid* (fourth-century manuscript). FROM *HANDBOOK OF GREEK AND LATIN PALAEOGRAPHY*, BY EDWARD M. THOMPSON, 1893.

Early Documents:
Cues for Oral Performance

The function of the earliest manuscripts, until the invention of printing, seems to have been to provide cues for reading aloud. The best known such activity would be the reading of saints' lives to the assembled community in a monastic refectory. Thus the model for medieval text was, in effect, a linear string (i.e., a purely aural phenomenon), broken on the page only according to the arbitrary termini of lines and pages—in other words, only by the accidents of manuscript production rather than according to sense. These texts presented to the eye a succession of letters, such as the page from a copy of Virgil's *Aeneid* shown in figure 9.1. It was up to the reader to distinguish the breaks between words—not particularly difficult once a text became familiar.

Gradually, once word-division (the next most obvious requirement) became standard practice, the early "speech for the eyes" acquired rudimentary punctuation, usually consisting of one stop mark, as illustrated by the *Anglo-Saxon Chronicle* of 1045 C.E. (figure 9.2). Manuscripts of the monastic period (very roughly from the seventh century until printing became common in the mid-fifteenth century) display very clearly the long-term progression: separation of words was followed by rudimentary sen-

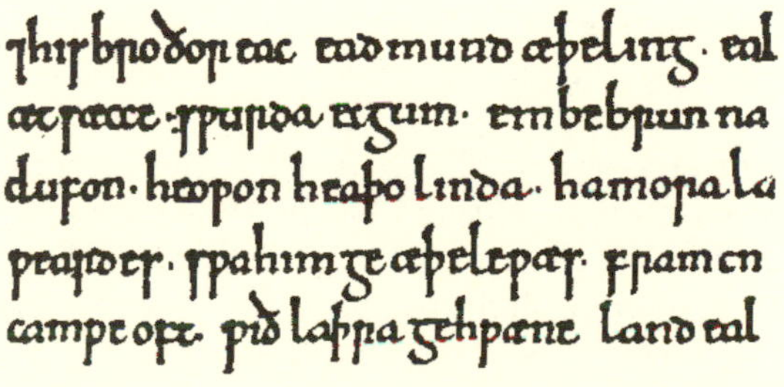

◆ **FIGURE 9.2** ◆

One-mark punctuation: *The Anglo-Saxon Chronicle* (1807). FROM *HANDBOOK OF GREEK AND LATIN PALAEOGRAPHY*, BY EDWARD M. THOMPSON, 1893.

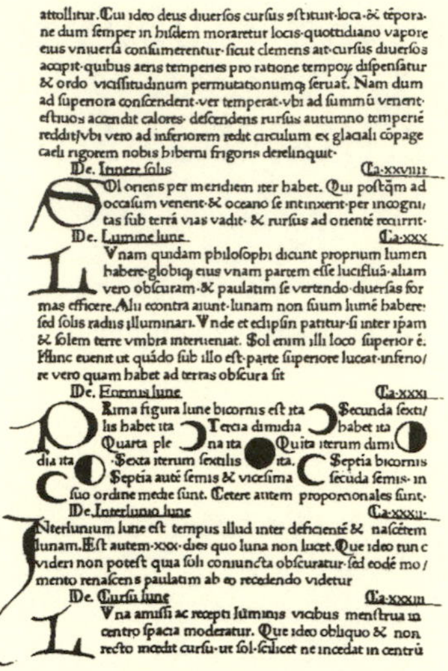

◆ **FIGURE 9.3** ◆

Paragraphs as chapters: Isidore of Seville, *Etymologiae* (1473). Courtesy of the Newberry Library, Chicago.

tence and clause punctuation, and eventually by paragraph and chapter divisions appearing on the two-dimensional page.

THE PRINTED WORD AND FIFTEENTH-CENTURY FORMAT

Around 1450, the Gutenberg Bible standardized print technology for the first time in Europe, and so it may be taken as fairly representative of contemporary ideas on standardized punctuation. Printing in this period displayed verses, with capital initial letters and with two marks of punctuation: a period (like our comma in appearance) at the end, and sometimes a caesura break (looking like our colon) in the middle of the verse.

The first stage in the development of chapters in secular material was for each short paragraph to be labeled as a chapter. Isidore of Seville discusses in his *Etymologiae* (1473, figure 9.3) the path of the sun, the light of the moon, the shape of the moon, the new moon, and the moon's orbit, all in chapters (numbered 29–33) of one paragraph each.

Only one more step was needed to arrive at the paragraph-and-chapter format, the pattern of prose text that has become the most prevalent from the Renaissance down to the present (and now gradually giving way to the Web page). The chapter of about ten to twenty pages became more common as a superordinate level of organization above the short, paragraph-length chapter, which had by then lost its numbers and headings. Where previously the punctuated linear string had been enhanced with only one two-dimensional feature above the sentence level, now there were two: the

CHAPTER 1

Introduction

L ogic, conceived today as the science of validity of thought, and as the term for the canons and criteria that explain trustworthy inferences, was in the English Renaissance a theory not so much of thought as of statement. For all practical purposes, the distinction between thoughts and statements is not a very real distinction, since the latter are merely the reflection of the former, and the former cannot be examined without recourse to the latter. But what distinction there is consists in a differentiation between mental phenomena and linguistic phenomena, the assumption being that the thing to which either set of phenomena refers is reality itself. Logicians of the twentieth century are primarily interested in mental phenomena as an interpretation of the realities of man's environment, and in that part of mental phenomena which we call valid or invalid inference. Logicians of the English Renaissance were primarily interested in statements as a reflection of man's inferences, and in the problem of the valid and invalid statement. Thus Renaissance logic concerned itself chiefly with the statements made by men in their efforts to achieve a valid verbalization of reality. Since such statements were the work of scholars and scientists, not of laymen, Renaissance logic founded itself upon scholarly and scientific discourse and was in fact the theory of communication in the world of learning. The data upon which this theory rested were all learned tractates of that and earlier times. The theory itself attempted on the one hand to explain the nature of these tractates, as to language, sentence structure, and organization, and on the other to offer assistance to the learner in his effort to master learned communication, as part of his entrance fee to the scientific and philosophical world.

Rhetoric, popularly taken today as a term for the sort of style you happen personally to dislike, was less subjectively construed in England during the sixteenth and seventeenth centuries. Rhetoric was then regarded as the theory behind the statements intended for the populace. Since the populace consisted of laymen, or of people not learned in the subject being treated by a speaker or writer, and since the speaker or writer by his very office was to some extent a master of the real technicalities of his subject, rhetoric was regarded

[3]

◆ **FIGURE 9.4** ◆

Current chapter and paragraph format. FROM *LOGIC AND RHETORIC IN ENGLAND, 1500–1700*, BY WILBUR S. HOWELL, 1961.

paragraph and the chapter. The stabilizing, uniformitizing effect of print helped standardize the Renaissance model of expository text: paragraphs and chapters, with the relationships between elements that were shorter than the paragraph displayed not two-dimensionally, but by cohesive ties.

THE "CURRENT-TRADITIONAL" PROSE MODEL: PARAGRAPHS AND COHESIVE TIES

The first page of Wilbur Howell's (1961) *Logic and Rhetoric in England, 1500–1700* (figure 9.4) shows at its best the tradition, deriving from Renaissance humanism, of a text that makes clear the outline of its ideas through a battery of cohesive devices. The text proceeds by making careful definitions, and then subdividing those definitions, and by repeating concepts through "re-entry" (Michael Jordan's [1981] term for repeated words, pronouns, and synonyms). The chapter begins by expanding the "logic" and "rhetoric" of the title, with a view to making clear the differences in meanings between the Renaissance and the present day. Today, logic is concerned with thought; back then, it was more concerned with statements. This distinction is made in various ways about five or six times in the course of the first paragraph, and is finally clearly defined for the Renaissance as "the theory of communication in the world of learning" (Howell 1961, 3). In the second paragraph, rhetoric, the other element of the title, also has displayed its changes in meaning over time; it is introduced as having not its present meaning of "the sort of style you happen personally to dislike," but its Renaissance meaning of "the theory behind the statements intended for the populace" (Howell 1961, 3). In this paragraph, the popular audience for rhetoric is contrasted with the learned one for logic. The clear, balanced, and graceful distinction-making continues throughout the chapter and indeed the whole book. Howell's opening chapter (it would be easy to find many other examples also) exhibits the ideal features of any introduction in expository writing, including technical writing at its best; it functions as an expanded table of contents, or as an "advance organizer" (Ausubel 1978, 251) for the remainder of the book, as well as making distinctions and definitions and providing examples. In short, this chapter represents the best of what traditional style could do without greater use of two-dimensional aspects of text presentation.

This pattern has survived as a standard into modern times, especially in the humanities. So long as samples are taken at sufficiently great intervals to avoid the lesser cross-currents and eddies of regional and idiosyncratic variation, the mainstream of print history does seem to show progression towards the standard practice of today: chapter headings, paragraphs, sentences marked off with periods, plus a whole host of punctuation marks to represent finer divisions, such as the elements of compound sentences, the subordination of complex sentences, parenthesis, opposition, and the like. The logical, or cognitive, relationships among notions in the text are conveyed, not by further spatial subdivision of the text, but by a system of cohesive ties.

The exact nature of the cohesion in what I am calling "unillustrated" or "linear" prose (meaning that the linearity is broken only by line and passage breaks, chapter headings, and paragraphing) has been the subject of much work in linguistics. There have been various theoretical explanations of the way texts cohere, all giving various names to what seems to be the essential feature of coherence—the repetition of concepts. The work of Susan Haviland and Herbert Clark (1974) focused attention on the patterns of "given" and "new" material by which texts take readers from the known to the unknown. M. A. K. Halliday and Ruqaiya Hasan's (1976) highly influential *Cohesion in English* identified enough types of cohesion to fill a six-page list falling into five groups. Similarly, Michael Jordan (1981, 1984) devised a system of "re-entry" involving "associated nominals," which explains many of the same phenomena with slightly different terminology. The "Functional Sentence Perspective" of the 1970s Prague school of linguistics was presented in this country by William Vande Kopple (1982), attempting to extrapolate the work of Haviland and Clark "from pairs of sentences to natural paragraphs" by means of identifying and following the progress of "topic" and "comment."

"Current-traditional" prose is a hybrid, combining the two-dimensional features of paragraphs, chapters, and punctuation, standardized with the

invention of printing, with a linear system of syntactical and lexical cohesive ties. This system has done pretty well since the Renaissance to make
meaning plain to readers—provided, of course, that those readers first
undergo a fairly lengthy training program in schools and colleges. In literate societies, that is what "literacy" has tended to mean—the ability to
decode the system of punctuation and cohesion. The vast majority of the
population, however, finds this system quite difficult to learn. It is significant that in matters of extreme importance and danger, such as writing
instructions for landing a plane on an aircraft-carrier (a life-and-death matter if ever there was one), dependence on linear prose has been avoided in
favor of a prescribed text–image ratio, typically one image per page or per
heading (Halloran and Whitburn 1982, 59).

Apart from instructions, manuals, official forms, some textbooks, and
the like, most of the writing through which we attempt to come to terms
with our world and ourselves comes to us in the traditional linear format,
enshrining historically determined conventions. Tradition dictates (and
most material follows) that we should share our ideas on paper (or on
screen) in the same way that St. Augustine, Erasmus, and Francis Bacon
did—that is, by textual variations on a format established for quite a different purpose, not to display the pattern of ideas, but to serve as a series
of cues for reading aloud to others. This format has been adapted labori-
ously, but only partially, to the two-dimensional page over something like
fifteen centuries. Up to now, no system has evolved, or been designed,
according to what we now believe about the way texts are understood, in
which visual cues and illustrations contribute substantively to meaning.
And now we are faced with Web pages where we mostly read in the same
old way, in spite of the promise and possibilities of hypertext. Most often
the links merely take a reader from one page of traditional text to another.
The graphics found there may be attractive to readers, but they are seldom
essential to understanding the text's meaning.

Three Types of Text–Image Relations

The traditional paragraph-and-cohesion system of unillustrated text has
struggled halfway towards two-dimensional expression of ideas and their
relationships, but still relies, for full cohesion, on a system of verbal conventions within the linear string of text. For the relationships between text
and explanatory images, the story is very different. So far from a gradual
adaptation to the way the mind works, such as we see in the history of unillustrated text, we find that the same set of relationships between text and
image is found in all periods and in texts on all kinds of topics. In the interests of simplicity, I should like to present ancient and modern examples of
three somewhat oversimplified types, each representing an arbitrary point
on a continuum running from illustrations with no assigned relationship to

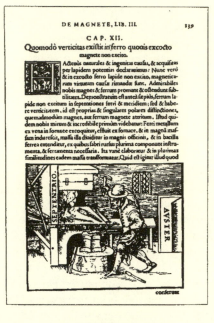

◆ **FIGURE 9.5** ◆

Ancillary illustration (early) from *De Magnete* (1600), by William Gilbert. Reprinted with permission of the Folger Shakespeare Library, Washington, DC.

a specific point in the text ("ancillary"), through illustrations with graphs or verbal links to the text ("correlative"), to text that is itself arranged in pictorial form ("substantive").

ANCILLARY IMAGES

In what I call *ancillary images*, two-dimensional material, usually pictorial, is placed in the neighborhood of relevant text (except in the case of title-page illustrations, frontispieces, and thematic colophons). The exact relationship of the image to the text, however, is left for the reader to determine. (It should be noted that extremely complex or technical material cannot be really effectively presented in this way.) Figure 9.5 shows an example from the Renaissance, and modern versions can be found in any contemporary popular-science magazine. The similarity over the centuries of ancillary relationships of this kind between text and image is striking; and, as we shall see, *correlative* and *substantive* relationships have likewise remained stable.

A very important subset of the ancillary mode is the slide-tape, movie, or video discourse, of which PowerPoint presentations are the most recent manifestation. This type of presentation, as opposed to print, combines clearly separable pictorial and linear elements—that is, pictorial elements

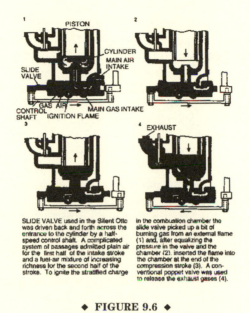

SLIDE VALVE used in the Silent Otto was driven back and forth across the entrance to the cylinder by a half-speed control shaft. A complicated system of passages admitted plain air for the first half of the intake stroke and a fuel-air mixture of increasing richness for the second half of the stroke. To ignite the stratified charge in the combustion chamber the slide valve picked up a bit of burning gas from an external flame (1) and, after equalizing the pressure in the valve and the chamber (2), inserted the flame into the chamber at the end of the compression stroke (3). A conventional poppet valve was used to release the exhaust gases (4).

◆ **FIGURE 9.6** ◆

Correlative illustration using captions, from "The Origin of the Automobile Engine" by Lynwood Bryant, in *Scientific Technology and Social Change* (1967). COPYRIGHT HELD BY *SCIENTIFIC AMERICAN*.

accompanied by "voice-over" or written text. The visual images in slide or computerized text-and-visual presentations are constantly in view, requiring us to continuously reconcile the picture with its script. In contrast, when we process illustrations in print documents, we relate the picture to the text according to our own needs or on the author's cue. In both cases, however, the visual element remains ancillary, in that the text, not the visual element, is expected to convey the message. In audiovisual media, sound and vision become two separate channels, with the ancillary video channel bearing more than merely ancillary meaning by reason of the constant attention it commands. Occasionally, text is added to the visual channel. The number of channels for conveying information is thus increased to three (image, text, and sound), with a correspondingly increased potential for either efficient cognitive reinforcement or for complete confusion. Adding print to the video portion of an audiovisual piece greatly complicates the task the reader or viewer must perform in order to adapt the linear audio to the two-dimensional pictures.

Ancillary or Correlative Illustrations Mediated by Captions. One very common type of modern illustration system uses captions to bridge the gap between text and image, whether the image is a picture without labels or a diagram with "callout" text correlating the parts of the picture with the captions and thence with the text via lines, as in figure 9.6. The most famous periodical to use this technique is the source of this figure, *Scientific*

American. The captions below the illustrations are short enough to focus the reader's attention on specific features of the illustration; the concepts must then be related to the text by the reader. This figure shows the process in action. The words "slide valve," "cylinder," and "control shaft" in the caption refer to specific features and are picked up in the labeled callouts on the illustration. The mechanism, which is the subject matter of the whole article, is also described in context in the article in slightly expanded form (Bryant 1974, 114).

The really interesting effect of this technique (which perhaps accounts for the amazingly long-running popularity of *Scientific American* on the newsstand) is that it allows meaning to be derived in three steps: first, the concepts and perhaps some of their relationships can be grasped from a survey of the pictures (*Scientific American* is justly famous for the quality of its illustrations); next this information can be expanded from the captions; and finally, dedicated readers can read the whole article, in which the concepts from the captions are repeated (often in the same words) and expanded upon. In this way, the captions constitute an expanded version of the abstract, leading the reader by easy stages as far as his or her time, interest, and expertise allow. It is probable that, for any given article, most readers perform only one or both of the first two steps.

CORRELATIVE (OR INTEGRATIVE) ILLUSTRATIONS

Correlative illustrations are usually associated with technical and scientific discourse and are characterized by keying illustrations to the text in a variety of ways. Certain rules, which are easily broken with a little inattention, must be observed if this technique is to be effective. As presented by J. C. Mathes and Dwight Stevenson (1976, 173), these rules are:

- All items in the text that need to be understood should also be shown and labeled in the illustration.
- All items labeled in the illustration should also be found in the text.
- The nomenclature in the text and in the illustration should be the same.
- The illustration as a whole should be cross-referenced to the text with a figure number and title, both of which are repeated in the text.
- The illustration should appear as near to the relevant text as possible.

This procedure was established very early in the history of printing, as we can see in a sixteenth-century example from Oronce Finé's *Protomathesis* (figure 9.7). The labels referring to the points of the geometric figure are repeated exactly in the text to facilitate the necessary switching back and forth from linear to two-dimensional reading, just as we do still.

◆ **FIGURE 9.7** ◆

Correlative illustration (early), from *Protomathesis* by Oronce Finé (1532). COURTESY
OF THE NEWBERRY LIBRARY, CHICAGO.

Figure 9.8 ("shoulder girdle of a vertebrate") represents a typical modern correlative illustration; it shows not only how the same method has
persisted into modern times, but since it is a complex labeling task, also
illustrates how error-prone the system is. "Callouts"—names repeated from
the text, set around the illustration, and linked with a line to the appropriate portion of the illustration—are almost universal in this type of situation.
Here, unfortunately, the system has not worked as well as it should. "Shoulder girdle," "ribs," and "sternum" are among the concepts named in the text
but not called-out in the illustration. "Pubis," "ischium," and "ilium" are
named on the illustration but not mentioned in the text (the illustration was

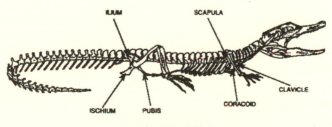

◆ **FIGURE 9.8** ◆

Correlative illustration (modern): shoulder girdle of a vertebrate. FROM *LABORATORY
ANATOMY OF THE ALLIGATOR* BY R. B. CHIASSON (1962).

intended by the editors to serve double duty as an entry on the "hip-girdle" as well). Writers underestimate the opportunities for such errors; attention has to be carefully carried from the linear format to the two-dimensional format and back again.

Just as the dynamism of the development of unillustrated text may suggest a certain amount of cognitive inappropriateness, so does this correlative type of text–image relationship itself hint at difficulties. It is so elaborate and prone to error that it does not seem, intuitively at any rate, to conveniently match human cognition. We might look at the system as one that rigorously and determinedly builds so many ties that it essentially admits the need for bridging—acknowledging a deficiency and going to great lengths to do something about it.

SUBSTANTIVE ILLUSTRATIONS

In the kind of relationship between text and image that I call *substantive*, there is no need for the reader to build bridges between image and text, as with ancillary illustrations, nor for a writer to construct elaborate and misunderstanding-prone bridges out of callout lines, numbering, or labels, as with correlative illustrations. If the words (or numbers) used with substantive illustrations are laid out two-dimensionally on a page so as to display structurally the relationships between them, then text and image are one. Identity of text and image is more effective (and certainly a lot simpler) than integration of them.

Substantive illustrations present assertion and support materials so that their relationships are immediately visible through the eye directly to the mind, without needing the reader to process them into quasi-pictorial form for storage. Particulars in support of generalized assertions, especially numerical ones, can be displayed in graphs and charts. Quantity and other relationships, such as modification and opposition, can be shown graphically, as can very complex relationships between concepts that would take a great deal of text to explain.

Although substantive illustrations in the form of numerical tables were not common before the Industrial Revolution, examples of substantive illustrations that include words are found in the earliest manuscripts and printed texts. In his *Etymologiae*, Isidore of Seville diagrams (figure 9.9) his version of the medieval system showing the interrelationships among the four elements of the earth in the outer ring (titled "Mundus"), the seasons of the year in the next inner ring ("Annus"), and the four humors of the human body in the innermost ring ("Homo"), all arranged according to their qualities of heat, cold, moisture, and dryness (also labeled in the outer ring). The diagram encapsulates a great deal of medieval physics, cosmology, medicine, and theology in a very small compass. A modern layout consisting of a similar pattern of named concepts with their functional relationships displayed spatially is typified by the common flowchart. In substantive illustrations, both late medieval and modern, words represent

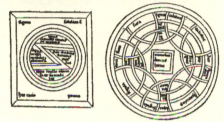

◆ **FIGURE 9.9** ◆

Substantive illustration (early), Isidore of Seville, *Etymologiae* (1473). COURTESY OF THE NEWBERRY LIBRARY, CHICAGO.

concepts in a cognitively significant spatial configuration. To explain the diagrams in words alone would be much less efficient.

Polemical Conclusion:
From Paragraph to Spatial Prose

If we can learn (as most of us have) how to translate linear text into our own mental imagery for processing and understanding, why am I proposing a two-dimensional approach to writing for the educated reader? The answer is that the more efficient the system, the more complex the ideas that can be conveyed to more people. The fact that we have been trained to cope with a 70-percent efficient system (more or less) need not mean that the system is fully efficient or sufficient, any more than the fact that a butterfly can flap successfully from one cabbage to another necessarily means that it can fly as well as an eagle. Only those with an investment in obfuscation (not, I hope, those in academia) would oppose the idea of text displaying its cognitive relationships spatially.

Why should not the ability of pictures (still, sequenced, or moving), charts, diagrams, and tables to display the relationships among ideas meaningfully be combined with the cohesive ties of conventional text to gain the advantages of both traditional and cognitively more effective discourse?

The dynamic history of unillustrated text, with the gaps between progressively larger units of thought becoming visually marked, almost suggests that users of text have been "striving" for something. With the advent of standardized print technology the process appears to have been frozen before it had dealt with clause-sized units of thought. Thus two-dimensional formatting was left with a limited cognitive role—dividing the discourse into paragraphs and chapters, but leaving sentences, clauses, and words in a linear, word-wrap string format of no cognitive significance. In the absence of a text system of full cognitive efficiency, our species has created what computer engineers disparagingly call a "kludge" to do the job—a system that patches up, rather than replaces, an inadequate one. The traditional chapter-and-paragraph system that generations of students have learned with blood, sweat, and tears, and by which, admittedly, skilled practitioners can with reasonable clarity convey relationships through punctuation and cohesive ties, seems just this kind of arrested, partially evolved, kludge-like system. Circumstantially but insistently, the combined histories of unillustrated print and of text–image relationships imply the primacy of the imagistic representation of information.

The time may be ripe to set our text practices on a firmer footing, applying what we currently believe about how we understand print. Although traditional structures should not be abandoned for light and transient causes (following Thomas Jefferson's precepts for political revolution rather than Thomas Kuhn's for scientific revolution), there is no reason why nonthreatening changes in print practices that can be easily effected, say through use of a simple word processor without recourse to PageMaker or similar desktop-publishing software, should not be fostered. Changes of this kind are not unthinkable; the present system, after all, enshrines earlier adaptations: that of spoken material to writing and print technology. Now that desktop-publishing software have made innovative, even nonrectilinear text design easier, it is imperative to consider what the next developments in text practice should be.

Such changes in our ways of representing meaning should not be much of a stretch for technical writers or writing teachers either. Writing for important manufacturing, business, or military situations has for a long time made use of headings, white space, lists, matrices, tables, charts, and diagrams. Admittedly, such writing (other than purely numerical tables and charts) tends to make use of what I have been calling *correlative* rather than *substantive* information design. Nevertheless, textbook publishers, especially of business, the sciences, and engineering, are becoming more willing to employ two-dimensional text for the exposition of complex concepts. A review article by Ben and Marthalee Barton (1989) clearly charts the emerging trend toward a visual mode in verbal materials.

What would such documents look like? I offer two answers. First, where text is to be written, write better text, following the example from Howell, with its "table-of-contents" paragraphs and topic sentences, with plenty of signposting and repetition of the signposts. Second, strive for substantive visual discourse wherever the relations between ideas (opposition, addition, example, numerical increase or decrease, and so on) are to be shown. The latter might mean laying out prose with plenty of white space to show the structure of complex sentences (rather like diagramming them, but according to the rules of logic rather then the rules of grammar). These precepts are especially important to writers working on Web documents, considering the impatience of readers of these documents.

Can current technical and scientific writing, with its strong two-dimensional element, be said to be any "better" than the predominantly linear current-traditional prose it claims to replace? And what of the promise of hypertext, the standard method for the display of ideas on the Internet? At present, in spite of the hype, there is not much to choose between paper and electronic presentations. The best of each surpasses the worst of both in cognitive efficiency. Most Web pages (even the award winners) today merely present a series of linked prose pages using the same old structures, mostly units of paragraph size or greater. The hypertext that most people see carries advertising, like a magazine, and will presumably carry more as time goes by. Web pages tend to be broken up by intrusive advertisements with brightly blinking colors and cute postage-stamp animations. What we may soon meet whenever we hit a URL is a magazine with a different (but not necessarily easier) way to flip the pages, and with less portability, at least for a decade or two.

It is fair to say that no matter how much more potential for two-dimensionality we find in hypertext, little progress has been made in using two-dimensionality to improve the clarity of written concepts at the sentence and clause level. That is still completely dependent on the kind of old-fashioned writing skills that old-fashioned "English" teachers teach.

What kind of document would I like to see? One that uses a lot of white space (or in the case of a Web page, a lot of links connecting short "pages"), and a lot of advance organizing, spatially showing relations of subordination, support, opposition, equivalence, cause and effect, and so on. I don't think it much matters *how* these elements are put together as long as they're there. Web sites sometimes take us to another screen and then leave us with only one idea, when what we actually wanted was to put two ideas together in some sort of spatial relationship in the mind. The prominent accessibility of the "Go Back" button is no accident. Most Web-page design seems to me almost as much of a kludge as the awkward text–image integration seen in many textbooks. And I don't think the current-traditional ideal of "good writing" with headlines and cohesive ties by any means ought to be abandoned as an ideal, but should in fact be integrated into Web-page design.

It is true that current print-publication procedures require that "substantive" text (that is, graphics with text displayed spatially to indicate logical relations) be treated with the same rather complex routines as pictures. I would like to suggest, however, that while current-traditional prose has no real means of deploying its ideas spatially, a two-dimensional format with punctuation and spacing easily done with a word processor or even on a typewriter could be applied to linear prose, to the great enhancement of both. Imagine, for example, the exemplarily lucid cohesive system of Wilbur Howell (figure 9.4) enhanced with progressive indentation, or with columns or fields, to display the grammatically and logically parallel elements (such as "logic" and "rhetoric") side by side rather than in linear prose. Or imagine it "cyberfied" or "htmlated" as a Web page. It is precisely my point that it is the structure of the writing of this kind of piece, characterized by subdivision of concepts and headings developed in branching fashion, that are necessary for easy transfer to a Web page at all—or for note-taking or, for that matter, even understanding. If we first take care of the logical processes such as parallelism and subordination, clarity will emerge whether we are writing an article or a Web page. There is no reason why, more than five hundred years after the beginnings of the paragraph-and-chapter system, we should not break the linear string and let our texts take full possession of the page; and also (now that hypertext has given us the opportunity to reapply some basic rules of good writing to a new and lawless frontier) take full possession of the computer screen.

Acknowledgment

The author wishes to thank the editors of *Technical Communication Quarterly*, in whose predecessor *The Technical Writing Teacher* (vol. xvii, no. 3, Fall 1990) an earlier version of this chapter first appeared, for permission to revise the article for republication in this volume.

References

Ausubel, D. P. (1978). In defense of advance organizers: A reply to the critics. *Review of Educational Research* 48: 251–57.

Barton, Ben F., and Marthalee Barton. (1989). Trends in visual representation. In *Technical and Business Communication: Bibliographic Essays for Teachers and Corporate Trainers*, ed. Charles H. Sides. Urbana, IL: National Council of Teachers of English and Society for Technical Communication.

Bryant, Lynwood. (1974). The origin of the automobile engine. In *Scientific Technology and Social Change*, ed. G. Rochlin. San Francisco: W. H. Freeman. (Originally published in *Scientific American*, March 1967.)

Chiasson, Robert B. (1962). *Laboratory Anatomy of the Alligator*. Houghton, MI: Michigan Technological University.

Finé, Oronce. (1532). *Protomathesis*. Paris: Gerardi Morrhij and Ioannis Petri.

Gilbert, William. (1600). *De Magnete*. London: Peter Short.

Halliday, M. A. K., and Ruqaiya Hasan. (1976). *Cohesion in English*. London: Longman.

Halloran, S. Michael, and Merrill D. Whitburn. (1982). Ciceronian rhetoric and the rise of science: The plain style reconsidered. In *The Rhetorical Tradition and Modern Writing*, ed. James J. Murphy. New York: Modern Language Association of America.

Haviland, Susan E., and Herbert H. Clark. (1974). What's new? Acquiring new information as a process in comprehension. *Journal of Verbal Learning and Verbal Behavior* 13: 512–21.

Howell, Wilbur S. (1961). *Logic and Rhetoric in England, 1500–1700*. New York: Russell & Russell.

Isidore of Seville. (1473). *Etymologiae*.

Jordan, Michael P. (1981). Some associated nominals in technical writing. *Journal of Technical Writing and Communication* 11: 251–64.

———. (1984). *Fundamentals of Technical Description*. Malabar, FL: Robert E. Krieger.

Mathes, J. C., and Dwight Stevenson. (1976). *Designing Technical Reports: Writing for Audiences in Organizations*. Indianapolis: Bobbs-Merrill.

Saenger, Paul. (1982). Silent reading: Its impact on late medieval script and society. *Viator* 13: 367–414.

Thompson, Edward M. (1893). *Handbook of Greek and Latin Palaeography*. Englewood Cliffs, NJ: Prentice-Hall. (Originally published by D. Appleton & Company.)

Vande Kopple, William. (1982). Functional sentence perspective, composition, and reading. *College Composition and Communication* 33: 50–63.

chapter ten

THE CONCRETE WORD
text and image
in the theater

lisa a. brock

A NY DISCUSSION OF TEXT AND IMAGE as they operate in the theater must begin with the premise that it is in the interrelationship between language and image that theater exists. The text or play, taken by itself, is not theater; rather it is a piece of literature that provides a map or blueprint for theater. It becomes theater only when it exists in the present tense, within a context of images, as in an actual production. The nature of this imagistic context, moreover, is mutable. The use of image in the theater can range from the simplicity of a body in motion on a bare stage to the complexity of a computer-driven Andrew Lloyd Webber spectacle. It can seem almost an afterthought, an embellishment of the text. Or it can magically transform the text into a theatrical event beyond the realm of words.

The various ways in which image is used in relation to text in the theater are significant, because these uses can intimate a culture's or society's vision of the value of both word and image. For example, theater artist Robert Lepage has found, while touring his works internationally, that different countries and cultures approach the very act of being an audience in different ways, depending on their vision of the relationship of word and image:

> There's an English-speaking culture that calls the public an audience.
> They go there to hear stories, and you go there to tell stories. However

visual you are, it goes through the ears. . . . And you have a part of the world that calls the public spectators, like in France. When they describe shows they've seen they talk about the story visually, even if they have heard the words. . . . The reason why I'm so fascinated by Japanese and Chinese culture is because they seem to have a three-dimensional concept of what things are, and their way of writing is both a sound and an image . . . the Japanese theatre and Chinese opera is the most refined three-dimensional, sculptural hologram form of theatre, because stories are told on these two levels all the time. (quoted in Delgado and Heritage 1996, 144–45)

Generally speaking, the relationship between word and image has taken a hierarchial form in Western theater at least since the advent of classical Greek drama, with the word being privileged over the image. In his *Poetics*, Aristotle summed up the use of image in the theater dismissively:

The Spectacle has, indeed, an emotional attraction of its own, but, of all the parts, it is the least artistic, and connected least with the art of poetry. For the power of Tragedy, we may be sure, is felt even apart from representation and actors. Besides, the production of spectacular effects depends more on the art of the stage machinist than on that of the poet. (1951, 29–31)

Beginning in the late nineteenth and early twentieth centuries, however, various philosophical debates about the relationship of language to image challenged and, in some cases, toppled this conventional hierarchy. Many of these philosophic challenges were first proposed in terms of the visual arts, but their arguments were quickly co-opted by the theater. At the same time, major technological advances in lighting and scenic design allowed for an immense expansion of the possibilities for creating images onstage. Theater artists began reimagining the stage in terms of a new visual code. In addition, with the advent and ubiquity of film and television, audiences began acquiring a new visual vocabulary, one that the contemporary theater is still struggling to incorporate. The result has been that in a culture that has become significantly more visual and nonlinear in its perceptions and more sophisticated in its artistic expectations, today's theater more and more frequently views text and image through juxtaposition rather than in a hierarchical relationship.

The Roots of Modern Theater

Prior to the 1870s, the text was central to Western theater and the stage itself was dominated by the proscenium arch and perspective scenery, which had developed in the Italian theater during the Renaissance. The visual focus of theater was firmly ensconced in a picture frame. Within this frame, settings were typically generalized and nonspecific, a trend influenced philosophically by the neoclassical demand for universality, and in practical terms by the possibility of reusing sets for a variety of different productions. Scenery was two-dimensional, painted on canvas, with three-dimensional elements like chairs added only when absolutely necessary. The visual result was a virtual nonrelationship between text and image, since the set operated merely as a backdrop or static image against which the actors recited the text.

By the early nineteenth century, illusionism began to come into vogue. A forerunner of realism, illusionism strived for a greater reality in scenic elements in order to enhance the illusion created by the text. Illusionism brought about an increased historical accuracy in costumes and experimentation with a variety of special effects such as moving panoramas used in conjunction with treadmills to create a sense of space and movement. Gas lighting began to be used in theaters in the 1820s, and by 1850, with the introduction of the "gas table," stage light could be controlled from one source, allowing for a greater degree of realism in lighting. The box set, which would become the standard unit for realistic set design, came into widespread use in the 1830s. Based on Diderot's concept of the "fourth wall," the box set attempted to replicate a room, including furniture, and it brought a certain amount of dimensionality to the stage picture, although many of the details of the setting were still represented through painting.

Certain artistic developments and technological innovations converged in the second half of the nineteenth century to move scenic design from illusionism to realism. Probably the most important technological advance was the development of electricity, since it not only had a sweeping impact on stage lighting, but also made it possible to power extensive stage machinery. The electric control board began to replace the gas table in the 1880s, while more advanced forms of floodlights, spotlights, and colored lights made it possible to control the direction and intensity of stage light to a greater extent than could previously have been imagined. At the same time, electric motors allowed for the creation of such scenic devices as elevator stages and revolving stages, which in turn allowed for larger and more realistic sets.

Artistically, Henrik Ibsen and Émile Zola became figureheads for realism and naturalism in the theater, creating through their writing a school of thought that saw an interrelationship between human beings and their environment. This thinking spurred a design revolution in which stage sets sought to mimic reality in every detail. André Antoine, who founded the Théâtre Libre in 1887, was one of the foremost proponents of naturalistic staging. The box set had previously been designed to make a concession to the viewpoint of the spectators, with furniture, props, and actors "cheated" toward the audience. To achieve a greater degree of realism, Antoine took the "fourth wall" concept one step further: he designed his box sets with completely realistic placement of furniture and objects and then decided which wall to take out, making no allowance for sightlines. His sets also employed the greatest possible realism in furniture, costumes, and props. The most famous example of his concern for detail was his use of real carcasses of bloody, dripping beef in a production of Fernand Icre's *The Butchers*. He also darkened the auditorium to increase the audience's sense that the play was an illusion of reality, an innovation in French theater at that time although Wagner had introduced the darkened auditorium at Bayreuth ten years previously. All aspects of Antoine's scenic design worked toward allowing the spectators to forget that they were watching a play.

In a sense, the work of Antoine and other proponents of realism continued and even enhanced the hierarchy of text over image in the theater, because the motivation for their scenic design was to flesh out and reveal the script. In the first decade of the twentieth century, however, several artistic movements arose in a backlash against realism. These movements disputed the heretofore accepted premises of Aristotelian-based dramatic theory and practice; the dominance of language over image, linear plotting, the aim of creating an illusion of reality onstage—virtually all previous theatrical conventions—were called into question as these various movements explored new modes of perception.

CHALLENGING DRAMATIC CONVENTIONS

Expressionism is perhaps the most well-known of these movements, and over time it has had as great an impact on the use of image in the theater as realism. Because expressionist drama attempted to portray a subjective reality, it called for a highly nonrealistic visual appearance, expressed through exaggeration and distortion in scenic elements and the use of lighting to suggest mood and emotion. Indeed, the overall visual appearance of the production became central in expressionist drama—an unsurprising development considering that expressionism as a movement first appeared in the visual arts. Ernst Toller subtitled his expressionist play, *Man and the Masses*, "A Play of the Social Revolution in Seven Pictures" and stated in the stage directions that "the Second, Fourth, and Sixth Pictures are visionary, projections of a dream" (1921, 57). His play calls for characters' faces to dissolve from one to another and for actors to walk through walls. In fact, many of the techniques of expressionist drama were appropriated by cinema, a medium more easily able to achieve some of the effects dramatists were calling for. In her essay "Film and Theatre," Susan Sontag points out that during this period, scenic and lighting experiments were actually passed back and forth between the two mediums; she cites Max Reinhardt's stage production of *The Beggar* as providing the inspiration for the lighting of Robert Weine's film *The Cabinet of Dr. Caligari* while asserting:

> The accomplishments of the "Expressionist film" were immediately
> absorbed by the Expressionist theatre. Stimulated by the cinematic tech-
> nique of the "iris-in," stage lighting took to singling out a lone player, or
> some segment of the scene, masking out the rest of the stage. Rotating
> sets tried to approximate the instantaneous displacement of the camera
> eye. (1966, 34)

At the same time, expressionist plays displaced the centrality of language
with texts that often consisted of mere fragments of sentences and disjointed words. Walter Hansclever's *Humanity* (1918), for example, proceeds primarily through pantomime, punctuated by one- or two-word sentences; the five-act text is only thirty pages long.

Two other movements that had significant influences on the use of
images and scenic elements in the theater were Futurism and Dadaism.
Futurism, first proclaimed by Filippo Tommaso Marinetti in 1909 and most
vividly realized onstage by director Enrico Prampolini, introduced the
concepts of simultaneity and multiple focus to scenic design. Prampolini
also called for a multidimensional stage rather than the two-dimensional
painted flat still common in scenic design, and intermingled actors with
geometric marionettes. Interestingly, Marinetti was also one of the first
theorists to consider the use of film as part of a theater that he conceived
of as "a final synthesis of all the arts" (Sontag 1966). Dadaism, which was
closely related to futurism, was characterized by texts that were nonlinear, alogical, and antiliterary. In Tristan Tzara's *The Gas Heart* (1920), for
example, the characters are all parts of a head—Ear, Eye, Nose, etc.—and
the script is a series of nonsensical non sequiturs.

Surrealism built on Dada as it co-opted many of its dramatic techniques, particularly the use of discontinuity and juxtaposition in both texts
and scenic design. Guillaume Apollinaire's *The Breasts of Tiresias*, first
produced in 1917, vividly demonstrates many of these ideas: the events in
the script are wildly illogical, the action is meant to surround the audience, and a variety of media, from music to acrobatics to painting, are
involved in the total experience. In his preface to the play, Apollinaire
states that his working premise is that "the stage is no more the life it represents than the wheel is the leg" and that he wrote the play "to protest
against that 'realistic' theatre which is the predominating theatrical art
today. This 'realism,' which is, no doubt suited to the cinema is, I believe,
as far removed as possible from the art of drama" (1917, 747). One of the
most famous Surrealist productions of the period was *Parade*, written by
Jean Cocteau, with music by Erik Satie and sets and costumes by Pablo
Picasso. Presented by the Ballets Russes in 1917, the production employed
collage and simultaneity in every element and succeeded in thoroughly
outraging its audiences.

CREATING A VISUAL VOCABULARY

By the second decade of the twentieth century, nevertheless, scenic design had advanced only a little beyond the two-dimensional pictorial style that August Strindberg argued against in his *Preface to Miss Julie* in 1888: "There are so many other conventions in the theater which we are told to accept in good faith that we should be spared the strain of believing in painted saucepans" (Strindberg 1888, quoted in Block and Shedd 1962, 97). Even in 1904, W. B. Yeats was complaining that "ever since the last remnant of the old platform disappeared, and the proscenium grew into the frame of a picture, the actors have been turned into a picturesque group in the foreground of a meretricious landscape painting" (1904, quoted in Dukore 1974, 658). Shortly after this period, however, the ground-breaking design theories of Adolphe Appia and Gordon Craig became widely known, particularly after their work was displayed as the centerpiece of the International Theatre Exposition in Amsterdam in 1922.

Appia was the first theater designer to meld all elements of design into a cohesive whole, envisioning the stage as a three-dimensional space that unified light, mass, and movement. His sets were characterized by ramps, platforms, pillars, and drapes, as he eliminated all but the most necessary scenic elements and created a spare, evocative atmosphere. He was also the first designer to incorporate the stage floor into the overall scenic design. Perhaps most importantly, he conceived of light as a means of expressing and enhancing the tone and meaning of the text of a play. Designer Lee Simonson eloquently explains the effect Appia's scenic designs created:

> The stage is no longer a space symmetrically split by flat picture planes against which an actor gestures; it is a three-dimensional area *through* which he moves in a carefully calculated pattern. Light is not an even flood spilling down from parallel borders or upward from a row of footlights. It is three-dimensional, has depth and defined limits so that actors move in or out of it, or, if they do not move, light moves on or off them. Light determines form. The playing area is contracted or expanded by fluctuations of light; a setting is no longer a picture seen in its entirety from one side of a frame to another. Light models the form of a stage setting with the accent of highlight and shadow, the balance of concentration and diffusion. The planes of a stage set are planned primarily to frame motion and to reflect light. Color is not absolute but relative, changing its hue with the light that ebbs and flows over it. In this envelopment a three-dimensional actor and a three-dimensional setting are fused. But their relation is not static; it is in continuous flux. Light confines movement, defines it, expands playing areas or blots them out. (Simonson 1950, 28)

Gordon Craig's visual conceptions, while developed independently of Appia's, bear some striking resemblances. Like Appia, Craig conceived of the stage as a three-dimensional space to be sculpted and defined by light. His sets employed the same spare simplicity, evocative use of color, and strong horizontal and vertical lines. He also introduced large mobile screens that he envisioned as moving fluidly from scene change to scene change, their appearance constantly altered by placement and lighting. (Unfortunately, the technology of his time was not yet advanced enough to allow him to realize that vision.) Where he parted company from Appia was in his belief that the hierarchial supremacy of text and actor should be done away with. While Appia felt that scenic design should serve and enhance the text, Craig proposed substituting a theater of silent movement for a text-based theater and using *ubermarionettes*, giant puppets manipulated by a master artist, instead of actors. In this sense he was closely related to the more extreme dramatic theories that were developing in the 1920s and '30s. Despite their differences, however, both Appia and Craig had an immeasurable effect on modern scenic design and contemporary culture's perception of stage images. Due to their work, the stage came to be universally conceived of as a three-dimensional space and, ultimately, they created a new visual language for the theater that has not yet been superseded.

OVERTHROWING DRAMATIC CONVENTIONS

The most extreme voice for a philosophic reimagining of the theater, however, came from Antonin Artaud in the 1930s. Although the roots of many of his dramatic theories can be found in earlier and concurrent movements such as Futurism, Dada, and Surrealism, as well as in the visual conceptions of Craig, Artaud took these theories to an extreme that turned the basic premises of Western theater upside down. In a series of manifestos and essays written from 1931 to 1936 and collected under the title *The Theater and Its Double* in 1958, Artaud launched an all-out assault on the theater of his day, a theater in which, in his perception:

> This idea of the supremacy of speech in the theater is so deeply rooted in us, and the theater seems to such a degree merely the material reflection of the text, that everything in the theater that exceeds this text, that is not kept within its limits and strictly conditioned by it, seems to us purely a matter of *mise en scenè*, quite inferior in comparison with the text. (Artaud 1958, 68)

In place of this theater, Artaud offered his own vision of a Theater of Cruelty "to put an end to the subjugation of the theater to the text, and to recover the notion of a kind of unique language half-way between gesture and thought" (p. 89). The Theater of Cruelty as he envisioned it served a holy and mythic purpose, purging and purifying society. He espoused a total theater in which the physical barriers between actor and audience would be broken down and the audience completely surrounded by and part of the action. In place of text and language, this theater would employ what Artaud called "a concrete language." His theater would be a total "spectacle" by which he meant that

> [e]very spectacle will contain a physical and objective element, perceptible to all. Cries, groans, apparitions, surprises, theatricalities of all kinds, magic beauty of costumes taken from certain ritual models; resplendent lighting; incantational beauty of voices, the charms of harmony, rare notes of music, colors of objects, physical rhythm of movements whose crescendo and decrescendo will accord exactly with the pulsation of movements familiar to everyone, concrete appearances of new and surprising objects, masks, effigies yards high, sudden changes of light, the physical action of light which arouses sensations of heat and cold, etc. (p. 93)

In essence, he proposed a theater driven by the senses, and primarily the visual sense, in place of a language-driven theater.

It is important in assessing Artaud's call for the reinvention of theater to acknowledge the influence of film on his theories. Significantly, in *The Theater and Its Double* he included a short critique of a Marx Brothers film, *Animal Crackers*, which he describes as "the liberation through the medium of the screen of a particular magic which the customary relation of words and images does not ordinarily reveal" (p. 142). Indeed, he not only acted in numerous films, but also wrote film scenarios and scripts, including *The Seashell and the Clergyman*, which was produced by Germain Dulac in 1926, and *The Butcher's Revolt*. Unsurprisingly, he identified with silent film and became disillusioned with the "talking cinema," which he viewed as the "negation of cinema itself" (1958, 131–32). His approach to theater production itself was highly cinematic, which partially explains why he never successfully realized his theatrical reforms within the context of his own stage productions. In *The Theater of Cruelty (Second Manifesto)* (p. 131), for example, he describes a scene from *The Conquest of Mexico*, which he intended to be his first production:

> Lights and sound produce an impression of dissolving, unravelling, spreading, and squashing—like watery fruits splashing on the ground . . . and like a tidal wave, like the sharp burst of storm, like the whipping of rain on the sea, the revolt which carries off the whole crowd in groups, with the body of dead Montezuma tossed on their heads like a ship.

While it requires a stretch to imagine this scene on either stage or screen, clearly many of its elements evoke cinematic techniques—particularly in the necessity to change focus rapidly and cut from one image to another.

Artaud's own experiments in Theater of Cruelty—which culminated in a production of *The Cenci* in 1935—were ultimately failures and had virtually no effect on the theater of his time. On one level, this failure was due

to practical considerations; as Christopher Innes points out in *Holy Theatre* (1981, 109):

> First, the gap between his unrealistically idealistic theory and what he
> actually practiced raised expectations in his audience that his work was
> not even designed to meet. Secondly, his stage effects relied on complex
> technology and a high degree of control in the acting. His productions are
> conceived in terms of lighting which did not exist, scenery which was too
> costly for an *ad hoc* group to build effectively, and a precision of chore-
> ography that required long-term commitments by an expert troupe.

But in a larger sense, they failed because the theater that Artaud advocated is essentially unrealizable. As Jacques Derrida points out in *La
parole soufflé*:

> The theater of cruelty is not a new theater destined to escort some new
> novel that would modify from within an unshaken tradition. Artaud
> undertakes neither a renewal, nor a critique, nor a new interrogation of
> classical theater: he intends the effective, active, and nontheoretical
> destruction of Western civilization and its religions, the entirety of the
> philosophy which provides traditional theater with its groundwork and
> decor beneath even its more apparently innovative forms.

In his essay, *The Theater of Cruelty*, Derrida goes through an inventory of
the kinds of theater that would not be considered faithful to Artaud's conception of theater of cruelty, only to arrive at the conclusion that "in thus
enumerating the themes of infidelity, one comes to understand very
quickly that fidelity is impossible. There is no theater in the world today
which fulfills Artaud's desire. And there would be no exception made for
the attempts made by Artaud himself" (1978, 246–48).

Nevertheless, since the publication of *The Theater and Its Double* in
1938 and, more specifically since its translation into English in 1958,
Artaud's vision has had a significant impact on contemporary theater.
While it can be cogently argued that his dramatic theories are more a synthesis of earlier movements and ideas—Futurism, Dadaism, Surrealism,
the "total theater" envisioned by Wagner, the lighting and scenic principles
of Appia and Craig, developing cinematic techniques—than innovations of
his own, yet he has come to be seen as a symbol of an image-based, rather
than a text-based, theater—a theater that is a total revolt against realism,
a complete multimedia spectacle. That none of his conceptions seem particularly shocking or new in today's theater speaks to the totality of the co-
optation of his theories. And while Derrida is correct in his assessment
that no theater embodies, or ever has embodied, Artaud's principles in any
true sense, yet a variety of theater artists have claimed his mantle in justifying their own forays into a nontextual theater. Ultimately, Artaud's theories seem to have had the effect of authenticating nontextual theater.

Word and Image in Postmodern Theater

In the second half of the twentieth century, the combination of these various philosophic challenges to a word-oriented, linear dramaturgy, in combination with the technological challenges that enabled these challenges, have acted as a catalyst for some significant revisionings of the relationship between word and image within the theatrical space. Moreover, just as the visual art of painting underwent a series of reactions to the ramifications of the advent of photography, so the ubiquity of film and television has forced the theater to metamorphose in myriad ways to justify its continued existence. All theater artists, to one degree or another, have had to grapple with the challenges and possibilities for image-making that late twentieth-century technology has presented them.

REINVENTION IN THE FACE OF TECHNOLOGY

Advances in technology over the past hundred years or so enabled, to a large extent, the major revolution in dramatic forms that created what we call "modern theater." Thus it seems logical to assume that the technological advances we have seen in the past twenty-five years alone will continue to enable another major theatrical revolution. Indeed, they already have in the area of scenic design. Computerized-memory light boards, which arrived in the mid-1970s, allowed for a huge expansion of the use of lighting in stage productions, as designers could program countless miniscule and subtle alterations in color and intensity. Vari-Lites, which are computer-controlled automated lighting instruments, and fiber-optics are two other developments that increased the possibilities of controlling light onstage. Computer-assisted design programs are commonly used by both set and lighting designers. The scenery itself has also become automated and computer-controlled, dramatically speeding up scene changes and giving set designers more freedom in creating movement within the stage space. One of the results of these new resources is that they have allowed designers to transpose cinematic techniques to the stage. David Mitchell's set for *La Cage Aux Folles* in 1983, for example, theatrically recreated a tracking shot:

> The curtain rose on a painted backdrop of the harbor with a free-standing
> building in the foreground. The building tracked downstage and opened
> to form the buildings along a street and to reveal the facade of the night-
> club. The street units then moved offstage, the nightclub unit moved
> downstage and a white curtain dropped in behind. (Aronson 1985, 128)

Interestingly enough, such innovations are received uneasily by many theater artists, who find the use of such dramatic effects somewhat suspect. In *Towards a Poor Theatre*, director Jerzy Grotowski (1969, 53) cogently summed up part of the paradox these artists face in dealing with the possibilities technology has created:

To the stage-designer, the theatre is above all a plastic art and this can have positive consequences. Designers are often supporters of the literary theatre. They claim that the decor as well as the actor should serve the drama. This creed reveals no wish to serve literature, but merely a complex toward the producer. They prefer to be on the side of the playwright as he is further removed and consequently less able to restrict them. In practice, the most original stage-designers suggest a confrontation between the text and a plastic vision which surpasses and reveals the playwright's imagination. It is probably no mere coincidence that the Polish designers are often the pioneers in our country's theatre. They exploited the numerous possibilities offered by the revolutionary development of the plastic arts in the twentieth century which, to a lesser degree, inspired playwrights and producers. Does this not imply a certain danger? The critics who accuse the designers of dominating the stage, put forward more than one valid objective argument, only their premise is erroneous. It is as if they blame a car for traveling faster than a snail.

Essentially, since realism has, in effect, been usurped by film and television, theater designers have been granted far more freedom and eclecticism in the way they use images onstage. Which is not to say that they should not go further. The mass appeal of these two forms has essentially altered the way in which audiences view images, a concept that the modern theater is still struggling to process. As Robert Lepage, one of the world's leading figures in nontextual theater, points out:

> We tend to do theatre in a manner where we're using an old way of telling stories because we think people are obtuse, and that they only have this old-fashioned way of understanding a story. In fact people are extremely modern. . . . They have a very modern way of connecting things; they watch TV, they know what a flashback is, they understand the codes of a flash-forward, they know what a jump cut is. . . . And if you don't use that, you don't trigger that, of course they're bored. They have gymnastic minds now and a gymnastic understanding of things . . . and we tend to pretend they're idiots. (quoted in Delgado and Heritage 1996, 148)

Interestingly, there was far more exchange of techniques between theater and film in the early part of the century, as previously discussed. Today, the implementation of new visual techniques seems to originate almost solely in film and then, only secondarily, to be borrowed by the theater. Dominic Serrand, one of the founders of Théâtre de la Jeune Lune, sees this one-way street as a serious flaw in the contemporary theater:

> We need to bring the editing of images back into the theater where it began. In most theaters the editing process that is seen on stage is outdated because it is still so logical, whereas our minds have developed a more advanced process. I think that's why people don't go to the theater anymore—it's too old, it doesn't talk to them. (Serrand 1984)

It is significant that both Serrand and Lepage have established theaters that place a primary emphasis on the visual aspect of drama, rather than the textual, thus making themselves part of one of the most important developments to come out of the reconsideration of word and image.

A VISUAL THEATER

The attempt to create a nontextual theater has been one of the great theatrical experiments of the past few decades, drawing on a legacy of thought that extends back to Artaud. In the 1960s and '70s, the Living Theatre, founded by Judith Malina and Julian Beck, the Open Theatre, begun by Peter Feldman and Joseph Chaikin, and the Performance Group, founded by Richard Schechner, were three high-profile theaters that have attempted a variety of explorations of improvisation and nonverbal drama. Peter Brook has also made some of the most radical ongoing experiments in the use of text and image in the theater. His production of *The Tempest* in 1968 cut the majority of Shakespeare's text and used the remainder primarily for the effect of juxtaposition or as ritualistic chanting. The essence of the play was intended to be expressed through imagery: an opening scene created through pantomime in which the actors became both the ship and the sea; a simulated orgy in which Prospero is devoured by an animalistic Caliban; scenes in which the main action is mirrored by pairs of actors. For *Orghast*, Brook had poet Ted Hughes create a special language for the text that would create specific intuitive emotions through sound. "The intention," Innes explains in his analysis of *Orghast* in *Holy Theatre*, "was not to create a conceptual language which described a situation, but to compose blocks of sound that would have the status of physical action and be indecipherable by intellectual analysis" (1981, 139).

More recently, Robert Lepage has created a series of stunning productions that deemphasize text in favor of a striking visual language. Lepage's work is informed by a sense that language imposes a linear, chronological form that is more suited to film, while visual imagery creates a nonlinear vertical effect that can be more successfully achieved in the theater.

A particularly fine example of image-driven theater is the work of the British-based company Théâtre de Complicité. Founded in 1983 by Simon McBurney and Kathryn Hunter, this group has been highly influenced by the mime work of Jacques Le Coq. One of their recent works, *The Street of Crocodiles* (based on the writings of Polish author Bruno Schultz), epitomizes the way in which Théâtre de Complicité uses physical images as a wholly visual expression of the text. The play opens with an actor sitting onstage sorting books. Water drips somewhere offstage. Suddenly a man walks casually down the back wall of the theater from the ceiling to the floor. Another person climbs out of a barrel. A third clambers out of an impossibly small box. In moments, the stage is peopled with actors dashing hither and thither. The books they carry become a flock of birds, wheeling in flight. Objects take on lives of their own. The language, what there is of it, is elliptical, almost an afterthought. Théâtre de Complicité's treatment turns the text into a nonlinear visual language that ranges with lightning speed from the real to the surreal to communicate the essence of Bruno Schultz's work.

One of the problems this kind of theater must constantly face, how-ever, is what Robert Wilson identifies as the lack of "an adequate visual book for a theatre of literature. . . . When I was in Shanghai, I saw a fifteen-year-old girl sing an aria for an hour and forty minutes. She had 550 dif-ferent ways of moving the sleeve of her dress. . . . It's a visual language that parallels the text that she has to speak or sing" (quoted in Delgado and Heritage 1996, 304). Trying to create a visual language in Western culture, which has no dominant tradition of a visual, nonlinear theater, requires a demanding amount of trial-and-error and/or extensive borrowing from other cultures. Either way, the artist constantly runs the risk of creating art that remains inaccessible to the audience through the lack of a com-mon vocabulary.

THE COLLAGE EFFECT

More common at the end of the twentieth century than a theater of pure image has been a theater colored by a postmodern sensibility that is demonstrated through the unexpected, and often clangorous, juxtaposi-tion of word and image. As designer Arnold Aronson (1985, 128) explains from a purely design point of view:

> Whereas modern design sought an organic and aesthetic unity in which the stage picture functioned as a metaphor for the world of the play, post-modern design cries out that unity is impossible in the contemporary world. Postmodern design is a kind of pan-historical, omnistylistic aes-thetic in which the world is seen as a multiplicity of competing, often incongruous and conflicting, elements and images. Using discordance, juxtaposition and even ugliness, postmodern design often makes refer-ence to other productions, to other works of art and to the world beyond the play, with only the stage frame as a unifying element.

From a theoretical point of view, this multilayered, seemingly chaotic and strikingly visual approach to a text is motivated by some specific re-imaginings of the function of text. First, this approach questions the valid-ity of traditional linear structure as a reflection of human experience. Secondly, it examines the ways in which an image or icon can cause a word or a text to take on a new or renewed meaning by being set in jux-taposition to it. Images within this context operate on a variety of levels and gain richness and meaning from these levels, while words are treated in many cases like a form of image.

In "Unbalancing Acts" (1992), Richard Foreman discusses his rationale

for undermining linear narrative in his work as a means of more completely capturing the essence of actual human experience:

> Society teaches us to represent our lives to ourselves within the frame-
> work of a coherent narrative, but beneath that conditioning we feel our
> lives as a series of multidirectional impulses and collisions. . . . I like to
> think of my plays as an hour and a half in which you see the world
> through a special pair of eyeglasses. These glasses may not block out all
> narrative coherence, but they magnify so many other aspects of experi-
> ence that you simply lose interest in trying to hold on to narrative coher-
> ence, and instead, allow yourself to become absorbed in the moment-by-
> moment representation of psychic freedom. (quoted in Drain 1995, 68)

The specific way in which Foreman seeks to achieve a vertical or multilayered representation rather than a linear, horizontal one is through the
use of visual elements that function as icons on a variety of levels:

> For example, if an actor is at the back of the stage sitting against a suit-
> ably painted wall, the scene may seem to be realistically domestic. But if
> he then runs downstage to grab a handle at the end of a pole that rises
> from the floor and starts to spin it madly, since that pole is not something
> you would expect to find in a living room, it suggests that he must have
> left that domestic situation. . . . The next thing that character did in *What
> Did He See?* was to run to the top step of a platform and sit upon a
> throne. . . . The physical resources of the set made possible the specific
> actions that enabled me to jump from psychological level to political
> level to metaphysical level, and so on. (quoted in Drain 1995, 69–70)

This use of scenic images is closely related to Jan Kott's analysis of
images as collage in *The Theater of Essence* (1984). He identifies stage
images as literal, mimetic, and symbolic and examines the ways in which
these images can be used in layers and in juxtaposition to communicate a
more powerful message than could be conveyed by the text alone. He uses
as an example the concept of the surrealistic collage, like the familiar fur-
lined teacup or bandaged violin:

> The things that make up collages are similar to "surrealistic objects" in
> that both are stripped of their meaning, their "gestalt," and their inner
> structure undergoes destruction; the become pure *objets d'art*, icons. Yet
> from their mutual juxtaposition, from their arrangement arises a new
> icon which is not only a literal sign, but which has, or can have, symbolic
> value. In Tadeusz Rózewicz's, Ionesco's, and especially in Beckett's plays,
> the dramatic situation as image is similar to that of the surrealistic col-
> lage. The shoes which Vladimir and Estragon take off and put on, the tree
> which blossoms, Krapp's tape, the mirror, the revolver, and all the objects
> which Winnie takes out of her purse, are literal signs. From their juxtapo-
> sition and arrangement come symbolic signs. (Kott 1984, 135)

Much of this focus on the juxtaposition of text and image was prefig-
ured by the work and theories of Polish director and designer Tadeusz
Kantor. In "Impossible Theatre" (1972), he espoused what he specifically
called the "collage method" of approaching a dramatic text, explicating it
thus:

> The principle: to link up the segments of the text and the precise notions
> contained in them with completely different, or even contrary, situations
> and behavior taken from current reality or "the stuff of life"; a condition
> deprived of all illustrative or symbolic function. Everything was based on
> the break-up of logical links; the process was to superimpose, to "tot up,"
> in order to create a new reality. (quoted in Drain 1995, 65)

One of the directors who has made the most radical and ongoing use
of collage and a postmodern sensibility in his approach to theater and
opera is Peter Sellars. He places all of his productions in a contemporary
setting, his rationale being that

> [d]rama exists only in the present tense. You're either feeling it now or
> you're not. It has to be grasped at the moment by both the performers
> and the audience. So it helps to give it whatever immediacy one can.
> Rembrandt's religious paintings, for example, are all done in contempo-
> rary clothing—they are all completely present tense. . . . The historical
> situation is only of interest to you because history is continuous and
> ever-present and we own it. (Sellars 1984)

He thus set his controversial 1994 production of *The Merchant of
Venice* in Venice Beach, California, and scattered television monitors
throughout the stage and auditorium, juxtaposing live and televised
action. In *The Magic Flute* (designed by Adrianne Lobel), the set was comprised of a series of projections of garish holiday postcards, while his *Così
Fan Tutti* was located in a roadside diner. His *Hang on to Me*, produced
at the Guthrie Theater in 1984, combined Gorky's turn-of-the-century
drama *Summerfolk* with the music of George and Ira Gershwin. Sellars's
productions are distinguished in part by his innovative use of various new
theatrical technologies that have become available. In *Merchant*, for
example, he used television monitors and microphones to demonstrate
the multiple points of view inherent in the text and mimic cinematic close-
ups. Ultimately, he is aiming at capturing "simultaneous levels of experience" through a confrontation between text and image (Delgado and Heritage 1996, 228).

JoAnne Akalaitis also employs an experimental approach to text and
image in the theater. One of her more provocative creations, *Red and
Blue*, consisted of a conversation between red and blue light bulbs. The
set, designed by John Arnone, was comprised of nine 2-feet-by-3-feet
rooms, all variations of one room, that were stacked on top of one another.

As three actors talked offstage, the light bulbs illuminated different rooms. Her production of Beckett's *Endgame* was set in a disintegrating subway station and used a multiracial cast, two innovations for which she was attacked by the playwright himself. When she directed Büchner's *Leon and Lena (and Lenz)*, she gave the play an American Southwest setting and incorporated dance, music, video, and film into the production. Deborah Saivetz points out that Akalaitis embraces the concept of chaos, rather than an Aristotelian-based, linear conflict-and-resolution concept, as the essence of theater, and integrates direction and design to create an "image-filled atmosphere" onstage (1998, 151).

A New Way of Seeing

In *Towards a Poor Theatre* in 1969, Grotowski posed the question of how to create a necessary theater? He was speaking within the context of a world that seemed to be dominated by the images created through television and film, and his own response was that theater had to reinvent itself as its own form rather than try to imitate another form. Thirty years later, Ben Cameron, the executive director of Theatre Communications Group, posed essentially the same question about the relevancy of theater in a technological age in *American Theatre*: "Could it be that as guardians of an art form that traditionally makes use of linear/narrative structures, we are failing to tell stories in ways that this young audience is prepared to receive?" (p. 6). The answer to Cameron's question is quite possibly yes. As a look at the history of the development of the modern theater has shown, the form can only remain vital so long as it continues to reshape itself in response to the world around it. When the audiences for theater have learned a new way of seeing, a new way of processing both visual and textual information, theater must also learn a new way of seeing and of creating confrontations between text and image to remain viable.

Equally important is the need to develop new critical paradigms and language to approach the theatrical work that these confrontations create. Too often, critical vision in America continues to be bound by theories and ideas that were shaped for a theater that existed in the past. Among these conventional approaches are three that Susan Sontag (1966) delineated in her essay, "Marat/Sade/Artaud" in *Against Interpretation*: that theatrical works be assessed primarily as texts or works of literature; that theater be based on psychology or realism; that theater be idea-based or, in other words, be *about* something. Another lack is that the theater and those who view theater critically have not yet developed a thorough-going critical language that can meet the demands of a new way of perceiving image-making on the stage. Instead, just as theatrical image-making still borrows from cinematic image-making, so cinematic language is borrowed to make up for the lack of a comprehensive visual theatrical language.

The juxtaposition of word and image that marks much of the leading edge of a postmodern theater and the questioning of traditional hierarchic perceptions and privileging that this juxtaposition embodies seem to offer the possibility of reinventing theater for a new audience, one whose perceptions of word and image have been inexorably altered by the effects of technology.

References

Apollinaire, Guillaume. (1917/1974). Preface to *The Breasts of Tiresias*. In *Dramatic Theory and Criticism*, ed. Bernard F. Dukore. New York: Holt, Rinehart & Winston.

Aristotle. (1951). *Theory of Poetry and Fine Art*, trans. S. H. Butcher. New York: Dover Publications.

Aronson, Arnold. (1985). *American Set Design*. New York: Theatre Communications Group.

Artaud, Antonin. (1958). *The Theater and Its Double*, trans. Mary Caroline Richards. New York: Grove Press.

Cameron, Ben. (1999, April). Something's coming. *American Theatre* 16(4): 6.

Delgado, Maria, and Paul Heritage (Eds.). (1996). In *Contact with the Gods? Directors Talk Theatre*. Manchester, UK: Manchester University Press.

Derrida, Jacques. (1978). *Writing and Difference*, trans. Alan Bass. Chicago: University of Chicago Press.

Foreman, Richard. (1992/1995). Unbalancing acts. In *Twentieth-Century Theatre: A Sourcebook*, ed. Richard Drain. New York: Routledge.

Grotowski, Jerzy. (1969). *Towards a Poor Theatre*. New York: Methuen.

Innes, Christopher. (1981). *Holy Theatre*. Cambridge: Cambridge University Press.

Kantor, Tadeusz. (1972/1995). Impossible theatre. In *Twentieth-Century Theatre: A Sourcebook*, ed. Richard Drain. New York: Routledge.

Kott, Jan. (1984). *The Theater of Essence, and Other Essays*. Evanston, IL: Northwestern University Press.

Saivetz, Deborah. (Summer 1998). An event in space: The integration of acting and design in the theatre of JoAnne Akalaitis. *Tulane Drama Review* 42(2): 147–53.

Sellars, Peter. (1984, May 12). Personal interview.

Serrand, Dominic. (1984, April 4). Personal interview.

Simonson, Lee. (1950). *The Art of Scenic Design*. New York: Harper & Brothers.

Sontag, Susan. (Fall 1966). Film and theatre. *Tulane Drama Review* 11(1): 24–37.

———. (1966). Marat/Sade/Artaud. In *Against Interpretation* (pp. 163–74). New York: Dell Publishing.

Strindberg, August. (1888/1962). Preface to *Miss Julie*. In *Masters of Modern Drama*, ed. Haskell M. Block and Robert G. Shedd. New York: Random House.

Toller, Ernst. (1921/1969). *Man and the Masses* (trans. Louis Untermeyer). In *Avant-Garde Drama*, ed. Bernard F. Dukore and Daniel C. Gerould. New York: Bantam Books.

Yeats, William Butler. (1904/1974). The play, the player, and the scene. In *Dramatic Theory and Criticism*, ed. Bernard F. Dukore. New York: Holt, Rinehart & Winston.

chapter eleven

"THE WAY OF
THE SORCERER"
an etiology of two images
from a lost graphic novel

◆

heinz insu fenkl

WITH ART AND COMMENTARY BY MIKE DRINGENBERG

Introduction

F OR THE TYPICAL COLLABORATIVE TEAM, the process of producing a comic
book is simultaneously frustrating and magical. In most cases, the
visions of the various members of the creative team never quite mesh, but
occasionally each new layer of input can seem to be the slow disclosing of
some divinely inspired masterwork that no single member of the team
could have imagined alone. Good collaborations succeed and bad ones fail
due largely to what happens in the workings of this "third mind" that takes
over the process.

The general public tends not to devote much thought as to how comics
are actually produced, and even semi-informed collectors are often surprised by how complex a system is behind the typical comic book (whose
fate is to languish—treasured—in an acid-free, airtight Mylar bag). The
truth is that comic books have been hardly read in the last fifteen years,
and most of those who did bother to read the books they collected tended
to perform a cursory once-over, scanning the pictures and text to get only
a general sense of the story (which, in most cases, hardly needed the text
to support it). Ironically, after the collapse of the collector's market in the
mid-1990s, comic books have survived with a far smaller but more serious

198 ♦ Chapter Eleven

readership. But the issue of reading comic books has never been a topic of much interest in the general comic-book culture.

It is understood, of course, that devout fans of superhero comics ("fan-boys") will read comics very closely, memorizing the textual and visual minutiae so as to retrieve them in arguments and nit-picky letters to editors. But even among the professionals who write, draw, letter, color, and edit comic books, the act of reading does not require sophistication in the academic sense; indeed, it wasn't until the late 1980s, with the publication of Scott McCloud's *Understanding Comics* (in comic-book form) that the industry even began to have a general and consistent critical language beyond that of production and professional shoptalk. For the past twenty years, a single publication called *Comics Journal* has been vainly attempting to elevate the level of comic-book criticism, but its readership is still highly selective.

A typical superhero comic book such as *Spiderman* involves an elaborate production team comprised of the following members:

- the *creator(s)*, responsible for the original concept
- the *writer(s)*, responsible for the plot and the script
- the *penciller*, responsible for the pencilled artwork
- the *inker*, who inks the pencil lines
- the *colorist*, who colors the artwork
- the *letterer*, who letters-in the word balloons and caption boxes placed by the inker
- the *cover artist* (sometimes the same as the interior artist)
- the *editor*, who orchestrates the above team.

Anyone with a cursory knowledge of other collaborative processes (like film-making) will realize from the above list that it would be unlikely, or impossible, for a comic book to retain the single vision originating with its "creator." There is actually quite a lot of overlap in the list: the creator may be an artist, writer, or editor; the penciller might ink some or all of his own work; the penciller might do the cover art in full; the editor might also be involved in touch-up art. In any case, the typical comic book's textual and visual narrative sort of aggregates as more and more people read, interpret, and respond to various stages of its production. The process is thus inherently a recursive one: in the best case, the recursion causes the original ideas to become amplified and therefore more powerful for the final reader; in most cases, the recursion is both hit and miss, and the final book might have little resemblance to its original conception (if a coherent concept even existed to begin with). As a critical reader might expect, most of the meaningful explication of the content in a particular comic book occurs after the fact and is projected retroactively into the process of its creation and production. There is only a handful of comic-book artists and writers who could explain the meanings behind a particular story and then execute it to carry out those meanings.

There is, however, a small class of comics produced by what the industry often terms "auteures," creators like Frank Miller, Dave McKean, and Dave Simmons. These comics are highly unusual because they are written and illustrated by the same person. (In the case of Simmons's lifework, *Cerebus*, the book is even published and marketed by the same person—himself!) In the comic-book industry, it is typically these creators who can offer close readings of their own work, usually in the context of interviews with other comic-book professionals; unfortunately, these interviews are hardly ever read by the sort of academic audience who would benefit from them, largely because they are published in nonacademic venues.

In this chapter, I am exploiting my own connection to two generally divergent contexts by discussing a project that died in the comic-book world and so will never be the topic of thoughtful interviews in that context. The work I will be discussing is not an auteur work, but it has stylistic similarities to a certain category of comics executed in mixed media by a group of artists once referred to as "art fags" by other traditional comic-book artists within the industry. The derogatory label was due largely to the fact that these artists had formal artistic training (in both art history and technique) from places like the Pratt Institute and tended to apply a "high culture" approach to their work. The artists in this group tend to be characterized by the obvious stylistic and thematic influences of the Pre-Raphaelites, Gustav Klimt, and Egon Schiele; their work is also rather distinct on a comic-book rack because it tends to be painted in watercolor, oil, or acrylic (a list of representative works of this type are listed in the appendix to this chapter). I will be reflecting on a work from this latter category, often generically classified in the business as a "painted" book. I was the creator and writer (scripter, plotter) for this project, and Mike Dringenberg (best known for his work on the early issues of DC's *The Sandman*) was the artist. The project existed under several different names before it was finally put on a production schedule as *The Way of the Sorcerer*.

Sorcerer, which had originally been proposed as a one-shot graphic novel of approximately 186 pages, was finally approved to be produced at a length of 96 pages, to be published in two 48-page perfect-bound books. After we started the project, certain long delays ensued, and finally, when we were in a position to complete the work, the publisher canceled the line under whose imprint *Sorcerer* was to be released. Later, after the publisher was under its second new ownership, the original art could no longer be located. Needless to say, *Sorcerer* is now a work that will never be completed in its intended form, and so it has developed a sort of mythic reputation in certain circles. It is the great graphic novel that could have been, resonant with the same sort of mystery as the lost film of some master film-maker.

My aim in this chapter is not to focus on the sequential art, though a few examples of the collaborative process are illustrated by my thumbnail sketches and notes accompanied by the final pages of Dringenberg's illustration. What I dwell on below are two particular images—paintings—that represent two radically different stages in the evolution of a collaborative comic-book work. The first image, "Don Jose" (figure 11.4), is the one that Dringenberg painted as a concept piece after he had read my proposal for the project, and it is the image that accompanied the proposal packet as an example of the style and substance of the art that would illustrate the story. It was highly effective as a concept piece representing Dringenberg's competence as a watercolorist (though his earlier work was done in typical comic-book media); the proposal was bought within a few weeks by the first (and only) editor who saw it. The second piece, "Teller" (figure 11.6), is the painting Dringenberg completed as the cover of the first issue of *Sorcerer*. This was done three years after "Don Jose" and represents the product of an intuitive collaborative process that had, over time, become highly conscious and willful. One might conveniently characterize "Don Jose" as the intuitive piece, and "Teller" as the conscious and analytic one.

Sorcerer—the graphic novel itself—had already become a sort of condensed symbolic narrative for me even before I put a proposal package together, so what I discuss below is how "Don Jose" and "Teller" both took on the qualities of summarizing symbols during two very different phases of the collaborative process. The two paintings represent what was an unpredictable convergence of the unconscious and conscious intentions of Dringenberg and myself, and the result is highly overdetermined images that retain a strong resonance, even for the viewer/reader who only responds to a few aspects of their symbolic content.

"The Way of the Sorcerer"

The Way of the Sorcerer was sparked by the single image of a panel (figure 11.1) taken out of context from a black-and-white comic strip by Joel McCrea, an artist who worked at a pie shop in Davis, California, in the late 1980s. The image resonated with me, because it reminded me of plant fiber, like strands of hemp, woven into rope. The style also recalled for me the strangely rendered transparent and multilayered anatomies of Hans Bellmer, who performed a sort of visual Freudian commentary on sexuality by overlapping male and female bodies or various organs and appendages.

At the time I originally conceived *Sorcerer*, El Salvador was a prominent topic in campus leftist politics and was much on my mind. So were the issues of Vietnam and Nazi Germany, since I happened to be thinking of my father's military history in the process of rewriting an autobiographical novel as I pursued graduate studies in anthropology. In my

◆ **FIGURE 11.1** ◆

The cover idea for the original proposal. This shows Teller in his transformed
state, after he has been moldering in the tree at the center of the Circular Ruins.
Plants have taken root in his flesh, and he has a permanent spot on his forehead
through which his kundalini shines like a light.

teaching of creative writing and later in running anthropology discussion
sections, I also made use of a range of texts that eventually became the
subtexts for *Sorcerer*: Joan Didion's *Salvador*, the El Salvador poems in
Carolyn Forche's *The Country Between Us*, Carlos Castaneda's descriptions of dream practice in his series of pseudo-ethnographic books, and
Douglass Truth's *The House of the Magician*. All of the subtexts addressed
Central or South America from some point of view, and they constituted a
sort of supersaturated solution for which Joel McCrea's image served as a
seed crystal.

The narrative that ensued was initially described, in the proposal package, as follows (I quote at length to show some of the ideas that eventually
influenced Dringenberg's illustrations):

Introduction

[*Sorcerer*] is a hybrid work drawing on the conventions of numerous genres including science fiction, horror, and magical realism; it is tempered
and contrasted by representations of the stark realism of politics in a
volatile [fictional] Latin American country. The mood and atmosphere
of the story range from the mundane to the hallucinatory.

The main character, Karl Teller, is a man who prides himself for his
rationality despite an almost religious obsession with torture. When he
confronts an ancient Indian sorcerer, who then becomes his mentor, he

begins a circular journey that takes him through the border worlds into the *tierra del ensueno* and back again into a transformed reality. In some ways the story is Karl Teller's confrontation with his own *Heart of Darkness*, his quest to redeem himself for all his terrible sins.

Synopsis

A transport plane lumbers down onto the runway of the Montenegro Aeropuerto Nacional. Onboard is a U.S. Army colonel, Karl Teller, nicknamed "The Sorcerer" for his uncanny abilities as an interrogator.

Like the periodically active volcano that gives the country its name, the political situation in Montenegro is on the verge of a violent eruption. Peasant guerrillas have been fighting the "democratic" military dictatorship for a long time, but now that the government has lost two key figures to international drug busts, things have become difficult for El Presidente. He needs to find a quick way to quash the rebels and their elusive new leader, Manito Mendez. The United States has sent him Karl Teller, an elite "technical advisor," in answer to his request for special assistance. In Montenegro, Teller will work closely with the local strongmen to interrogate prisoners who might have information on the identity and whereabouts of Manito Mendez; he does his job with a perverse pleasure and a fanatical zeal.

Teller believes he can liberate the souls of his victims by making them experience "transcendent pain," a sensation that serves to purify as much as pleasure can corrupt. Teller believes that when indulging in physical pleasure, people ignore their spiritual needs, and so his philosophy is that by causing the body excruciating and constant pain, he can force his victims to retreat to the only place that remains for them— their souls. As one might predict, those who suffer Teller's form of spiritual salvation usually end up dead.

Teller's mission is untenable. As he tortures prisoners he turns up information that always leads to some peculiar dead end, suggesting he has just lost Mendez once again. Finally, the death squad brings in an ancient farmer named Don Jose, who gives Teller a strange feeling. Not only is he vaguely familiar, but there is an almost palpable sense that this man possesses true knowledge. If anyone knows the whereabouts of Manito Mendez, it is Don Jose.

The questioning begins and Teller is disgusted because the old man doesn't make even a token attempt at resistance. He weeps from the pain, he grovels, and he speaks all-too-freely. He is the first to tell the truth: Manito Mendez is an illusion. Of course, no one believes him, and in his contempt for the old man and his weakness Teller kills him most brutally. They throw the old man's body out in the infamous "dump" and he is quickly forgotten. One of the death-squad goons mentions that Don Jose was rumored to have been a sorcerer. Everyone laughs.

A few days later, while Teller is in his office, he is visited by a familiar obsequious old man. It seems that Don Jose has come back to life. At first Teller is incredulous—after all, he does not believe in ghosts. But the uncanny resemblance gives him pause, and he goes after the old man, only to see him vanish. Teller writes off this odd incident as a product of his overworked state, but strange things continue to happen. He begins to experience unexplainable dreams and synchronicities, and all of the memories of his past seem to come rushing back at him, as if his life were trying to flash before him in preparation for death.

When Don Jose, who is, indeed, a sorcerer, finally comes for Teller, he finds him in a state of confusion and paranoia. Don Jose snatches him out of this world and sends him on a quest into the jungle to find the ancient Mayan circular ruins, to dream himself a new body and a new life.

Because of his long and intense fixation on the nonexistent man, Karl Teller has imagined the mythical rebel leader more profoundly than anyone else. Through his dreaming in the circular ruins and his sojourn among a group of natives, Karl Teller the torturer unwittingly *becomes* Manito Mendez, the rebel leader he has been seeking.

Along with the above text, I sent a copy of my own thumbnail pages and production notes (figure 11.2) to Dringenberg for his use in coming up

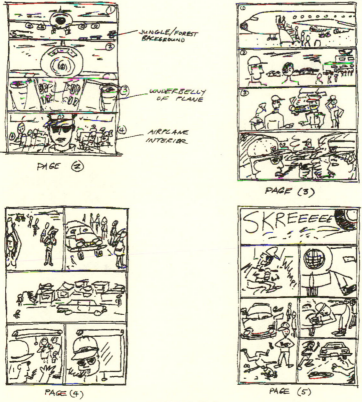

◆ **FIGURE 11.2** ◆

Fenkl's thumbnail sketches for the opening pages of *The Way of the Sorcerer*. These show the plane landing, Teller meeting the local strongman, and the drive to through a shantytown that ends in an accident.

with a concept piece for the proposal package (these same pages were later sent to the editor to give an idea of the sequential art before Dringenberg began his illustrations). The finished pages of art that Mike returned corresponded only generally with my own notes and thumbnails (which I had done in case I was working with a literal-minded artist). Dringenberg's realistic watercolor paintings would entirely change my approach to *Sorcerer*. The finished pages (shown in gray scale in figure 11.3) were done after the concept piece "Don Jose"—after we had begun our explicit discussions of symbolism and iconography—but I have provided them to show how they correspond to the thumbnails upon which they were based.

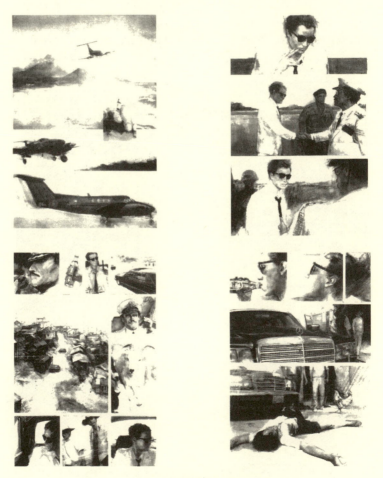

◆ **FIGURE 11.3** ◆

Dringenberg's finished artwork corresponding to Fenkl's thumbnails. Note the cinematic quality of the panel arrangements and the dramatic changes in the composition.

◆ **FIGURE 11.4** ◆

"Don Jose"—Dringenberg's concept painting for the proposal package.

THE CONCEPT PAINTING ("DON JOSE")

Since Don Jose is one of the central characters in the story, Dringenberg made him the central image in the concept painting (figure 11.4), using the bright halo-like glow in his shock of white hair as a focal point in the composition. The Catholic priest to his left is intended to be a reflection of Don Jose, but not in the literal sense; he is meant to "mirror" the pre-Christian shamanic tradition, and both his stature and expression suggest the simultaneous presence and tentativeness of Christianity in the deep consciousness of the local culture. The birds were merely a decorative element at first, designed to fill up dead space, but in later conversations Dringenberg began to reflect on the archaeology of religious tradition in Mesoamerica—Catholicism built over the Mayan sun-worshipping religion built over older shamanic and anamist cultures. He noted the strange syncretism in the region and suggested that perhaps Don Jose was like a St. Michael blended with a native deity, a sort of degenerate Hermes.

Comments from Dringenberg

The trees in the background are just tropical trees to provide a backdrop appropriate for the setting. The two figures are standing behind the peasants partially for compositional reasons, but also because the two reli-

gious traditions are in the background of the peasant culture. The bird
wing and the chicken, again, are a reflection of the native tradition. The
chicken is just a chicken—a source of food. But it's also used in ritual,
and here I associated it with some sort of almost angelic ritual. Don Jose
is the spiritual center of the story. He's the spirit guide that leads to Teller's enlightenment. The priest is standing to one side, so there's room on
the other side for another wing.

Lots of smoke. Shamans use tobacco smoke of different kinds for
ritual cleansing. The figures on Don Jose's chest are from Australian Aboriginal sources because I personally find them more primal and more
easily keyed into archetypes, so I figured that they would be less obscure
than South American and African motifs and easier for a general reader.
There's also a great deal of sky imagery—wind, spirals, birds, etc.—an
unconscious statement of rising above, achieving the sky. There's both a
suggestion of a desire to rise and the presence of means by which to do
so. You could read Don Jose's hair like a crest on a rooster, a sort of
Jungian commentary.

In the opening sequence, there's a volcano below the plane that sym-
bolizes the land merging with the sky, another reflection of the theme of
spiritual enlightenment.

Since the concept painting, at first glance, seemed only peripherally
linked to the story, my response was to read it carefully. It was clearly resonant and compelling, but in a way that I had not anticipated or meant to
deal with. What it offered was the symbolic product of Dringenberg's personal response to *The Way of the Sorcerer*, and though the elements in the
painting didn't immediately make sense as an *illustration* of the story, I
could see how they formed another layer of associations I could then
respond to myself, and then work back into the text of the story. Adding
the specific images in the concept painting to my own accumulated
imagery, I could more clearly see how I had to deal with the central
themes in the text.

In a good comic book, the text and visual images are resonant, not
redundant. Although the words might actually reiterate the visual imagery
at times, they do so to amplify and not to compete. Likewise, the visual
images do not simply illustrate the text (although there is a certain pressure for the artist to do so in the production process).

Since the concept piece did not come from one of my thumbnail
sketches, I read it carefully to come up with what might have been Dringenberg's implicit textual thumbnail. I read it as if it were the visual text
of a dream that Dringenberg had had in response to the proposal package
for *Sorcerer*.

MY READING OF DRINGENBERG'S CONCEPT PAINTING

There are three major pairings in the painting: the chicken and the
wing, the two peasants, and the contrasting figures of Don Jose and the
cardinal. The most striking thing about the painting is the use of white,

which ends up highlighting the peasants and Don Jose, particularly his head (which has a sort of misty quality to it, as if he were in the process of dematerializing or materializing out of some spiritual light substance). The darkest figure in the painting is the cardinal.

I couldn't help but read thematic meanings into the composition. The cardinal, sort of lurking in the dark background, has a vague guilty cast to him. Though he should also be bathed in light, the rhetoric in the painting is that the Catholic religion is dark compared to the shamanic tradition represented by Don Jose's light figure. Don Jose is more appropriately associated with the peasants, whose white outfits reflect the bright tropical light in the same way that Don Jose's head seems to project light. Dringenberg is siding with the peasants and Don Jose, problematizing the role of Catholicism, which is the latecomer tradition responsible for the decimation of the indigenous culture.

Don Jose ends up by having an odd angelic quality to him (i.e., he is a figure bathed in light), but in an ironic gesture, Dringenberg gives us half of a wing, a rather dark one, simultaneously providing and dismembering the angelic symbol. (This reminded me of Marquez's short story, "A Very Old Man with Enormous Wings.") The chicken in the foreground provides another layer of ironic commentary—it's the mundane and worldly bird figure whose stature is parallel to that of the other bird figure, the cardinal. But whereas the cardinal is a parasite on the culture, or an oppressive force cowering behind Don Jose, the chicken is a nurturing source of food. That Don Jose is associated with one wing also suggests that there is something incomplete about him, and that points to the missing character, Teller, who arrives in the country on an airplane that comes down through the clouds with the volcanoes in view. (There is also another ironic layer in the painting, because the dark mass of the cardinal can be linked, behind the figure of Don Jose, with the dark mass of the single wing, making him also one-winged and serpent-like.)

All the bird imagery in the concept painting made me consider the bird in its many symbolic roles in Mesoamerica. This was one of the reasons I included a quetzal bird in one of the key scenes in the story. The quetzal bird represents the god Quetzelquatl, the feathered serpent, and serves to symbolically link the reptile imagery I had already incorporated in the story with the theme of transformation and enlightenment. The feathered serpent is a Christ figure, but he is also associated with the coming of a white man (Teller). In evolutionary terms, it would be the transitional animal in the evolution of reptiles into birds (the damned into the saved, in Christian terms). It also completed the underlying caduceus imagery I had in mind, which required a reptile wrapped around a tree, and then wings emerging from the top of the tree. (This would be the shamnic process as one of both spiritual and physical healing.)

In any case, reading Dringenberg's painting made conscious for me many of the things I had been dealing with intuitively, particularly when it came to meaningful iconography and symbols in the story. It revealed to me the parameters of the symbolic palette I was drawing on for *Sorcerer*, and it allowed me to make that palette more economical and focused.

Of course, both Dringenberg and I realized that all of this deep reading and encoding of symbols in the art would not cause the readers of *Sorcerer* to begin deconstructing our work the way we did ourselves. What we were hoping to achieve was simply to charge the work with a high level of resonance and a recursive vocabulary so that if a reader, at some point in the story, suddenly saw some of the symbology at work, he or she would suddenly appreciate the story at another level of sophistication. (Much as the reader of Hemingway's "Hills Like White Elephants," who suddenly sees the symbolic charge of what at first appeared to be mundane details once he or she realizes that the story is about the possibility of an abortion.) To this end (though we did not discuss it in these terms), what we wanted was to overdetermine the symbolic language of the story both in the text and in the visuals.

At an early point in the collaboration, because I both trusted his ability to illustrate and his tendency to intuitively anticipate my own visual imagery with uncanny accuracy, I simply provided Dringenberg with a screenplay-style script without accompanying thumbnails or elaborate descriptions of the panel art.

THE COVER (TELLER)

Once we had completed a significant part of the graphic novel, the editor asked Dringenberg to do a cover piece for the first issue. He chose to refer to a scene called "In the Circular Ruins."

In the Circular Ruins

Teller is in the ceiba tree at the center of the Circular Ruins, the gateway to *tierra del ensueño*. He has been there for a long time, and his body has already turned into a fibrous thing that looks like coils of rope. Plants have taken root in his flesh, and he has a permanent spot on his forehead through which his Kundalini shines like a light. The gigantic python and the beautiful, green-plumed quetzal bird keep him company.

Teller is un-dreaming his identity, dreaming himself anew. Don Jose had instructed him to center his attention on the one thing that occupied him most intensely, and now, in this strange state, what guides his transformation is his hatred of Manito Mendez. He remembers scenes from his childhood. More of his father, his mother, Auchwitz, the trials at Nuremburg, moving to America, the academy, the army, Saigon. These are final flashbacks that exhaust his memories of life as Karl Teller. After each memory flashes it is gone forever, burnt permanently out of the consciousness that was Teller. And now the new dreams pervade the space left by the memories—hallucinations, visions, fantasies, hopes. Because the one thing that has preoccupied Teller most intensely during the past months is Manito Mendez, that becomes the focal point of his dreaming. Under the plant fiber, from the bleached and hairless flesh of the man

SETTING SUN

RIVER

LEAF

CROW

BODY MOSSY

FOLIAGE IN B/G.

◆ **FIGURE 11.5** ◆

Fenkl's thumbnail sketch for "In the Circular Ruins." This is the primary model for Dringenberg's cover painting, "Teller."

who was Karl Teller, the mythical Manito Mendez slowly comes into being.

Dringenberg also referred back to some of my initial thumbnails and accompanying notes, but based his painting mostly on a combination of motifs from the initial "In the Shadow of the Sorcerer" piece (figure 11.1) and my central thumbnail sketch for "In the Circular Ruins" (figure 11.5).

Comments from Dringenberg

The cover is a much more elaborate painting, and the elaborations are more deliberate, less automatic [than in "Don Jose"]. I actually displayed the entire underworld as what it is—the roots of the tree as Xibalba, going through the nine levels of the Mayan underworld from the lowest to highest, until the tree breaks through the ground to the surface world and then reaches up to the sky. I also created an allegorical wedding of male and female principles. The dividing stripe is a representation of the boat of death [the figures with their hands on their foreheads are the dead]. It's like the boat on Styx, but in the Mayan underworld, the realm of death is clear water.

I was thinking of the male and female creative principles that weave through the different characters and plot lines of *Sorcerer*, and I started thinking of different aspects of the story. Teller represents a man with a weak personality who gradually becomes stronger through Don Jose's intervention. One way is by being wrapped in the tree—a phallic womb symbol; it's upright, but it's also feminine and of the earth. The fact that the tree stretches into the sky and has a crown of green leaves [in the same] way [that] Don Jose has a crown of light poses Teller as Don Jose's spiritual son. The snake also illustrates the similarity between rivers and serpents. It represents knowledge of the underworld, it's a symbol of the

◆ **FIGURE 11.6** ◆

"Teller"—top detail of Dringenberg's cover painting for what was to be the first issue of *The Way of the Sorcerer*. Note how he has been selective in his adaptation of motifs from the thumbnail sketch and has devoted more attention to showing the layered cosmological ideas suggested in the story.

labyrinth, it's associated [with] the intestines and the lower regions of consciousness. So for me, the snake in the tree was like the path between the earth and the labyrinth.

The composition reminded me later of the fact that Xibalba [the Mayan underworld] is said to have a mouth. There's actually a large cave—I think it's near the ruins of Uxmal—that's womb-like, but inside it there's a large hole through which a tree was growing out of the cave and out into the air of the upper world. That's the literal symbol I link the illustration to at the moment, a symbol of ascending from the lower to the upper world. (See figure 11.6.)

Since I prefaced Dringenberg's commentary with my own initial sketches and notes, it is not necessary for me to present my reading (especially since my reading of the painting did not change my ideas for the story in the way that "Don Jose" did when I received it as the concept piece). But "Teller" has an entirely different kind of visual force than "Don Jose." Both paintings create a visceral resonance, but "Teller" is far more powerful. In the end, both Dringenberg and I attribute the symbolic power of "Teller" to the fact that it represents a much more fully conscious application of symbolic rhetoric. Here, the collaborative process seems to mesh rather seamlessly, although the painting is ultimately the product of a great deal of explicit and implicit dialogue between artist and writer. Dringenberg's impulse to use more accessible symbolic allusions (ranging from the Garden of Eden to the shamanic cosmic tree) is here more pronounced than in the concept painting in which he used an Australian Aboriginal motif in one case, but composed much of the rest of the painting rather idiosyncratically. Of course, the format of "Teller" also contributes to its visual power, paralleling its underlying rhetoric of ascension and the joining of worlds with its vertical composition, but our reading is that much of the power is due to the fact that the reader/viewer, being more familiar with the symbolic allusions, has the chance to be more attentive at a deeper level. At the same time, the allusions are not so overt as to be visual clichés (which would cause the reader/viewer to become less attentive).

"Don Jose" and "Teller" are, on the one hand, products of an entirely different set of collaborative parameters, and yet they also retain enough similarity to be recognizable as images from the same work. What makes them particularly interesting for both of us is that the sequence of their creation and the method underlying their formulation and composition end up paralleling the theme of *Sorcerer*. At one point in our exchanges I found it especially gratifying that Dringenberg would identify so strongly with Teller as to go through a transformation in his art parallel to Teller's "enlightenment" in the story. I wanted to take credit for this process, since I was the writer of *Sorcerer*, but it became clear to me that in writing the final script of *Sorcerer* (the text that would have been printed over the artwork), I had also been profoundly influenced by Dringenberg's art. In fact, at some deep level, I found it tragic that his work would have to be marred by caption boxes and word balloons.

Conclusion: The Fate of "Sorcerer"

When the imprint planning to publish *Sorcerer* was cancelled, Dringenberg and I were left with few options, because of the dismal status of "painted" projects in the world of comics at the time. When the art was lost, our options diminished even further, but we were moved by an involuntary need to innovate. Our first thoughts were to take the color photo-copies we had on hand and scan them to produce an online comic book. That option became less and less attractive to me when I saw that the time it took to view a particular page—even on the fastest browsers—entirely destroyed the interaction of text and image that comics were designed to rely upon for effect. Having fully formatted and lettered pages might work with *Sorcerer* on CD, but not on the Internet. We eventually rejected the idea and moved on to a more viable medium—hypertext.

Our plan was to scan the work panel-by-panel and then rework the entire story in a way that would take advantage of the interplay of structure and meaning in a hypertext. We had not decided whether we wanted a sim-ply-organized hypertext that merely strung together a series of text/ image pages into a linear narrative (except in the shamanic and hallucinatory sec-tions of the story), or whether we wanted to take full advantage of the uncertainty principle of hypertexts to create an explicitly nonlinear multi-media narrative with a range of multiple readings. Ironically, while we were still considering our options, the technology of the Internet and the mem-ory and processing speed of the average computer advanced by a quantum leap, and now the initial liabilities I had seen in the online comicbook for-mat are not as much of an issue. We are now formatting *Sorcerer* to be read in a more-or-less linear fashion, panel-by-panel with text (and background sound), taking advantage of the rudimentary cinematic effects (e.g., fades, panning, zooming) provided by Flash animation. We see this form of *Sor-cerer* as an intermediate step toward a nonlinear hypertext, which we still plan to produce; and given the speed at which Internet technology devel-ops, we will probably be able to do this hypertext entirely online. (Exam-ples of works in this form can be found on the SciFi Channel web site: <http://www.scifi.com>. Click on "SciOriginals" under the heading for On-line Series. The direct link is: <http://www.scifi.com/scioriginals/>.)

In a way that parallels Teller's journey in *Sorcerer*, the project itself has died in its intended form; it has been forcefully shifted, by circumstances beyond the creators' control, into a more ethereal medium. What Dringen-berg and I have discussed regarding the composition of the two paintings now serves as the new and unanticipated starting point for the evolution of *Sorcerer* into its next incarnation as multimedia hypertext. Perhaps it is better, in the end, that *Sorcerer* never became the comic book it was intended to be.

Appendix

The following list is a sampling of graphic novels that represent the "high culture" of American comics in the past fifteen years. Most of these works incorporate watercolor, oil, acrylic, or mixed media. Visually, they are immediately distinct from the typical comic book.

DeMatteis, J. M., and Jon J. Muth. (1985). *Moonshadow*. New York: Marvel, Epic.

DeMatteis, J. M., and Kent Williams. (1987). *Blood*. New York: Marvel Comics.

Gaiman, Neil, and Dave McKean. (1990). *Black Orchid*. New York: D.C. Comics.

McCloud, Scott. (1992). *Understanding Comics*. Northampton, MA: Tundra Publishing.

McKean, Dave. (1992). *Cages*. Northampton, MA: Tundra Publishing.

Miller, Frank, and Bill Sienkiewicz. (1986). *Elektra: Assassin*. New York: Marvel Comics.

Morrison, Grant, and Dave McKean. (1989). *Batman: Arkham Asylum*. New York: D.C. Comics.

Morrison, Grant, and J. Muth. (1994). *The Mystery Play*. New York: D.C. Comics.

Pratt, George. (1990). *Enemy Ace: Wary Idyll*. New York: D.C. Comics.

Rieber, John Ney, and Kent Williams. (1992). *Tell Me Dark*. New York: D.C. Comics.

Sienkiewicz, Bill. (1988). *Stray Toasters*. New York: Marvel Comics.

PART THREE

visual and verbal features
in digital spaces: new visions
for transformed contexts

Words and images interconnect all around us, sometimes working together in mutual support and sometimes colliding. Electronic communication has only made their relationships more prominent and our need to understand them imperative as reader/viewers participate more overtly in the meaning-making, even in the text-building, processes. Yet the corporate and professional worlds struggle with the ways in which words and images should interact, and how those interactions and the employees who handle them should be managed. Similarly, the teachers of future professionals strain to find good ways to prepare their students to enter the professional world. The discussions in part 3 concern issues that arise when we work in or read/view works presented in electronic media. The topics range from guidelines to effective design to literary efforts and corporate presentations; the authors speak from their professional experience with current multimedia tools and with training others to use words and images.

Working in multimedia opens doorways. Writers can add dimensions to documents to enhance their appeal and usability in various ways. But as opportunities usually do, these also present challenges. There are many kinds of electronic spaces, and writer/designers need to know how these spaces compare to one another and to paper spaces for the tasks and purposes they want to achieve. If the choice of medium isn't controlled by use limitations, writer/designers may need to determine which medium—say, CD-ROM or the Web—is more appropriate to their topic and purpose. They also need to know how their materials should be presented differently if they adapt, for example, a CD-ROM document to the Web. No one wants to end up with "shovel ware," a document that seems to have been shoveled from one medium to another without the reconsiderations necessary to adapt it appropriately.

As George Landow (1991) said and Ron Fortune reminded us: "Hypermedia, which changes the way texts exist and the way we read them, requires a new rhetoric and a new stylistics" (1991, 81). This theoretical stance translates into a host of skills. Today's electronic document writer/designers need to know what constitutes good design in terms of both aesthetics and effectiveness. And, of course, all of this must be done within the constraints of time, money, and technological capability. In chapter 12, "The Digital Design Revolution," Jonathan Allen, president and head author for Shuffleware Media Co., and Greg Simmons, graphic artist and Web designer at Whitlock Business Systems, draw on their experiences as professional writer/designers to provide guidance on issues that arise while working in multimedia. They compare designing for print and digital media in terms of image quality and color, interactivity, usability, and maintenance, creating examples to illustrate the rationale that guides decisions as they work.

As we use resources on the Web, we recognize that some Web sites are helpful, some are visually pleasing, some are easy to use, and some are none of these. When we browse a Web site, its design makes a visual impression on us that pleases and leads us on, or discourages and sends us clicking off to another possibility. There are more subtle issues, however, that work on us just as surely, though perhaps without our conscious knowledge. These include both aesthetic and ethical issues that we need to understand in order to know how they are influencing the meaning we derive from a site's content. Amy Kimme Hea, who teaches business and technical communication at the University of Arizona, explores just such issues in chapter 13, "Articulating (Re)Visions of the Web: Exploring Links among Corporate and Academic Web Sites." Kimme Hea uses the images, text samples, and links of one corporate Web site to make visible to us the ways in which Web sites inform and are informed by a reader/viewer's particular lens. She shows us how interpretive strategies can be situated differently for different users and describes the political implications and ramifications that may result.

Computers as a medium for texts have changed not only what we read and where we read it, but also how we read. For example, one way that we now often find ourselves reading is with others in a group at a presentation. When we need to make a presentation—to a professional organization, community group, club, or corporate audience—we have various options to consider for making our points clear and memorable. Many conference presenters rely on overheads or slides that show their major points. In this way, the presentation gives the audience visual as well aural input on the main points, and it provides the speaker with an outline to guide the talk. Others strongly object to this sort of duplication as, at best, a waste of time, and, worse, an insult. PowerPoint, a presentation tool from MicroSoft, is the option that is becoming standard for presentations to a group within corporate settings. It operates somewhat like an outline, with images and color to attract our attention. It also involves audience members in a group activity as they read together, whether they are a group of two or two thousand. Consequently, with PowerPoint presentations, we should consider issues of group activity and development, the constraints and influences of technology on the presentation, and the role and skills required of the speaker in this multimodal setting. In chapter 14, "Reading PowerPoint," Rich Gold, leader of the Research in Experimental Documents group at the Xerox Palo Alto Research Center, invites us to attend his lecture as he explores the software's features and the ways in which PowerPoint slides have become items of "folk art" within corporate culture. He also focuses particularly on issues of group reading, relationships between projected text, projected graphics, the spoken word, and the aesthetics of computerized presentations.

Neil Kleinman, dean of the College of Media and Communication at the University of the Arts in Philadelphia, concludes part three by summarizing many of the issues faced by professionals who work with words and images. To place these issues within context, Kleinman relates them to problems faced by the University of Baltimore faculty in developing curricula for the School of Communications Design, of which he was formerly co-director, and its doctoral program. In chapter 15, "Mixing Oil and Water: Writing, Design, and the New Technology," Kleinman begins by recounting a story of the confusion created when one of the program's graduates, who combined theory and skills for working with both text and graphics, arrived at his new professional position. The corporation was at a loss in deciding where to place a person with skills in both areas. Kleinman asks whether we, as a society, have moved much further, whether we can actually envision a postliterate culture in which knowledge and wisdom emerge from a love of reading, writing, and design that depends less on print and more on new media for expression and meaning. Are there places, he asks, where writing and design meet and work harmoniously? His answer—well, maybe, someday.

Reference

Landow, George P. (1991). The rhetoric of hypermedia: Some rules for authors. In *Hypermedia and Literary Studies*, ed. Paul Delaney and George P. Landow. Cambridge: Massachusetts Institute of Technology Press.

chapter twelve

THE DIGITAL DESIGN
REVOLUTION

jonathan allen and greg simmons

T HROUGHOUT HISTORY, COMMUNICATION has been shaped by the available technology. From the first shapes carved onto stone tablets to the development of digital media, the way we communicate has been profoundly influenced by the tools we use. The simple, angular glyphs carved into stone by ancient humans were dictated by the materials at hand. The nature of the message conveyed was also influenced by these factors, as the relative difficulty of carving in stone limited the recording of information to only the most important events. Once words and symbols could be recorded on paper, this much simpler, portable medium for communication was adopted, and the base of shared knowledge grew. Further radical change in communication came in the 1450s with the invention of movable type. This cheap uniform printing tool not only changed the way people communicated, it helped alter the very structure of Western civilization.

The end of the twentieth century witnessed yet another revolution in communication. The creation of media intended specifically for the digital realm, namely CD/DVD-ROM and Web sites, has all but overturned the legacy of the printed page. When asked about the impact of the computer on design,

Leslie Becker, program chair for the California College of Arts and Crafts in San Francisco, states: "No, it's not a tool. It has fundamen-tally changed the way we do things, it's changed the way we think about things" (McCarron 2000, 33). This fundamental shift in the way designers work has created a whole new set of opportunities and problems for those who work with text and images. To understand the nature of these new challenges, it would be wise to first explore some of the issues that face designers in contemporary printed media. Doing this will provide some insight into the mind sets and predispositions of both professional and student designers working within the digital arena.

The impact of a technology upon communication is best understood by examining the limitations the technology places on those using it. Despite operating under the same basic principles for hundreds of years, the print industry has undergone many transformations due to changing technology, and each time, old limitations have disappeared only to be replaced by new ones. At each transformation, however, the limitations imposed by the technology have lessened, allowing more practical and conceptual freedom for the designer. The current state of printing technology allows unprecedented choices; there are thousands of typefaces for the computer, thousands of photographic and illustration resources, and, with the advent of digital printing presses, full-color printing available to customers of modest means, all due to the relative ease and speed of production afforded by a digital press. Despite a few inevitable problems, the environment that greets the print designer is an almost boundless frontier of possibilities.

The blank page is a perfect object, an unspoiled landscape for potential combinations of words and images. Even the proportions used for page sizes and shapes, now mimicking those proportions commonly found in nature, have been honed over hundreds of years by trained eyes. Ironically, it is the job of print designers to spoil this state of perfection, forcing structure and content into the page to suit the requirements of the project. It is often useful to think of the printed product as a container, able to hold a finite amount of text and pictures. Moreover, once filled (i.e., carved, printed, etc.), this container cannot be emptied and refilled. A good designer must be willing to let the fixed container dictate the proper relationships of words and images. This characteristic is an underlying principle of page layout and speaks to every decision the designer makes—and, not insignificantly in modern design, to every decision the customer makes. Fortunately for the print designer, these difficult tasks are not made harder by the technology with which printing is produced.

The design and production of printed media are based upon time-tested principles and have their foundations in generations of practical experience. Most of the early tools for designing in the digital media, however, have come not out of the crucible of the designer's experience, but from the relatively pragmatic sensibilities of software programmers. Not surprisingly, many current Web sites and CD-ROM titles are quite poor from a design standpoint. This is partially due to the lack of adequate tools to create well-designed digital pieces, and partially due to a lack of established standards. There is a recent, increasing awareness of the need for well-designed digital media, accompanied by a growing group of digital designers with a solid background in design. Despite this, there is still no consensus about what constitutes good Web site and CD-ROM design. This is the challenge for the next generation of designers.

Designing Digital Media

Digital technology has had a revolutionary effect on communication. The changes can be seen in both the projects themselves as well as the way in which they are designed. One of the most commonly seen effects of digital technology on publishing is the use of multimedia. Projects combine the advantages of several different media types to achieve a more profound result. Take, for example, a book describing how to change a tire on a car. When using just text, the author may spend several pages describing how to replace the lug nuts in a star pattern, whereas a simple animation with appropriate effects zooming into areas of focus can show this concept with a much higher degree of correctness in just a few seconds. Multimedia has greatly increased the number of possibilities open to designers, giving them much more control over how they make their points.

Multimedia is often regarded as new and is associated with high technology. However, we, as users, have been experiencing multimedia for years as movies and television shows. The difference that the new technology brings is that these advantages are now available to a much broader range of developers. The power and affordability of the equipment necessary to produce high-quality multimedia has become available to anyone who has an idea and the desire to make it happen.

More importantly, however, digital publication has brought a new type of media to the table. Designers can now allow the user to interact with the project. This new mode of expression has proven very powerful for the effectiveness of communication, and is currently unique to those in the digital realm. The user has the ability to control what material is being communicated to them and at what speed. This increases their level of comfort with the project, and therefore the effectiveness of the experience and the chance of a return trip. However, designing interactivity effectively is not necessarily a simple thing.

Just as with any other style of communication, the designer of an interactive project is trying to convey some message to the user. Giving users complete control over what they are viewing would most often destroy the original intent of the project. Therefore, interactivity must be designed into the project in such a way that users gain the benefits from the comfort of control, but are only given the choices that the designer wants them to have. This concept can be thought of as similar to a stroll through the woods. The user is given complete control to choose which path they follow; however, the designer must carefully plan where the paths will lead and which forks will be available at which points along the trail.

Even though designing digital media shares many issues with designing printed media, there are some significant differences. The most important variable between them is that not all digital media are created equal. This phenomenon stems from the fact that digital media must be viewed on some sort of computer, other than the one upon which it was designed. The effects of technology on design discussed thus far have stressed the technology at the disposal of designers as they build projects. With digital media, however, the designers not only have to deal with the limits due to their own technology, but also those of the technology available to the end-user of the project. Differences from one computer to the next in drive speed, processor speed, display size, and color depth as well as many other hardware and software features make for a giant guessing game at the planning stages of digital media.

Data throughput, the speed with which information is moved from the storage area to the computer monitor, is such an influential problem involving digital design that it alone has caused a separation in this new field. Some designers feel that they need the highest-quality media to express their ideas. To this end, the final product exists on some local container, such as a CD-ROM or a hard disk drive, within the computer so that the highest possible rate of data throughput can be achieved. Other designers, however, are more interested with the volatile nature of digital media and prefer to take advantage of instantaneous upgrades of information available through the Internet. Still others attempt to achieve the best of both worlds by calling-up files to a local disk from their Web sites. It is this throughput concern that must first be addressed to determine which type of project will be made. Once the design team knows whether they are producing for a static program or the internet, then they can begin to specialize their project.

The end-user's computer display is another important aspect to take into account when planning a digital project, as this is the definitive interface through which the user will see the message. There are several features related to the display that must be taken into account during the planning stages. The most important of these is color. Digital projects have a great advantage over printed material when dealing with color in that designers have access to any combination of colors and gradients imaginable. Since it does not cost any more to show a pixel as black and white or as color, designers do not have to worry about cost when adding color to a digital document. They do, however, have to set a cutoff limit for how many colors the project can have. Some displays can show so many colors that the human eye cannot differentiate among the small details, while others can only manage a few. Some operating systems prefer one color set over another, forcing the designer to choose one set or to make a hybrid set.

Color is a very valuable design tool that digital media are able to take advantage of. Consequently, within the last few years, we have seen a huge growth in the acceptability of high-color graphics for digital media. Even though some limits must be taken into account, they are becoming a concern of the past, and digital designers are increasingly able to reap the full benefits of dazzling color in their documents. As the speeds of computers and their visual hardware continue to increase, concerns about color may become obsolete. Even the slowest of computers will be able to handle the full spectrum.

Another limit, which is introduced by the fact that the project must be projected onto a screen, is the actual physical size of the display. When preparing a project for print, designers can decide to use whatever size paper they see fit for the final look, budgetary issues not being taken into account. This freedom is not available to the digital designer. In fact, often the size of the end-user's screen will be unknown. Therefore the digital designer must decide how to build size into the project. For some, this means that they must pick a size, put everything inside those boundaries, and leave the rest as blank space. For others, this may involve designing the layout so that it will look correct when conformed to fit whatever size the user chooses or is able to display.

This issue has actually been important enough that it has made a fundamental change in communication. In the past, the text has played the most important role in the overall message, while the images have been used as support for what was being conveyed. Therefore we see large blocks of text explaining several issues occupying most of a page or chapter, similar to the one you are reading now. With digital publication, these roles have been switched. The graphics are now the major source of information, with the text providing a supporting role. Typically, the rules of grammar are ignored, with text being presented as bulleted lists or phrases rather than in large blocks of text. Furthermore, the information to be communicated is separated much more finely. Each screen is designed to portray a single thought, rather than dealing with an entire chapter at a time. Many screens can be combined to form a full message, but each screen is given one main idea.

Local Media

The first type of digital publishing we will describe in detail is *locally stored media*, such as a project on a CD-ROM or DVD-ROM disk. For purposes of this discussion we will call this "local media" or "local digital media." Publishing in this manner is simply a natural progression of communication design. These types of projects are fundamentally the same as publishing printed materials, such as books or magazines, in the way that the project is conceived and delivered. What sets local digital media apart from the current standard is how technology directly affects the way that the designer communicates. As mentioned earlier, digital media have many advantages over printed media, such as in the use of multimedia and interactivity, but they also add some new concerns like screen size and image quality. When designers choose to produce their project as locally stored media, they are making some immediate decisions about these new criteria.

Locally stored digital media are simply the next step in the linear evolution of communication. Like its ancestors, a local media project is a physical, tangible item. Once the person or team has finished developing the product, it must be delivered as an entity to someone for them to use it. Similar to book or magazine publication, this process requires mass production, packaging, and delivering of the product to the end-users. Once users have their copies, they may do with them what they wish. Furthermore, once the project goes to print, it is a finished product. No more changes can be made without creating major problems and extra costs. Unlike a book or magazine, however, this product is merely a carrier for the media, and not the media itself. If you were to enter your favorite book store and purchase a copy of a book, you can open it up and read it there, or anywhere else that pleases you. It is a complete usable package unto itself, as long as you can read the language in which it is written. With a digital publication, the physical object that you carry with you is only the receptacle, similar to a video cassette. The user must have a piece of equipment in order to use what is inside.

When designing a project to be used from a local disk, the designer knows how the media will be delivered to the computer. For example, say you are designing a project on how to bake brownies, which is to be delivered on a CD-ROM. Immediately you know a few things and must make a few decisions. You know that your project will be stored on a standard CD-ROM. This means that you have 650MB available for the finished product. You must use this information to make a few decisions about quality versus compatibility. Not every user will have the same CD-ROM drive. Therefore you must plan according to your lowest common denominator. This limitation comes into play when deciding both platform dependence for the operating system as well as quality of the media.

First, you must decide if your project is going to be delivered to one operating system or to many. Similar to the decision of whether to publish a book in multiple languages, this decision regarding the operating system has a major effect on the size of your audience and consequently the complexity of the project. If you limit your project to one operating system, you need only to plan for one type of computer. This is much easier in the design and production phase, but becomes more difficult when trying to market the finished product. If you decide to produce your project for more than one system, you must take the limits of each one into account and build them into your project. Also, you may find that you need multiple copies of some files, or extra files for one system that would be useless on another. This can quickly take up space on your CD-ROM, where you know you have a space limit. However, you must let the nature of the project be a factor when making this decision. The need to bake brownies is rather universal among computer operators, so it would seem that you would want to construct this project for multiple systems, whereas if instead you were discussing how to install a hard drive on a particular computer, you may find your audience to be narrower. Once you have made this operating-system decision, you then need to take the limits of the computer itself into account.

Typically, the CD-ROM drive is the major bottleneck when delivering your project to the screen for the user. The processor, RAM, hard drive, and other factors can also be accountable, but usually you will find that these are all minor when compared to the speed of the CD-ROM drive. For example, you may think that digital video is the most effective way to show how to bake brownies. Naturally, you would like these movies to look as good as possible. However, the better the quality of the movie, the more space it takes up on the CD-ROM and the more data that needs to be taken from the disk to play the movie. If you use the best-quality video, you may find that your 650MB of space is filled while you still have your brownies in the oven. Or you may find that these movies are of such high quality that only a very high-speed drive can read them fast enough so that they will play smoothly. Conversely if you make the file size and data rate too small, you may find that the movies are illegible and useless for communication. You as the designer must decide a cutoff point so that you can maximize both your movie quality and the number of people who can effectively use the product. This decision must be made for every type of media used in the project, and for the project as a whole. You must combine the images, movie, sound, and any other media together when figuring your lowest common denominator. As mentioned before, there can be many factors that affect the output of your project. The only way to be certain that everything is working well is to test your project during development, as well as when it is finished, on as many different configurations of computers as you possibly can.

The Tangled Web

Designers have all the advantages of digital publishing available to them when producing local media projects. Furthermore, many experienced print publishers can step right into the design of local media, because many production basics are the same. Digital media provides the design world a major twist, however, when it comes to the Internet. At first glance, Web sites appear to be just another form of digital media. When it comes to designing and maintaining a site effectively, however, the rules have changed. As stated by Chris Edwards, vice president of design, Art Technology Group: "Today, a UI [user interface] designer has to be pretty far advanced in his knowledge because the challenges of interface design are complex. And likewise, Web designers have a whole set of issues they're dealing with that have no relation to print design" (Adams 2000).

While Web-site designers are still at the mercy of serious technological limitations, they are no longer constrained by many of the physical impediments that hamper the print designer. If the printed page can be thought of as a container, the Web site must then be thought of as a conduit. Rather than containing words and images in a fixed, permanent state, the Web site transmits words and images in a fluid, open way that can be altered again and again as the designer sees fit. As with any new method of doing things, this opens a frontier of possibilities and problems for the designer.

The primary effect of the fluid nature of Web sites is on the structure of those sites. The Web designer has no need to choose a fixed size for the pages of the site, and can fit as many or as few words and images into a page as is deemed necessary (figure 12.1). In fact, dictating the exact size and proportions of the individual elements of the site are practical impossibilities. The size of the screen on which the site is viewed can vary greatly, thus altering the flow of text and the placement of images. The effect of this uncertainty is that many site designers find any attempt to exert control over their site frustrating. Added to these structural ambiguities of Web design is the fact that certain choices by the designer such as colors of links and fonts to be used, can be overruled or misinterpreted by the preferences in the viewer's system. If Mr. Smith sets up his browser to always show links in bright red, it doesn't matter that you intended for the entire site to be in soft, pastel colors.

With diligence and foresight the designer can learn to exert a reasonable amount of control over the layout of the pages. These structural problems must not be thought of as inherent characteristics of Web sites, but rather as limitations of the current tools used to create them. Without doubt, as the tools improve, more control will be put into the hands of the designer. Some would frown upon the designer of Web sites having more control, saying that the beauty of the Internet is that each person sees things a little differently according to his or her own preference and equipment. This view is somewhat naive. Ultimately, the purpose of Web sites,

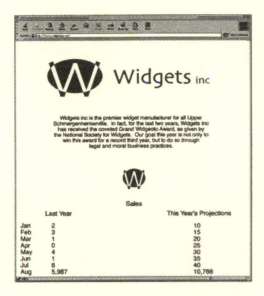
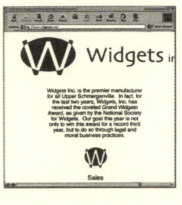

◆ **FIGURE 12.1** ◆

These two images show a typical Web page, with a large logo header, some introductory text, and some more in-depth information in tabular form. Depending upon how the page is scaled, large variations can occur to the structure and look of the page. For example, here a change in size results in reflowing of the text and cropping of the gif or jpeg logo and the table. Steps can be taken to mitigate this problem, but at present they are cumbersome.

like any form of design, is to convey a message and given the opportunity, designers will always gravitate toward tools that allow them tighter control over that message. In contrast with the print designer, who must let the fixed proportions of the page dictate the relationships and proportions of text and images, the Web site designer must be willing to force structure onto a variable, unfixed "page," and any technology that helps them to do this will be welcome.

The real power of Web-site words and images, regardless of any technical considerations that might dilute it, comes from color. Web designers enjoy almost total freedom in this respect and can include a graphic with a dozen colors as easily and for the same cost as a graphic with two, whereas the print designer pays a premium for each added color. Currently, the color aspect of Web graphics is hampered by the mode of transmission in use; with the limited transfer rates now available it is in the best interest of designers to use specialized palettes of a few choice colors to achieve the desired result. Using an image-editing software application such as Photoshop™ gives the diligent Web designer exacting control over the colors that end up in each image file. When skillfully handled, this can result in huge reductions in the memory size of the graphic file, with no obvious

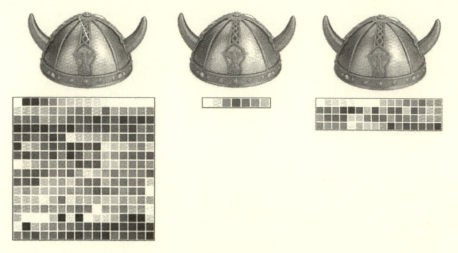

◆ **FIGURE 12.2** ◆

The helmet to the left was saved with an indexed 8-bit palette, meaning a total of 256 colors (or shades of gray) were designated for the image's pixels, some of which may be duplicates or near duplicates. This image looks good, but will take a long time to appear on a site due to its large file size. The middle helmet was saved with a 3-bit palette, which means that only eight shades were allowed to remain. The file's memory size is small, but the image is severely degraded. Finally a 6-bit palette was determined to give good image quality while keeping file size down.

decline in image quality (figure 12.2). This reduction of size lessens the time it takes for the image to load onto the page. In Web designer's terms, this concept is the lifeblood of an effective site. A site with many complex graphics will be seen by only the few patient enough to wait the several minutes it takes to load the pages. Again, this limitation is one created by the current technology and is not an inherent flaw in Web-site graphics. This issue will also disappear as better tools lift the restrictions on color.

The other problem associated with color freedom is the potential for anarchy. Without the proper use of color theory, a Web site can quickly become a chaos of hues. The total freedom of choice regarding imagery can be a major pitfall. Images can easily overpower words, and the temptation to overuse images in Web sites affects many designers. Added is the fact that images can be animated and that video with sound can be included; the potential for images to overwhelm the very message they are trying to convey becomes clear.

As if the unprecedented power of images on Web sites wasn't enough, the sad current state of Web typography makes the sins of print typography seem minor. Current methods of font usage require the same tolerance for ambiguity on the designer's part as do the tools for layout discussed earlier (figures 12.3–12.5). The designer can specify a font for the

> # "TYPOGRAPHY
> # IS GOOD STUFF"

◆ **FIGURE 12.3** ◆

This example shows a simple block of text set to be "centered" and using the default values for kerning (space between individual letters) and leading (space between lines of text). This is how this text would typically look in an HTML environment—somewhat cramped and seriously unbalanced, despite the centered setting.

> # " TYPOGRAPHY
> # IS GOOD STUFF "

◆ **FIGURE 12.4** ◆

This example shows the same size and style of type with some adjustment to the space between letters (kerning), and more space between lines (leading), to ease the cramped feel of the all-capital letters. Also, some hand-tweaking of the centering gives much more visual balance to the block. HTML treats all figures the same for the purposes of centering, not taking into account that components such as quotation marks carry much less visual weight and should be dealt with differently.

> # " TYPOGRAPHY
> # IS GOOD STUFF "

◆ **FIGURE 12.5** ◆

Finally, we see a very symmetrical block of text (not necessarily better looking than figure 12.4, just different). This look was achieved by further manipulating the kerning and width of letters. The manipulation must be done with a light touch, or it can come across looking just as clumsy and heavy-handed as in figure 12.3. These subtle typographical effects can be "faked" on Web sites by creating the text in a good text-editing program, and then turning it into an image for use in the site.

site to call up, but if the viewer doesn't have that font in his or her system, the designer can only specify more generic parameters to go by, such as the font Arial, which almost everyone has, or even more generally, a sans serif font. Other aspects of font usage such as kerning, indents, and leading, are not even dealt with in HTML, and can only be faked through cumbersome means. Even the fonts that were designed to meet the limited visual capabilities of contemporary monitors are affronts to true typography. Once again, however, we can see that these problems for Web-site words will be corrected by improved tools. This is not to say that the problem of text marginalization is not real; on the contrary, text is given diminished power and flexibility on the Web and will always face an uphill battle due to the power of imagery in this medium. Issues related to text are truly a problem inherent to web sites and must be dealt with by those who wish to create lasting, quality Web design.

The Internet has changed the character of our communication, but it does not have to change the quality of it if we are willing to listen to the lessons our traditional media have to teach. As the tools for making Web sites improve, we may be surprised to find that these sites look increasingly like the classic printed page, with well-planned use of color and blocks of well-set type that complement the images with which they share their space.

Looking to the Future

The visions of a good designer always reach beyond what he or she is capable of actually producing. It is this gap between the imagination and reality that pushes the development of new technology, finding ways to make those visions come to life. In only a few short years we will scarcely recognize the media that are now in their infancy. Most, if not all, of the inconveniences that current digital media carry with them will no longer exist. Of course, there will be new problems facing the next generation of digital designers, but the continuing process of technological growth will give us ever-more powerful and versatile tools for communication.

References

Adams, Eric J. (2000). Striking the perfect balance: Here's how four top creative managers juggle their challenges. 2000 Publish Media, LLC <http://www.publish.com>.

McCarron, Carolyn. (2000, March–April). School of thought. *Adobe Magazine* 11: 31–36.

chapter thirteen

ARTICULATING (RE)VISIONS OF THE WEB
exploring links among corporate and academic web sites

amy c. kimme hea

As Nancy Allen's introductory chapter to this volume suggests, images and words cannot be examined devoid of the medium in which they appear. The interpretive history of images and words chronicles the ways in which images have contested traditional textual media such as the academic essay, and words have challenged traditional visual media such as art. With the World Wide Web (WWW), the line between images and words blurs as text becomes graphical art and images become links integral to finding other nodes of the Web site. Jay Bolter and Richard Grusin (1999) argue that the WWW refashions almost all other media from print-based texts to television and video (p. 197). Hypertext theorists, too, have urged us to understand how hypertext refigures our literate practices (Bolter 1991; Johnson-Eilola 1993, 1994, 1997a; Joyce 1995; Moulthrop 1991; Moulthrop and Kaplan 1994; Selber 1997). Still other computer composition theorists have explored areas of images and words from the iconographic metaphors of the graphic user interface (GUI), word-processing software, and Web graphics to the textual interpretations of listservs and chatspaces (Hawisher and Sullivan 1999; Johnson-Eilola 1997b; Johnson-Eilola and Selber 1996; Romano 1993, 1999; Selfe and Selfe 1994; Takayoshi 1994, 1999). Many of these works attend not merely to the technical structures of these electronic media, but also to their ideological impact.

These critical engagements on media also present a way for us as educators and Web designers to consider our own Web pages. In his discussion of images and words and their meaning, Gunther Kress (1999) emphasizes the designer's role as "meaning" maker and thus his or her responsibility in shaping our social and cultural environment (p. 87). In other words, rather than exclusively focusing on design elements or users as separate from ideological concerns, to be socially responsible designers we must explore contextualized versions of our pages and thus produce Web documents that are not only functionally sound but also ideologically aware. In my own discussion, I seek to connect the ideological implications of images and words and their position in relationship to other aspects of the Web medium in order to understand the roles of Web designers and users.

To begin questioning the demands presented by the discourses on Web technology and the medium itself, I will focus my exploration on one of these constituencies—the corporation. By interrogating corporatization as a set of operations, we as educators and Web designers can better determine how corporate constructions affect and inform our teaching of and authoring on the Web. Here, I am using "corporatization" to mean the possible effects of corporate Web-design practices and standards on other areas of Web design, including academic Web pages, home pages, or other Web sites.

In this chapter, I will first posit articulation as a methodology for interrogating the discourses of and on the Web. Then, through an articulation of Union Pacific Corporation's Web site, I will operationalize a definition of corporatization. Finally, using this definition, I will illustrate articulation through my own pedagogical materials created for a technical writing course taught during the fall of 1998 at Purdue University. This exploratory process is not to advocate a universalized method for teaching Web research, authoring, and reading, but rather to propose a rearticulated approach to teaching and working with the Web.

Complicating the Corporate/Academic Split

Before outlining my methodology, I want to acknowledge an issue with the term *corporatization*. Within academic settings, corporations often are seen as being remote to academic pursuits and goals. Traditionally, within college and university settings, knowledge creation and intellectual development are not fostered for the profit of a corporation or even corporate interests. Further, many academics avoid all business models and references in relationship to their roles as scholars. As Lester Faigley (1999) reminds us in his most recent discussion of technology and education, the academy cannot be positioned as being outside or even beyond all connections to economic systems or their various entities (p. 132). Research grants, scholarships, and even scholarly conferences often are funded in part or whole by corporate endowments. Sometimes this support is a gift and other times it is a partnership between the corporate entity and the university community. My claim is not that these interrelationships are inherently negative or that they should be avoided to retain a sense of "pure" scholarship. To the contrary, my hope is to outline my methodology and then to enact that methodology in order to understand the ways in which corporate institutions interact with academic ones in material and figural ways, and to consider how such interactions relate to pedagogies of the Web.

I will be using the term *corporatization*, defined as: the standards and assumptions by which various corporate entities develop goals and ideals for what it means to be successful in the marketplace. While this definition does not prevent all complications in discussing corporate and academic relationships, it highlights my desire to focus on the enactment of certain corporate practices. These practices, however, are dynamic and cannot be fixed by a strict set of terms.

Constructing Articulation Theory as Methodology

A critical methodology designed to address the partial and dynamic nature of experience must be more than merely a set of techniques. Jim Porter and Patricia Sullivan (1997) suggest that methodology is rhetorical (p. 11). A researcher's methods are infused by his or her interpretations of social relationships and the context of those relationships. To frame a methodology is to foreground the ways in which we position ourselves as researchers in relationship to cultural practices, but this framing also acknowledges how our research projects are shaped by our own interpretations of those practices.

Considering both methodology as situated practice that needs to be foregrounded and the project of questioning and refiguring existing practices and structures of Web authoring and teaching, I believe that articulation theory[1] holds the potential to enact such a methodology. Articulation theory can be understood as a heuristic to interrogate the interrelationships among corporatization, the academy, and the Web as a technology. Articulation seeks to contextualize a set of terms rather than to create a universalized definition. Such a process temporarily connects otherwise unrelated ideas and concepts to allow us to enact both critical analysis and critical reconstruction of the relationships among those ideas and concepts.

While articulation's reliance on temporal, nonnecessary connections makes it difficult to assert a simple definition, it can be defined in relationship to certain elements that are vital throughout the works of scholars practicing and theorizing articulation. These elements include an emphasis on ideology; a claim to dynamic, contingent, and multiple practices and structures; an acknowledgment of difference as integral to understanding those practices and structures; and a call for political imperatives. Although these elements are not exhaustive, most of the theoretical approaches and practical applications of articulation highlight them, because they complement articulation theory's grounding in cultural-studies commitments. Articulation theory originates with the work of cultural-studies scholars who have sought a means to combat essentialist and reductivist conceptions of Marxian theory and to posit a framework for analyzing and reworking specific, contextualized power relations (Grossberg 1992; Hall 1985, 1986, 1989; Laclau 1977; Laclau and Mouffe 1985; Slack 1989, 1996). These power relations are not simply an aspect of *one* particular context; rather *all* contexts can be explored to make visible the otherwise normalized subordinate and dominant positions of their given situations. In turn, each situation becomes a starting point to reconceive of relations that are more equitable and to inquire into the ways cultural practices come to stand for certain cultural norms or structures. My contention is that in conceiving of articulation in methodological terms, we, as educators and Web designers, can make important connections between our work and corporatization. We can reflect on the ways in which corporatization informs our roles as scholars and educators and how corporate images and words relate to the images and words of the academy and the Web.

Understanding Corporatization in Practice

To make responsible Web-design choices we must understand the ways in which corporatization constructs Web representations, and how those constructs position us and our work with students and other professionals. Some of us are charged with the job of preparing our students for their careers—careers in which many of them will bear the responsibility of "managing" other persons. Others of us must produce sound Web-based documents that not only shape but also reflect the goals of our clients. The expectations circulated about work, the role of the corporation, the Web, technology, and education all need to be explored as a set of relationships. Because both teachers and professionals are implicated in a system where corporatization often can be assumed as the invisible standard for Web development and use, we need to make visible these otherwise normalized practices and structures.

My chosen site, Union Pacific Corporation's (UPC) Web site, comes from my own experiences working for Union Pacific Railroad (UPRR), one of UPC's largest operations. UPC's Web site does not vary dramatically from other corporate sites in either its content or form. Consequently, this Web site can serve as a good example for applying articulation in order to illustrate a definition of corporatization in relationship to Web-site development and maintenance. Significant to my selection of UPC's Web site is also this corporation's role in industrialization and postindustrialization. UPRR's history is iconographic in its contribution to westward expansion and even romanitization of industrialism. Also, Union Pacific Technologies (UPT), a more recently developed operation that produces transportation-control technologies, can demonstrate the postindustrial, technological developments associated with shifts in our economy. This company's history affords us a wider perspective on how corporatization changes yet retains commitments to certain assumptions and values. My exploration focuses most prominently upon UPRR and UPT as parts of the larger corporate Web site, and upon the images and words that are used to develop their pages. The selection of UPC's Web site affords insight into not only corporatization, but also the effects of corporations on persons. Quite apparently, my investment can be traced directly to my former co-workers and others who participate in the functions of the railroad and its maintenance. My interest also extends to the ways in which this corporation is an example of how corporations have shaped, and continue to shape, other persons and institutions through both historical and even current operations.

To articulate UPC's Web site, we must consider issues of hypertext as a technology that affects content and form. Both the ways in which hypertext is structured and the ways in which text and images support that structure allow for a richer understanding of corporate standards for the Web. In elucidating these interrelationships, I focus on text, images, links, the design of individual nodes and the larger site, and the interactivity of the nodes and the site. These elements of the Web site are not easily divisible, in that images and links are components of the Web-site design just as the content addressed within the Web site relates to the choice of images. These components of Web sites are examined in order to provide insight into how a Web site can enact certain practices and figure certain structures.

As many hypertext theorists have noted, reading a hypertext document differs from reading a print-based text. Through linking, nonlinearity, and nodes, Web readers also can be considered Web writers as they actively "write" the text by choosing certain links to traverse across nodes or Web sites. These connections and the politics of such connections are dynamic and contingent, changing with each new Web reader/writer and even each reading/writing of the Web site. In Andrew Feenberg's (1991, 21) often-quoted discussion of technology and how it functions, he posits that

> [t]echnology is not a thing in the ordinary sense of the term, but an "ambivalent" process of development suspended between different possibilities. This "ambivalence" of technology is distinguished from neutrality by the role it attributes to social values in the design, and not merely the use, of technical systems. On this view, technology is not a destiny but a scene of struggle. It is a social battlefield, or perhaps a better metaphor

would be a parliament of things on which civilizational alternatives are debated and decided.

The negotiation process involved in being a Web reader/writer and the tensions among the ways in which technology is being designed, implemented, and used can be applied directly to UPC's Web site, and other Web sites as well.

Exploring Union Pacific's Web Site

As suggested, articulating UPC's Web site allows for an operationalized definition of corporatization that can be applied to ways of re-envisioning Web research and authoring for educators and designers. UPC's starting node adheres to certain corporate conventions in that it emphasizes its corporate history and background, operations, and financial information. Through these various nodes and other sections of the Web site, UPC constructs its corporate image and announces its corporate culture; the political ideals of UPC are elaborated in its Web-site text, and the ideological implications of these ideals also are revealed in the design of its page. (See figure 13.1.)[2]

Some of those ideals reveal a concern with specialized practices rather than concerns for the persons implementing them. The discussion of these practices ignores the agents performing the actions and their experiences, or it renders their experiences as secondary to the goals of a project. For UPC, one project that focused on specialization rather than the agents was westward expansion, which UPC (1999a) represents through its careful use of images, words, and links. From UPC's starting node, a Web reader/writer can choose the link to a "Brief History," where it states that

[i]n 1868, Andrew J. Russell . . . was commissioned by Union Pacific to photograph its construction crews as they laid ribbons of steel across the plains and through the mountains and valleys of the western territories. This endeavor was the nineteenth-century technological equivalent of the space program a century later. Russell's pictures are a testament to this breathtaking achievement—hailed as "The Great Work of the Age"—and to the heritage of Union Pacific. (Union Pacific Corporation 1999b)

Indisputably, UPRR helped to expand the West and commerce within our country. This description of the process as a triumphant engineering marvel, however, elides some of the various complications with specialization: the deemphasis of the effects of specialized processes on those workers who deployed them and a reverence for the technologies that enabled and even recorded them. (Note that the only "named" person in the above quote is the photographer.) In addition, the choice to tell this history rather than portray it through images also masks the human agents

◆ **FIGURE 13.1** ◆

Starting nodes for Union Pacific Corporation (Union Pacific 1999a), Union Pacific Railroad (Union Pacific 1999d), and Union Pacific Technologies (Union Pacific 1999g).

who helped orchestrate the expansion. Thus the corporate entity, UPRR, becomes the sole agent of the narrative.

Later, text within this same node states that

[a]mong the men who built the Central Pacific from the West Coast, left, and Union Pacific, right, some returned home to their families, but many stayed with the Railroad to build expanding branch lines. Still others were among the tens of thousands of new settlers who began to carve homes, farms, ranches and eventually new states from the wilderness between the Missouri River and the Pacific Ocean. Union Pacific has been serving the United States ever since, hauling billions of tons of autos, trailer and container traffic, chemicals, coal, grain, lumber, and an almost infnite [*sic*] variety of consumer goods. (Union Pacific Corporation 1999b)

Union Pacific's revelry in its development of the West emphasizes the contributions of certain engineering works. This node also reveals a photograph of the famed completion of the transcontinental railroad (see figure 13.2), but what is stressed in this description and image is the way in which specialized knowledge, as instantiated both then and today through certain technologies, creates a heritage to be valued and a consumer service to trust. The irony of this focus on UPC's ability to produce specialized

◆ **FIGURE 13.2** ◆

Andrew Russell's photograph of the completion of the transcontinental railroad (Union Pacific 1999b).

◆ **FIGURE 13.3** ◆

Another of Andrew Russell's photographs of the completion of the transcontinental railroad. CALIFORNIA STATE RAILROAD MUSEUM.

practices is its deemphasis on the persons who implemented and per-
fected the practices of UPC's engineering vision. This separation of the
specialized knowledge from the workers participating in its implementation is best illustrated by works found in the Web archives of the California State Railroad Museum. There, another of Andrew Russell's photographs of the scene (see figure 13.3) is displayed with the explanation that
it is of "the Chinese laborers who were excluded from the larger group pictures" (California State Railroad Museum 1999). Both in written and pictorial form, this version of the history of UPC's contributions privileges the
corporation's specialties of engineering and commerce over any discussion of the workers' backgrounds or working conditions while engaging in
the development of an engineering marvel that rivals the technologies of
the later space program. Rather than mentioning the lives lost, disparate
working conditions, or labor and management tensions, this historical
account discusses the men as having various opportunities after their
experiences building the transcontinental railroad. Rather than providing
space in the site for alternative views of this historical development, and
thus expressing its commitment to diversity, UP presents a limited—even
an inaccurate—historical perspective, all of which is achieved by the
design of the Web page itself. The images, words, and links help to preserve the corporate history of UP rather than tell the history of the workers of UP.

The concept of specialization depicted by this section and others of the UPC site does not make the corporation corrupt. Obviously, the corporation is representing itself to a specific audience, and it chooses to do so by highlighting its ability to create specialized services that prove invaluable to historical and technological development. Such specialization can be found in a variety of corporations and academic fields, but the importance of considering how such purposes inform our representations and our concepts of ourselves as educators and professionals should be considered when designing Web-based materials. When specialization and emphasis on the tools of specialization prevent us from making connections between our standards and practices and the persons with whom we engage, then we must consider more carefully the potentials of such standards and practices to ignore certain psychological, intellectual, and material effects. As Jennifer Terry and Melodie Calvert (1997) suggest, a privileging of the "tool" concept of technology, where the technological object encompasses the limits of the technology, tends to ignore the relationships among the designers, users, and technological objects (p. 3). In UPC's brief history, racial difference is elided in favor of a narrative that celebrates the tools of progress—progress of the railroad, commerce, and even men who were claimed to be bettered by their experience in this history-making moment. By including a broader view of the history of the railroad's development, UPC could emphasize and even celebrate its commitment to issues of diversity now and in its future relationships. UPC could then acknowledge to its current employees, customers, investors, and railroad enthusiasts that the company values difference and actively constructs a workplace where prejudice will not be tolerated. Thus by changing the images and words of its Web-based narrative, UPC could, in effect, change the history-making function of its pages.

By choosing two other links from UPC's starting node, the Web reader/writer can discover UPC's perceptions of three of its largest operations—the UPRR, UPT, and Overnite Transportation (OT). These three operations are overviewed by the corporation in terms of their contributions to the parent corporation and to America. In the link to the profile of UPC and its operations, it is asserted that "Union Pacific Corporation is dedicated to being an industry leader in quality customer service, the most advanced technology, and the highest degree of employee involvement" (Union Pacific Corporation 1999c). The Web reader/writer is given the choice to read/write further about these three holdings. And, based upon the claim of attentiveness to persons, customers, and employees and to technological advances, the reader/writer might expect to find more developed discussions of the human and technological interactions forwarded by the corporation. By choosing any of the links, however, the reader/writer will find the conflation of persons and machines—or more accurately, the absence of persons as agents. In its more extensive discussion of UPRR, UPC stresses the following about this operation:

Union Pacific's customer responsiveness, highly advanced computer systems, superbly maintained track, powerful, computer-monitored alternating-current locomotives, and versatile freight cars have consistently set industry standards. . . . At the heart of the Railroad's system is one of America's most sophisticated communications networks. A central dispatching center in Omaha—the largest in the world—monitors and controls the 1,200 trains operating daily on Union Pacific's 24-state network. . . . A unique customer service center in St. Louis handles requests 24 hours a day, seven days a week, via a nationally accessible 800 number. And computers are used to assign cars, direct the assignment of crews, keep track of the progress of shipments, handle all shipping instructions and billing, and provide data for detailed cost analyses, among many other tasks. . . . In a very real sense, such railroads as Union Pacific form an indispensable circulatory system that constantly pumps new life and vitality into the American economy. In the years ahead, Union Pacific Railroad will continue to innovate, to achieve optimum levels of operating efficiency, and to put new technologies to work to maintain the leadership position of its system. (Union Pacific Corporation 1999c)

This extensive quote denotes UPC's mechanization in that the systems discussed and the inquiries processed are not performed by employees but rather by technologies. The requests processed also are agentless. The description makes it seem as if the processes are carried out by the mechanisms—the technologies—rather than persons, and this mechanization is supported further by the lack of images that depict any agents. The promise to the reader/writer is that this corporation will continue to implement ever-new systems that will perpetuate its dominance.

Strikingly, the persons who were touted as significant in UPC's "Operations Overview" node are constructed as mere components of the mechanized "circulatory" system that UPC provides to the betterment of all America. This conceptualization is best described by Feenberg's insight that "[i]f one ignores most of the connections between technology and society, it is no wonder that technology then appears to be self-generating" (Feenberg 1995, 8–9). Here, such a move to construct technology as self-perpetuating and inevitable is critiqued for its unconscious concern for the potential effects that technology has on persons, and that persons have on technology. Critical technological theorists assume that technological systems are made up of persons and machines, and that choices about implementation and design are not inevitable or always necessarily better than existing uses and designs. The lack of UPC's critical insight into its own positioning of both its employees and even its customers in relationship to its technologies can be related to obscurantism, or the refusal to speculate on traditional methods or practices and even the negation that such speculation could produce any necessary social change (Ferre 1995, 37).

What seems apparent from these two examples in UPC's Web site is the corporation's need to be efficient. Even the text-heavy design of the Web page itself illustrates this efficiency, in that text is more expediently loaded by most Web browsers than image files. Developing better, faster, more progressive methods and technologies that can enhance the performance of its employees and gain its market share—these goals, as stressed before, are not unique to corporate plans for success.

To demonstrate its need to develop better methods, UPC emphasizes its current and historic contributions to technological development through transportation technologies and the railroad, respectively. From either of the nodes—the "Brief History" or the "Operations Overview"—the Web reader/writer can select a link that leads directly to UPRR's history or to its starting node for UPRR from which he or she could link to UPRR's history section. This history section provides a more substantial history of the transcontinental railroad's development than the history that is given on UPC's page. The connection between them, however, is in the tone of these two histories. In a section of the history provided by UPRR, it suggests that "[t]he Indians repeatedly attacked without warning, and the UP acted as its own army" (Union Pacific Corporation 1999e). Here, UPRR admits the tension between Native Americans who inhabited the land being territorialized by the railroad and the railroad workers developing the transcontinental line. Later, in this same section, it states that

> [h]e [General Dodge of the UPRR] wrote to General Sherman, commander of the Military Division of the West "We've got to clean the Indian out, or give up. The government may take its choice." There was no mystery about how to do the job. The solution was practically larger than life. Sherman knew that the bison was the source of food, clothing and shelter for the plains tribes. The railroad, by bisecting the great herds of bison, provided a source of transportation for hunters, thus speeding up their [bison] elimination. Eradicating much of the bison population provided an earlier end to the hostilities than otherwise might have been the case. (Union Pacific Corporation 1999e)

This history pays homage to the need for efficiency at all costs. The assumption is that the technological and engineering breakthroughs of the railroad take precedence over the lives of the persons, and the bison, who inhabited the land being territorialized. The passive attack on these persons is justified by the assumption that this method was "better" than any other that might have been deployed.

More odd than this historical perspective is the merchandise offered by the railroad. If the Web reader/writer selects the merchandise link provided by UPRR, he or she can purchase photos such as the one shown in figure 13.4 from the UPRR's site.

The Native Americans who survived became "merchandise" for the UPRR (Union Pacific Corporation 1999f). The use of words and images on the history page and the Native American archive of images page demonstrates UPC's equating of persons with profits. The need for efficiency, and even the desire to make profits, are acceptable goals for corporations, but

◆ **FIGURE 13.4** ◆

"American Indians on horseback at Buffalo Run, Yellowstone, ca. 1924" (Union Pacific Corporation 1999e).

here, technological efficiency and merchandizing provide UPRR with a means to write a glorifying and profitable version of its history. Feenberg (1995) argues that "fetishism of efficiency ignores our ordinary understanding of the concept [of efficiency] which alone is relevant to social decision making" (p. 15). In other words, to calculate the costs involved with technological policies and codes designed to achieve efficiency, we must consider noneconomic values such as quality of life and government and corporate responsibility. These codes and policies, after all, are situated within a cultural context along with the technologies that are being administered.

In relationship to such policies, codes, and values of technological implementation, UPT has developed a software program that will allow corporations to judge the worthiness of their projects. From UPC's starting node, the Web reader/writer can choose a link to UPC's "Productivity Quality Management" node. In this node that explains the software, UPT asks: "Is your software project destined to succeed or doomed to fail?" (Union Pacific Corporation 1999i). Then, based upon the amount of resources channeled to corporate projects, UPT asks why:

> Thirty-one percent of those projects get cancelled before completion? Fifty-three percent cost 189 percent of their original estimates? Only 16 percent get completed on time and on budget?* [*from Standish Group International, Inc.]. Maybe it's because project managers have never had a tool to measure key metrics related to project success . . . and maybe it's time to manage expectations and insure your own success. (Union Pacific Corporation 1999i)

This discussion of faulty and costly projects relates to the need for standard quality practices that can be implemented within a corporation. To

PQMPlus Highlights

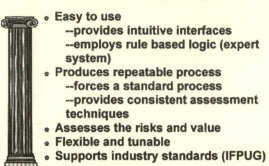

- **Easy to use**
  - **--provides intuitive interfaces**
  - **--employs rule based logic (expert system)**
- **Produces repeatable process**
  - **--forces a standard process**
  - **--provides consistent assessment techniques**
- **Assesses the risks and value**
- **Flexible and tunable**
- **Supports industry standards (IFPUG)**

◆ **FIGURE 13.5** ◆

PQMPlus highlights (Union Pacific Railroad 1999i).

gain insight into such practices, UPT has developed "PQMPlus" software to plan and determine which projects are most feasible and cost effective. An image link that explains the benefits of PQMPlus provides some interesting ideas about how standards can be determined by software (Union Pacific Corporation 1999i). (See figure 13.5.)

The image reveals that the software is "easy to use" and "intuitive" and has a "rule-based logic," but it also claims to "force a standard process" and "provide consistent assessment techniques." Later, the image suggests that the software is both "flexible and tunable" and "supports industry standards." The coupling of intuitive characteristics that provide flexibility with standard processes and consistent assessment is contradictory; however, the potential contradiction of the individual goals of employees or even companies in relationship to a universalized set of standards is not acknowledged. To the contrary, this software attempts to quantify procedures and processes in terms of standards that also circumscribe the abilities of certain persons or corporations to act.

Inflexibility is further emphasized in the design of the page. The image in effect "fixes" the text of this display. To change the text on this page, the Web designer would have to create an entirely new image. Thus the universality that is advocated by this software diminishes the opportunity for workers and management to negotiate standards in relationship to categories outside the universalized system described. This sense of isolating and quantifying variables in a system where the values are determined by the software engineers and designers of the program can be seen as technical determinism. Social agents must adapt to certain technological imperatives, and thus this decontextualized stance becomes the "foundation" for our actions (Feenberg 1995, 6). Instead of positioning technologies as relating to the persons who design, implement, and even develop

◆ **FIGURE 13.6** ◆
Union Pacific Technologies (Union Pacific Corporation 1999h).

new uses (other than those intended by the developers), UPC develops a view of technology as inevitable.

Articulating UPC's Web site has involved an examination of the content—the text and images of the nodes—and the form—the design of the pages themselves. Other considerations in relationship to this Web site are its self-contained status; from my exploration of the UPC, UPRR, and UPT areas of the Web site, I found no links "outside" the Web site. All links that I traversed were connected to the parent corporation or to its operations. Further, the standards and procedures for the technological development were highlighted in multiple ways, but each time the narrative remained consistently associated with technology as a tool. UPC's sense of technology, specifically Web development, centers on one or all of the categories of corporatization: specialization, mechanization, efficiency, and standardization. UPC's sense of technology can best be demonstrated by the image provided (see figure 13.6) (Union Pacific Corporation 1999h). The hovering globe is aptly labeled "Union Pacific Technologies," and the transportation companies of UPC are all leading into the computer terminal of the UP system. These company symbols coalesce to stand for the new manifest destiny of the horizon of technology, where progress and efficiency are highly valued. This image plays into the celebration of technology and its mastering of the global marketplace. Here, the industrial train meets with the postindustrial computer to shake nature into submission.

The political imperative of this corporation is none less than to be the world leader in the transportation industry. This imperative, as illustrated in this complex image, diminishes the significance of certain practices on persons both directly and indirectly involved in its pursuit of this goal.

Applying Corporatization to Developing Web-Site Materials

Using my definition of corporatization with its emphasis on specialization, mechanization, efficiency, and standardization, I want to consider how such constructions relate to my own Web-based pedagogical materials and their design. Neither technology nor corporatization should be viewed as deterministic screens that disallow agency in relationship to educational or professional practices. In order to understand how certain practices become normalized and are reproduced even in university pedagogies (generally, considered to be "removed" from direct corporate intervention), I want to critique my own pedagogical Web-based materials developed for my fall 1998 technical writing course taught at Purdue University. Unlike UPC's extensive Web site, I have a much more limited number of nodes and sections within my site: approximately twenty-five nodes and three sections. The technical writing course for which these materials were developed is a junior- or senior-level requirement for many students in the school of technology at Purdue.

At the point at which I designed and published these Web-based technical writing materials I had two years of experience with both technical writing teaching and Web authoring. My Web-based materials for this course are, however, the first Web documents that I had created exclusively for my teaching. While the Professional Writing Program at Purdue requests that all staff members provide at least a Web version of their syllabi, I began to offer additional Web-based assignment materials during this semester, since doing so would allow students the opportunity to access more easily the documents that they would need for their participation in the course, documents that otherwise would be available only through a university-established server mount point. In addressing issues of Web design and development, I do not claim to hold expert status as a professional Web developer, but I do see a connection between the roles of instructors creating and maintaining their own Web resources and the roles of professional Web developers. Both instructors and professionals working in the hypertext medium encounter and contribute to the expectations of how the Web should "serve" their specific constituencies. These expectations are informed by cultural factors that advocate technology's acceptable uses and are often translated in the words and images of their Web pages.

Part of my own impetus for implementing more Web-based pedagogical materials was in the name of efficiency for students and myself.

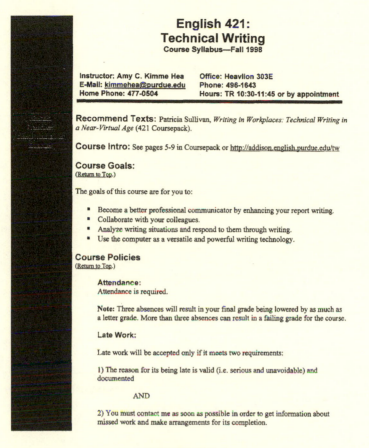

**English 421:
Technical Writing**
Course Syllabus—Fall 1998

Instructor: Amy C. Kimme Hea   Office: Heavlion 303E
E-Mail: kimmehea@purdue.edu   Phone: 496-1643
Home Phone: 477-0504   Hours: TR 10:30-11:45 or by appointment

Recommend Texts: Patricia Sullivan, *Writing in Workplaces: Technical Writing in a Near-Virtual Age* (421 Coursepack).

Course Intro: See pages 5-9 in Coursepack or http://addison.english.purdue.edu/tw

Course Goals:
(Return to Top.)

The goals of this course are for you to:

- Become a better professional communicator by enhancing your report writing.
- Collaborate with your colleagues.
- Analyze writing situations and respond to them through writing.
- Use the computer as a versatile and powerful writing technology.

Course Policies
(Return to Top.)

Attendance:
Attendance is required.

Note: Three absences will result in your final grade being lowered by as much as a letter grade. More than three absences can result in a failing grade for the course.

Late Work:

Late work will be accepted only if it meets two requirements:

1) The reason for its being late is valid (i.e. serious and unavoidable) and documented

AND

2) You must contact me as soon as possible in order to get information about missed work and make arrangements for its completion.

◆ **FIGURE 13.7** ◆

Starting node for English 421: Technical Writing (Kimme Hea 1999a).

Despite my critical engagement with technologies as a part of my own research work, I admit to creating Web-based documents that relate to corporatization. Regardless of my theoretical grounding in critical pedagogy and theory and practical experience in teaching writing rhetorically, I can find many incidences in my own pedagogical materials where I fail to assert my goals of being a critical educator. On the first node of my pedagogical materials (see figure 13.7), I describe the students' responsibilities in relation to the course technologies by suggesting that "[b]ecause the exchange of information and materials in this class will be almost entirely electronic, familiarity with certain technologies is crucial for participation and success in the course. Thus by the end of the first week, you should be able to attend to the responsibilities in the list below. If you need any assistance now or at any point during the semester, please do not hesitate to ask" (Kimme Hea 1999a).

In this description of their technological responsibilities, I provide no rationale to students for how and why the course technologies (listserv, Web-based materials, course mount point, email, etc.) will be useful except as a "required" means for information exchange. Rather than providing a contextualized view of technology, I present these technologies as mere delivery systems that can seriously affect students' "success" in the course. This description sets the precedent that the technologies only affect learning processes in relation to their use value and the effectiveness of such uses. As with UPC's pull toward efficiency, in my own desire to provide a more efficient classroom space, I reduce the technologies of the classroom to devices and tools that if they are not "mastered" can adversely affect students' standings in the course. Instead of reinforcing a deterministic view of classroom technologies, I could have focused on the political and rhetorical choices related to the use of these technologies in the classroom context. Rather than contributing to a normalized view of technology, I could have provided students with contextual information for how and why certain classroom technologies are integral to the course and how using them will affect the classroom dynamics. Thus my choice of terms and the design of this page could have led to critical engagement with technology—one of the goals of the course—rather than mask the possibility for such engagement.

As with UPC's Web site, standardization also can be seen in the design of my assignment pages. In order to create a consistency in the ways in which students engage the materials, I set a structure for the project nodes that allows for linking among particular components of a single project, but none of the projects themselves are linked to one another.

To demonstrate this standardization, I have provided an example node (see figure 13.8) of the design layout used for the nodes of the Web-based client project. This "Oral Progress Report" node is linked to the starting and other component nodes of the "Web Solutions Project" and back to the "Syllabus" node. The design of this node, which closely resembles the electronic versions that are available through the course folder, yields consistency but also universalizes the projects for the course. I could have provided more contextualized cues as to which project students are viewing; for example, one simple addition could have been images as visual cues to particular projects. Instead, the text-heavy design of these nodes privileges a sense that each of the projects is similar in its objectives and criteria; this is not the case. Moreover, the project materials themselves outline objectives and provide some aspects of the purpose of the project and its components, but even these discussions prevent a more connected view of how the individual assignments relate to one another and the overall pedagogical goals of the course. As with UPC's site, the design of these nodes privileges the text-based description versus an image- or icon-driven design. This privileging relies heavily on the misguided assumption that text is inherently more direct, clear, and even professional. Rather than combating this assumption, however, my Web-based materials advocate this idea.

Oral Progress Report

Your 15-minute, scripted oral progress report for Web Solutions should provide an introduction to your client's organization including information about your client's needs and resources. Further, it should include specifics concerning the field research your team has conducted in order to analyze your client's context and web needs. Each team member must participate equitably both the planning of the oral report and its delivery to the class. This presentation must include not only verbal but also visual components.

Purposes

This presentation allows your team to:

- update me and other members of the class on analysis of your client's organizational context and web communication needs.

- discuss the field research your team has conducted in order to formulate feasible recommendations for your client.

- share ideas with and receive feedback from your peers.

- gain more experience in giving polished, professional presentations.

Components

Your oral progress report is due on either W, 11/18 or F, 11/20 and should include both verbal and visual components.

- Project Overview

- Field Research

- Preliminary Data Analysis

- Remaining Tasks

- Visuals

Description of Components

Project Overview
Your team should give an overview of your client context and an indication of what you will address in your presentation.

Field Research
Your team should discuss the methods you have used to collect information about your client, including interviews, observations, and textual analyses.

Preliminary Data Analysis
Your team should highlight the points from your data that are most relevant to your formulation of feasible recommendations. That is, you should analyze how and why the information that you highlight is significant to the recommendations that your team will offer to the client.

Remaining Tasks
Your team should outline the steps needed not only to generate potential recommendations but also to confirm the feasibility of those recommendations before finalizing your report.

Visuals
Your team should integrate visuals throughout the presentation. Your visuals should not only have a professional appearance but also enhance the rhetorical effectiveness of your discussion.

Return to Syllabus.

Return to Web Solutions.

Return to Client Proposal.

Return to Rhetorical Analysis of Websites.

Return to Points to Consider for Oral Progress Report.

Return to Recommendation Report to your Client.

Return to Top.

✉ Email Instructor.

◆ FIGURE 13.8 ◆

"Oral Progress Report" node of the "Web Solutions Project" (Kimme Hea 1999b).

The concept of specialization also complicates the students' abilities to engage fully with the Web-based materials provided to them. The pedagogical goals for the course, which are provided on the starting node, suggest the focus of the course (Kimme Hea 1999a). The goals of this course are for you to:

- Become a better professional communicator by enhancing your report writing.
- Collaborate with your colleagues.
- Analyze writing situations and respond to them through writing.
- Use the computer as a versatile and powerful writing technology.

These goals illustrate some of the major goals of Purdue's Professional Writing Program. The program offers technical and business writing courses focused on contextualized writing projects that center on rhetorical principles. Rather than presenting traditional genre-based pedagogies, the program asserts that writing is a complex social act. Students are asked to conceive of writing as part of a situated set of actions and practices that inform and are informed by relationships among persons, standards, technologies, and so on. In my own sections of the technical writing course, students are required to conduct extensive field research—document collection and response, observation and field notes, and interview and interview transcript. Students analyze all of these data components in order to create a written report about how writing functions within their field, and what this functioning might mean for them as professionals.

Because of the complexity of this project, students often are challenged by its demands and frustrated by the research expectations. This frustration can be related to the difference in our disciplinary backgrounds (theirs most likely in technology or engineering, and mine in rhetoric and composition) and to expectations coming out of those different fields. Without totalizing their experiences, I want to suggest that our disciplinary frameworks demand different conceptualizations of processes and products. Many students assume that writing is almost exclusively about a product, so asking them to consider writing as a complex process that relates to persons, technologies, and professions seems odd at best. This tension can be productive if addressed in relationship to the demands of this assignment; however, I do not address it in the materials that I provided to students. In class, I attempt to discuss professionalization in terms of their experiences and mine and to interrogate the similarities and differences in how professional expectations and assumptions are articulated within particular professions. The Web-based materials, however, situate the research aspects of this assignment as "normal" activities that students should be willing to participate in without question. This stance is similar to the view of specialization demonstrated in UPC's Web site, in that it takes the agents for granted. More specifically, my Web-based description ignores the students' perceptions of research as it is situated within their professional context, which is somewhat ironic considering that one of the goals of this project is to ask students to determine what counts as knowledge-creation in their fields. The project materials shift attention to the products that students will produce and the process in which they will engage, rather than acknowledging their roles as agents in the knowledge-making process. One simple addition could have been a collaboratively produced resource page with a collection of links to Purdue Web sites that feature students' majors, and other Web pages related to their fields and future professions.

My Web-based materials also relate to the problematic of mechanization. Within my course Web site, students are offered very few links—only three in fact—to "outside" Web sites: Purdue's Professional Writing Program Web site, Purdue's On-line Writing Lab APA style guide, and the National Highway Traffic Safety Administration (NHTSA). These links are

considered resources that students should access either to understand the
goals of the course better or to conduct and prepare research components
of the course. Despite my awareness that students often construe the
course as being about written products rather than processes, the
research links that I provide assert that writing can be narrowed to a few
"key" resources, a seemingly self-defined process. These resources are the
tools to build effective writing. Rather than presenting students with further opportunities to critique Web resources, I have narrowed the process.
Ideally, for students to build a more critical view of hypertext resources, I
could have provided them with strategies for determining which resources
might be best for their projects and for analyzing Web design such as
words, images, layout, and links of pages. By directing them to a Professional Writing Program link without any additional comment on its content and/or purpose, I am mystifying the ways in which programmatic
goals for the course relate to those highlighted in my Web-based syllabus.
Based upon the placement of these links, both the research and program
processes can be construed as inevitable principles that direct the shape
of the class without question.

Additionally, such mechanization is supported through the lack of interactivity provided within my Web-based materials. Other than students'
option to email me, which is a link provided at the bottom of every page,
students are not offered other means by which to assert agency. Similar to
UPC's agentless technologies, my Web-based pedagogical materials seem
to stand for themselves. These links, which are buried within the standardized form of the assignment materials, do not imply the need to communicate with me about the materials unless students "misunderstand" them.
During the fall semester of 1998, none of the forty students, to my knowledge, used these links to email me. Despite the presence of these links, the
expectation is that the materials "speak" for themselves without need for
critical exploration or even interrogation. I am not suggesting that the
classroom context for the course does not complicate the materials provided or that classroom discussions do not highlight more critical inquiry
into writing, technology, and professional contexts. Rather, I am stressing
that the Web-based pedagogical materials that I provided to the fall 1998
technical writing students presented a sense of containment and universality that does not effectively illustrate the critical focus of my course.

Rearticulating Web-Based Pedagogical Materials

By applying the critical lens of corporatization to my own Web-based
materials, I am not suggesting that the design of my Web site and its content are devoid of value. My critique of both UPC's Web site and my own
is not to suggest that educators or professional writers design, implement,

and maintain pages that lack consistency or create a sense of "confusion" for their readers/writers simply to complicate the role of technology in the classroom or to highlight the role of agents in industry. My goal, instead, is to offer a different conceptualization, one that seeks to negotiate a design model that provides information and interactivity, connections and complicated critique, and resources and critical consideration of Web resources.

We must be critical of the Web-design standards that we implement in the development of our pages. Becoming more critical of the design factors that we deploy in the coding of our Web sites is necessary if we are to create Web-based materials that relate to project goals. Many guides, handbooks, and even design tools such as text editors offer little guidance to Web designers, especially educators. These resources often are written for and by corporate designers, and we should consider how the advice provided in them relates to the wider goals of a corporation and to the specific needs of instructors and students. By seeking out Web-design resources that take into account an educator audience, instructors can conceptualize new methods for not merely delivering information to students, but also engaging them in complex learning processes. Similarly, professionals given the responsibility to design and maintain Web pages can seek out ways to represent a more complex relationship between the acts of composing pages and the readers who engage those pages. The potentials for alternative structures and designs of Web pages should encourage us to experiment with issues of content and form.

To shift the emphasis from a standard corporatized model, instructors and professionals should develop Web-based materials that can be user-tested by students and clients. Feedback from these audiences can be incorporated into the form and content of the page. Web-based materials also should provide opportunities for students and clients to contribute to the development of the Web site through links to their own pages, contributory images or links for existing nodes, and suggestions for how the pages can better serve their needs. By making critical inquiry into the technology applicable to the materials and projects that students contribute to the class and clients contribute to the companies, educators and professionals can lessen the sense that technologies function as "tools" and emphasize the cultural aspects of the design, use, and implementation of technologies.

Our classroom and professional discussions of the technology of hypertext also should provide opportunities to complicate technological determinism or obscurantism. In other words, in order to prepare students and consumers to be critical agents of technology, we must be willing to discuss technology in sophisticated ways rather than assume the stance that technologies "teach" themselves. Providing rhetorical education and employing rhetorical principles in terms of design, layout, content, and publishing of Web-based documents would mean asking students and clients to consider the set of human and technological relationships. A shift to a more critical view of technology does not mean, however, that we should ignore all design conventions. Instead, a critical view asks us to create strategies for interaction and interrogation of Web authoring and researching practices that take into account the complexity of design and learning.

Notes

1. Throughout this work, "articulation" and "articulation theory" will be used interchangeably to stand for this theorized practice.

2. Because many of the figures in this chapter are copied from the WWW, they will not reproduce clearly here. The images, with higher visual quality, may be viewed directly on the UPC Web site at <http://www.uptWeb.com/>.

References

Bolter, Jay David. (1991). *Writing Space: The Computer, Hypertext, and the History of Writing.* Hillsdale, NJ: Lawrence Erlbaum.

Bolter, Jay David, and Richard Grusin. (1999). *Remediation: Understanding New Media.* Cambridge: Massachusetts Institute of Technology Press.

California State Railroad Museum. (1999). *Building the Transcontinental Railroad* (Web site) <http://www.csrmf.org/transbuild.html>.

Faigley, Lester. (1999). Beyond imagination: The Internet and global digital literacy. In *Passions, Pedagogies, and Twenty-First-Century Technologies,* ed. Gail E. Hawisher and Cynthia L. Selfe (pp. 129–39). Logan: Utah State University Press.

Feenberg, Andrew. (1991). *Critical Theory of Technology.* New York: Oxford University Press.

———. (1995). Subversive rationalization: Technology, power, and democracy. In *Technology and the Politics of Knowledge,* ed. Andrew Feenberg and Alastair Hannay (pp. 3–22). Indianapolis: Indiana University Press.

Ferre, Frederick. (1995). *Philosophy of Technology.* Athens: University of Georgia Press.

Grossberg, Lawrence. (1992). *We Gotta Get Out of This Place: Popular Conservatism and Postmodern Culture.* New York: Routledge.

Hall, Stuart. (1985). Signification, representation, ideology: Althusser and the post-structuralist debates. *Critical Studies in Communication* 2: 91–114.

———. (1986). On postmodernism and articulation: An interview with Stuart Hall. *Journal of Communication Inquiry* 10(2): 45–60.

———. (1989). Ideology and communication theory. In *Rethinking Communication,* vol. 1: *Paradigm Issues,* ed. Brenda Dervin, Lawrence Grossberg, Barbara O'Keefe, and Ellen Wartella (pp. 40–52). London: Sage Publications.

Hawisher, Gail, and Patricia Sullivan. (1999). Fleeting images: Women visually writing on the Web. In *Passions, Pedagogies, and Twenty-First-Century Technologies,* ed. Gail E. Hawisher and Cynthia L. Selfe (pp. 268–91). Logan: Utah State University Press.

Johnson-Eilola, Johndan. (1993). Control and the cyborg: Writing and being written in hypertext. *Journal of Advanced Composition* 13(2): 381–99.

———. (1994). Reading and writing in hypertext: Vertigo and euphoria. In *Literacy and Computers: The Complications of Teaching and Learning with Technology*, ed. Cynthia Selfe and Susan Hilligoss (pp. 195–219). New York: Modern Language Association.

———. (1997a). *Nostalgic Angels: Rearticulating Hypertext Writing*. Norwood, NJ: Ablex.

———. (1997b). Wild technologies: Computer use and social possibility. In *Computers and Technical Communication: Pedagogical and Programmatic Perspectives*, ed. Stuart Selber (pp. 97–128). Greenwich, CT: Ablex.

Johnson-Eilola, Johndan, and Stuart Selber. (1996). Policing ourselves: Defining the boundaries of appropriate discussion in online forums. *Computers and Composition* 13: 269–91.

Joyce, Michael. (1995). Siren shapes: Exploratory and constructive hypertexts. In *Of Two Minds: Hypertext Pedagogy and Poetics*, ed. Michael Joyce (pp. 39–59). Ann Arbor: University of Michigan Press.

Kimme Hea, Amy C. (1999a). *English 421: Technical Writing* (Web site) <http://wcic.cioe.com/~kimmehea/syllabus.htm>.

———. (1999b). Oral progress report (Web site) <http://wcic.cioe.com/~kimmehea/oprreport.htm>.

Kress, Gunther. (1999). "English" at the crossroads: Rethinking curricula of communication in the context of the turn to the visual. In *Passions, Pedagogies, and Twenty-First-Century Technologies*, ed. Gail E. Hawisher and Cynthia L. Selfe (pp. 66–88). Logan: Utah State University Press.

Laclau, Ernesto. (1977). *Politics and Ideology in Marxist Theory: Capitalism–Facism–Populism*. London: Atlantic Highlands Humanities Press.

Laclau, Ernesto, and Chantel Mouffe. (1985). *Hegemony and Socialist Strategy: Towards a Radical Democratic Politics*. New York: Verso Books.

Moulthrop, Stuart. (1991). The politics of hypertext. In *Evolving Perspectives on Computers and Composition Studies: Questions for the 1990s*, ed. Gail E. Hawisher and Cynthia L. Selfe (pp. 253–71). Urbana, IL: NCTE and Computers and Composition Press.

Moulthrop, Stuart, and Nancy Kaplan. (1994). They became what they beheld: The futility of resistance in the space of electronic writing. In *Literacy and Computers: The Complications of Teaching and Learning with Technology*, ed. Cynthia L. Selfe and Susan Hilligoss (pp. 220–37). New York: Modern Language Association.

Porter, James, and Patricia Sullivan. (1997). *Opening Spaces: Writing Technologies and Critical Research Practices*. Greenwich, CT: Ablex.

Romano, Susan. (1993). The egalitarianism narrative: Whose story? Which yardstick? *Computers and Composition* 10(3): 5–28.

———. (1999). On becoming a woman: Pedagogies of the self. In *Passions, Pedagogies, and Twenty-First-Century Technologies*, ed. Gail E. Hawisher and Cynthia L. Selfe (pp. 249–67). Logan: Utah State University Press.

Selber, Stuart. (1997). Hypertext spheres of influence in technical communication instructional contexts. In *Computers and Technical Communication: Pedagogical and Programmatic Perspectives*, ed. Stuart Selber (pp. 17–44). Greenwich, CT: Ablex.

Selfe, Cynthia, and Richard J. Selfe. (1994). The politics of the interface: Power and its exercise in electronic contact zones. *College Composition and Communication* 45(4): 480–504.

Slack, Jennifer Daryl. (1989). Contextualizing technology. In *Rethinking Communication*, vol. 2: *Paradigm Issues*, ed. Brenda Dervin, Lawrence Grossberg, Barbara O'Keefe, and Ellen Wartella (pp. 329–45). London: Sage Publications.

———. (1996). The theory and method of articulation in cultural studies. In *Stuart Hall: Critical Dialogues in Cultural Studies*, ed. David Morley and Kuan-Hsing Chen (pp. 112–27). London: Routledge.

Takayoshi, Pamela. (1994). Building new networks from old: Women's experiences with electronic communications. *Computers and Composition* 10(4): 11–26.

———. (1999). No boys allowed: The World Wide Web as a clubhouse for girls. *Computers and Composition* 16: 89–106.

Terry, Jennifer, and Melodie Calvert. (1997). Introduction: Machine lives. In *Processed Lives: Gender and Technology in Everyday Life*, ed. Jennifer Terry and Melodie Calvert (pp. 1–19). New York: Routledge.

Union Pacific Corporation. (1999a). *Union Pacific Corporation* (Web site) <http://www.up.com>.

———. (1999b). *Union Pacific Corporation: A Brief History* (Web site) <http://www.up.com/overview/history.htm>.

———. (1999c). *Union Pacific Corporation: Profile* (Web site) <http://www.up.com/overview/today.htm>.

———. (1999d). *Union Pacific Railroad* (Web site) <http://www.uprr.com>.

———. (1999e). *Union Pacific Railroad Historical Overview: Construction* (Web site) <http://www.uprr.com/uprr/ffh/history/hist-ov4.shtml>.

———. (1999f). *Union Pacific Railroad Photo Gallery: American Indian* (Web site) <http://www.uprr.com/uprr/ffh/photos/NativeAmerican>.

———. (1999g). *Union Pacific Technologies* (Web site) <http://www.uptWeb.com>.

———. (1999h). *Union Pacific Technologies' Background* (Web site) <http://www.uptWeb.com/uptdefin.htm>.

———. (1999i). *Union Pacific Technologies' PQMPlus* (Web site) <http://www.uptWeb.com/uptpqms1.htm>.

———. (1999j). *Union Pacific Technologies' PQMPlus Highlights* (Web site) <http://www.uptWeb.com/pro3.gif>.

chapter fourteen

READING POWERPOINT

rich gold

Thank you very much for inviting me to speak with you today. It is a great honor.

Before I begin my talk there are several things I want to briefly mention. The first is that I have constructed this entire talk within Microsoft Office, primarily using Word and PowerPoint. The images you see were all produced from scratch in PowerPoint using only its own drawing tools. This is worth noting, for I believe (and this is not an unusual belief) that a medium powerfully affects the creative process, and so we could say that this talk is not just about PowerPoint, but it is also shaped by it.

Second, I would like to emphasize that this is not a scientific paper. Rather, it is a reflection, or perhaps a meditation, on certain activities I have engaged in and have been part of over the past decades. By far the most prominent is that during the last eight years, as a researcher at Xerox PARC, I have become a heavy PowerPoint user and have even become known for my presentations. I have ghost-written other people's Power-Point slides. I could even say I have at last found my medium. I think in PowerPoint.

And last, and most important, I have drawn deeply from my colleagues at PARC, particularly those in my RED group (Research in Experimental Documents). This a group of researchers who are currently studying *reading* and how it has changed over time and how it will continue to change in the digital age that we have so haphazardly stumbled into. I look at PowerPoint as a central, and powerful, form of reading in this new era.

READING/WRITING

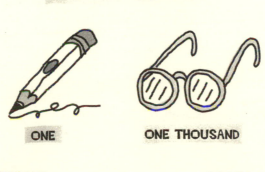

ONE   ONE THOUSAND

RICH GOLD   SLIDE TWO

Our culture privileges creativity, the making of new stuff, so greatly that we often think of writing as far more important than reading. To us, writing is the creative act, the formative act, the act of genesis. At best, we think of reading and writing as unequal equals, as mirror-like siblings that we take together as a single system. We might even imagine, as many do, that reading will disappear with the onslaught of multimedia. But we imagine that writing will remain, if for no other reason than to create the scripts for the video games.

The truth of the matter, of course, is that we read—oh, who knows, perhaps a thousand times more than we write. In every city there are only small handfuls of writers churning out the texts that the millions will read. In most of our jobs, writing takes only a fraction of our time, while reading, in all its forms, is ubiquitous. Even in my small office there are millions of printed words to read, and not just in the expected books, magazines, Web pages, and brochures. Words crowd and cover every object and surface from keyboard to telephone, from white board to poster, from etched award to my shirt's label, from the colorful boxes of shrink-wrapped software to soda cans. Words are even printed on the skin of the orange I will snack on. I am in a state of constant reading.

Our *untagged* concept of reading—that is, how we think of "reading" free of modifiers—is that of scanning pure words on white, unadorned pages. For example, try to picture the sentence: "*Jane reads.*" Most of us form an image of something like a woman sitting in a chair with a *non-illustrated* Grisham novel in her lap, *alone* and *silently* taking in the words. But most textual reading actually occurs within fields of illustrations that alter and bend the meaning of the words. In newspapers, magazines, textbooks, and on billboards, signage, and T-shirts, words appear next to, and interpenetrated by, images. Even nineteenth-century novels were illustrated (as are the covers of contemporary books). And we read everywhere, not just in armchairs. We read while driving, we read at conference tables and kitchen tables, we read in the movies, and we read on the Internet. Reading is not even necessarily silent. We read out loud to our children, to God in our churches, and to one another at conferences. Yet the image-free, silent, solitary definition of reading is so deep that it is hard for most people to even think of watching a PowerPoint presentation as reading. But within the contemporary workplace it is an extraordinarily central form.

Within today's corporation, if you want to communicate an idea to your peers or to your boss or to your employees or to your customer or even to your enemy, you use PowerPoint. PowerPoint is how companies read. I don't know if the novel is dead, but the memo certainly is. In its place rises the *slide*.

A MATRIX

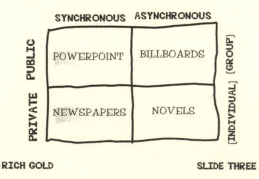

Call me a structuralist, but I often find two-by-two matrixes to be helpful. They are particularly useful here in trying to shatter the stereotype that reading is a solitary act performed silently, while prone in bed, with no pictures accompanying the words. (Just as a data point, it is good to be reminded that eight hundred years ago monks read standing up, in groups, out loud, and from illustrated texts.)

The first dimension of this matrix sweeps from top to bottom between public reading and private reading. This first dimension concerns itself with the architecture of the read word. The second dimension sweeps between synchronous reading (multiple people reading a given text at the same time) and asynchronous reading (multiple people reading a given text at different times). This second dimension is more social than architectural, but not wholly so. (There is another dimension that sweeps between group reading and individual reading that is similar to, but not completely isomorphic with, the public/private.)

The perfect example of public reading is a billboard. Other examples might be movie credits, posters, crawling stock market quotes, cereal boxes at the supermarket, or a Monopoly™ board at a party. The usual example of private reading is a book. Newspapers are mostly private, but can be read over someone's shoulder, making them a little more public. PowerPoint is quite public, but usually not as public as a billboard. So here's a good place to make the other distinction: PowerPoint is *group* reading, and the sense of the group is important. The billboard, though public, is read *individually*, each reader being alone in a vehicle.

The second axis sweeps between synchronous and asynchronous reading. To use this last example again, billboards are read asynchronously, while PowerPoint presentations are primarily read synchronously. Chat lines are synchronous, while books are read asynchronously. Newspapers are read more or less synchronously (at least on the same morning), while magazines are slightly less so (same week or same month). Reading psalms in church is highly synchronous, while reading the telephone book is asynchronous.

A PowerPoint presentation is, then, typically synchronous, group, and semiprivate—a powerful form of reading and one well suited to the hierarchical, group-oriented, and highly social nature of most corporations.

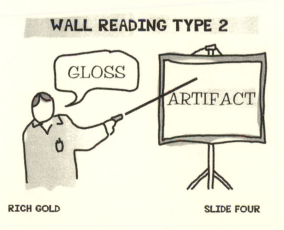

WALL READING TYPE 2

GLOSS

ARTIFACT

RICH GOLD   SLIDE FOUR

There is an interesting distinction to be made between cultures that read primarily from private documents (*bibliographic*) and cultures that read primarily from walls (*epigraphic*). Reading PowerPoint is wall reading, is group reading, is synchronous reading, is semipublic reading. The corporate shift from memos to walls is profound, for it reflects or prefigures, or constructs, a society of sociality over individuality. This tugs both ways on our national- and class-value systems, for if the isolated memo reader was alone, gray, and disconnected, he or she was also unique, self-motivated and self-determined. In the sweaty, hormone-steeped conference room, when all eyes are on the PowerPoint presenter with his or her slides dissolving from one to the next, the emphasis is on group, consensus, team, collaboration, comprise, unity.

There are two basic forms of wall reading. The first is primarily asynchronous and public: It includes billboards, road signs, posters, airport arrival/departure signs, building exit maps, you-are-here maps, storefront signage, and the like. The second group is *vocally glossed* wall reading, and it includes teachers pointing at blackboards, coaches explaining play diagrams, generals barking orders over military maps, museum tour guides pointing to painting signage, and art directors caressing new advertising campaign boards on flip charts. PowerPoint is not only in this second group, but has colonized much of it.

While it is often assumed that PowerPoint slides simply help the reader/listener to follow the speaker's argument, I propose that their actual function, as in most vocally glossed reading, is somewhat different. The slides externalize the *truth* and allow the audience to analyze it separately, but simultaneously, from what the speaker is saying *about the same truth*. The slide is not simply an opinion, it is a written artifact on a wall owned in common by all in the room—even if, as is usually the case, the speaker wrote the words in the first place. It is for this reason that it is considered a faux pas for the speaker to simply *read the slides*. For a speaker to read the slides is to attempt to make private what is now perceived as public. It is also for this reason that for the speaker to simply *read directly from notes* without extemporizing while the slides click by is also considered to be a faux pas. For a speaker to read from notes is to say that the speaker is not commenting about the commonly held written artifact, but is rather reporting on some previous, private musings.

UBIQUITOUS COMMUNICATIONS

RICH GOLD   SLIDE FIVE

Like all rituals, PowerPoint presentations arose from precursor ritu-als—shifting them, enlarging them, engulfing them. What was once minor, off-to-the-side, primitive, uncritical becomes central, expansive, elaborate, sophisticated, core. Such shifts can occur for social/political/economic reasons, and for technical reasons. The technical shift in this case was the personal computer (PC). Once the PC loomingly situated itself on the average worker's desktop, the latent social forces were in a position to re-formulate an old, minor form of reading (group presentations) into the behemoth of PowerPoint.

The driving social need leading to the rise of PowerPoint was—no sur-prise—corporate communications. It is simply mind-bending how many thousands of people and how many tens of companies, working together, it takes to make even the simplest object. To achieve these remarkable feats (and it is achieved over and over as the tens of thousands of objects in our world attest) requires more than just communication (the exchange of information); it requires common purpose and direction.

As a result (or a necessary condition) corporate workers swim in a thick soup of communications ranging from voice mail to email, from brochures to video conferences, from annual reports to Web pages, from memos to meetings, from corporate speeches to hallway gossip. Each communication form takes a different amount of time to construct (hall-way conversations are constructed in real time; annual reports might take six months to produce) and a different amount of time to consume (the hallway conversation takes as long to consume as to construct).

What PowerPoint brings to the table is not efficiencies in time. Power-Point slides are actually quite time-consuming and difficult to produce. And the *information* (to use that compromised word) contained in a forty-five-minute PowerPoint presentation can usually be contained in a short memo. What PowerPoint dramatically inspires is unifying direc-tional community formation, much as a war dance inspires the fighting power of a tribe about to go to war. If everyone is focused in the same direction, it is far more likely that whatever the company is manufacturing will get manufactured. When the PC made verbally glossed wall reading not just possible but easy, ubiquitous PowerPoint was the result.

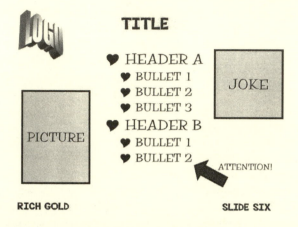

There are three primary formal elements to a PowerPoint presentation: the slides, the presenter, and the audience.

The *slides* are usually projected onto a wall or screen behind the presenter. That they are projected behind the presenter creates one of the few nettlesome problems in the PowerPoint ritual, for the presenter must decide how to deal with imagery *behind* him or her. How to point to specific elements on the slides, without either blocking the audience's view or losing eye contact with it, is not an entirely resolved problem. There is another place where the slides and the presenter rub across a rough edge: the presenter must *change the slides*, either by placing new overheads on the projector, by pressing a hand-controller, by using the "PgDwn" key on the laptop, or by calling out "next" to an unseen compatriot. This extra-textual activity can on occasion disrupt the flow of the gloss.

The wall writing itself is structurally divided into discrete *slides*, which are clicked through in a monotonic order. While contemporary versions of PowerPoint offer transition effects (fading, blending) and limited forms of animation (bullet points that come flying in), the concept of the discrete slide remains firm and is the scaffolding on which the reading hangs.

Each slide contains a combination of words and images, though either can attenuate to zero on any given slide. Although there is great variation in word and image, there are certain defining formalisms, deeply embedded within the construction parts of the PowerPoint program, that make a PowerPoint slide instantly recognizable. On the word side, there is the title, usually in boldface and placed across the top; there are numbered or dingbatted lists, usually in a terse form of PowerPoint English; there are asides or quotes or miscellaneous short blocks of text set apart for their emphasis; and there are ownership and numbering texts placed across the bottom.

Both in slide construction and in slide consumption (except for anomalies such as cartoons with speech bubbles) the graphics are distinct from the text. The graphics are either *clip art*, which are drawn with scalable vectors and fill, or *pictures*, which are bitmaps. The relationship between graphics and text can be highly varied and serve many purposes: graphics can emphasize a certain piece of text; they can illustrate a point; they can be the object of the textual references; or they can be an aside (humorous or serious). The graphics can also occupy, on occasion, the entire slide— for example, a picture of a new product—in which case any explanation must come entirely from the presenter.

In a well-formed talk, the slides have a common background image—a kind of floating landscape providing tone and cohesion, with a small number of fonts used in a consistent manner and an overall graphical style. However, as we shall see, the semiunderground economy in individual slides often results in a potpourri or potluck style instead.

POWERPOINT AS JAZZ

RICH GOLD   SLIDE SEVEN

As in most verbally glossed wall writing, the *presenter* is expected to explain the artifacts on the wall, often pointing and gesturing at them, as the talk progresses. Because they are wall writings, the audience has already reviewed much of the writing, but has not fully comprehended it. The role of the presenter is to explain these artifacts, to fill them out, to make them comprehensible. The presenter is also supposed to give the images and words appearing on the screen a truth value by reprocessing and explaining them in real time.

Hence, the role of *notes* in a PowerPoint presentation is highly ambiguous. PowerPoint itself gives a method of adding notes to each slide that can be printed out, along with thumbnails of the slides, to create a kind of cheat sheet for the speaker. Other methods of maintaining notes are by using the paper separators between the acetate slides or by using heavily annotated printouts of the slides. Typically, notes are hidden on the lectern or placed precariously on the overhead projector table. In any case, these notes are not intended to be read from (or seen by the audience), but exist only to remind the presenter of what he or she should think about, and then comment upon, in real performance time.

Presenting PowerPoint slides is, then, much like playing a sax in a jazz band. The slides (and notes) provide the bass, rhythm, and chord changes over which the melody is improvised. Clearly, the chops required to do this have been practiced and studied, but they are laid down afresh for each presentation.

When a presenter is really cooking, he or she enters *flow* (as Mihaly Csikszentmihalyi calls it in his 1991 book *Flow: The Psychology of Optimal Experience*), that state of unthinking in which each moment follows naturally from the previous in a highly intelligent manner. In flow, the presenter locks into the audience, locks into the slides, locks into the ideas, and produces a gloss that takes the obscured and fragmented wall writings and makes a whole.

UNFOLDING OF THE ARTIFACT

RICH GOLD   SLIDE EIGHT

It is an unresolvable question as to whether close listening to formally presented speech is a form of reading or not. (It is really a matter of how we want to define it.) We read books to our children; we listen to books on audio tape in our cars; poetry jumps on and off the page; before Gutenberg, almost all writings from Homer to the Bible were listened to and not looked at; the blind hear their books (when not touching them). Let's say that such listening is reading.

The *audience* reads, synchronously, the PowerPoint presentation while reading with both eyes and ears. With all facing the presenter and his or her slides, the audience enters into a deep reading reverie. Audience members' eyes read the slides and decode the images. While the slide makes sense on one level, it is only by listening to the gloss, provided by the presenter, that the deeper levels are revealed. This unfolding, this unlayering, can be quite powerful for it replicates, in a speeded-up fashion, one's own thought processes.

Like the presenter in a truly great talk, the audience also reaches flow where the visual reading and the auditory reading merge. Two things are supposed to happen. First, an understanding is reached with the presenter. Second, wholly *new thoughts* arise in the listener's mind, improvising one octave up from the speaker, like a clarinet over the sax. When all of this works, as in any synchronous reading, a community spirit is founded upon a common heartfelt experience.

Depending on the kind of presentation, the audience can ask questions either during or after the talk. Questions during the talk are truly a test of the speaker, for he or she must maintain flow, and for that reason such intratalk questions are often forbidden (or limited). On the other hand, questions at the end are extremely common, almost required, and serve a number of purposes, but primarily they are concerned with whether group consensus has been reached. These clarifications, questionings, appreciations, additions, attacks, rephrasings, shared new thoughts, and all the other interrogatives spoken by audience members are really tests of, or attempts to create or attempts to prevent, group formation. These group-formation efforts usually continue into corridors and cubicles after the talk is formally over and the audience disperses.

Unlike what happens with a memo, and to acknowledge its theatrical roots, the audience often claps at the end of a PowerPoint presentation. For the presenter, who is often in a peer or near-peer relationship to the audience, this clapping is proof of acceptance and having passed a severe test of membership.

SECONDARY READINGS

RICH GOLD   SLIDE NINE

The PowerPoint presentation is the preferred or privileged form of reading PowerPoint, but it is not the only one. Depending on the nature and context of a PowerPoint presentation, it may not even be how most readers read the slides. A slide set can be read off the Internet (or the "sneaker net"); it can be emailed to one or a thousand people; it can be printed as thumbnails and handed out (it is, in fact, a common request after a talk to ask for the paper version); or it can be placed on the Web where hundreds or millions can read it.

The obvious problem with reading PowerPoint slides *sans* presenter is, as we have seen, that it is the *verbal gloss* that contains the critical information to make the slides meaningful. The slides are often intentionally obscure (or at least so distilled as to be not more than the essence of the talk) precisely so that the verbal gloss will illuminate them. Furthermore, to the reader, without being part of an audience in the process of group formation, the slides become dry and dusty historical artifacts, the interpretation of which becomes almost arbitrary. In other words, read alone, PowerPoint slides are missing both the crucial commentary and the mammalian pack-formation pheromones.

This is known as the PowerPoint reading problem and is dealt with in various ways. First is by textually glossing the printed slides—that is, by placing narrative text next to or under the slides. This text is intended to replicate to some degree what would be verbally glossed during a presentation. Often these are simply the notes of the presenter, though more elaborate. Second, and less commonly in my experience, is that the presenter can create two versions of the slides, the second version being much more verbose and self-explanatory (that is, traditionally readable) and is the version that is distributed. Lastly, the author can leave it up to the reader to mentally add in the missing verbal gloss and read the slides *as if* both were present, much the same way that one can read poetry silently, *as if* it were being read out loud. This is difficult if you don't know what the slides are supposed to mean.

In any case, that the slides will be read after the presentation, minus the gloss, puts considerable pressure on the slide creator to make them useable without the verbal gloss even though this can diminish the performance itself. Like many art forms, PowerPoint is filled with compromise.

A GIFT CULTURE

RICH GOLD   **SLIDE TEN**

Because the *slide* in PowerPoint is so stable and formalized, and the means of PowerPoint production are so ubiquitously distributed on most PCs, and it is so easy to electronically exchange slides, and we live in an age of appropriation, annotation, and quotation within most corporations, there is a brisk trade and economy in slides. It is not uncommon to see presentations composed primarily of slides produced for other talks by other people. While this can produce a jarringly ugly and disjointed visual experience, it does not matter as much as you would expect so long as the verbal gloss, which is the heartbeat of the presentation, flows.

Within a corporation itself, just who owns a slide—the employee or the corporation—is a slippery question. Each slide certainly is another corporate asset that can and should be used to maximize ROI (Return on Investment) in multiple ways. On the other hand, each employee within a corporation is an independent agent, with his or her own career track and elaborate set of social relations. To simply use someone else's slide in your own presentation, while not illegal, is, within this context, unethical.

What arises as the resultant vector is an elaborate *gift culture* in slides. "Can I use one of your slides in my presentation?" is an oft-repeated phrase in any company. The answer is almost always "yes," but it sets up, or adds to, a balance sheet of favors that over time must get reconciled. If the favor is considered large, or if the two participants are of unequal status (either way, it turns out), the phrase "I will give you credit" is appended to the request. Eventually, a network of slides and favors bonds together entire departments and can form the basis of corporate cultural identity.

It is not uncommon, for instance, for a certain slide to be used so often, by so many different people, that it completely breaks free of its original owner and is considered an "ur-text" of the company. Such texts, because they remain in PowerPoint (unlike slides produced in Illustrator, for instance), are highly malleable and can be seen to mutate over months and even years as they are cast and re-cast into different presentations. A knowing audience can read these changes, as Soviets used to read the appearance of Politburo members on the balcony, for changes in the corporate wind.

SECONDARY CHARACTERISTICS

RICH GOLD   SLIDE ELEVEN

No art form can exist for long without creating a surrounding *aesthetic* that both modulates the new construction of it, and deeply affects the reading of the art. This aesthetic is broader than the *content* of a talk. We have all seen presentations that were *good* but lacked content, and likewise *bad* talks that had lots of content. And we can imagine two talks, both with the same content but where one was *better* than the other. These aesthetics are not neutral when judging the *effectiveness* of a presentation—that is, how much it alters subsequent behavior in a desired direction—but are critical to it. No one considers it a surprising thing to say that an aesthetically pleasing presentation is also an effective one. And in that direction lies personal success within the corporate milieu.

Just being able to successfully create an aesthetically pleasing presentation is *a secondary success characteristic* in that it suggests that the creator can also be successful in other endeavors. In that sense, it is important that it not be too easy to create a good PowerPoint presentation, for it would then cease to be a worthy test. We need not worry, of course, for to create a good presentation requires a firm grasp of content, a good graphical sense, a good written-language sense, and, most importantly, good real-time performance skills. And the bar continually inches upward with each new version of PowerPoint and with the addition of new and improved audiovisual "aides."

PowerPoint presentations, particularly at the upper levels of the company, often are ghost-produced (but they can never be ghost-presented in anything like the same sense). As the graphical aesthetics become more sophisticated, it becomes necessary to turn the task of the slide production over to professional graphic artists. But managing graphics artists is itself a difficult task (and perhaps a worthier test of corporate skill than that of centering text).

Great presentations can arise out of a corporation and gain national or even international fame. In the lucrative conference circuit, audience members pay thousands of dollars to attend sessions that have become in essence PowerPoint marathons, in which presentations can be compared for aesthetic and content quality.

EVEN ARCHITECTURE

OLD   NEW

RICH GOLD   **SLIDE TWELVE**

PowerPoint has transformed the modern corporation from a document-reading environment of individuals to one of group, synchronous wall reading. In so doing it has transformed the social forces that bind the corporation and give it direction and unity. It has also brought with it a sense of aesthetic art and performance, of theater and theatricality that had been largely missing. But the times are not stagnant and we can expect still further changes.

There is a growing tendency to include video within presentations, which is highly problematic because video drags the attention away from the presenter's gloss. The gloss must either be loudly spoken over the video's soundtrack or be delayed until the video is over.

As video conferencing becomes more common (primarily as a solution to the high cost of travel), PowerPoint presentations are often broadcast as part of these virtual meetings, the techniques and aesthetics of which are still to be largely worked out. To the remote viewer, the graphics and gloss collapse into a single, distanced video, which may need its own local gloss. In any case, they are often painful to watch.

Like all other media, PowerPoint is merging with the Web. It is not uncommon these days for PowerPoint-looking talks to be given directly off the Web in HTML. It is assumed that in the near-future Microsoft will migrate PowerPoint directly onto the Web, thereby collapsing this distance to zero. While I see this as a difference in media, the genre remains pretty much the same.

While there are perceptual changes in equipment (from noisy overhead projectors to finicky laptops), PowerPoint is now, most amazing, directly affecting the very architecture of corporate buildings. Until recently, conference rooms were dominated by the oval table, perfectly suited for a document-based culture. Companies are now in the midst of remodel fever, replacing the ovals with "U"s, the open end of which faces a wall of white screens, perfect for a wall reading society.

Just as Gutenberg's printing press changed what and how we read and what a library looked like, PowerPoint is changing how the neurons of business carry information, and even what their office buildings look like.

Thank you, for allowing me speak to you today. I will now take questions.

READING POWERPOINT

Thank You

RICH GOLD   SLIDE THIRTEEN

Reference

Csikszentmihalyi, Mihaly. (1991). *Flow: The Psychology of Optimal Experience.* New York: HarperCollins.

chapter fifteen

MIXING OIL AND WATER
writing, design, and the new technology

◆

neil kleinman

Prologue

L ET ME START WITH A STORY. Sean Cohen graduated from our master's program in publications design after arriving with an undergraduate degree
in painting and English. A man of many talents, he is a writer, graphic
designer, and Web designer, who also teaches courses in interactive design.
The story begins with a telephone conversation on the day he started his
new job as multimedia specialist at the Hubble Space Telescope Project.
  Here is his story in his own words:

Boss: Hi, I see here on your resume that you are a designer.
Sean: Sure, but I code too, uh, you know and I also write. [Screaming inside,
  "THAT IS WHY YOU HIRED ME!"]
Boss: Are you a programmer?
Sean: Well, not really, I do Javascript, lingo, etc. I do scripting . . . not C++
  or Java coding. I also write the narrative and captions that go with
  the site.
Boss: [a pause] Are you a programmer or a designer or a writer?
Sean: I like to be in the place where programming, writing, and design meet.
  [Using his "I believe in happiness" voice.]

Boss: They don't meet.

Sean: I'm sorry?

Boss: They don't meet. That is what I am trying to get from you.

Sean: I am sorry, somehow I am not understanding.

Boss: [sigh] The programmers work on the left side of the building. The designers work on the right. And the writers work in another building altogether.

Sean: Oh.

Boss: They don't meet. We were wondering who to put you with. If you go with the programmers, you'll be in their meetings.

Sean: And if I go with the designers?

Boss: They don't talk to the programmers. They don't meet.

Sean: And if I go with the writers?

Boss: They don't talk to the programmers or the designers.

Sean: Are we talking about who shows up to what meetings?

Boss: Yes. And also where your office will be.

Sean: I get an office?

Boss: No. A cubicle. Sorry. [She actually sounds sorry.]

Sean: Is there any cubicle space in the middle?

Boss: What do you mean?

Sean: Is there any space in the middle, you know, where I could go and talk to programmers OR designers OR writers if I wanted?

Boss: Why would you want that?

Sean: Uhm, heh heh. [He begins to panic.] IS there space in the middle?

Boss: Maybe we should discuss this in person. [She sounds a little miffed.]

Sean: Ok, uh—

Boss: No, we'll just put you in another division, ok?

Sean: Uhmm—

Boss: That's how we will solve this. [And then a clipped] Thank you.

So that is how Sean Cohen (1995) got to be in his own division.

Something's Happening

I tell you this story because it explains a great deal about what is happening around us: the changing requirements for jobs and the new experiences, expectations, and talents people bring to their work. The new digital media—first, desktop publishing and, now, Web design and digital editing in all media—are reshaping what we know about writing, reading, and design (Kleinman 1997, 30). They are making us rethink how we express ourselves, make our ideas public, and incorporate words, images, action, and sound (Kleinman 1997, 51–57).

Is there a place where programming, writing, and design meet? That is not something one would have asked even as recently as five years ago. The nature of our discourse is changing; perhaps, in fact, it has already changed. The skills we need to communicate, create, and teach are changing too. Few of us now can work without our computers and word-processing programs, without access to the Web for research and the Web for classwork and professional work space, and without email to communicate short notes and lengthy essays.

These changes signal more than changes in the tools we use to write. Bit by bit, we are discovering that the new media are changing the way we express ourselves: what we think to say, how we think to say it, and the audience we say it to. We don't limit our public and private narratives to type on paper (Nunberg 1996, 133). With that, we must learn a new way of telling stories, as well as learn a new way of reading them. We are able now to write, design, and display ideas using a rich range of media that incorporate sound, image, words, motion, and hypertext links. There is a growing body of literature that exists in electronic space, that was written to fit "naturally" in that environment. It now needs to be read, needs to be understood, and needs to be explained. The problem is that most readers will need to rethink the way they read, and need to recreate the way they evaluate what they are reading. What is called for are forms of analysis different from those many of us learned when we were students. We shall all need to get prepared—producers of this new work, teachers, and students alike.

New forms of analysis? That seems rather extreme. To understand why it's not, remember the way we were first taught to analyze a poem. After reading "Sir Patrick Spence," the teacher asked what now seems the obvious question: "The poem begins with a scene at the royal court. Does the rest of the poem break up into scenes? What are they?" (Brooks and Warren 1950, 14).

The question means little in a world of hypermedia. Where does one find the beginning? It seems to change each time one starts. How does one look for the orderly progression of scenes? Scenes, sections, or phrases emerge often by surprise and not in a regularly predictable pattern. Later, when we are asked to study a poet's intention and meaning, we face the same dilemma. Shown two versions of a poem, one an early draft and the other a version that "is approaching the finished form," we're told to "write an account of the development of the poem" (Brooks and Warren 1950, 625). The question assumes that we can tease out the author's intent—it assumes, in fact, that there is an author who is in charge: "For better or for worse, the poet is responsible for his poem. He can always reject any ideas, images, phrases, etc., that come into his head. . . . And in the end, if a poet feels that a poem doesn't represent him . . . he can always burn it. His veto is absolute" (Brooks and Warren 1950, 610–11). For the moment, we are asked to weigh in on the side of the author, the rights he has and the powers he's likely to assert. The reader is only a bystander. He can twiddle his thumbs but can do little else since it's the author who must decide that the work is finished and fixed. By the time the reader gets his hands on it, the composition phase is complete. It's only then that the reader's job begins.

What, though, if we were to weigh in on the side of the reader? That is, after all, what hypermedia encourages us to do. "Hypertext . . . creates an active, even intrusive reader" (Landow 1992, 71), a reader who leans across the author's desktop and suggests, just as the work is being "composed," how it might be arranged or changed. Here is a very different attitude towards the author, the reader, and the text itself. Nothing is final. Nothing is fixed, and the author's role is something short of absolute.

What of the teacher's original assignment? *Write an account of the development of the poem?* It is nearly impossible to point to "a finished form," and equally difficult to decide who is responsible for the poem's development. Things have become a lot more fluid.

The requirements of the new media and their effect on the analysis of graphic design are equally apparent. Read, for example, Jan White's book, *Editing by Design* (1974). Writing about how to design to tie facing pages together, White presents an elegantly designed two-page spread: on the left, we see a young boy peering through a cut-out in a wall; the boy is looking towards the outer trim of the book. On the right, we find the text which begins with a nicely balanced heading, "Look ahead" (White 1974, 27); the heading is positioned to look in a direction opposite to that of the boy's gaze. The rule, we are told, is: "Link facing pages by implication of meaning" (White 1974, 27). This is classic print-design advice. Design enhances the story. The facing pages contain and define the words and image; they establish meaning through fixed form, fixed comparisons, and fixed contrasts.

Good print design stops us so we can admire each spread, so we can follow the story that is unfolding as we read. Web design is up to something else: it wants to get the reader to move, to jump from layer to layer, to skip and bounce from one part of the "information structure" to another. It encourages us to navigate easily, quickly, and confidently among levels of information. What can be more different?

A page of print is a container, inviting us to stop awhile so we can appreciate the meaning that's right in front of us. A Web page is a "portal," suggesting passage somewhere else. Where that trip leads is not easy to predict since it is not entirely in the hands of the designer or writer. After all, in hypermedia, the "user" has some authority to decide what's next. He can "choose his . . . way through the metatext . . . and . . . create links between documents written by others" (Landow 1992, 71).

What remains of the old aesthetic and the traditional authorities we have normally associated with the roles of author and designer? What aesthetic rules do we have to help us understand how to promote navigation, "readability," and a visual balance that successfully ties dynamic pages? Like their students, many faculty members will need to learn a form of analysis that makes sense in this medium.

———◆———

Sometimes the literature of this new media seems incomprehensible, frustrating, annoying, even downright perverse (Kleinman 1997, 31–33). Sometimes, its humor, wit, and surprising connections remind us of ideas and ways of seeing that seem dreamlike and liberating. Perhaps most often, reading work in the new media is exciting because it suggests new ways of saying things that we might try.

First, though, we need to learn how to read all of these visual, verbal, and aural messages so that we can help ourselves and our students exploit them. Where is Pound's (n.d.) *ABC of Reading* when we need it? Until we have such a book, we shall have to proceed by trial and error. People will learn what they need to learn so that they can do what they must do. As in most enterprises, the aesthetic standard remains a few steps behind the practice.

Sean Cohen can't do the kind of Web design that's required of him if he does not know how to design, program, and write. But once he knows how to design, program, and write, he will find that there are things he can say— things he *wants* to say—that he could not say when he was working only at one level of the "text." At the same time, as he works in a medium that is more accessible to a variety of users, he'll find that what he *wants* to say will change as he recognizes the variety and differences in his audience.

Something Happened

How did we get here? For several generations, literature was read as being the best thoughts; as Alexander Pope (1711/1966) explained, "ne'er so well expressed" ("An Essay on Criticism," line 298) or, as Matthew Arnold (1865/1962) proclaimed 150 years later, "the best that is known and thought" ("The Function of Criticism at the Present Time," in Super 1962, 283). One didn't "teach" literature because that was, to put it simply, what gentlemen read. The book was an extension of culture because it was the language of culture. One learned about literature, especially contemporary literature, in the same way one learned the social graces—by participating in "society."

By the late nineteenth century it was becoming apparent that there were simply too many books being written and too few men of discernment available to sort out the better ones. What such a proliferation of bad literature might mean for culture was anyone's guess, but some suspected that it did not bode well. It argued for critics and for anthologies so that some "authority" might regulate this state of affairs. So explained Francis Turner Palgrave (1861/1991), whose *Golden Treasury* was the best seller of its time:

> Reading tends to become only another kind of gossip. Everything is to be read, and everything only once; a book is no more a treasure to be kept and studied and known by heart, as the truly charming phrase has it. . . .
> Really, the more books, the better possible selection for the readers; but each fills so little time in an age when everyone reads, that it is natural to turn to the next on the table. I may notice that this summary process, this inability to read even novelties more than once, leads to a truly mean and miserable false judgment on many books once justly studied and enjoyed. (p. 453)

By the late nineteenth century it became clear that anthologies by themselves would not suffice, and, early in the twentieth century, Sir Walter Raleigh of Oxford University was named the first professor of English. As he somewhat apologetically explained to a friend (quoted in Kernan 1990, 1):

> If any young man could found a society where people speak only what they think and tell only what they know—in the first words that come to hand—that would be, at last, a school of literature.
> But of course we must carry on. Prophets are no good: they get pupils and imitators and start silly fashions. God forgive us all! If I am accused on Judgment day of teaching literature, I shall plead that I never believed in it and that I maintained a wife and children.

Raleigh was arguing for a new study of literature—the study of "living literature"—which he thought should replace the study of the classics. It seemed rather revolutionary at the time.

What was central to the agenda of Raleigh, Palgrave, Arnold, and Pope was that each, in his own way, emphasized the text, the printed document in which the best thoughts were fixed in literature and then transmitted from one generation to the next. This emphasis was true for succeeding generations and succeeding revolutions. Thus when Cleanth Brooks and Robert Penn Warren first published *Understanding Poetry* (1938), the book that helped to establish New Criticism as *the* literary approach of the 1950s and '60s, they explained that the "emphasis should be kept on the poem as a poem" (Brooks and Warren 1950, ix),

> though one may consider a poem as an instance of historical or ethical documentation, the poem in itself, if literature is to be studied as litera-

ture, remains finally the object for study. Moreover, even if the interest is in the poem as a historical or ethical document, there is a prior consideration: one must grasp the poem as a literary construct before it can offer any real illumination as a document. (p. iv)

They meant to cut away what they took to be the overgrowth of irrelevant commentary, social interpretation, and classical comparisons that had been the contributions of Raleigh, Arnold, and Palgrave, but like them, they also based their criticism on the printed object, the "literary construct," as the thing that should be examined. A new aestheticism? Perhaps. But still it was one that depended upon the same medium that the Victorians built their criticism on. It turns out that it is difficult to build an entirely new edifice when one must use the stones from the last one.

So successively, each generation of teachers of literature has centered its discussions on print-based literature (Bolter 1991, 153–56; Kernan 1990, 9, 15). What else might one do, since so much of the literary record had been fixed in print for the last five hundred years? It is true, though, that the literary tradition was fraying at the edges—for a number of reasons. The impact of the new media of television, radio, and print advertising was becoming more apparent, as McLuhan (1964) and others reminded us during the 1960s and '70s. The tools of a new technology were being taken more seriously as anyone who thumbed through the *Whole Earth Catalog* (Brand and Warshall 1968/1998) was bound to see. And the "literature of the streets," mediated by television, street pamphlets, and folk music, culminated in the summer of 1968 and moved the 1960s generation even further from a text-based literature. At every turn, we were told, or shown, that technology, media, culture, and art—not to mention politics and social change—were connected.

Still, departments of English and literature did not budge. Their curriculum was fixed in the literary approaches of the previous generation. Even postmodern criticism is a print-based discourse, developing analyses of the text, discussing intertextuality using the printed medium, talking about the death of print and print-bound literature even as the postmodern critics used the print medium to publish the obituary (Bolter 1991, 161–64; Kernan 1990, 213; Landow 1992, 2–7, 30–34). The first hint of change was to come when, as George Landow (1992, 3) put it, "critical theorists . . . have . . . a new laboratory, in addition to the conventional library of printed texts, in which to test their ideas of critical theory." The laboratory was the personal computer and the software associated with hypertext and hypermedia. For many, the Apple computer, which became available in 1977, gave them their first chance to see what such a lab might look like, although it would be another decade before they heard about hypertext.

Beginning Somewhere

Sometimes beginnings start in the oddest places. In 1978, the University of Baltimore—a small "upper-level" university—started a graduate program that "integrated" writing and design and used, as best it could, some of the early computer-based design and typography systems then available. Looking back, we can rationalize why we created this program: our sense of where things were going, our curiosity, our interest in the ideas of McLuhan, and our desire to "play" with these new forms of expressions.

Many of us also felt a certain degree of powerlessness: no one seemed to care what English teachers had to say; English majors graduated with a depressing lassitude and passivity (who wanted what they knew?); and some of us felt that our writing was too often taken over by designers who shaped it in ways that seemed to make what we wrote unreadable. Like factory workers of the nineteenth century, we only asked to control the means of production. A curriculum that taught writers "how to design" or, at least, "how to talk to designers" seemed the solution, and a curriculum that taught designers "how to behave" when dealing with words seemed useful.

What was, probably, the most important force to make us take a chance with such a risky curriculum was that we needed to figure out a way of surviving. Issues of survival always have a way of getting one's attention. Because we were an upper-division university, we had no composition and rhetoric courses to justify our existence. And, therefore, we couldn't have been a service program even if we'd wanted to be! Because our university was small and appealed to working-class students interested primarily in a practical education, we had few majors. Without students interested in what we taught, there seemed to be little time left before we would dwindle to nothing.

There was good news too. Because we were a small university, we had no art department, communications programs, not even a computer-science program, so we had no one to compete with. Like Defoe's Robinson Crusoe, we built our curriculum taking pieces from the debris we found about us. No one stopped us as we created our curriculum in writing and design, because no one thought it would work and no one cared.

By the mid-1980s we added video to the mix, and in the mid-'90s we added hypermedia, multimedia, and, more recently, Web design. In 1998 we started a post–master's-degree program, a doctorate in communications design that takes up questions of marketing, business development, and entrepreneurship and considers how to develop new publications that take advantage of the new and old media, at the same time that students polish their skills in design, writing, and digital technology.

To absorb all of this, we've grown. Starting in 1978 with a faculty of about eight in a small English department, we now have seventeen faculty members teaching in the programs offered within what's now named the School of Communications Design. This faculty teach in a range of disciplines: creative writing, technical and professional writing, graphic design, videography and radio, communications theory and practice, literary criticism and theory and language analysis, social and economic history, law, electronic publishing, hypermedia and interface design, and business practices and marketing. Along with this faculty, the school now has three professionals with significant competence in computer graphics, interface design, computer programming and systems management, and video and audio production. In addition we have three labs—in graphics, video, and hypermedia.

The change has been considerable. Literature and writing faculty now teach with faculty trained in videography, design, hypermedia, and programming. Faculty used to blackboards, typewriters, and pencils now work in an environment of computer labs and video- and digital-editing suites. Words and images are treated together, and both faculty and students try to learn a language that attempts to combine very different aesthetics, assumptions, and values. It appears that we've been able to fashion a place where programming, writing, and design *do* meet.

Telling the Truth and Moving On

It all sounds pretty impressive. The truth is a bit more complicated than the rhetoric. Like so many experimenters, we've managed to build a laboratory, but we've not yet created what we hoped to—an environment in which we integrate word and image, create a new language and a new form of expression, and understand the theory behind this integration. Perhaps there is one simple reason—an explanation that tells us much about the transition we are all going through: as a program, we are still very much influenced by the "print culture" that we grew up in.

Many in our English literature faculty were trained in New Critical theory, and that theory is still embedded in our nervous systems. It reveals itself almost reflexively when we look at a "text." We read and teach the postmoderns. Nevertheless, somewhere in our literary psyches many of us still look to the "literary construct" as the object to be studied. Our design faculty members are also locked into the print culture. Their design aesthetic has been shaped by five hundred years of print and print typography. They too feel a bit uncomfortable when forced to deal with dynamic pages of hypermedia, limited arrays of typographic forms, and an inability to "fix" their design so that they can predict what the "viewer" will see.

Where Do We Go from Here?

Although we have come a long way in the last twenty years, it is important to admit that we still don't have answers to many of the questions. Far from it! In fact, we are only now beginning to learn some of the questions. There are so many questions to deal with, but two of the most important relate to the passionate, often ferocious, interaction between two forms of discourse: the first represented by the way we communicate when we write, and the second represented by the way we communicate when we design.

IS IT POSSIBLE TO INTEGRATE THE WORD AND THE IMAGE?

It is unpleasant to admit this, but integrating words and images is a rather subversive act, especially if the images begin to move and the words are both text and sound. W. J. Thomas Mitchell (1986, 43) neatly describes the struggle:

> Among the most interesting and complex versions of this struggle [between word and image] is what might be called the relationship of subversion, in which language or imagery looks into its own heart and finds lurking there its opposite number. . . .
>
> [T]he relationship between words and images reflects, within the realm of representation, signification, and communication, the relations we posit between symbols and the world, signs and their meanings. We imagine the gulf between words and images to be as wide as the one between words and things, between (in the largest sense) culture and nature.

Sometimes the gulf between words and images seems pretty wide and very deep.

Taken together, words and images create an unstable tension between the narrative structure of verbal and visual material. The verbal presents ideas in a time-bound discourse: the reader does not take in information instantly; he must be both patient and curious—sufficiently curious to want to wait to hear the story as it unfolds. The visual is instantly displayed and instantly understood. The viewer takes it all in at one glance and begins to draw conclusions from what he or she sees. One *feels* the tension between these two when students present their work to be judged. The writers feel unloved and unread. Because it takes so long to appreciate what they've achieved, they are greeted by polite silence. In contrast, the designers receive instant gratification—and applause.

When the two are placed together, the verbal is, too often, at a distinct disadvantage. It does not have sufficient power over the imagination, perhaps because the imagination is fueled by the energy of our dreams that are, for the most part, visual (Freud 1965, 347).

If the verbal is almost always overwhelmed by the visual, then why would we want to teach ourselves and our students to "integrate" writing and design? The easy answer is that we have no choice. The new media makes such integration inevitable. Fewer and fewer writers and readers over the next decade or so will be comfortable with text that is merely limited to typographic form. They will insist upon the dynamic of the visual and verbal being connected. (Once the eye is trained or prepared for this integration, it becomes difficult for the eye to return to the rather placid forms of simple text on paper.)

The easy answer to why we've begun to work among these forms, as I've said, is that we had no choice. The hard answer is that this is the time for people who have been trained to think about creative expression, rhetoric, and persuasion to think about the aesthetic that these new media demand. If we don't, who will? The software engineer? The writer lamenting the lost authority he or she once took for granted? The designer in control of "the work" but timid around declarative statements? If we believe that there are aesthetic values, narrative traditions, and ways of telling stories that we would like to see continued in the new media, we must learn how to use that media and help to shape it as a creative and humane form of expression.

IS IT POSSIBLE FOR DESIGNERS, WRITERS, HYPERMEDIA DESIGNERS, AND TEACHERS OF LITERATURE TO WORK TOGETHER?

The tension between the verbal and the visual repeats itself in the relationship between the commentators or critics and the makers or designers. This tension is reflected, writes Mitchell (1986, 43), in a "compulsion to conceive of the relation between words and images in political terms, as a struggle for territory, a contest of rival ideologies." He is right. If the struggle between word and image is "political," you can only imagine what it must be like between writers and designers. It is even more difficult to mix those who are committed to the *craft of producing* new work—whether they are designers or writers or poets—with those who find pleasure in *commenting on the work* that others have produced. One finds, as Mitchell predicts, "a struggle for territory and a contest of rival ideologies" (1986, 43).

Put simply, the critic analyzes and describes. At its best, his or her criticism or commentary provides a descriptive overlay that points to an action—the act of making or presenting that which was made. The designer (or the creative writer) makes and presents objects that are more nearly action. Perhaps, in fact, the Web designer comes closer to true action when he works in the dynamic, almost mimetic space of the Web.

Designers and critics seem to operate in two very different worlds. How can they work in the same department or teach the same students? If we don't learn how to collaborate in this new media, we will have learned nothing—although the price and pain of collaboration are high. Those who follow "a craft" generally have a low opinion of theorists; how, they wonder, can anyone know what the work means if they can't *do* it? "Oh, yes, they can talk the talk, but can they walk the walk?" On the other side, those who follow theory often see practitioners as blind moles who dig their holes in the earth without a larger sense of purpose and plan. Yes, they say, each piece is good, but *how* will it fit into other work and other purposes? And if it does, *why* and to *what end*? "Good technique, but nothing to say!"

It is because of the differences between the makers and the commentators, between creators and critics, that there is every reason to struggle to keep them together, talking and making. Like linking Aristoleans and Platonists, one ends up with an education that combines an appreciation of the particular and an understanding of the whole. Again, Professor Mitchell (1986, 44–46) provides part of the answer as to why it is important to bring writers and designers together:

> [The struggle between word and image] carries the fundamental contradictions of our culture into the heart of theoretical discourse itself. The point, then, is not to heal the split between words and images, but to see what interests and powers it serves. . . .
>
> Perhaps the redemption of the imagination lies in accepting the fact that we create much of our world out of the dialogue between verbal and pictorial representation.

The electronic space pushes us to maintain that dialogue and forces us to learn how to appreciate the inevitable struggle between these two forms of discourse. This struggle—a civilized version of combat—is probably impossible to simulate in a classroom if both writers and designers, critics and creators, those committed to print and those engaged in the digital, are not in the classroom together. Who would take seriously an argument in which the two contenders are not present to deliver the blows and receive them in turn?

Why?

If the struggle is so hard, the rules so vague, and the principles so easily questioned, what's to recommend an attempt to integrate writing and design? Any student might reasonably wonder how she is to learn both. Teachers and professionals, who have already mastered one craft, will no doubt ask why they should become amateurs again simply to learn another one. To the teacher, the student, or the professional the task will appear all the more daunting, perhaps even foolish, when he or she understands the time it takes to acquire skills not normally taught in writing and design programs—skills connected to the "quantitative" and algorithmic disciplines of computing, information architecture, and dynamic databases rather than those connected to the creative and expressive arts.

The requirements (and possibilities) of cyberspace are becoming apparent to anyone who lives, publishes, or creates in this environment.

> [Writers] must . . . become software testers, since pages designed for Netscape on a Wintel machine will look different when viewed with Internet Explorer or on a Macintosh. . . . They need to become programmers and designers, with technical expertise rarely learned in humanities . . . programs. (Rosenzweig 2000, B5)

> "Digital journalists" are needed who not only can write and report stories for online publications but can pepper them with video, sound clips, and links to related resources. (Career Opportunities 1995, 77–78)

> When industries are competing at equal price and functionality, design is the only differential that matters. (Mark Dziersky, president, Industrial Designers Society of America, quoted in Gibney and Luscombe 2000, 69)

> Exploiting qualities unique to digital technology, digital worlds cannot exist independently of a computer. *They are worlds that could not even be conceived without digital technology.* These are the worlds that soon will define and fill ethereal cyberspace and that represent an unexplored frontier of human expression. (Holtzman 1997, 16)

> In the new media we work in an era of constantly shifting technological and business boundaries and following change is the only constant. . . . [Our] efforts to keep pace with the evolving business have led us to recruit from a wide variety of backgrounds . . . radio, television, film newspapers, magazines, software engineering, and museums. (John Sanford, design director, Discovery Online and Discovery Publishing, writing in support of proposed doctorate in communications design, 1996)

WHY MAKE THE ATTEMPT TO COMBINE THE WORD AND THE IMAGE IN A NEW TECHNOLOGY?

The answer to the skeptical teacher is simple: The ability to integrate writing and design, especially through the new medium, is going to be important to expression in the next generation. I do not say that it will be the only way to express ideas and create new ones. I only say that it will be a primary force for those who wish to create or communicate in the years ahead. It is time to reflect on that change, what it promises and what it threatens so that students are prepared to engage in the creative dialogue that is beginning to take shape around them (Kleinman 1997, 33–39).

The answer to the skeptical student is equally simple: The marketplace needs people who can write and design and can take advantage of digital media. For the practical, this means remarkable job prospects. But money aside, there is an even more compelling reason to embrace this new media and to learn how to find a space that brings programming, writing, and design together. The new media provides an opportunity to walk on a field of "new snow" that has few, if any, foot prints. For those who are creative, this means that they have been given the rare chance to experiment, create, and lead before they are weighed down by the burden of tradition and convention.

Samuel Johnson, who knew something about writing, reading, and publishing, once remarked that "you can never be wise unless you love reading" (quoted in Kernan 1987, 219). Here is a wonderful and curious thought. Certainly it is one worthy of the great dictionary-maker, the man who'd read "every" printed book of his time so that he could catalog and organize their words. But for us now, it would be odd to believe that civilization is based upon the printed word or that knowledge can only come from reading. "We—readers of books . . .— are so literate," Walter Ong (1982, 2) reminds us, "that it is very difficult for us to conceive of an oral universe of communication or thought except as a variant of a literate universe."

The question now is: Can we envision a postliterate culture in which knowledge and wisdom emerge from a love of reading, writing, and design that depend less on print and more on new media for expression and meaning? To say that wisdom only comes through reading is to forget the role of Socrates or Homer or others who played their lives out in a preliterate time. Perhaps we will find wisdom in a "postliterate" culture, one that combines words, images, and sound in a quite different syntax from the one we now use. Until then, we shall need to work to build more places where programming, writing, and design meet.

Acknowledgments

For this chapter, I am in debt to Sean Cohen—both for his story and his disagreements. He reminds me that the integration of words and images is possible—if not now, soon.

An earlier version of this chapter was given as a presentation at the

1998 Conference on Programs in Technical and Scientific Communication and appears in that conference's proceedings.

This chapter is dedicated to Bill Kinser (1931–1999), a designer who loved reading and writing: He was there at the beginning.

References

Arnold, Matthew. (1865/1962). The function of criticism at the present time. In *Lectures and Essays in Criticism*, ed. R. H. Super (pp. 258–85). Ann Arbor: University of Michigan Press.

Bolter, Jay D. (1991). *Writing Space*. Hillsdale, NJ: Lawrence Erlbaum.

Brand, Stewart, and Peter Warshall (Eds). (1968/1998). *Original Whole Earth Catalog, Special 30th Anniversary Issue*. San Rafael, CA: Whole Earth.

Brooks, Cleanth, and Robert P. Warren. (1950). *Understanding Poetry*, rev. ed. New York: Holt.

Career Opportunities. (1995, October 30). *U.S. News & World Report*, 77–78.

Cohen, Sean. (1995, September 24). Personal communication.

Freud, Sigmund. (1965). *The Interpretation of Dreams*. New York: Avon Books.

Gibney, Frank, and Belinda Luscombe. (2000, March 20). The redesigning of America. *Time* 155: 66–73.

Holtzman, Steven. (1997). *Digital Mosaics: The Aesthetics of Cyberspace*. New York: Simon & Schuster.

Kernan, Alvin. (1987/1989). *Printing Technology, Letters and Samuel Johnson*. Reprinted as *Samuel Johnson and the Impact of Print*. Princeton, NJ: Princeton University Press.

———. (1990). *The Death of Literature*. New Haven, CT: Yale University Press.

Kleinman, Neil. (1997). The digital revolution ain't so bad. *CEAMAGazine* 10: 30–59.

Landow, George. (1992). *Hypertext*. Baltimore: Johns Hopkins University Press.

McLuhan, Marshall. (1964). *Understanding Media*. New York: McGraw-Hill.

Mitchell, W. J. Thomas. (1986). *Iconology*. Chicago: University of Chicago Press.

Nunberg, Geoffrey. (1996). Farewell to the information age. In *The Future of the Book*, ed. G. Nunberg (pp. 103–33). Berkeley: University of California Press.

Ong, Walter. (1982). *Orality and Literacy*. New York: Methuen.

Palgrave, Francis T. (1861/1991). On readers in 1760 and 1860. In *The Golden Treasury*, ed. C. Ricks (pp. 451–54). London: Penguin.

Pope, Alexander. (1711/1966) An essay on criticism. In *Pope's Poetical Works*, ed. H. Davis (pp. 64–85). London: Oxford University Press.

Pound, Ezra. (n.d.). *ABC of Reading*. New York: New Directions.

Rosenzweig, Roy. (2000, March 17). The riches of hypertext for scholarly journals. *Chronicle of Higher Education* 46: B4–B5.

Sanford, John L. (1996, October 28). Letter of support for proposed doctorate in communications design. Available from the School of Communications Design, University of Baltimore (1420 N. Charles Street Baltimore, MD 21201).

White, Jan. (1974). *Editing by Design*. New York: Bowker.

AFTERWORD

experiments with image and word

———◆———

F OLLOWING BIOLOGY'S MODEL for "studying" a subject, Neil Kleinman has developed eight experiments, or as we call them in writing classes, exercises, for awakening our senses to visual elements and the ways that they relate to words. (Professor Agassiz, famous for teaching about fish, would be proud [Cooper 1945, 65].) These experiments, found in appendix A, are divided into work at three levels—novice, more experienced, and advanced—to benefit students and professionals who would like to practice and improve on their skills.

In addition to these experiments, Kleinman has outlined five courses that can be used to form the core of a curriculum intended to develop theoretical concepts and skills for working with words and images. This model curriculum is found in appendix B. These courses are modeled on a curriculum developed at the University of Baltimore's School of Communications Design.

Reference

Cooper, Lane. (1945). How Agassiz taught professor Scudder. *Louis Agassiz as a Teacher*. Ithaca, NY: Comstock Publishing, 55–61.

APPENDIX A

exercises and experiments for the workbench

———◆———

"**I**F WE'RE NOT CAREFUL, we'll only talk and have done nothing!" says the student. In reply to that the clever teacher should say, "The proper METHOD for studying . . . is the method of contemporary biologists, that is careful first-hand examination of the matter, and continual COMPARI-SON of one 'slide' or specimen with another" (Pound n.d., 17). Like that teacher, I don't know any better place to begin. What follows are some slides to start with. (The culture will provide many more.)

The order of these exercises moves from observation to action, from thinking to making, from texts others create to those we create for ourselves. But no student or teacher should feel obliged to follow that order. In some things, we are novices. In others, we are advanced. We must decide this for ourselves.

FOR NOVICES

1. *Telling, Pointing, Holding—it's all in the way we do it and in the way we describe it.*

Look at the magazines, books, or Web sites you normally read. Have they a linear structure with clearly defined beginnings, middles, and ends? Are they "portals"—an entrance that links you to alternate paths, each path taking you in a different direction with the likelihood that you'll not return to where you began? Or do they serve as "containers" in which everything is connected but connected to keep you in one place (like a page or a printed magazine or book) so that you don't wander off?

Linear structures, portals, and containers have been with us a long time, although with different names. They are ways of telling a story, and they are ways of thinking. We're used to *linear* narrations and find them in much of nineteenth- and twentieth-century storytelling (e.g., Tolstoy, Stendhal, Eliot, James, and Hemingway).

The *portal* is not new, although with the advent of the Web it has been given a new life. The digressive structure of Swift's *Tale of a Tub*, Sterne's *Tristram Shandy*, or Cervantes's *Don Quixote* is very much like a portal: one idea takes us on to another, each footnote or digression takes us to another text. The images of Escher are forms of portals. Our eye cannot stop. Just as we think we see "closure"—the form that frames everything— we see a new dynamic, a new way of looking, and we move on. The stories of Borges in his book *Labyrinth* are also forms of portal storytelling. What is a labyrinth but an infinite portal? Just as we think we understand the shape, there's another layer, another direction, and another way to go.

It's not hard to find *containers*. They are all about us, especially in the classroom. Anthologies, literary collections, and, in fact, books like the Bible are nothing more than containers. They collect a range of ideas and texts meant to refer to one another and, by thus referring to one another, define the pieces they are collected with.

2. *Voice, Audience, and Point of View—if I only knew my audience, I'd know what to say.*

Compare an issue for the same week of two different news magazines and contrast the way each one treats the same news event. Move a photograph, a paragraph, or a caption from one article to another or add something created by you. Then consider the change of voice, tone, and purpose.

The language, the visuals, and the layout we use combine to create "an attitude"—a voice and tone. The "style" of a magazine has been shaped to address a specific audience: old people, young people, hip people, singles, couples, and so on. Each magazine has a different point of view—a political, social, or cultural bias, even if it is carefully hidden. It is possible to tell who the audience is by taking apart the language, voice, and images being used, just as it is possible to build a magazine by knowing the kinds of voices, images, music, and language your target audience likes. Publications are carefully wrapped packages of words and images that frame a story in a distinctive way. Change one of the elements, and you change the tone, voice, point of view, and meaning.

3. *Selection and Editing—it's what is* <u>*not*</u> *there that counts. We define everything by what we omit.*

Select a photograph and list what is and what is not shown.

The easy part will be to describe what is present. It will be harder to imagine what might have been in the picture but is not. Why is something *not* there? What does the decision *not* to include material that "could have been there" tell us about the picture and the story that's being told?

4. *Words and Images—I gotta use words when I talk to you.*

Select five minutes of a video. Listen to it with the sound off and write a short script or story describing what you see. Then create a few different stories, each with a different purpose and meaning. If you are more advanced, run the tape backward and write a story or script that gives yet another meaning to the action. (Alternatively, take two or three photographs from the newspaper and write new captions, describing what you—not the editor—want us to "see.")

In the world of images, we underrate the power of language to give meaning. Especially when things are surprising or don't look ordinary, language becomes the important tool used to give significance. A text can be used to undercut the image or redirect the eye of the reader, making him or her see what is not obvious. If the context makes the language seem too weak, you can slow down the eye of the viewer by creating images that startle or mystify: that will give purpose to the language being used. To startle, you'll need to learn how to "distort" the image—slow it down, speed it up, cut it up—so that the reader or viewer needs to rely on the text to find meaning.

FOR THE MORE EXPERIENCED

5. *Metaphor-Making—these are a few of my favorite things.*

Start a scrapbook that combines "found" art—photographs, postcards, matchbooks, napkins, envelopes, ticket stubs; and "found" language—passages from books, magazines, poems, advertisements, direct-mail pieces, commercial prose, and snatches of conversations overheard. Organize everything so that each page has a meaning. Then include, where you need it, a commentary so that the reader sees what you want him or her to see.

Start simple and then get more complex. The simplest way to start is to put things together that seem similar (everything connects!), and then put things together that seem different (everything is unique!). You'll see the tug-of-war between images, between images and words, and between words and words. Most importantly, you'll see the way in which two "different" things—whether word or image—make a "new meaning." It's what Aristotle meant in the *Poetics* (chapter 22) when he said that "a good metaphor implies an intuitive perception of the similarity of dissimilars" (Aristotle 1941, 1,479). It's the ability to make a real metaphor—to see how a visual and verbal "idea" are similar—that is the test of designers and writers who hope to speak to each other.

6. *Moving Images and Still Text—everything is the same; everything is different.*

Compare two Web sites for different companies that sell the same product—computers, books, cars, whatever.

What's the difference between the "look and feel" of each of the sites? Do you find it easier to "read" one of the sites? Do you think the sites have a different purpose and a different audience in mind?

Pay attention to how you read each site. You may find that you jump from visual image and link to the next visual image and link, paying little attention to the text. On the other hand, some sites have found ways of making the text readable, appealing, and attractive. Think about which is more powerful on these sites: the word, the image, or both. Good site designers shape the space, the visual material, and the language so that you will understand where you are and how to follow the line of thought.

FOR THE ADVANCED

7. *Time and Speed—time is but a stream I go a-fishing in.*

Look at Picasso's painting *Guernica* and then write a narrative that puts the "events" you're looking at in an orderly structure—first this happened, then this, finally that. *Guernica* is "frozen" time. Everything—past, present, and future—is frozen in one instant.

The narrative you wrote will seem too orderly, too slow, and not sufficiently dramatic. You will be tempted to overcharge the verbs and overuse adverbs or to describe things that are not present. Don't! Is there another way to "tell" the story so we can "see" it and not lose the visual impact but still retain the narrative voice? What Picasso has done in *Guernica* is slow the viewer down so that the image requires more than a blink. Such images serve the text well, because the viewer has been given time and inclination to process something very complicated.

8. *The Final Exam—being both an author and a reader.*

Edit this book, first as an author and then as a reader.

This is the exercise for the enterprising student. He or she is no longer passively engaged, but active like any author. What's to be done? Change the order of the chapters. Add to the text (notes, images, references to other books, links from one essay to another, etc.) so that the point is easier to understand, so it sounds more academic, so it sounds like something written for a beginner. Think about the design. What does a "scholarly" book look like? And what would a book that's "sheer entertainment" look like? Finally, if you were putting this book onto the Web, how might you structure it for that space?

References

Aristotle. (1941). *The Poetics.* In *The Basic Works of Aristotle,* ed. R. McKeon (pp. 1,478–80). New York: Random House.

Pound, Ezra. (n.d.). *ABC of Reading.* New York: New Directions.

APPENDIX B
a model curriculum

N O ONE CURRICULUM CAN TEACH everything that is to be learned. But for those who are in search of a curriculum, here is a model that we have developed at the University of Baltimore's School of Communications Design.

1. *Integration of Forms.*

   This is a course that *must* be taught by both a writer and a graphic designer, or by a writer and a videographer, or by a writer and a Web designer. (Sometimes the writer can be a technical writer, a creative writer, or a professional writer. Like the different kinds of designers, each kind of writer brings a different take on his or her craft and its purpose.) So much of learning how word and image come together depends upon examples and watching the battle between people who are highly visual and those who are highly verbal. There is no easy truce, but there are some interesting solutions. Here, you would learn the role of subject, voice, and audience and the relationship of these to visual and verbal forms.

2. *Media Design.*

   This is a course that examines light, space, motion, and sound and shows students how to manipulate and use them in order to shape messages.

3. *Design Principles and Strategies.*

Since text is so important in bringing the word and image together, this course teaches basic typography: how to use type to solve complex programs, create information hierarchies, and integrate text into a visual layout.

4. *Language and Form.*

This course illustrates the relationship of verbal patterns and forms to questions of voice, audience, and meaning.

5. *Design for Interactive Environments.*

This course explores electronic publication environments, showing how to create interactions among people, machines, and media, and structuring a fluid space for the unforeseen and the (often) unpredictable user. Realistically, it is two or three courses in one: one must learn how to design and code; how to build hierarchies of information; and how to evaluate useful structures and create a style.

Plus advanced work and skills

In addition to these courses, students who want to know how to integrate the word and the image need to take additional advanced-level courses in writing, design, videography, and hypermedia production. They must also learn how to exploit a range of desktop-publishing software, Web-authoring tools, and digital-editing software both for video and audio.

SELECTIVE
BIBLIOGRAPHY

Arnheim, R. (1969). *Visual Thinking*. London: Faber & Faber.

Barthes, R. (1977). *Image, Music, Text*, trans. Stephen Heath. New York: Hill & Wang.

————. (1981). *Camera Lucida: Reflections on Photography*, trans. Richard Howard. New York: Noonday Press/Farrar, Straus & Giroux.

Berger, A. A. (1989). *Seeing Is Believing: An Introduction to Visual Communication*. Mountain View, CA: Mayfield.

Bolter, J. D. (1991). *Writing Space*. Hillsdale, NJ: Lawrence Erlbaum.

Drucker, J. (1998). *Figuring the Word*. New York: Granary Books.

Gandelman, C. (1991). *Reading Pictures, Viewing Texts*. Bloomington: Indiana University Press.

Goodman, N. (1968). *Languages of Art: An Approach to a Theory of Symbols*. Indianapolis: Bobbs-Merrill.

Hall, S. (1986). On postmodernism and articulation: An interview with Stuart Hall. *Journal of Communication Inquiry* 10(2): 45–60.

Haraway, D. (1997). *Modest_Witness@Second_Millennium. "Femaleman" Meets Oncomouse: Feminism and Technoscience*. New York: Routledge.

Holtzman, S. (1997). *Digital Mosaics: The Aesthetics of Cyberspace*. New York: Simon & Schuster.

Johnson-Eilola, J. (1997). *Nostalgic Angels: Rearticulating Hypertext Writing*. Norwood, NJ: Ablex.

Kosslyn, S. M. (1980). *Image and Mind*. Cambridge, MA: Harvard University Press.

Kress, G. (1998). Visual and verbal modes of representation in electronically mediated communication: The potentials of new forms of text. In *Page to Screen: Taking Literacy into the Electronic Era*, ed. I. Snyder (pp. 53–79). London: Routledge.

Landow, G. (1992). *Hypertext*. Baltimore: Johns Hopkins University Press.

Manguel, A. (1996). *A History of Reading*. New York: Penguin Books.

McCloud, S. (1992). *Understanding Comics*. Northampton, MA: Tundra Publishing.

———. (2000). *Reinventing Comics*. Northampton, MA: HarperPerennial Library.

McLuhan, M., and B. R. Powers. (1986). *The Global Village: Transformations in World Life and Media in the 21st Century*. New York: Oxford University Press.

Mitchell, W. J. T. (1986). *Iconology: Image, Text, Ideology*. Chicago: University of Chicago Press.

Schapiro, M. (1996.). *Words, Script, and Pictures: Semiotics of Visual Language*. New York: George Braziller.

Selber, S. (1997). Hypertext spheres of influence in technical communication instructional contexts. In *Computers and Technical Communication: Pedagogical and Programmatic Perspectives*, ed. S. Selber (pp. 17–44). Greenwich, CT: Ablex.

Selfe, C., and R. J. Selfe. (1994). The politics of the interface: Power and its exercise in electronic contact zones. *College Composition and Communication* 45(4): 480–504.

Slack, J. D. (1996). The theory and method of articulation in cultural studies. In *Stuart Hall: Critical Dialogues in Cultural Studies*, ed. D. Morley and C. Kuan-Hsing (pp. 112–27). London: Routledge.

Stephens, M. (1998). *The Rise of the Image, the Fall of the Word*. New York: Oxford University Press.

Tufte, E. R. (1997). *Visual Explanations*. Cheshire, CT: Graphics Press.

White, J. (1974). *Editing by Design*. New York: Bowker.

INDEX

Abstract, abstraction, 3, 7–8, 10, 13, 26, 28–40, 57, 70–71, 108, 128, 134
Abstract expressionism, 1
Actor, 186
Adams, Eric J., 226
Aesthetics, 10, 16, 120, 131, 135, 216–17, 268–69, 275, 277, 279
Affordances, 31–40
Akalaitis, JoAnne, 194–95
Allen, Tina, 2, 138
Alphabet, 3, 6–8, 75, 78, 105
  Greek alphabet, 78
Alphabetic
  scripts, 68
  writing, 7–8
Animation, 72, 221, 262
Antoine, André, 182–83
Appia, Adolf, 185–86
Apple Computer, 277
Appolinaire, Guillaume, 184
Arago, Dominique François, 142–44, 147
Argument, 10, 12–14, 17, 29, 81, 86, 119, 121, 123, 136, 138, 140, 142–44, 155, 181, 282

Aristotle, 4, 121, 181, 282, 290
Arnheim, Rudolph, 11, 26, 80–88, 93, 124, 127
Arnold, Matthew, 275
Aronson, Arnold, 189–92
Arrows, 60, 66, 71–72
Art, 208, 268
Artaud, Antonin, 186–88
Articulation theory, 233–34
Artificial intelligence, 28
Artists, 189, 199, 211
Astrophysics, 140–42, 162
Audience, audiences, 3, 14, 16, 119, 121–22, 180–81, 186, 195–95, 217, 240, 252, 260–62, 264–69, 275, 288
Author, auteures, authoring, 15, 80, 90, 92, 101, 110, 126, 199, 216, 232–33, 236, 246, 253, 266
Author, intention, 273
Avedon, Richard, 14

Backdrop, 182
Background, 112
Bars, 64–67, 71–72

ABOUT THE EDITOR
AND CONTRIBUTORS

JONATHAN ALLEN is the founder/president of the Shuffleware Media Company, an internet based multimedia development/design firm. Prior to starting the company, he was a multimedia developer and project coordinator at Purdue University for the Biological Sciences and Materials Sciences and Engineering departments. While at Purdue he inaugurated the Interactive Multimedia Development Center.

NANCY ALLEN is associate professor of written communication in the English Department at Eastern Michigan University. She teaches courses in professional communication, rhetoric, research methods, and computers and writing. She has published in professional journals, including the *Technical Communication Quarterly*, *Computers and Composition*, *IEEE Journal of Computer Documentation*, and *Journal of Business and Technical Communication*, and in books on technical communication. She is a member of the editorial advisory board for *Computers and Composition*.

LISA A. BROCK is a Twin Cities playwright and arts critic. She is a regular contributor to *Minnesota Women's Press* and the *Star Tribune*. Her play, *The River Wife's Daughters*, has been produced in Minneapolis, Ashland, Wisconsin, Philadelphia, and Edinburgh, Scotland. It was chosen by the *Twin Cities' Reader* as one of the ten best productions of 1990, and was nominated for a "Fringe First" Award in Edinburgh. She has also worked for several years as a stage manager, scenic artist, and properties designer.

MIKE DRINGENBERG, best known for his illustrations for DC Comics' *The Sandman* series (written by Neil Gaiman), lives in Salt Lake City. He is currently at work on covers for the new edition of J. R. R. Tolkein's *The Silmarillion* and a culture and art column for *PULP*, an American magazine devoted to Japanese manga.

HEINZ INSU FENKL is the author of *Memories of My Ghost Brother*, a Barnes and Noble "Great New Writer" selection and Pen/Hemingway finalist in 1997. He has written graphic novels, screenplays, and hypertexts, and is co-author (with Terri Windling) of the Folkroots column in *Realms of Fantasy* magazine. He currently teaches in the Milton Avery MFA program at Bard College in upstate New York.

RONALD FORTUNE is professor and chair of the English Department at Illinois State University. His work focuses on intersections between writing and reading, and especially on ways in which computer technology participates in these intersections. Currently, he is investigating relationships between the distributed perspectives on writing in manuscript and hypertext cultures. His essays have appeared in *ADE Bulletin*, *Computers and Composition*, *Style*, *Journal of Advanced Composition*, and *Journal of Teaching Writing*, and in essay collections. He has directed a number of projects with support from NEH.

ARTHUR M. GLENBERG is a professor of psychology at the University of Wisconsin–Madison and the former associate editor of the *Journal of Experimental Psychology: Learning, Memory, and Cognition*. He is a central figure in the development of the theory of embodied cognition based on the principle that cognition's major function is control of the interaction between body and environment.

RICH GOLD is the manager of RED (Research in Experimental Documents) at Xerox PARC. RED studies and creates new genres and document types centered around new technologies. It is particularly interested in the process of authoring the medium and the content simultaneously, forming resonant evocative objects.

RICHARD JOHNSON SHEEHAN is an assistant professor at the University of New Mexico, where he is director of the professional writing program at the graduate and undergraduate levels. His research areas include the rhetoric of science, visual rhetoric, and sophistic rhetoric. He teaches courses in hypertext, visual rhetoric, rhetorical theory, and the rhetoric of science.

JAMES KALMBACH is a professor of English at Illinois State University, where he teaches courses in technical writing and Web authoring. He is the author of *The Computer and the Page: Publishing, Technology, and the Classroom* (Ablex, 1997), and has had articles appear in *Computers* *and Composition, Journal of Computer Documentation, Journal of Reading, Technical Communication,* and *Technical Communication Quarterly.*

AMY C. KIMME HEA is an assistant professor at the University of Arizona. Her research is in the areas of the discourses and practices of Web-based teaching and learning for first-year composition. She recently published an essay exploring articulation as a methodology in the international journal *Educare/Educure.* At present, she is working on a forthcoming article about critical Web-based teaching for a special edition of *Computers and Composition* about power and the WWW.

NEIL KLEINMAN is professor of communication and media and dean of the College of Media and Communication at the University of the Arts in Philadelphia. He is author of a book on German propaganda and writes on law, literature, and technology. For the last two decades, he has developed and taught in programs that have as their primary focus the integration of words, images, and technology.

BARRY PEGG is associate professor of literature in the Department of Humanities at Michigan Technological University. He has published on the two-dimensional aspects of text, on polar exploration, and is now working on a translation of Dmitry Shparo and Aleksandr Shumilov's history of lost expeditions in the Russian arctic.

GREG SIMMONS is a graphic designer with Clarkston Graphics in Clarkston, Michigan. His academic training and professional development have been in the fields of art and design. He has an extensive working knowledge in all areas of print design, as well as expertise in Web-site design and maintenance.

BARBARA TVERSKY is professor of psychology at Stanford University. Her primary interests are in spatial thinking and language, memory, and categorization. These theoretical interests have taken her to study cognitive maps, diagrammatic reasoning, human–computer interaction, design, and eyewitness testimony among other topics.

GREGORY A. WICKLIFF is an associate professor of English at the University of North Carolina at Charlotte, where he teaches courses in technical/professional writing. His current research is in the area of photographically illustrated nineteenth-century scientific and technical texts.